GEOGRAPHIES OF PRIVILEGE

What role does space play in the control and distribution of resources such as housing, education, leisure, sex, and safety? *Geographies of Privilege* presents case studies from around the globe that provide analyses of power as it operates within local, national, and global networks. How are social inequalities (racial, sexual, economic, occupational) experienced, reproduced and challenged in local, global and transnational spaces?

Twine and Gardener have given us an interdisciplinary collection that provides empirically grounded case studies that reveal the ways that a nuanced analysis of space (domestic, institutional, transnational) is crucial in analyses of intersecting social inequalities. The contributors to this volume analyze how power is transferred and transformed into economic, social, symbolic, and cultural capital.

The volume's contributors take the reader to compelling global and local sites including brothels, blues clubs, dance clubs, elite schools, detention centers, advocacy organizations, and public sidewalks in Scotland, Italy, Spain, United Arab Emirates, Mozambique, South Africa, the United States, and the European Union. *Geographies of Privilege* is the perfect teaching tool for courses on social inequality in Geography, Sociology, Anthropology, American Studies, European Studies, and Global Studies.

France Winddance Twine is Professor of Sociology at the University of California Santa Barbara. She is an ethnographer, a critical race theorist and a documentary filmmaker who earned her degree at the University of California- Berkeley. She has published more than 60 books, journal articles, book reviews and essays. She is the author and an editor of 8 books including *Geographies of Privilege* (forthcoming, 2013) *A White Side of Black Britain: interracial intimacy and racial literary* (2010), *Outsourcing the Womb: race, class and gestational surrogacy in a global market* (Routledge, 2011a), *Retheorizing Race and Whiteness in the 21st Century* (with Charles Gallagher, 2011b) and *Feminism and Antiracism: international struggles for justice* (New York University Press, 2000). She has served as Deputy Editor of American Sociological Review: the official journal of the American Sociological Association. Twine currently serves on the international editorial boards of the journals *Ethnic and Racial Studies*, *Sociology*: the official journal of the British Sociological Association and *Identities: Global Studies in Culture and Power*.

Bradley Gardener earned his Ph.D. in the Earth and Environmental Sciences Program at the CUNY Graduate Center. He has taught at several CUNY schools and has been employed as writing fellow at Medgar Evers College in Brooklyn, New York. His research focuses on the intersections between race, migration, place, and identity.

This compilation of inter-disciplinary, trans-national research reveals the fundamental connections between space and privilege through richly contextualized ethnographic and qualitative data. Examining diverse institutional settings, from neighborhoods to civil rights organizations to schools, *Geographies of Privilege* elucidates how the social reproduction of privilege occurs in geographies of land, identity and the body. A must read for all who study privilege and inequality!

—Wendy Leo Moore, Sociology, Texas A&M University

Geographies of Privilege is an innovative treatment of how privilege gets reproduced through space and how space shapes privilege. The essays are must-read material for those interested in inequality, power and privilege.

—Joyce M. Bell, Sociology, University of Pittsburgh

GEOGRAPHIES OF PRIVILEGE

France Winddance Twine and Bradley Gardener

Routledge
Taylor & Francis Group

NEW YORK AND LONDON

First published 2013
by Routledge
711 Third Avenue, New York, NY 10017

Simultaneously published in the UK
by Routledge
2 Park Square, Milton Park, Abingdon, Oxon OX14 4RN

Routledge is an imprint of the Taylor & Francis Group, an informa business

Library of Congress Cataloging in Publication Data
Geographies of Privilege / France Winddance Twine and Bradley Gardener. — 1st Edition.
 pages cm
 Includes bibliographical references and index.
 1. Social classes. 2. Elite (Social sciences) 3. Race awareness. 4. Whiteness (Race identity) I. Twine, France Winddance, 1960–, editor of compilation. II. Gardener, Bradley, editor of compilation.
 HT609.G46 2013
 305.5—dc23
 2012029343

ISBN: 978-0-415-51961-8 (hbk)
ISBN: 978-0-415-51962-5 (pbk)
ISBN: 978-0-203-07083-3 (ebk)

Typeset in Minion
by EvS Communication Networx, Inc.

SUSTAINABLE
FORESTRY
INITIATIVE

Certified Sourcing
www.sfiprogram.org
SFI-00555
The SFI label applies to the text stock.

Printed and bound in the United States of America by Walsworth Publishing Company, Marceline, MO.

This book is dedicated to the global Occupy Movement and to other social justice movements that support the 99%, who struggle to support their families, friends, and communities without the privileges that transnational elites take for granted.

Contents

   *The sex industry in Dubai includes migrant women from Sub-Saharan
   Africa, East Asia, Eastern Europe, and the Middle East (North Africa).
   This chapter examines the hierarchy of desire, that is the demand for
   "whiter" and lighter skinned women. This ethnic hierarchy is structured by
   the locations within the city where they perform their labor. It privileges
   Iranian and Moroccan women who are perceived as more desirable and
   allows them to provide sexual services in safer, elite neighborhoods in
   the city. Anti-trafficking discourses also produce a form of privilege for
   Euro-Americans who can "rescue" sex workers who are classified as either
   villains or victims depending upon their national origin and how they are
   racialized.*

*This chapter draws on field research in a bar and dance club in
Pietermaritzburg, South Africa, to outline a critical approach to place-
identity that moves beyond the rhetoric of inclusion-exclusion. This
chapter offers an analysis of gender privilege by examining the emotional
or "affective" realm of privilege in a middle- to upper middle-class
heterosexual dance club where women are privileged as customers in order
to provide subjects for male consumption.*

*This chapter provides an analysis of a black-owned blues club on Chicago's
South Side that is currently undergoing a transformation. How are elite
patterns of consumption shaping the decisions of black blues clubs' owners?
Located in a two-mile area that is in the core of South Side's black "ghetto,"
blues clubs are under pressure to "upscale"—to transform their clubs into
a more marketable commodity that provides pleasurable experiences
for elites. How do the owners of these clubs decide what kind of social
milieu they will cultivate as they seek to "produce pleasure and identity-
nourishment for themselves and others in the club"? Will they transform
their club into "a new playground for reverie and spectatorship for white elites"?*

*This chapter draws upon field research in Johannesburg to ask the question
"What does the transition from apartheid tell us about privilege?" During
the apartheid era (1948–94) the state consolidated white racial privilege
through the management and production of racially exclusive spaces
of work, residence, and leisure. The urban environment was used as a
resource to construct and maintain white racial privilege. During the two
decades since apartheid ended, space continues to be a key resource by
which privilege is constructed and maintained.*

This chapter provides an analysis of elite transnational mobility among white South Africans with colonial ancestries. The "visa whiteness machine" refers to a set of visa and passport arrangements available to white South Africans, constituting a machine that attracts and repels bodies, and thus produces white privileged bodies. The ability of bodies to move in particular transnational spatial circuits is linked to earlier colonial migrations of white Europeans. Drawing upon semistructured interviews with white residents of Durban, an industrial city of 3 million in South Africa, and the only region in South Africa where English-speaking whites constitute the majority, the author analyzes whiteness as a "passport of privilege" that enables South Africans to migrate to the UK. Racially privileged bodies have the capacity to move with ease between the UK and South Africa. Many South Africans have the right to visas to live and work in the UK due to their ancestors' colonial migration histories during the apartheid and segregationist era.

Bringing the critical geography literature on place and identity into dialogue with critical race scholarship focused on the African diaspora, this chapter examines the spatial contours of privilege and belonging in Turin, Italy through the vantage point of first-generation Italo-Africans and the transcolonial interweavings of Europe and Africa.

Which bodies can move freely within the EU and across its borders? At the borders of the EU, a powerful and security-obsessed distinction between travelers is increasingly being constructed between those who "belong to" the EU and those who do not, based on their national origins. This chapter examines how the creation of a so-called white and black Schengen list in the EU, recently relabeled a "positive and negative" list, is used as a criterion for visa applications. A significantly high number of Muslim and developing states are listed on the "negative" list. This chapter provides an analysis of the EU's "war on migrants" and how it has produced a border industry that has changed the landscape into barbed wire surveillance and detention camps. A form of global apartheid has been produced through EU policies that define "security" in terms of keeping the world's poorest out of the European zone.

Why do some migrant bodies feel more comfortable in certain spaces because they perceive themselves as already belonging there? Lifestyle migrants from the Nordic countries and from the UK are very attracted to southern Spain as a destination for expatriate living. In this chapter, Lundström draws on interviews with Swedish women living in southern Spain, to argue that "the institutionalization of whiteness" in southern Spain recruits subjects who feel that they are part of an "international community," thus belonging, but resulting in divisions between migrants from northern Europe, non-European migrants, and locals from Spain. Class inequality also structures the experience of Swedish migration with the lower-income migrants experiencing downward mobility in southern Spain while middle-class Swedes were able to retain their class privileges. There is a postcolonial identification with Anglo-Saxon countries and disidentification with (former colonial powers) in Southern Europe.

How do welfare-dependent white mothers negotiate the stigma of poverty while trying to secure housing in middle- and upper-middle-class residential neighborhoods? Drawing upon interviews with twenty-five welfare-dependent white women raising families in the Greater Boston area, this article uses Erving Goffman and Pierre Bourdieu to argue that whiteness is a resource that facilitates movement into higher income, racially segregated neighborhoods for poor families. We identify six benefits that welfare-dependent white women (in contrast to their black and brown peers) gain by concealing their welfare status, including access to safer neighborhoods, social resources, symbolic capital, and educational resources.

*White flight was not a phenomenon unique to American cities in the 1960s
and 1970s. It also happened in some African cities after European colonial
rule ended. This chapter asks "what happens to racial privilege when there
is no longer a privileged race?" Maputo, Mozambique, a sizable African
city, was developed for the exclusive use of white European settlers during
Portuguese colonial rule. After independence from Portugal in 1975, there
was rapid white flight from Maputo. The rapid abandonment of this city
left no time for a transition. However, Maputo remained a zone of privilege
and provided a nascent Black African middle class with opportunities to
become privileged urban dwellers for the first time.*

*This chapter argues that within antiracist workshops as well as the
academy, white privilege is reinforced, rather than challenged by practices
such as "confessing" that one possesses privilege. This article details and
describes ideological obstacles to meaningful social and political change by
examining how Native Americans are constituted as "subjects."*

*The political, social, and legal application of civil rights is dependent upon
the organization and conceptualization of physical spaces by Muslim
civil rights advocates. This chapter provides a comparative analysis of
two Muslim American civil rights organizations: Council on American
Islamic Relations (CAIR) and Karamah: Muslim Women Lawyers for
Human Rights. Karamah focuses on issues such as domestic violence and
sexual harassment that are neglected by CAIR, which uses a masculine
understanding of the social world that privileges public spaces over
private spaces.*

*How do upper middle-class adolescent males experience bullying as it
intersects with masculinity and privilege in an elite boarding school?
What do they learn about privilege in these elite spaces? This chapter
analyzes the culture of bullying as it is practiced in sports locker-rooms,
classrooms, and student clubs. Drawing upon research interviews with
ten faculty (administrators, teachers) and ninety-six classmates in ninth
through twelfth grade, the author shows how particular performances of
masculinity are privileged and learned.*

*How are the bodies of young girls classified as outside normative standards
for physical appearance? In other words, what do girls whose bodies are
classified as "dis-abled" learn about "privileged" bodies versus "dis-abled"
bodies? This chapter examines the expectations and experiences of Scottish
girls and young women who encounter a number of obstacles to sexual
agency, marriage, and motherhood. They are taught that their bodies are
not "normal" and therefore they are not expected (and are not socially
trained) to desire an active sexual life or to become mothers.*

Acknowledgments

The idea for this book originated in a session organized for the 2010 meetings for the Association of American Geographers in Washington, DC. The original participants of that session, which was organized by Bradley Gardener, included: Doreen Fumia, Jennifer Johnson, Joseph Nevins, Serin Houston, and Janet Gray. We thank the participants as well as a number of scholars who have both inspired us and worked with us over the past two years but were not able to contribute to this volume. In this vein we thank: Setha Low, Koni Benson, Doreen Fumia, Joshua Inwood, Deborah Martin, Serin Houston, Rachel Heiman, Jen Giesking, Janet Gray, Abby Ferber, Michelle Billies, and Joseph Nevins.

During the past two years we have expanded the geographic and thematic scope of this volume to address a wide range of sites, nation-states, and mechanisms through which privileges are activated and intersect with racial/ethnic, religious, class, and postcolonial power geometries. We have received guidance, insights, recommendations, and support from a number of scholars. In this vein we thank Allen Isaacman, Jan Nederveen Pietersee, Michelle Fine, and Cindi Katz.

We thank the contributors to this volume who patiently worked with us to revise and reshape their chapters so that we could achieve our goals of producing an innovative, interdisciplinary volume that is theoretically provocative yet lacks the obtuseness that often prevents scholarship from traveling across academic borders to reach a wider and more diverse readership. We have tried to balance theoretical innovation with empirical case studies that illuminate the complex ways that privilege operates on both sides of the Atlantic.

Bradley Gardener thanks Valerie Rose for her initial suggestion that he embark on this project. He thanks France Winddance Twine for everything she has taught him about professionalism, the academy, and producing edited volumes. He is grateful to his family, friends, and colleagues. Interactions with these groups of people helped him conceptualize this volume and inspired him to see it through to its completion.

France Winddance Twine thanks Paul Amar, Ingrid Banks, Zsusza Berend, Stephanie Baptiste, Esther Lezra, George Lipsitz, Melissa MacDonald, Paola Bacchetta, Tanya Golash-Boza, Jan Nederveen Pieterse, Maria Charles, Geoff Raymond, Leila Rupp, and Verta Taylor for their support while preparing this volume. I thank the following for softening the blows of racism and other forms of domination that I negotiate daily as a first generation academic from a working-class family: Steve Twine, Allan Cronin, Joseph Jewell, Howard Winant, Victor Rios, Debbie Rogow, Lisa Hajjar, Elizabeth Bernstein, and Constance Penley.

Finally, we thank Lynn Goeller and Margaret Moore for their patience and professionalism during the production process.

France Winddance Twine
Bradley Gardener

Foreword

Geographies of Privilege presents a compelling and groundbreaking collection of essays that analyze how social actors normalize and rework privileges through space and how space makes privileges. It is also about the creeping power of neoliberal capitalism, modes of governing, and the operation of consumerism as lived, felt, and desired by social actors. The persistence of ontologies and landscapes of privilege, the rearticulation of embodied transnational whiteness, and the devaluation of bodies deemed out of place and time thread through these fascinating and clearly written essays. Unfolding through diverse global locations, the volume launches an interdisciplinary encounter of exceptional depth and clarity grounded in a critical focus on the social, spatial and cultural manifestations of privilege as it is deployed materially and discursively.

Over the past decades there has been considerable debate in anthropology, sociology, and more recently in geography in an effort to make sense of the persistence and negotiation of racial, gender, class, and other axes of social inequality and power. But these studies have frequently spoken past instead of in dialogue with each other. This interdisciplinary volume of essays is needed to push beyond established orthodoxies and nourish new understandings of privilege, to test and put geographical theorizations of race and other privileges front and center through rich, historically situated ethnographic analyses.

For structures of privilege are resilient. Racial divisions have been reinforced and further expanded globally in recent years, in spite of the end of state sanctioned apartheid in South Africa, the many gains of the Civil Rights Movement in the United States and the election of its first black president. W.E.B. Dubois' classical insight that "the problem of the 20th century" will be the "problem of the color line" is in the 21st century as Manning Marable argues, "the problem of global apartheid" through widespread racialized division and the stratification of resources, wealth, and power that separates Europe, North America, and parts of Asia from the billions of people of color across the world (Marable 2008). And yet in both popular and scholarly registers these structures of power are plausibly denied through officially declared commitments to "color blind" policies, while forms of class and racial segregation escalate. In the United States, the triumph of gender equality is lauded while an all-out assault is being waged against gender expression and identity and young people are encouraged to look upon the gains of the "sexual revolution" with suspicion.

Such evasions of racial, ethnic, gender, class, and other privileges stretch well beyond the national boundaries of the United States. Michael Herzfeld has suggested in his work on Rome, that a kind of global neo-cultural politically correct language has rendered expressions of "racial intent" more easy to disguise in the highly charged Italian society in which immigration has been a hot button issue for over a decade now (Herzfeld 2009, 316n35). In spite of the silencing, racialized and elite privileging has in practice accentuated deepening through obfuscation and aversion, and, as a number of essays in this collection suggest, expanding through the diffuse policies justified in the name of the "war on terror." In the European sphere following unification and the emergence of the "war on illegal migration" the EU promotes what Van Houtum (chapter 7, this volume) characterizes as a "gated community" via a profoundly hierarchical and dehumanizing border machinery that scans and codes bodies for entry or rejection on the basis of where they were born. The renewed focus on territorial identity and the production of colonial like frontiers in Europe have led to the diffusion of border anxiety and practices in everyday life, the making of separate spheres of activity and meaning between us and them, here and there, physically identifiable permanent non-members and unmarked members.

We have been conducting research in Turin, Italy, for more than two decades, where in daily lived reality, many now face encounters with negative images of blackness expressed in micro-aggressions in shops and public spaces and the insinuation that there is kind of cultural dissonance/distance that naturally divides local people from people of apparently non-western or northern European origins. With the economic downturn, migrants are the first to experience distress, and for those without stable housing the situation is even more difficult. Subject to housing shortages and chronic underemployment, much of it *lavoro nero* or off the books, they must also face the indignities of being considered "out of place," in an Italian cultural space that is imagined as white.

Life has become increasingly more difficult in Black Europe. On a summer's day in 2010 with the sun reaching its zenith, we made our way to a former school which was the makeshift home of some fifty refugees from the Horn of Africa to speak with Somali and Eritrean refugees, one of the many Black Spaces or anti-detention camps that had been occupied by African refugees or asylum seekers who could find no other place to live (Merrill forthcoming). We arrived at the door and two young men greeted us with hesitation. The young man we were looking at was speaking with a group of his countrymen in the shade of a few trees in a small piazza opposite the "house." We reached him shortly after news of our arrival. We did not fit the profile, a white women and an African perhaps journalists, no we were American researchers not working for the papers. Despite media attention, only a few charitable organizations offer help in the form of meals and a place to shower, "They all talk to us and it's the same thing, nothing happens. They come, they take their interviews and nothing changes for us." Forced by Dublin Treaty agreements to stay in the country of their initial arrival in the European Union, the refugees have little choice but to remain in Italy, although they know that conditions might be better for them elsewhere in Europe. The occupation of various urban sites is a manifestation of protest of their treatment. At the close of the conversation, the young man pointed to his arm, "No one is going to do anything for us because of the color of our skin," he said as if it were a final offer at communication. No longer placing hope in the officials of any state, these refugees spend their days reading and discuss the Koran, staying in contact with others in the international diaspora, and building relationships with other migrants.

For female refugees, conditions are even less hopeful. In July, 2010 a group of twenty Somali women dressed in black abayas and cheap flip flops sought shelter from the scorching summer sun by taking craft and Italian language courses in the women's inter-ethnic center in Turin, Alma Mater. In a language tinged with deep pain and anger, they spoke with us out of a desperate desire to be heard, as they wanted us to carry the story of their degraded lives in Europe to the United States. Sleeping in homeless shelters that opened their doors at 8 pm and pushed them out at 8 am each morning, they spent weekday mornings at Alma Mater and the rest of the day and weekends walking the urban pavement or sitting in the shade of a park tree. They described living in the frigid winters as even more brutal, when they struggled to hold onto each other for warmth in single digit temperatures. Each woman, several holding infants, told the story of her life in Mogadishu, a "lawless place, where you go to sleep at night and don't know if in the morning you will be alive." Risking their lives to escape Somalia by crossing the Gulf of Aden into Yemen or overland through

Ethiopia and Sudan, journeys that take the lives of hundreds each year, they found themselves in Italy in a state of placeless limbo, or as one put it, "We don't exist." They described the peculiarities of their situation as women made vulnerable to the dangers of homeless shelters where there was constant threat of being robbed and raped. They were without enough money to survive, without hope of finding stable housing or work, and left to roam the streets. Permitted to enter Europe yet then left virtually without resources to do more than barely survive, these women were faceless figures in the landscape of European privilege. Born in the "wrong country" and the "wrong body" they lacked embodied symbolic capital without which people can be easily rendered invisible.

In *Navigating the African Diaspora: The Anthropology of Invisibility* (2010) Donald Martin Carter explores what he calls the modalities of invisibility, a "power to establish or manifest a state of invisibility for specific categories of persons in a given space, location, time or position" (Carter 2010: 22). The conferring of invisibility implies a kind of sub-personhood, the devaluation or dehumanization of the person as the great cultural critic James Baldwin once wrote, this is a basic diminishment of "human reality . . . human weight and complexity" (Carter 2010 ibid). When people come to be seen this way, they become from the perspective of a certain cultural logic "superfluous," imponderable as a human presence, and are therefore rendered invisible. Carter argues that invisibility operates through the state and its functionaries, manifest in concerns with the control and disposition of bodies and embodiment, and through popular and scholarly discourses. The lack of representations, histories, and knowledge about African and African American soldiers in the Second World War would be an example of this type of erasure. Invisibility is a way of making the seen disappear in plain sight; domestic workers, migrants and others can essentially disappear, for those who employ them become part of a set of operations such that the dispositions that constitute their work effectively reinforces the process of their disappearance as socially relevant subjects. Slight changes in address or ritual greetings can signal such a difference. At some college and universities, for instance, grounds workers are rarely spoken to directly by students or faculty, leading them to complain about being taken-for-granted or being invisible. Acknowledgement even begrudging creates a kind of sociality. Such techniques are often played out in spatial registers, for instance materially forcing people considered to be inferior off a sidewalk was an old Jim Crow practice so routine it often went without mention among the great repertoires of othering practices.

Invisibility is often coupled with hyper-visibility as with the case of Muslims in many western countries today who are from the single aspect of security hyper-visible but often are not considered integral members of the societies in which they live. When we fail to see the migrant, the refugee, the person with disabilities and others, these people begin to become for us less socially relevant and essentially invisible. Invisibility is however merely a small archipelago in the expansive geographies of privilege.

Studying privilege is a complex pathway to an understanding of the forms of social inequality that are often masked by such ideologies as color blindness and post-racialism. For privileges are tangibly felt in everyday lives, tied to many socioeconomic factors such as life expectancy, health, education, work, wealth accumulation, and mobility. One of the most salient forms of privilege in the making of the contemporary global context appears to be a certain re-articulation of "whiteness," infusing postcolonial, and post-apartheid societies with differential capabilities for international travel and affective linkages with pan-ethnic communities in the European Union, the United States, and Canada to name only a few of the possibilities. Migrants or even refugees from the Horn of Africa, one of the regions in which the turbulence of daily life has cast many into disapora share no enabling affinity with privileged portions of the Western world and are subject to a relatively diminished motility and social invisibility as a consequence. The ability to cross borders remains dependent on access to powerful countries and regions of the world that replicate well-worn geospatial pathways and privileged cultural "heritage" or the social capital of whiteness passed from one generation to the next.

In *The Miner's Canary*, Lani Guinier and Gerald Torres confront a host of stumbling blocks in North America largely due to the legacy of the unfinished business of social justice as it relates to race, pointing to such markers as the unequal distribution of wealth that spans generations, an alarming rate of incarceration of black and Latino youth and a declining desire to extend the benefits of a universal education. Calling at once for incisive political work that might address the insinuation of "colorblind" thinking in North America, they liken the fate of black and Latino youth to the miner's canary, since the distress of the canary signals the worsening of conditions for all those in the mine as the air becomes too poisonous to breathe. We might look at the treatment here of privilege in a similar manner since the distress of those subjected to the expansive geographies of privilege are the first sign of a danger that threatens us all (Guinier and Torres 2003). We must examine that threat through the ruins of colonial projects and world development schemes and the great race for supremacy on the world stage.

Now in the aftermath of global economic failures and regional proxy wars, the old rhythms and rituals of the world capitalist order seem resilient. We face the emergence of a new state of play perhaps of a very old game. As we stumble towards the future, who are the subjects/agents that dependent upon social, local, national, and regional contexts. We cannot understand race privilege without considering generation (age), gender, sexuality, citizenship status, religious affiliation, national origins, and economic status. Specific cases cannot be subsumed into abstract categories of white/black or male/female (Housel 2009).

Fourth, privilege must be understood in relation to the groups it oppresses or harms as well as those it benefits. As scholars of privilege, our aim is not only to point out where privilege exists, but also who or what pays for privilege. The class privilege of the wealthy is made at the expense of low-wage laborers with few benefits (Higley 1995; Darby 2000). Racial or ethnic privilege is inextricably linked to the disinvestment of poor communities where stigmatized ethnic minorities live (and of course not all racial and ethnic groups are perceived as marginal or experience the same forms of economic discrimination) (Berman 1996; Surgue 1996; Wyley and Holloway 2002).

Finally, privilege is a flexible resource and is embedded in relationships that can mutate over time and space (Housel 2009). The categories under which privilege operates and is experienced are dynamic and always in motion. Who benefits and who loses is always a contested process in which the meaning given to categories and the categories themselves are in flux (Goldberg 1993; Kurtz 2006). Second, privilege is by no means a fixed relation, and both privileged subjects and those who are oppressed by privileging processes are struggling against power relationships (Robinson 1983; Woods 1998, 2007).

Occupy Wall Street and Privileged Spaces

On Saturday, September 17, 2011 a group of anarchists and protesters in their twenties established a camp in Zuccotti Park (also known as Liberty Plaza), a privately owned public space near the New York Stock Exchange. By that evening 300 people went to sleep in that space and launched a six-week occupation to call attention to economic inequality and social injustice that has cost millions of Americans their homes and jobs, and caused a worldwide economic crisis. The mainstream media essentially ignored and failed to report on this economic justice movement for two weeks. It was not until the mass arrests of protesters on the Brooklyn Bridge on October 1, 2011, that the media began to cover it, although much of the reporting misrepresented Occupy and caricatured the Occupiers.

How will Occupy Wall Street be remembered one hundred years from now? Will it be remembered as simply another movement organized and directed by whites? Will it be seen as an unsuccessful, if well-intentioned movement that lacked a coherent set of goals as some of the Baby Boomer critics have argued? Was it doomed to failure because it was too reliant upon a particular urban space, Zuccotti Park, as a symbolic space of protest, rather than going to working class neighborhoods where people of less privileged backgrounds lived? Was it able to incorporate children, women of color, the working class, the disabled, and those who had social reproduction responsibilities?

This volume is timely because it synthesizes an amazing breadth and depth of different kinds of places that include border control (van Houtum, chapter 7), blues clubs (Wilson, chapter 3), dance clubs (Durrheim et al., chapter 2), brothels (Madhavi, chapter 1), antiracist advocacy organizations (Love, chapter 12 and Smith, chapter 11), domestic spaces (McFarlane and Hansen, chapter 14), elite all-male schools (Stoudt, chapter 13), rental housing (MacDonald and Twine, chapter 9), transnational motility (Andrucki, chapter 5), and public plazas (Merrill, chapter 6). Not only does its international focus meet challenges of scholars critical of privilege and whiteness study who argue that these studies are too North American focused, but the authors also consider how many different scales are connected (Bonnett 2000; Levine-Rasky 2002). As the authors in this volume deal with their particular slice of the world they attempt to understand the link between people and the way they make place, not unlike the way Manissa Maharawal (2011), a student organizer, experienced Occupy Wall Street, and link them up to the broader abstract processes that explain how the world works. Taking issue with the way organizers at Occupy Wall Street were conceptualizing race, she said, "we needed to tell him about privilege and racism and oppression and how these things still existed, both in the world and someplace like Occupy Wall Street" (Marharawal 2011).

A focus on space and materiality allows us to see how categories change and reform. Simply understanding that white or male bodies are always benefitting in the same kind of ways, and simply crying privilege without anything to substantiate it is a serious issue. A focus on space allows us to see how privileged processes unfold, and the best way to deal with them.

One of the foundations of privilege studies is that privilege is multi-faceted, or as Peggy McIntosh says, "interlocking." Jasbir Puar argues that intersectionality, the idea that different aspects of identity must be understood in relation to each other, intertwined, but existing as separate entities, is problematic (J. Puar 2007). Specifically, she argues that sorting out, naming, and making legible different aspects of identity such as race, gender, and sexuality leads to a reification of categories used by the state to produce and reproduce powered and privileged relationships. She says, "As a toll of diversity management, and a mantra of liberal multiculturalism, intersectionality colludes with the disciplinary apparatus of the state—census, demography, racial profiling, surveillance—in that difference is encased within a structural container that simply wishes the messiness of identity into a formulaic grid" (212). For Puar, breaking out of the grid that nurtures these categories is a necessary component of altering privileged social relationships.

Similarly, in a discussion of whiteness Peter Jackson argues against the reification of racial categories. He argues that:

> Concepts of Whiteness should continue to be theorized within a radicalized context, whereby some identities are privileged over others, providing a powerful basis for racialized exclusion. This should not lead us to submit to a simplistic form of racialized thinking, where whiteness is automatically opposed to blackness. Instead the preceding argument has sought to repudiate such binarized ways of thinking and to focus on the complex cultural politics of all such racialized categorizations. (Jackson 1998, 104)

Jackson argues against privileging some racial identities over others, specifically black and white, the traditional categories of racial privilege and exclusion. He advocates a nuanced understanding of how privilege works. A focus on space, particularly in a myriad of different contexts, in our case at the international scale, can reveal the ways in which privilege works and can be transformed.

Conclusion

This volume breaks new ground by engaging in public debates about privilege taking place on the streets, in university classrooms, and organizing spaces like the Occupy Wall Street movement. Second, it brings notions of spatial hierarchy into discussions of privilege. In our view, this is essential to rethinking how to reduce inequality, racism, and poverty by implementing a more democratic distribution of resources. This volume moves between the local and the transnational, thereby revealing some dimensions of privilege which are relatively invisible to those who possess them.

An analysis of privilege is approached using different theoretical traditions. In chapter 11, Andrea Smith pushes the reader to rethink privilege by examining some of the ways that white privilege is replicated in the discourses employed in the context of antiracist organizations. For Smith the individual confessional white subject is unable to see his or her privilege while it is actually being performed and deployed in an effort to promote social change. Furthermore, Smith argues that a concentration of privilege on the individual scale produces the reification and concretization of problematic categories of identity. A second approach in this volume involves analyzing the obstacles to geographical mobility across neighbor-hoods (MacDonald and Twine, chapter 9) and across nation-state borders (Merrill, chapter 6, Leonard, chapter 4, and van Houtum, chapter 7). Sev-eral contributors analyze the ideologies and practices that "privilege" some bodies over others. This enables privileged bodies to convert their racial/ colonial ancestries and national origins into forms of currency (access to visas, resident permits, jobs, and housing) that enable them to travel and reside in Europe with ease. The absence of fear and the ability not to be detained is a form of privilege in intra-European travel.

Third, contributors focus on how privilege operates in the marketing or selling of pleasurable experiences and access to specific leisure spaces and in neighborhoods located in middle class as well as racialized and impoverished urban communities in the United States and South Africa. David Wilson provides an analysis of the ongoing transformation of Chi-cago South Side blues clubs during a period of economic development. He analyses the discourses and practices employed by a club owner as she negotiates the larger structural changes occurring in the city and balances the club's economic survival with marketing the club to a more privileged and racially diverse clientele. Pauline Leonard offers an analysis of the rebranding of Johannesburg to appeal to more progressive, post-apartheid whites (chapter 4).

Forth, the issue of what types of spaces are prioritized in civil rights advocacy is addressed by Erik Love in his comparative analysis of two dif-ferent Muslim American Civil Rights advocacy organizations (chapter 12). He highlights the important role that gender plays in structuring which types of spaces are visible in the discourses and legal projects of one Mus-lim American organization that is dominated by men and another that focuses on semipublic or private spaces. This complements the analyses offered by Andrea Smith (chapter 11) which focus on antiracist organiza-tions that are run by and primarily for whites. Finally, the issue of mas-culinity and gendered practices that are privileged in an elite school is examined by Brett G. Stoudt (chapter 13). We learn how elite schools are spaces where young boys are socialized into aggressive forms of masculine behavior and into patterns of upper-middle-class entitlement. This occurs in specific spaces that are outside of the classroom and constitutes what would be called "the hidden curriculum."

Geographies of Privilege is not intended to be an exhaustive analysis of all dimensions of privilege; rather, it is intended to provide compelling, contemporary, and innovative analyses of different forms of privilege as they operate across the globe. This book is a tour through an exciting global landscape in which people struggle to acquire, utilize, and transfer different resources (social, educational, economic, material, erotic) that in turn, are used to reproduce, resist, challenge, and reinscribe different types of spatial privileges, some of which are visible to them and some that are taken for granted.

Notes

1. After serving for two consecutive terms as the President of the Catholic Interracial Council and thus becoming a lay spokesperson for progressive Catholics in Chicago, Twine stepped down. In 1972, Paul Twine died in Chicago at the age of 52. In his obituaries, which were published on April 13, 1972 in the *Chicago Tribune* (the white press) and in *The Chicago Defender* (the black press), he was described as "former President of the Catholic Inter-Racial Council" and an employee of the Chicago Transit Authority.
2. John T. McGreery provides an insightful analysis of the political struggles around race and racism for urban Catholics in several major cities including Chicago. For an analysis of this and to understand the significance of lay Catholic activists such as Paul Twine (who is quoted in this book), see (McGreery 1998).

References

Anderson, Kay. 1991. *Vancouver's Chinatown: Racial Discourse in Canada, 1875–1980*. Buffalo, NY: McGill-Queen's University Press.

Berman, Marshall. 1996. "Falling Towers: City Life After Urbicide." In *Geography Identity: Living and Exploring Geopolitics of Identity*, edited by Dennis Crow, 172–92. College Park, MD: Maisonneuve Press.

Bonnett, Alastair. 2000. *White Identities: Historical and International Perspectives*. Harlow, UK: Prentice-Hall.

Brodkin, Karen. 1999. *How Jews Became White and What that Says About Race in America*. Piscataway, NJ: Rutgers University Press.

Collins, Timothy, Sara Grineski, Jayajit Chakraborty, and Yolanda McDonald. 2011. "Understanding Environmental Health Inequalities through Comparative Intracategorical Analysis: Racial/Ethnic Disparities in Cancer Risks from Air Toxics in El Paso County, Texas." *Health and Place* 17 (1): 335–44.

Creswell, Tim. 1996. *In Place/Out of Place: Geography, Ideology, and Transgression*. Minneapolis: Regents of the University of Minnesota.

Darby, Wendy. 2000. *Landscape and Identity: Geographies of Nation and Class in England*. Oxford, UK: Berg.

Delaney, David. 2002. "The Space that Race Makes." *The Professional Geographer* 54 (1): 6–14.

Dwyer, Owen, and John Paul Jones III. 2000. "White Socio-Spatial Epistemology." *Social and Cultural Geography* 1 (2): 209–22.

Essed, Philomena. 1991. *Understanding Everyday Racism: An Interdisciplinary Theory*. London: Sage.

Feagin, Joe, and Melvin Sikes. 1994. *Living with Racism: The Black Middle-Class Experience*. New York: Beacon Press.

Fox, Maddy, and Michelle Fine. 2012. "Circulating Critical research: Reflections On Performance and Moving Inquiry into Action." In *Critical Qualitative Research Reader*, edited by Shirley Steinberg and Gaile Cannella, 153–166. New York: Peter Lang.

Gilmore, Ruthie. 2007. *Golden Gulag: Prisons, Surplus, Crisis, and Opposition in Globalizing California*. Berkeley, CA: University of California Press.

Goldberg, David. 1993. *Racist Culture*. Malden, MA: Blackwell.

Hamnett, Chris, and Tim Butler. 2011. "'Geography Matters': The Role Distance Plays in Reproducing Education Inequality in East London." *Transactions of the Institute of British Geographers* 36 (4): 479–500.

Hartigan, John. 1999. *Racial Situations: Class Predicaments of Whiteness in Detroit.* Princeton, NJ: Princeton University Press.

Harvey, David. 1996. *Justice, Nature, and the Geography of Difference.* Malden, MA: Blackwell.

———. (1982) 2007. *Limits to Capital.* New York: Verso.

Hayden, Dolores. 1980. "What Would a Non-Sexist City be Like/ Speculations on Housing, Urban Design, and Human Work." *Signs* 5 (3): S170–S187.

Higley, Steven. 1995. *Privilege, Power, and Place: The Geography of the American Upper Class.* Lanham, MD: Rowan and Littlefield.

Housel, Jacqueline. 2009. "Geographies of Whiteness: The Active Construction of Racialized Privilege in Buffalo, New York." *Social and Cultural Geography* 10 (2): 131–51.

Jackson, Peter. 1998. "Constructions of Whiteness in the Geographical Imagination." *Area* 30 (2): 99–106.

Kobayashi, Audrey, and Linda Peake. 2000. "Racism out of Place: Thoughts on Whiteness and an Antiracist Geography in the New Millennium." *Annals of the Association of American Geographers* 90 (2): 392–403.

Kurtz, M. 2006. "Ruptures and Recuperations of a Language of Racism in Alaska's Rural/Urban Divide." *Annals of the Association of American Geographers* 96 (3): 601–21.

Lefebvre, Henri. 1976. "Reflections on the Politics of Space." *Antipode* 8: 30–37.

———. 1991. *The Production of Space.* Oxford: Blackwell.

Levine-Rasky, Cynthia. 2002. *Working Through Whiteness: International Perspectives.* Albany, NY: SUNY Press.

Lipsitz, George. 2011. *How Racism Takes Place.* Philadelphia: Temple University Press.

Marharawa, Manissa. SO REAL IT HURTS: Notes from Occupy Wall Street. *Racialicious* October 3, 2011. http://www.racialicious.com/2011/10/03/so-real-it-hurts-notes-on-occupy-wall-street/.

Massey, Douglas, and Nancy Denton. 1993. *American Apartheid: Segregation and the Making of the Underclass.* Cambridge, MA: Harvard University Press.

McGreery, John T. 1998. *Parish Boundaries: The Catholic Encounter with Race in the Twentieth-Century Urban North.* Chicago: University of Chicago Press.

McIntosh, Peggy. 1995. "White Privilege: Unpacking the Invisible Backpack. In *Women: Images and Realities*, edited by Amy Kesselman, Lily Mcnair, and Nancy Schniedewind, 264–67. Mountain View, CA: Mayfield.

Merrifield, Andy. 1996. "Social Justice and Communities of Difference: A Snapshot from Liverpool." In *The Urbanization of Injustice*, edited by Andy Merrifield and Eric Swyngedouw, 200–19. New York: New York University Press.

Merrill, Heather. 2011. "Migration and Surplus Populations: Race and Deindustrialization in Northern Italy." *Antipode* 43 (5): 1542–72.

Moore, Sarah. 2012. "Garbage Matters: Concepts in New Geographies of Waste." In *Progress in Human Geography* http://phg.sagepub.com/

Pager, Devah. 2009. *Marked: Race, Crime and Finding Work in an Era of Mass Incarceration.* Chicago: University of Chicago Press.

Puar, Jasbir. 2007. *Terrorist Assemblages: Homonationalism in Queer Times.* Durham, NC: Duke University Press.

Puar, Nirmal. 2004. *Space Invaders: Race, Gender and Bodies out of Place.* Oxford, UK: Berg.

Pulido, Laura. 2000. "Rethinking Environmental Racism: White Privilege and Urban Development in Southern California." *Annals of the Association of American Geographers* 90 (1): 12–40.

Robinson, Cedric. 1983. *Black Marxism: The Making of a Black Radical Tradition.* Chapel Hill, NC: University of North Carolina Press.

Roediger, David. 2007. *The Wages of Whiteness: Race and the Making of the American Working Class*. rev. ed. London: Verso.

Rose, Gillian. 1993. *Feminism and Geography: The Limits of Geographical Knowledge*. Cambridge, MA: Polity.

Said, Edward. 1994. *Culture and Imperialism*. New York: Vintage Books.

Shapiro, Thomas, and Melvin Oliver. 1997. *Black Wealth/White Wealth*. New York: Routledge.

Soja, Edward. 1980. "The Socio-Spatial Dialectic." *Annals of the Association of American Geographers* 70 (2): 207–25.

———. 1989. *Postmodern Geographies. The Reassertion of Space in Critical Social Theory*. New York: Verso.

———. 2010. *Seeking Spatial Justice*. Minneapolis: University of Minnesota Press.

Steinberg, Steven. 2001. *The Ethnic Myth: Race, Ethnicity, and Class in America*. Boston: Beacon.

Surgue, Thomas. 1996. *The Origins of the Urban Crisis: Race and Inequality in Postwar Detroit*. Princeton, NJ: Princeton University Press.

Twine, France Winddance. 1996. "Brown-Skinned White Girls: Class, Culture and Construction of White Identity in Suburban Communities." *Gender, Place & Culture* 3 (2): 205–224.

Woods, Clyde. 1998. *Development Arrested: Race, Power, and the Blues in the Mississippi Delta*. New York: Verso.

———. 2007. "'Sittin' on Top of the World': The Challenges of Blues and Hip Hop Geography." In *Black Geographies and the Politics of Place*, edited by Katherine McKittrick and Clyde Woods, 46–81. Cambridge, MA: South End Press.

Wyley, Elvin, and Steven Holloway. 2002. "Invisible Cities: Geography and the Disappearance of Race from Mortgage-Lending Data in the USA." *Social and Cultural Geography* 3 (3): 247–82.

PART I

Privileged Bodies in Pleasure and Leisure Spaces

Sex, Music, and Dance Clubs

CHAPTER 1

The Geography of Sex Work in the United Arab Emirates

PARDIS MAHDAVI

On May 11, 2009, the doors of "City of Hope," a United Arab Emirates (UAE) based women's shelter, were closed following almost two years of public controversy. Beginning in late 2007, Cheryl,[1] the founder and director of the shelter, was locked in an almost constant battle with locals, the government, and other activists that was staged at the global level through the use of media outlets such as *The New York Times, The New Yorker,* and the BBC. An American woman who had married an Emirati and created the organization "in her living room," Cheryl was a very vocal and outspoken activist in Dubai who began with domestic violence as her primary cause, but became passionate about "fighting trafficking" when trafficking became part of a sensationalized media and political frenzy following the passage of the U.S. Trafficking Victims Protection Act (TVPA) in 2000 and, later, its international component, the *Trafficking in Persons Report* (TIP) (U.S. Department of State 2001). Through conversations with reporters, researchers, and antitrafficking advocates in EuroAmerica, Cheryl publicly castigated the UAE for what she viewed as major governmental shortcomings in the "war on trafficking."

In early 2007 Cheryl partnered with the Middle East Partnership Initiative (MEPI), a development initiative founded and funded by the Cheney family, which only heightened the negative attention she had been receiving from locals and locally based grassroots activists. Throughout the

course of her work with City of Hope, Cheryl worked with several antitrafficking groups from the United States and secured funds from a variety of
American development agencies. In 2008 Cheryl was accused of abusing
the women in her shelter, selling their children, and often subcontract-
ing their services. Though she dismissed the claims as defamation, several
reporters and researchers (myself included) who spoke with the women
from her shelter confirmed reports of abuse. In May of the following year
she was exiled from the UAE and told that she could never return. Subsequently, the shelter was abandoned abruptly leaving the residents without
electricity or running water, in search of a new shelter and assistance.

As one Middle Eastern women's rights activist told me in 2011 reflecting on the story of City of Hope, "Cheryl and her organization are a classic
example of the problem with American approaches to development. As an
American who had moved to the Emirates and was working to 'save' the
women there, she fit the script perfectly. So perfectly, that no one thought
to look for accountability, to see what she was doing, and what she was
doing was wrong. I agree with the locals who feel that the U.S. supported
the wrong woman for the job." City of Hope, which Cheryl promoted as
the "first" women's shelter in the Gulf, and a leader in the "fight against
trafficking" in the UAE, is a striking example of development efforts constructed from a position of "privilege" or U.S. hegemony and empire, gone
terribly wrong. Locals and activists in the UAE agree that not only did
Cheryl perpetuate the gendered and racialized rhetoric embedded in the
"war on trafficking," but she actually harmed the people she purported to
help.

Migrant women face multilayered and multifaceted challenges. On the
one hand, they must confront the reality that women who move across
borders for employment are often underpaid compared to their male
counterparts, and more likely to face abuse in migration (Ehrenreich and
Hochschild 2008). Beyond the obvious gender stratification in employment demands and compensation, is the fact that women face increased
scrutiny in the form of policies, discourses, and development strategies
that aim to "help" or "rescue" them, highlighting the discursive, physical,
and structural violence they can be exposed to. The story of Suri, a domestic worker from the Philippines who had migrated to Morocco, exemplifies
these myriad challenges in a powerful way.

"I left Morocco because there was no work at home, and my husband
had left me with four children and a lot of debt," she recalled. Because of
increased scrutiny the Moroccan women had leveraged on migrant women,
however, Suri could not migrate legally due to the increased bureaucracy
the Moroccan state had enacted. She had decided to migrate to Dubai to
work in the sex industry because she had heard through friends that wages

for Moroccan women were high in the sex industry and that she could make a large sum of money quickly and return home. "For me, it was about making money as fast as possible so I could get back to my kids. That was it," she explained. But one night, after working in Dubai only one month, not long enough to pay back the debt her husband had accrued, she was rounded up on a "rescue mission" that an American based antitrafficking group enacted. She was arrested, raped, and abused in jail, before being deported, still in high debt, and now facing exile from her family.

My research examines the production of race, ethnicity, and sexuality through deeply flawed and highly privileged developmentalist efforts to address "human trafficking" in the UAE. The field of "development," development studies, and more recently, development anthropology has raised red flags for many anthropologists and been the topic of much commentary and controversy for at least the past two decades (see Escobar 2001). Scholars have critically examined the role of development in the furthering of empire in the neoliberal world order (Agustín 2007, 2008; Escobar 2001; O'Connell Davidson 2006), pointing to ways in which development efforts operate from a presumed position of privilege. While some foreground their concerns in the complicated responses and results of economic development, others focus on the role of "charity," or as Laura Agustín has labeled outreach efforts, as "the social" (Agustín 2007).

In the wake of the global "War on Terror" there has been increasing examination of the role of "development," "outreach," and "charity," especially as it pertains to the racialization of the Muslim world in the recent climate of Islamophobia.[2] The "War on Trafficking," which could arguably be seen as the feminized antidote to the hypermasculinized "War on Terror," has also generated much controversy, especially within the fields of anthropology, sociology, and geography. Scholars such as Denise Brennan (forthcoming), Carole Vance (2011), and Julia O'Connell Davidson (2006) have pointed out the shortcomings of the trafficking debate and the overdetermination of the word *trafficking*.

The widespread panic about transnational female labor, especially in the commercial sex industry has resulted in an elasticity of the term *human trafficking* especially as it is marshaled and deployed in policy and international conventions. As many have noted, it is a term that at once claims too much and too little (Constable 2010; Davidson 2006). Like a rubber band, the term *trafficking* stretches wide enough to encompass all forms of commercial sex work (whether by force, fraud, coercion or not),[3] but then shrinks to exclude forced labor outside the sex industry. Born out of an understandable sense of indignation regarding the types of abuse and exploitation that seem all too common in migrant women's worlds, the concept has been expanded beyond reasonable or feasible limits, becoming both conceptually and juristically obtuse, while narrowly gendered, sexualized, and racialized at the same time. Specifically, the misunderstanding that human trafficking refers only to women who are kidnapped by men and forced into the sex industry has, problematically, become the functional definition of the term in policy, media, and discourse. This has altered the way in which trafficking is represented, pursued, and prosecuted. The paradigm of human trafficking as it exists today, and critically, the disjuncture between the legal ambiguity and popular specificity with which trafficking has been defined, offers uncomfortable insight into the complex ways that gender and race permeate popular understandings of victimhood, vulnerability, and power. The wars on "terror" and "trafficking" conspire to produce moralizing rhetoric about those in need of policing and those in need of rescue, carving the world into victims and villains, both of whom require intervention from EuroAmerican forces.[4]

In this paper I aim to show how antitrafficking discourses constructed in EuroAmerica are raced, gendered, and sexualized while both operating and leading to a moralized type of development or outreach in the name of combating the war on trafficking. This antitrafficking type outreach, produced from a supposed position of privilege (as rehearsed through the rescue rhetoric[5] that involves "us," EuroAmericans, saving "them," the backwards global South) reproduces a racialized morality[6] on multiple levels.

First, it produces the UAE (and other Muslim majority countries) as "hotbeds" of illegal activity including smuggling, terror, and trafficking, which legitimates EuroAmerican intervention in the name of rescue, force, protection, or invasion. The second result, which can be seen worldwide but which has particular ramifications in constructing the geography of sex work in the UAE, is the production of women as either victims in need of rescue or villains who should be criminalized. Consenting female migrants who may or may not work in the sex industry are cast as villains deserving any fate that might befall them, while "victims" are those whose agentive capacity must be ignored or refuted.

In the case of the UAE, consent and agentive capacity are constructed along racialized and classed lines. Women's perceived complicity in determining their status (one that is assumed rather than based on actual accounts) correlates with the ability to script their subjectivities into programmatic paradigms of "victimhood."[7] A closer look at the developmentalist logic that undergirds antitrafficking initiatives reveals the production of gendered, racialized, and sexualized bodies within specific locales but also in the broader construction of empire. The antitrafficking script, constructed within a development framework, casts a trope of appropriate victims and villains which contributes to the production of these very categories.

Four years of extended trips to the Gulf framed ethnographic research with migrant men and women in the UAE (including sex workers, domestic workers, construction workers, and others), as well as those that provide services to them, and assessed the experiences of migrant women and sex workers, labeled as "trafficked" by the international community. Fieldwork in the Gulf was supplemented by nine months of fieldwork in Washington, DC interviewing policymakers and migration activists about discourses, laws, and policies relevant to trafficking, sex work, and migrants' rights globally.

This essay looks at how racialized and sexualized bodies are produced through the developmentalist logic of antitrafficking initiatives. Building on Foucaultian notions of biopolitics and biopower (Foucault 1978), I show how antitrafficking efforts, as a type of development response in conversation with the "War on Terror," have produced a kind of "development discipline" wherein certain bodies need to be disciplined through development efforts. I have found Mahmood Mamdani's (2002) concept of the production of the dichotomous "good Muslim" and "bad Muslim" in the post-9/11 climate of discourses on terror and trafficking useful in framing these analyses. I begin with an examination of racialized and gendered discourses about trafficking and the "rescue industry" these have generated, and then move to a discussion of the reverberations of antitrafficking discourses, policies, and development efforts in the UAE. By contrasting discourses about trafficking in the UAE with actual lived experiences and local grassroots efforts, I highlight the shortcomings of discourse, policy, and development, and the ways that the figures of victim and villain are constructed through hegemonic discourses. I conclude with ethnographic narratives of my interlocutors who describe the negative impacts of development efforts on their lives and experiences in the Gulf.

Victims and Villains

The first time I met Ziya she was living with a group of Indonesian and Australian real estate agents in the Jumeirah Beach Residences, a high end housing complex located in the southern, newer part of Dubai that has emerged as the more affluent part of town. "Here, I love. JBR very good," Ziya told me, referring to her current housing situation. "Me, I'm not liking Bur Dubai. Living on street, living in bus station. Bur Dubai dark, bad. Marina, nice," she said, contrasting the two very different parts of town she had inhabited since migrating to Dubai in 2007. She walked out to the balcony of her current home to show me the breathtaking view of the Persian Gulf and the accompanying Palm Islands as she settled in to tell her story.

Ziya migrated out of Addis Ababa in 2007 after her husband left her with two children and deeply in debt. Having heard from friends that there was an abundance of work in the Middle East and "a lot of money there," as she said, she decided to migrate to Dubai to pursue domestic work. When she arrived, however, she was placed with a family that was highly abusive toward her. "They burn my clothes, throw cups at me, very difficult," she explained. Domestic workers in the Gulf States fall outside the protection of labor laws, and due to the sponsorship system in the UAE (*kefala*) legal residency in Dubai is dependent on the sponsor-employers (problematically collapsed into the same category) who often retain employees' passports and legal working papers.[8]

When Ziya made the decision to run away from her abusive employers, she not only absconded from her job, but automatically became an illegal alien. "I run away, but no passport, no place to go," she explained, reflecting on a tumultuous time in her life not six months earlier. Without her passport (which her former employers still retain), legal work permits, or any money, Ziya entered the informal economy, working as a sex worker and sleeping in airport terminals, bus stations, or on the streets of Bur Dubai, the older part of town which is now somewhat of a working class neighborhood populated mostly by migrant workers of South and East Asian origin.

Lining the wide streets of the southern part of Dubai and the Marina area, gleaming skyscrapers are often spaced miles apart to allow for breathtaking views of the Gulf, the Palm, and the Marina. This urban planning contrasts sharply with the narrow winding streets of Old Dubai in the north, which is home to the neighborhoods of Deira, Bur Dubai, and the Bastakiya (or old fishing village) quarter. When making the drive from south to north on Sheikh Zayed road (the main highway connecting most of the seven Emirates), drivers can witness the spaces between buildings narrow incrementally the further north one moves.

After six months of living and working on the streets of Bur Dubai, where she faced regular abuse from clients, police, and sometimes others in the business, Ziya found an informal organization, supported by locals and expats alike,[9] that provided outreach to street-based sex workers and "trafficked"[10] persons. The members of this informal group mobilized to provide housing assistance for Ziya while they worked to sort out her legal paperwork so that she could procure a new working visa. When I last spoke with her in September of 2009 she had found a job as a nanny for a family in the same building as her temporary home. She laughed as she said, "I am happy to make money now like this to send home to my family. Next time I go home to Ethiopia, I am happy and proud."

The first time I met Maryam, a high end call girl from Tehran, she was also living in a modern high rise skyscraper overlooking Dubai Marina. By the time I left Dubai in 2009, however, Maryam was sleeping in a half built metro terminal in Bur Dubai (the metro system in Dubai was under construction during the summer of 2009 and had been slated to open the following fall) and trying her best to avoid the authorities, who had a warrant for her arrest. "I guess I'm a rags to riches story, but in reverse," Maryam told me when I talked with her on the phone shortly before my departure from the field that summer. "Remember when we first met? I was making thousands of dollars a night, living the good life. Now look at me. I can't stay here (in Dubai), I am in debt because of my legal cases, and I can't even go back to Iran. Worse yet, no one wants to help me here," she lamented. I had initially heard about Maryam through her friends and colleagues in Iran, while conducting field research for a book on sexuality in postrevolution Iran. I had met her friends in Tehran and followed them to Dubai in 2004, where they would make repeated visits to engage in transactional sex.

Women from Iran and Morocco belong to the two highest paid nationalities of sex workers and in highest demand in Dubai, consequently these women earned up to 12,000 Dhs (about $3,000) per night. Many of them lived in luxurious apartments paid for by their regular clientele, while others financed their own accommodations in more expensive parts of town with their high salaries. Maryam used the semiprivate space of the Internet to attract her customers, and up until 2009 had a steady flow of clients that allowed her to make more money than most of the businessmen I met while in Dubai. She and her friends enjoyed the relative safety provided by the discretionary nature of their work. "No one is going to find us here, and if they do, they can't prove anything, can't prove we are prostitutes so it's ok," Maryam had told me in 2005. When I asked about physical safety, she pointed to a series of cameras in her apartment and indicated that she and her friends had hired a full-time guard who would provide assistance should any problems arise. "We are living the life," her friend Sayeh told me in 2008 when I visited their five bedroom apartment, marveling at the view and prime real estate location near the Palm Islands.

In 2009, however, all of this changed when the jealous wife of one of Maryam's customers found out about her husband's activities and called the police. Maryam was arrested immediately, and spent most of one year's income on legal fees and posting bail. She was permitted to leave her holding cell in early 2009 but was told she could not leave the country while her case was pending. She was charged with the crime of adultery. When another client's wife found out about her, she charged her with a series of crimes ranging from espionage to theft. This time, however, the authorities couldn't find Maryam. She had lost her apartment when her friends had rented her room out to another young woman from Tehran in her absence and told Maryam not to return home due to unwanted attention she or her clients' wives might bring. Maryam was relegated to working in hotel lobby bars and clubs, and occasionally turned to street-based sex work to make ends meet. She began sleeping at the homes of clients or in airport or metro terminals. When she sought out assistance from informal outreach groups, she was turned away.

Why the discrepancy? Why was Maryam turned away, unable to access services and assistance while Ziya was taken in? The answers to these questions have everything to do with perceptions of female sex workers[11] based on their countries of origin, and the spaces in which they work. While women who work in street based sex work (located at this spectrum of the sex industry because of demand tied to perceived race) are seen as vulnerable and innocent, higher end sex workers such as Maryam are viewed as predatory, guilty, and a threat to the moral fabric of society by those who provide outreach in the form of social support and services. Their perceived complicity in determining their status (one that is assumed rather than based on actual accounts) correlates with the ability to script their subjectivities into programmatic paradigms of "victimhood."[12]

In addition to the construction of the ideal "antitrafficking" initiative, is the script of the ideal victim. The ideal "trafficked person" typically is a woman, usually working in the sex industry, often young, and in the UAE, usually street based and from sub-Saharan Africa. In Dubai, sex work is both racialized (or more appropriately, ethnicized, but locals refer to these various ethnic groups as "race" and thus I will deploy a similar vernacular, though cognizant of the social construction and problematic use of the term) and spatialized.

In recent years, the sex industry in Dubai has grown to include women from the Middle East, Eastern Europe, East Asia, and Africa. The increase in sex workers of different nationalities has produced a form of racism embedded in spatialized structures of desire constructing specific locations. In other words, the raced hierarchy of demand both structures and is structured by the locations within the city in which sex workers perform their labor. Women from Iran, Morocco, and some parts of Eastern Europe (described as lighter skinned women and labeled as "white") command the highest price, and thus invariably work in the higher paid, more comfortable environments of expensive bars in Jumeirah, Dubai Marina, and inside luxury apartments in wealthier parts of town. Women from East Asia, the Philippines, India, and Pakistan (perceived as "brown" women) form a middle tier (based on earnings) and often work in lower end bars and clubs in Deira or Bur Dubai, or else in brothels and massage parlors throughout the city. Finally, women from Africa (specifically sub-Saharan and East Africa—perceived as "black") are still conspicuously overrepresented in the poorest and most dangerous sectors of the trade, namely in street work. That each group is located in various imagined and physical spaces is a product of their racialization within the discourse, but is also caused by the construction of hierarchical demand. Causality between race, space, place, and demand is thus multidirectional. Ideal "victims" are typically those in street based sex work, while those working in higher end arenas of the sex industry are viewed as having consented and are cast as criminals, regardless of abuses faced or actual level of consent structuring employment situations.

"You can't win either way," said a Moroccan sex worker/activist I met in 2008. "If you are considered a trafficked person, usually the Ethiopians or Nigerians who work the streets or low end bars, then you get raided and rounded up by the police or people who are trying to 'help you,' supposedly. If you aren't, if you are someone like me, considered a criminal, you'll still get arrested by the police. Sometimes we all end up in jail cells together," she explained. The antitrafficking developmentalist discourse constructs appropriate "victims" who are painted as lacking in agency, and are in need of rescue, though rescue efforts can feel like abuse for many women I spoke with. Furthermore, the solution put forth for these "victims" is to send them "home," which for many women is not considered help. "What people don't understand is that we have often left our homes because 'home' is not a good place to be," said one Eritrean woman who fled threats of violence in her home country. "I cannot go back there, I cannot," she added. Others noted that they did not want to return home empty handed to face debts or questioning family or friends, while still others felt that deportation was a terrifying experience. Many of the local activists I spoke with indicated frustration at the way in which the trafficking rhetoric sought to create and produce categories.

"If you don't fit the idea of trafficking and you are a sex worker you are a criminal, and if you aren't a sex worker but you are an African woman, you are seen as a criminal," said Suad. If a migrant woman outside the sex industry experiences force, fraud, or coercion, she is often not considered "trafficked," and if she is, the outreach given to her is either deportation or detention. If a man experiences force, fraud, or coercion and seeks outreach in the name of having been trafficked, he is emasculated and often has no avenues to turn to.[13]

The rhetoric seeks to discipline bodies and this discipline is at the level of the state, outreach efforts, and migrant workers. The result of "development discipline" is that migrant women feel under increased scrutiny, and often fear the after effects of "rescue." Men are no longer considered a risk category, regardless of the myriad abuses they face. The UAE government is also put in a precarious position in that they need to perform a certain way in order to be perceived as being in adherence with U.S. antitrafficking policies. To conform to American expectations they have to show increased prosecutions of "sex traffickers" and demonstrate a commitment to fighting "sex trafficking" by increasing law enforcement and "tightening borders," regardless of whether this may increase challenges migrant workers face, or the fact that this eclipses the larger issue of migrants' rights.

Producing Panic, Necessitating "Rescue"

Over the past decade[14] there has been a growing moral panic (Cohen 1972) about the movement of female bodies across borders that feeds rhetoric about the need to rescue "victims of human trafficking." Around the world today, conversations about labor, migration, sex work, and trafficking have been on a collision course. Policy makers, academics, and activists working within these fields of concern have conflated issues of authoritarianism, race, class, and gender in ways that have served to marginalize the populations most affected by policies and portraits painted about their lives. Most notably, migrant Gulf residents, and particularly women, foreign residents, and "trafficked" persons have been excluded from the opportunity to contribute their own narratives to the programmatic paradigms that they have been scripted into. This research seeks to ameliorate this gap in our understanding while responding to the development efforts that deploy outreach in the name of "antitrafficking activism" to regulate and restrict the movement of certain bodies (gendered and racialized) in certain spaces and discuss ways in which existing narratives about the Gulf mask the complexity of the messy intersections of race, class, nationality, and gender in the rapidly changing urban and institutional spaces of the post petro-dollars Gulf states.

The constructions of "trafficked victim" and "sex worker" are highly gendered, raced, and sexualized. Labels such as "migrant" and "trafficked victim" are often placed on various populations without interrogation. It is for these reasons that many scholars (such as Denise Brennan 2013;Laura Agustín 2007; and Kamala Kempadoo, 2005) argue for a larger conceptualization of trafficking within a broader framework of forced labor and migration, while recognizing the race, class, and gender biases that may accompany such labels. It is useful to interrogate the terms we use to describe the experience of moving to work abroad. As we enter the 21st century, we find ourselves in an era where the movement of bodies, ideas, and discourses occurs rapidly. While the term *trafficked* is mistakenly used mostly to refer to women, usually in the sex industry, the term *migrant*, especially in the Gulf, has a very masculine connotation, and one that is classed as well. In the UAE, "migrant" typically refers to unskilled, low-wage male workers.

Unskilled female workers in the formal economy are referred to as housemaids (*khaddamah*) or nannies, or more commonly as "the help." So too the concept of "laborer" is often gendered, used to refer primarily to low-wage male workers, while women are viewed as "helping" in the domestic sphere. The concept of "laboring" should be expanded to include women's work as well. In the UAE, the term *migrant* is never used for workers of Western backgrounds, who are exclusively referred to as "expatriates." The term *expat* implies highly skilled, Western guest workers in the Gulf and can be applied to people of both genders who come from a certain class and country of origin.

The "War on Terror" and the "War on Trafficking" have both contributed to the production of gendered, racialized bodies perceived to be in need of protection/monitoring/control. As Junaid Rana notes, "the 'War on Terror' exacerbated migrant control, regulation and discipline to create deportable subjects racialized through notions of illegality and criminality" (Rana 2011, 137). The "War on Trafficking" is also racialized, gendered, and sexualized, and quite fixated on prosecution and criminalization. As many scholars have noted, the trafficking protocol is "framed within the convention on transnational organized crime ... packaged within a protocol on smuggling, [and] reflects a preoccupation with illegal immigration as part and parcel of a supposed security threat posed by transnational organized crime as opposed to a concern with the human rights of migrants" (Davidson 2006).[15]

Similar to the raced but faceless "terrorists," "trafficked" persons, migrant laborers, and sex workers have been problematically excluded from the opportunity to contribute their own narratives to the programmatic paradigms that they have been scripted into. Additionally, global rhetoric about human trafficking is markedly focused on sex trafficking and has constructed the issue (in the minds of the public and policy makers alike) in specifically gendered, raced, and classed ways. The archetypal trafficking victims are women, minors, or female minors who have been tricked or forced into "human slavery," often for the explicit purpose of sexual exploitation. Men, or women outside the sex industry, are not imagined as trafficked within the discourse that paints the image of a woman, victimized by her own circumstances. Most recently, this image has taken on a postcolonial, racialized dimension: women from the developing world, willing to take extreme measures in the face of dire poverty, make the "irrational" choice to expose themselves to risky migratory methods and partners (e.g., Bales 1999; Kara 2009; Hughes 1979; Barry 1996).

Individuals, particularly women from the global south, have been scripted in the trafficking framework as duped, or "victims of their global southness" (Shah 2011), a phrase that paints these women as lacking in agency.

Kemala Kempadoo astutely points out that the types of racism that function both within sex work and in framing sex work take two forms: that of "racisms embedded in structures and desires within specific local industries (i.e. the fact that the demand for sex workers for example in Dubai is based on their race/ethnicity) and that of cultural imperialism refracted through international discourses on prostitution" (Kempadoo 2005). Kempadoo and Mohanty go on to note that this second type of racism is less obvious, yet more dangerous. It has become embedded in neoliberal feminist discourse about non-Western women who are, according to Kathleen Barry, in desperate need of "saving" (Barry 1996).

Thus these non-Western women who migrate, possibly to engage in sex work, or who employ transactional sex as a survival or supplemental strategy and may or may not be exploited or trafficked, are constructed as lacking agency and are bearers of a distinctly unmodern subjectivity. The developmentalist logic framing this image, which operates from a position of privilege, excludes the space for self-representation by women from the developing world, and this absence is then cited as evidence of their helplessness and inferiority in comparison to Western female counterparts.

The human trafficking rhetoric, as explicated through policies such as the U.S. *Trafficking in Persons Report* (TIP), a global scorecard ranking nations throughout the world according to their perceived responses to trafficking, calls for commercial sex work to be acted on by the state, often in conjunction with EuroAmerican development efforts (U.S. Department of State, 2001). As others have noted (see Soderlund 2002; Agustín 2008; Bernstein 2010), a "rescue industry" has been crafted whereby members of the developed world mobilize efforts to ostensibly "rescue" or "save" "trafficked women"—usually in the developing world—contributing to the production of what Longva has called an "ethnocracy" (Longva 1995). A few examples of "rescue" efforts[16] that have their origins in the United States but now work to "save women" in countries around the world include the International Justice Mission (IJM) as well as the Coalition Against Trafficking in Women (CATW) whose mission is to "work internationally to combat sexual exploitation in all its forms, especially prostitution and trafficking in women and children, in particular girls (www.catwinternational.org). Evident in this mission statement is the focus on women (and the repetition of the phrase *women and children*, which as other scholars have noted has entered the global lexicon as womenanchildren to the point where women are seen *as* children), the desire to mobilize international efforts, and the focus on sexual exploitation.

There is a dramatic disconnect between policies on human trafficking, and the realities of lived experience. As a result, "antitrafficking" initiatives (most often originating in EuroAmerica) are having a detrimental effect on the lives of migrant men and women in Dubai and Abu Dhabi, and are contributing to a discourse about those in need of "rescue" and those who fall outside the "rights" paradigm. Only those whose narratives fit the "script" of trafficking deserve outreach, and often this outreach or "rescue" comes in the form of raids, arrests, and unwanted deportation.

In her description of the global moral panic about human trafficking and sex work which fuels the production of a rescue industry, Laura Agustín identifies a category of "the social" as those whose "jobs, whether paid or voluntary, are dedicated to improving the condition of society in a wide range of ways" (Agustín 2008, 4). She is critical of this category, however, arguing that "those declaring themselves to be helpers actively reproduce the marginalization they condemn" (Agustín 2007, 5) and in this way notes ways in which "the social" functions to harm those they purport to protect, while simultaneously fueling a racialized, gendered, and moralized discourse. In her book, *Sex at the Margins* (2007), she chronicles a history of gendered and classed relations wherein the figure of the "prostitute" was constructed as demonized in the eighteenth and nineteenth century in a deliberate attempt to create victims that needed "charity." Women of upper and upper middle classes then were able to create jobs and a "charity" industry to "save" the fallen women and the destitute, and this marked the beginning of the "rescue industry" which operates on a much more commercialized and commodified level today. Agustín notes that the "helpers" rely on a particular construction of "the victim" in order to legitimate their authority and work. As she notes, "the victim identity imposed on so many in the name of helping them makes helpers themselves disturbingly important figures" (Agustín 2007, 8). Nowhere is this more evident than in the construction of the trafficked person who is both portrayed as needing help or rescue and protection, while also needing to be controlled as a threat to morality and sovereignty. Agustín traces a genealogy of the rescue industry to follow Judith Butler's concept of genealogy as an investigation of "the political stakes in designating as an origin and cause those identity categories that are in fact the effect of institutions, practices and discourses with multiple and diffuse points of origin" (Butler 1990, ix). In constructing and tracing this genealogy, Agustín shows how those involved in charity work, outreach, and development specifically vis-à-vis sex work and migrants were actually active producers of identity categories of victims and thereby produced tropes of fallen women as victims and racialized men as villains. She concludes that "the social invented not only its objects, but the necessity to do something about them, and thereby its (the social) own need to exist" (Agustín 2007, 107).

As I have shown, the global trafficking rhetoric which is often constructed within a privileged EuroAmerican framework, is raced, classed, gendered, and sexualized thereby producing (while simultaneously being produced by) outreach, policies, development, or "charity" that are similarly sexualized, raced, and gendered. These efforts are disconnected from the needs of migrant workers and trafficked persons, and are functioning to the detriment of those in need while fueling Islamophobic rhetoric about certain countries' nefarious tendencies as hotbeds of illegal activity. As I will elaborate in the next section, antitrafficking initiatives such as the IJM (mentioned above) and to some extent the TIP are examples of the social operating to the detriment of migrant workers in the UAE. In my fieldsite, it was not just trafficked women who needed to be saved, but a "morally impaired" (read: backwards, unmodern) Muslim country that needed to be told how to manage the large influx of migrants within its borders, reflecting concerns about "good Muslims" and "bad Muslims," a type of racializing and moralizing rhetoric operating at the state level.

Trafficking and Development Gone Wrong

Throughout the 1990s, a movement had been building in the UAE to address the issue of migrants' rights. Groups of coethnics or coworkers began coming together to lobby the government for a reform of *kefala,* the sponsorship system that regulates all migrant work in the UAE.[17] Migrants' rights groups came together pushing for more rights and an eventual overhaul of the sponsorship system that they indicated was the root of impingements upon migrants rights. The *kefala* system ties all migrant workers to an employer/sponsor, problematically collapsed into the same figure, rendering the experience of working in the host country entirely dependent on one individual. For women who work as domestic workers, they are subjected to the rules outlined by *kefala* but enjoy none of its protections and many workers become illegal aliens in the instance of a dispute with their employer/sponsor leading them to abscond. Grassroots efforts to modify the sponsorship system had just begun receiving government attention when the war on trafficking took center stage. In 2005 the UAE was given a low ranking in the TIP report. Unlike its neighbors such as Iran, the UAE was vested in its international reputation, especially vis-à-vis one of its major trading partners, the United States. With the creation of the TIP report, a chain of events, cyclical and simultaneous at points, was put into motion. Apart from the racialized morality inherent in the crafting of the TIP report as discussed above, the TIP, with its focus on sex trafficking and prosecution, shifted governmental attention away from migrants' rights (which is the heart of what trafficking is about), and onto hyperscrutiny of the sex industry. Sex workers became the target of raid and rescue campaigns, and antitrafficking initiatives from the United States started making their way into the Emirates at the level of discourse as well as action. The TIP was very clear in its directives toward the UAE:

> The United Arab Emirates (UAE) is a destination country for men and women trafficked for the purposes of labor and commercial sexual exploitation ... government authorities continue to interpret the anti-trafficking law to exclude some who have been forced into commercial sexual exploitation of labor ... (r)ecommendations for the UAE: continue to increase law enforcement efforts to identify, prosecute and punish acts of sex trafficking (U.S. Department of State, 2008)

A snowball became an avalanche, escalating with its own momentum. Most importantly, perhaps, is that attention was directed away from reforming *kefala* and migrants' rights (which is at the heart of trafficking) and focus was placed exclusively on the sex industry. A secondary result was that U.S. antitrafficking efforts began to direct their attention toward "saving" the "poor women in the Gulf" as one Los Angeles based activist told me in 2008. Organizations such as City of Hope also began taking on a new mandate (with American support) to "fight trafficking." Locally, the Emirati response was to create a vice squadron within the police department to focus on "trafficked women." These police officers were imported most often from neighboring Bangladesh or Sri Lanka[18] and not trained to work with sex workers or trafficked persons. The result, as many sex workers told me, was increased abuse from police officers who conducted raids in the name of rescue. "What we needed were more labor inspectors, but the trafficking issue, when it took center stage, it was all about arresting women," explained a local migrants' rights activist in Dubai. "And when they increased police and increased raids, they actually increased abuse," added another volunteer who had herself experienced the abuses she discussed at the hands of imported police officers.

The conflicted and at times negative role of "the social" was evident on multiple levels within my fieldwork. Many migrant women I spoke with complained of hyperscrutiny on "trafficking" as producing a category of criminals to be prosecuted or victims necessitating rescue (and sometimes both simultaneously). More specifically, they noted that this "rescue" came in the form of raids, arrests, and deportation, which for some caused more problems and led to more abuse than the conditions under which they were working. Anya, a sex worker from Eritrea noted that "the police come, they say they come to save us, but they hurt us. So many of us have bruises from the police. But seeing bruises is good, because maybe then they let you go, you are lucky. The not lucky ones have to go home." Other women complained that the rescue rhetoric created a script, and if a woman sought outreach and was complicit in her migration, that she was not deemed a "trafficked person" and thus not seen as deserving assistance. Gloria, a domestic worker from the Philippines, was an example of a woman seen as outside the trafficking paradigm and thus ineligible for outreach or assistance from her Embassy. "I went to my embassy, I said, I am being abuse, I showed them the burn marks all over my body from where my boss put out his cigarettes on me," she explained lifting her shirt to show her wounds which have still not healed despite the fact that over a year has passed. When Gloria went to her Embassy, she was asked if she had contracted her job through the Ministry of Labor. "When I said yes, and when I said I am a domestic, he just looked at me and said, can you believe this? He said 'well, I'm sorry miss, there isn't much I can do for you because you weren't trafficked.' So because I contracted and I'm a domestic, I don't deserve rights?" she asked rhetorically.

Perhaps one of the most harrowing side effects of the trafficking discourse was the way in which local grassroots organizations such as migrants' rights groups and smaller organizations run by groups of three or four migrant workers were eclipsed in favor of American style antitrafficking development efforts. Not only did the antitrafficking discourse provide a script about appropriate victims and villains, but it also painted a picture of the ideal organization (with one series of negative after effects) to combat trafficking. A cascading series of missteps ensued from privileged U.S. based antitrafficking discourses (in the form of the TIP) and initiatives. The creation of a vice squadron within the UAE police department led to unwanted raids on street based and brothel based sex workers who reported abuse at the hands of imported, untrained police officers. American-supported efforts such as City of Hope actually increased challenges that migrant women were facing. And grassroots, smaller efforts that had been working with migrant women and men were eclipsed and ignored. The experience of Sama, a local grassroots activist who works with migrant women illuminates both of these after effects quite well:

In a café off of Sheikh Zayed Road, facing the soaring twin towers of the Dubai Financial Center, Sama sits at the table, takes a sip of her mint tea, and lets out an exhausted sigh before burying her face in her hands. She has brought a young woman named Meskit with her to the café this morning, and Meskit is accompanied by her son, a three-year-old boy named

Karim. Karim tears around the café while his mother smiles at him and adjusts her head scarf.

"I am tired," Sama says. "Not just today, but tired because this work is taking its toll on me, and it feels like my job is getting harder and harder to do." She clenches her hennaed hands into fists. Meskit slides over to Sama and puts her arm around her. "This woman is the reason I'm alive," she says. Meskit proceeds to tell her story, how she left Addis Ababa to work in Dubai as a domestic worker and was abused and raped by her employer. When her employer found out she was pregnant, he kicked her out of the house and she ended up in jail. After three weeks, Meskit found Sama's number and called for her assistance. Over the next three months Sama was able to persuade the authorities to let her out of jail and helped her to procure a new working visa. Today, Meskit is working as a nanny and lives in Dubai with her son. "She has helped so many Ethiopian women like me, but she is exhausted, it's getting harder and harder to do her kind of work."

Sama is tired from battling the global and local notions about human trafficking that combine to put undue pressure on female migrants in the UAE, while also eclipsing her efforts. She is tired because international policies as championed in the *Trafficking in Persons Report* have hindered her efforts to create and mobilize a civil society in the UAE to meet the needs of migrant workers, trafficked or not. Sama was born in Ethiopia and raised in refugee camps in Somalia and Italy. As an adult, she lived in Canada briefly before moving to Dubai in 2003. She says that it was her experience being a refugee and then a migrant worker in Italy and Canada that made her interested in forming an ad hoc social support group to help African women who have become migrant workers around the world. A tall woman with kind eyes, she speaks seven languages fluently and uses her linguistic skills to help translate for women who are facing legal troubles or are mired in court cases.

"The problem is that your George Bush and the Americans made trafficking so political. On top of that they made it so that all trafficking is sex trafficking, so what does that do? It makes people racist, it makes people think that any Ethiopian woman here is a sex worker, or has been trafficked, and is a criminal," she explained. Every day Sama works with Ethiopian women who have been arrested for absconding from their jobs, overstaying their visas, accruing debt, or working as sex workers. She says that the pointed focus on sex trafficking within the TIP and in United Nations documents such as the *UN Protocol to Prevent, Suppress, and Punish Trafficking in Persons* (2003) (which operates under the umbrella of the UN Office on Drugs and Crime) has constructed the trafficking issue as a criminal matter in the minds of locals and UAE law enforcement. Sama is frustrated that members of law enforcement assume that women from certain nationalities must all be guilty. She is angered that local and international authorities articulate and reproduce local racialized and gendered hierarchies rather than approaching labor and migration issues within a human rights framework. She is also angered by international policies, such as those advocated in the TIP report, that consider all abused migrant women to be sex workers and, by default, criminals. Thus any migrant worker seeking assistance is first taken to jail for questioning. "The worst part is that they don't even get good translators for these women. They—the police, or the judges—they have made up their minds about Ethiopian women, and they get people to translate for them into words that they want to hear, that they are guilty, that they are criminals. They don't even get a fair shot, that's why I insist on doing the translations, because it's just not fair," she explained.

Sama pulls out a photograph from her purse and hands it to me. In it, a frail Ethiopian woman not weighing more than ninety pounds is lying in a hospital bed. The woman is hooked up to an IV drip, but her arms are also handcuffed to the bed. I look up in confusion. Sama continues, raising her ordinarily soft voice for the first time: "Yes, can you believe it? She is handcuffed to the bed! She ran away because her employer was abusing her, she was a housemaid. She ran away and as she was doing so she was hit by a car and was taken to the hospital. When she woke up, she was chained to the bed. They assume that because she ran away, and because she is an Ethiopian woman, she is a criminal. Now how do you handle that kind of racism?"

Her voice once again becomes soft as she tells me that things weren't always this way; that people didn't used to be this harsh toward migrant women, and that doing her job used to be much easier. She acknowledges that there has been a long history of labor rights violations in the UAE, but stresses that in the late 1990s, migrant advocacy groups were beginning to make progress vis-à-vis the state; progress that was stunted, in her opinion, with the politicization of the trafficking issue. She emphasizes that it was only when the issue became political, when the UAE was put on the TIP watch list that female migrant workers became synonymous with sex workers and, as sex workers, became labeled as trafficking victims and seen as a dangerous, politically damaging population that demanded what some would call protection in the form of observation and surveillance. While Sama was one of my first interviewees to name the negative effect of international policy mandates on building civil society, she was not the only one to do so. As a result of the TIP, the individuals and organizations providing public services and raising awareness about the circumstances of migrants in need have come under harsh scrutiny by the government.

Local grassroots activists in Dubai also complain of the EuroAmerican desire to "rescue" morally impaired populations in the Middle East. The political potency of migration and human trafficking disrupted local outreach efforts in the UAE in three main ways: (1) through the pointed politicization of the issue of human trafficking, which brought migrant women under levels of increased scrutiny not previously experienced; (2) through the creation of the TIP report, which placed the UAE and other Arab countries onto a watch list and spurred unanticipated state involvement in what was developing as an organic, resident-directed movement to address the egregious lack of social support systems; and (3) through the strategic use of literature on the "absence" of civil society in the Arab world and in the Gulf in particular, that, in labeling/explaining how and why the UAE was "unable" or "noncompliant" in dealing with the trafficking issue, erased and silenced the activism that had been taking place for a number of years, while enabling the state's co-optation of the issue. "What bothers me most about the TIP," said Randa, a Palestinian lawyer who now lives in Dubai and works to advocate for domestic workers' rights in the UAE, "is that one of the things the Bush Administration was after was this bilateral trade agreement (here she is referring to the '1,2,3 Agreement'—a nuclear weapons agreement),[18] an agreement that would get them a better trading deal with the UAE, so they strategically used the trafficking issue to negotiate a better deal." Becoming more animated and agitated, she added,

> well, it also really bugs me that it seems like the TIP has an imperialist agenda. I mean it's a good thing to have human rights standards, but we must take into account how people come to those organically. In order for neoliberal feminists in the West to have their rhetoric, they must understand that neoliberal rhetoric is based on Western experiences and this rhetoric can be very condescending!

Heba and Maysoun, two Emirati women who donate money to various informal groups working with migrants, took Randa's sentiments a step further. When I interviewed them at a cafe in Abu Dhabi, the conversation began quietly enough. The quiet tones dissipated, however, once we began talking about civil society and the role of EuroAmerica in helping or hindering a civil society movement in the UAE. Pushing back the sleeves of her long black *abbaya* so she could gesture emphatically with her hands, Heba began talking about the reasons she believed that people in EuroAmerica react to Dubai the way they do;

> It's like this, like they couldn't conceptualize an Arab Muslim country doing so well, developing so rapidly and so successfully, and even having civil society, like it didn't fit into their little box that they had drawn about us. Now with things going a bit differently,

they are so excited to point to us and our problems and say, "see, I knew they couldn't be doing that well, or if they were, they did it in a sneaky and backward way." Like it's because since they didn't anticipate it, and that it didn't fit into their box, they are doubly happy to see us struggle. They point to us and say that we have a trafficking problem, that we don't have civil society. They want to see us fail. They want to keep us down somehow.

Her friend Maysoun continued, also becoming very animated to the point where her head scarf actually began slipping off:

They want to blame everything on Islam, they want to use something, to find something to point to the fact that us Muslims, there is something wrong with us, like that we need to learn to be better, like that we can't figure out our own way forward. I'm so tired of people trying to save us. Like save us from whom? And from what? Oh the poor Muslim women, you know what? I feel sorry for the poor Western women who don't know anything. Tell them to get off our backs!

Maysoun passionately conveyed her frustration at the way she felt that the UAE and Arab Muslim world in general had been painted in the academic and political discourse generated by EuroAmerica—or certain types of EuroAmerican "feminists." She felt it was unfair that the UAE was accused of having a "trafficking problem" that it supposedly did not know how to deal with when she knew from personal experience that there had been a push for civil society to address these issues, but that it was co-opted by the state, precisely because of the rhetoric as laid out in the TIP.

Conclusion

Antitrafficking rhetoric and initiatives that operate from a position of privilege seek to discipline certain bodies through development efforts. The result is a racialized morality and a series of tragic missteps that have rendered lived experiences of migration, forced labor, and sex work more challenging. Moralized development produces raced, classed, gendered and sexualized discourse, policy and intervention. It also feeds into rhetoric about the "moral decay" of the Muslim world, fueling "clash of civilizations" type rhetoric (Huntington 1996). Beyond xenophobic and misogynistic rhetoric, moralized development also mobilizes and supports efforts that operate to the detriment of migrant workers such as City of Hope while eclipsing the efforts of those people, like Sama, who are actually working to improve migrants' lives at the grassroots level. Privileged outreach efforts, operating as "the social," further harms migrant workers by creating categories that question migrant worker subjectivity. It is not clear who is being served by these efforts, other than the "rescuers." When establishing a moral sphere of regulation, it is important to interrogate what populations are being served and what the reverberations are to those most in need.

Acknowledgements

I am grateful to the Pomona College faculty research grant, the American College of Learned Societies, and the Woodrow Wilson International Center for Scholars for their support of this project. I would also like to thank my research assistants including Christine Sargent, Sarah Burgess, Abby DiCarlo, and Justin Gutzwa. I am also grateful to France Winddance Twine and Bradley Gardener, the editors of this volume for their inspiring work on this exciting project. Finally, I wish to thank my interlocutors who opened their hearts, homes, and lives to me.

Parts of this chapter have been published as an article entitled "Race, Space, Place: The Racialization and Spatialization of Sex work in Dubai." In *Culture, Health and Sexuality*. A few parts also appear in P. Mahdavi, *Gridlock: Labor, Migration and Human Trafficking in Dubai* (2011, Stanford University Press).

Notes

1. All names have been changed to protect the identity of the respondents.
2. For an excellent discussion of racializing Muslims, see Rana (2010).
3. The official definition of trafficking as outlined by the United Nations *Protocol to Prevent, Suppress and Punish Trafficking in Persons, Especially Women and Children* is: Colloquially, trafficking is defined as instances of force, fraud, or coercion.
4. For an in-depth discussion of ways in which the wars on terror and trafficking conspire to produce racialized Muslims requiring intervention, see Rana (2010) or Mahdavi (forthcoming).
5. For an excellent discussion of the rescue industry please see Agustín (2007, 2008) or Sodurlund (2002).
6. Ibid.
7. I place "trafficking victims" in particular in quotations to indicate the arbitrary nature of "victimhood." I do not deny that trafficked persons are often subjected to unscrupulous and criminal figures, and that migrants, trafficked or not, often are victim of macro- and microinstances of violence and exploitation. I am wary, however, of the term *victim*, because of the unequal power dynamic that is implied. By positioning trafficked women as "victims," the attention and power is then shifted to "rescuers," who set the terms for who gets to "count" as a victim and what they are understood to be a victim of. For an in-depth explication of the politics of the rescue industry see Soderlund (2005).

8. Dubai is not the only place where the *kefala* or sponsorship system governs the rules and experiences of guest workers. In fact, many of the Gulf countries have this same system in place. In these countries, the *kefala* system is problematic in that residence in the country is predicated on the sponsor-employer. Scholars such as Andrew Gardner have argued successfully that this system imposes a type of structural violence on migrant workers in the Gulf (see Gardner 2010). For domestic workers, the *kefala* system presents particular challenges in that while they are held to the rules of the sponsorship system, they cannot benefit from the protections of said system as their work is relegated to the "private realm" and there exists a specific clause in UAE labor laws that domestic workers are not protected by labor laws that protect construction or other migrant workers (http://www.uae-embassy. org/uae/human-rights/labor-rights). Domestic workers in many parts of the world face the dilemma of what scholar Rhacel Parrenas has termed "partial citizenship" (Parrenas 2001). However, domestic workers and many other members of the informal economy in the Gulf experience added challenges of not being able to seek out recourse for challenges incurred during their time as domestic workers due to a lack of formal structures in place to protect their rights. For an excellent discussion of domestic work in the Gulf see Longva (1999), Silvey (2004), or Gamburd (2000).

9. Note that the population of Dubai consists of only 8% Emiratis or locals (Government of Dubai, Statistical Center 2009). The remainder of the population is made up of noncitizens. Of these noncitizens, it is estimated that 70% are unskilled laborers from Asia and Africa, but most commonly from South Asia (for more statistics on demographics in the Gulf please see Andrzej Kapiszewski 2001). Male unskilled workers are typically labeled "migrants," female unskilled workers are referred to as "help" or "caretakers" while skilled workers, mostly of Western origin earn the more melodious term *expat* according to my interlocutors.

10. I use quotes to indicate the contested nature of a term that has no universal definition, rather various actors define the term *trafficked* in ways that are most convenient for their policies, academic discourses, or activist procedures. There has been an increasing amount of debate about the definition of trafficking, which is most often used to refer to the movement or transport of illegal contraband, specifically arms and drugs. "Trafficking in people" is defined as the transportation of people across long distances (which may or may not include crossing an international border) through some form of deceit, coercion, or force. It is for these reasons and more that it is important not to conflate the often sliding definitions of terms such as *trafficking*, *migration*, or *labor*. For an in-depth discussion of the strategic deployment of the term *trafficking* in the Gulf, please see Mahdavi and Sargent (2011).

11. Though several interlocutors described the presence of male sex workers in Dubai, I was unable to find any men during my time in the field. Therefore, while I acknowledge the presence of male sex workers in Dubai and the Gulf more broadly speaking, in this article I am focusing on women who work in the sex industry.

12. I place "trafficking victims" in particular in quotations to indicate the arbitrary nature of "victimhood." I do not deny that trafficked persons are often subjected to unscrupulous and criminal figures, and that migrants, trafficked or not, often are victims of macro- and microinstances of violence and exploitation. I am wary, however, of the term *victim*, because of the unequal power dynamic that is implied. By positioning trafficked women as "victims," the attention and power is then shifted to "rescuers," who set the terms for who gets to "count" as a victim and what they are understood to be a victim of. For an in-depth explication of the politics of the rescue industry, see Soderlund (2005).

13. For a full discussion of gendered trafficking paradigms please see Mahdavi and Sargent (2011).

14. Though as Kempadoo (2009) notes, much of this panic can be traced back to panics over "white slavery" as well as controversy about sex work across borders that have their roots in the late nineteenth and early twentieth century.

15. For an in-depth explication of the problems inherent with the EuroAmerican framing of the "rescue industry" please see Agustín (2007).
16. For further information about the *kefala* system and its shortcomings please see Longva (1995) or Gardner (2010).
17. In Dubai only 8% of the population are local Emiratis, therefore they do not have enough manpower to staff infrastructure such as law enforcement, and thus must import this labor.
18. For more information about the "1,2,3 Agreement" please see http://articles.cnn.com/2009-01-15/world/us.uae_1_nuclear-non-proliferation-treaty-nuclear-cooperation-nuclear-power-plants?_s=PM:WORLD

References

Augustin, Laura. 2007. *Sex at the Margins: Migration, Labour, Markets, and the Rescue Industry*. London: Zed Books.
———. 2008. "The Shadowy World of Sex Across Borders." *The Guardian*. http://www.guardian.co.uk
Bales, Kevin. 1999. *Disposable People: New Slavery in the Global Economy*. Berkeley, CA: University of California Press.
Barry, Kathleen. 1996. *The Prostitution of Sexuality*. New York: New York University Press.
Bernstein, Elizabeth. 2010. "Militarized Humanitarianism meets Carceral Feminism: The Politics of Sex, Rights, and Freedom in Contemporary Antitrafficking Campaigns." *Signs: Journal of Women in Culture and Society* 36 (1): 45–72.
Butler, Judith. 1990. *Gender Trouble: Feminism and the Subversion of Identity*. London: Routledge.
Brennan, Denise, and Pardis Mahdavi. 2013 *Rethinking Trafficking*. Durham, NC: Duke University Press,
Cohen, Stanley. 1972. *Folk Devils and Moral Panics*. London: MacGibbon and Kee.
Davidson, Julia O'Connell. 2006. "Will the Real Sex Slave Please Stand Up?" *Feminist Review* 83: 1, 4–22.
Dubai, Government of, Statistical Center. 2009. *Dubai in Figures*. Author.
Ehrenreich, Barbara, and Arlie Hochschild. 2008. *Global Woman: Nannies, Maids, and Sex Works in the New Economy*. New York: Holt.
Escobar, Arturo. 2001. Culture sits in places: reflections on globalism and subaltern strategies of localization. *Political Geography* 20: 139–174.
Foucault, Michel. 1978. *The Birth of Biopolitics: Lectures at the Collège de France 1977–1978*. London: Palgrave Macmillan.
Gamburd, Michele. 2000. The Kitchen Spoon's Handle: Transnationalism and Sri Lanka's Migrant Housemaids. Ithaca, NY: Cornell University Press.
Gardner, Andrew. 2010. *City of Strangers*. Ithaca, NY: Cornell University Press.
Huntington, Samuel P. 1996. *The Clash of Civilizations and the Remaking of World Order*. New York: Simon & Schuster.
Kapiszewski, Andrzej. 2001. *Nationals and Expatriates: Population and Labour Dilemmas of the Gulf Cooperation Council State*. Garnet & Ithaca Press.
Kara, Siddharth. 2009. *Sex Trafficking: Inside the Business of Modern Slavery*. New York: Columbia University Press.
Kempadoo, Kamala, ed. 2005. *Trafficking and Prostitution Reconsidered: New Perspectives on Migration, Sex Work, and Human Rights*. Boulder, CO: Paradigm.
Kempadoo, Kamala, 2009. "Centering Praxis in Policies and Studies of Caribbean Sexuality." In *From Risk to Vulnerability: Power, Culture and Gender in the Spread of HIV and AIDS in the Caribbean*, edited by Christine Barrow, Marjan de Bruin, and Robert Carr, 179–191. Kingston: UWIHARP and Ian Randle Publishers.

Longva, Ahn Nga. 1995. "Citizenship, identity and the question of supreme loyalty: the case of Kuwait". *Forum for Development Studies*, 2: 197–219.

Longva, Ahn Nga. 1999. *Walls Built on Sand: Migration, Exclusion, and Society In Kuwait*. Westview Press.

Mahdavi, Pardis. 2011. *Gridlock: Labor, Migration and Human Trafficking in Dubai*. Palo Alto, CA: Stanford University Press.

Mahdavi, Pardis, and Christine Sargent. 2011. "Questioning the Discursive Construction of Trafficking in the UAE." *Journal of Middle East Women's Studies*.

Mamdani, Mahmood. 2002. *When Victims Become Killers: Colonialism, Nativism, and the Genocide in Rwanda*. Princeton, NJ: Princeton University Press.

Parrenas, Rhacel. 2001. *Servants of Globalization: Women, Migration, and Domestic Work*. Palo Alto, CA: Stanford University Press.

Rana, Junaid. 2011. *Terrifying Muslims: Race and Labor in the South Asian Diaspora* Durham, NC: Duke University Press.

Shah, Svati. 2011. "Slumdogs, Brothels and Big Screen Rescues." Lecture delivered at Pomona College April 5.

Silvey, Rachel, 2004. "Transnational Domestication: State Power and Indonesian Migrant Women in Saudi Arabia." Political Geography, 23(3).

Soderlund, Gretchen. 2002. "Covering Urban Vice: The New York Times 'white Slavery' and the Construction of Journalistic Knowledge." *Critical Studies in Media Communication* 19 (4), 438–460.

———. 2005. Running from the rescuers: New U.S. crusades against sex trafficking and the rhetoric of abolition. *NWSA Journal*, 17(3), 64–87.

UN Office on Drugs and Crime. 2003. *UN Protocol to Prevent, Suppress, and Punish Trafficking in Persons.* http://www.uncjin.org/Documents/Conventions/dcatoc/final_documents_2/convention_%20traff_eng.pdf

U.S. Department of State. 2001. *Trafficking in Persons Report*. Washington, DC: Author. http://www.state.gov/j/tip/rls/tiprpt/

U.S. Trafficking Victims Protection Act. 2000. PL 106–386.

Vance, Carole S. 2011. States of Contradiction: Twelve Ways to Do Nothing about Trafficking While Pretending To. *Social Research* 78 (3): 933–948.

CHAPTER 2

Displacing Place Identity
Introducing an Analytics of Participation

KEVIN DURRHEIM, CLINTON RAUTENBACH,
TAMARYN NICHOLSON, AND JOHN DIXON

Recovering Affect from Place Identity

The construction and management of space has been an important means for securing social privilege. Nowhere is this more apparent than in the use of segregation to produce and maintain racial hierarchy (Cell 1982). The slogan of "separate but equal" was employed to defend both Jim Crow segregation in the United States and apartheid in South Africa, but it soon became clear that segregation produced inequality. Pettigrew (1979) described segregation as the linchpin of inequality, because mutually reinforcing circuits of segregation in housing, education, and employment ensured that a black underclass became locked into a spiral of poverty and social disadvantage, an idea confirmed by Massey and Denton's (1993) monumental analysis of racial inequality and segregation in the United States.

Although explicit, government enforced policies of segregation have all but disappeared, established patterns of segregation and privilege have been preserved. David Goldberg (1998) has characterized this new segregation as conservationist, peripherally organized, and class differentiated because it:

conserves and deepens the hold of segregation historically produced as if it were in the nature of things ... [and] is produced by
doing nothing special, nothing beyond being guided by the pre-
sumptive laws of the market, the determinations of the majority's
personal preferences (17).

In this model, segregation and privilege are instituted by the enactment
of personal preferences. Private vectors of choice—"the informalities of
private preferences schemes" (Goldberg 1998, 17)—have overtaken the law
and might of the state in maintaining geographies of privilege.

The concept of place identity has provided a useful analytic tool for
investigations of how such preferences are exercised in the defense, and in
some cases the extension of privilege. On the one hand, the concept of place
identity simply captures the phenomenological potency of belonging or
exclusion. Place identity is marked by a sense of social, physical, and autobio-
graphical "insideness" (Rowles 1983; Tuan 1974): an emotional, intellectual,
and even spiritual connection to place. On the other hand, place identity
can also be associated with a sense of threat, exclusion, marginalization, or
displacement (Tuan 1979; Durrheim and Dixon 2001). Particularly under
conditions of sociopolitical change, constructions of place identity may
justify the maintenance of the status quo, a theme documented by several
discursive psychological studies of everyday discourse about place.

The discursive approach to place identity was in psychology inaugurated
by extending the understanding of how places served as the grounds for
identity (Dixon and Durrheim 2000). Not only did place ground a sense of
belonging, it also served as a "rhetorical warrant through which particular
social practices and relations are legitimated" (Dixon and Durrheim 2000,
33). This focus on language and rhetoric allowed researchers to politicize
place identity, investigating the ideological traditions to which rhetoric
about place identity adhered (e.g., Hopkins and Dixon 2006; Manzo 2003;
Di Masso, Dixon, and Pol 2011). The personal, emotive, and psychological aspects of place belonging and attachment could be seen as doing the
work of shoring up privilege. Thus, for example, the sense of belonging and
nostalgia for places developed under apartheid needed to be understood
from the perspective of how it was being used and deployed in the broader
ideological projects of racial segregation and inequality (e.g., Ballard 2010;
Brown 2009; Durrheim and Dixon 2005b).

This work in discursive social psychology was part of a greater questioning of humanist accounts of the subject. In place of a "coherent, bounded,
self-aware and universal subject" (Pile 2010, 7), feminist and nonrepresentational geographers proposed not only that subjectivity was relational, fluid, and embedded in practice, but that subjectivity—thoughts,

emotions, feelings, and affects—were, strictly speaking, not represent-able (Thrift 1996). Expressions of subjectivity—narratives of belonging or displacement—were always to be viewed as occasioned and interested accounts that could not be taken at face value as reports of internal states (cf. Edwards 1997).

The idea that the subjective features of place identity were rhetorical and ideological constructions led to a threefold transformation of the field of place identity both in social psychology and in the social sciences more generally. First, research began to focus on how ordinary people talked about place. Such talk was viewed as occasioned and instrumental constructions of self and place, and was of interest for its rhetorical and political effects and not merely for what it described (Durrheim and Dixon 2005a). For example, when white suburban residents of a neighborhood of Cape Town complained that the emerging informal settlement of black "squatters" destroyed the "pristine beauty" of the place, the actual beauty of the place and the emotional reactions of the white residents were not treated as descriptions, but as elements of politically attuned rhetoric of exclusion (Dixon et al. 1994).

Place identity provided the grounds for private preference schemes that worked to secure white privilege and exclusivity. Second, as an immedi-ate consequence of the focus on talk, the attention to place-related affect, emotion, and feeling that had been so important in the phenomenological tradition was rendered problematic. These diverse and nuanced subjective elements of place attachment were now viewed with some suspicion, as ways of grounding exclusion and privilege in naturalized and thus apoliti-cal mental states. Third, the rhetorical approach to place identity was often concerned with constructions of belonging. Arguments about who did or did not belong provided the political impetus for this work. The focus on the rhetoric of place attachment, displacement, and belonging was informed by the idea that privilege and domination operated principally by means of an exclusion–inclusion dynamic (e.g., Dwyer 1999; Rose 1990; Sibley 1995). Consequently, much of the social psychological research on place identity in South Africa was primarily concerned with how vari-ous forms of segregation—such as informal segregation (Durrheim and Dixon 2005b), semigration (Ballard 2004), and gated communities (Hook and Vrodiljak 2002)—operate to maintain racial privilege. For example, Durrheim and Dixon (2005b) observed how white resistance to the end of beach apartheid focused on how beaches had been transformed from arenas of family and relaxation to arenas of fear, suspicion, and hypervigi-lance. Yet these feelings, thoughts, and emotions were of little direct inter-est. The focus was placed firmly on how these forms of subjectivity were utilized in arguments for exclusive spaces of racial privilege.

In the present chapter, we suggest that privilege does not only operate in the narrow field of practice marked by the rhetoric of inclusion–exclusion. First, research needs to move beyond concerns with rhetoric and representation to consider other "possibilities of performance" by which spaces are enlivened (Latham and Conradson 2003). In addition, we need to consider how these practices are implicated in relations of power and privilege that transcend a simple impulse to exclude the historically disadvantaged. To evoke the Foucaultian model, power is not merely repressive and exclusionary but is also productive of truth and of subjects (Foucault 1978, 1982). Privilege is thus maintained by modes and tactics of "governmentality" by which the conduct of free subjects is guided and shaped in ways that are socially inclusive, self-affirming, even pleasurable (Dean 1994; Hook 2007; Rose 1990).

The chapter thus has two aims. First, we want to outline a critical approach to place identity that transcends the politics of inclusion-exclusion, and second we want to acknowledge the subjective and affective aspects of privilege that ground place identity in places, bodies, and performance as well as in everyday discourse. To this end, we shall consider how gender privilege operates in the context of heterosexual bar and club culture. Rather than being unwelcome or excluded from these spaces, the presence of women is celebrated and guaranteed in practices that favor women, such as allowing women free entry, free drinks, ladies night, priority access, and, ostensibly, put women at center stage. We will argue that privilege does not operate via practices of exclusion, but through the engineering of affect and in the production of women as the subjects of male consumption.

Our interest in affect is derived from nonrepresentational human geography which, during the past decade, has sought to investigate the "*how of different emotional relations*" (Anderson and Harrison 2006, 334; emphasis in original). This emerging tradition does not signal a retrogressive return to a humanist phenomenology of emotions. Like discursive social psychologists, nonrepresentational geographers view emotions as ultimately unknowable; that is, in the psychological sense of interior "feelings" experienced and expressed by the autonomous individual. They are instead concerned with the "genealogies, conditionalities, potentialities and materialities" of affect, and in the "emergence of subjectivities from more or less unwilled affectual and emotional assemblages" (Anderson and Harrison 2006, 334). This is a Foucaultian project in the sense that it proposes no preexisting subject whose agency is grounded in untrammelled thought and feeling. It resonates with Butler's (1990) view of the subject, which suggested that "there is no 'being' behind doing, acting, becoming; the doer is merely a fiction imposed on the doing—the doing itself is everything" (25).

In this model, affect can be defined as "the property of an active outcome of an encounter [which] takes the form of an increase or decrease in the ability of the body and mind alike to act" (Thrift 2004, 62). The source of emotions is thus outside of individuals, arising within settings that choreograph trajectories for bodies and shape the nature of social encounters and exchanges. For example, aggression can be marshaled and channeled "through various forms of military training such as drill" and result in outcomes such as increased firing and higher kill ratios (Thrift 2004, 64). Similarly, when Durrheim and Dixon (2005b) interviewed holiday makers who were lying and sun tanning on Scottburgh beach, they all reported "feeling relaxed." These emotions had their place in a specific arrangement of events and things, times, places, and people. Being relaxed was a form of subjectivity produced through participation in the ritual of holidaying, tied to times, seasons, and place and performed through a series of ritualistic maneuvers and embodied practices of relocation away from home and work.

From this kind of theoretical grounding of affect in bodies and performance, cultural geographers such as Thrift, McCormack, and Anderson locate affects in transversals between bodies located in the materialities of space-time and in sites of inbetweenness that connect people and people as well as people and places (cf. Pile 2010).

> The emergence of affect from the relations between bodies, and forms of encounters that those relations are entangled within, make the materialities of space-time always-already affective. There is not, first, an "event" and then, second, an affective "effect" of such an "event." Instead, affect takes place before and after the distinctions of subject-world or inside-outside as a "ceaselessly oscillating foreground/background or, better, an immanent 'plane' (Seigworth 2000, p. 232)." (Anderson 2006, 736)

In a register of dialectics, we might say that affect is both the condition and outcome of action. However, Anderson refuses to use the language of cause and effect, inside and outside, so he says instead that affect is "enfolded in action" as an immanent plane of its possibility.

This geography of affect shifts the analytic focus from mind and the rhetoric of place identity to embodied practices and thus connects work in the field to broader developments in the so-called affective turn in the social sciences (e.g., Clough and Halley 2007). In so doing, it neither approaches subjectivity through phenomenological introspection nor treats it simply as a discursive or textual accomplishment. Instead, by the "spacing of emotion and affect" (Anderson and Harrison 2006, 334), subjectivity is seen as the product of specific forms of participation in the settings and routines of everyday life. The immediate advantage of this theory is that it widens the scope of political analysis to include a focus on affect. Hope, fear, joy, shame, boredom, and many other affects may constitute geographies of privilege in addition to or alongside boundaries and regions of inclusion-exclusion that have been of interest in the social psychology literature of place identity.

This offers new possibilities for political engagement which aims to understand and dismantle forms of relations and materialities of oppressive affects. The job is urgent for, as Thrift suggests, affect has become the site of social engineering:

> now affect is more and more likely to be engineered with the result that it is becoming something more akin to the network of pipes and cables that are of such importance in providing the basic mechanics and root textures of urban life. (Thrift 2004, 58)

This is a stark antihumanist vision in which docile subjects and vectors of privilege can be fabricated by setting up forms of relations and materialities—rerouting, rewiring, and renetworking the pipes and cables of affect—that channel human conduct and govern participation in social life.

Reconnecting Affect and Thought

There are problems, however, with this conception of the spacing of affect and the focus on emotional assemblages. Steve Pile (2010) suggests that "Affectual geography radically splits affect from thought … construct[ing] affect as the pure non-representational object: it cannot be known, grasped or made intelligible" (16). This creates a logical problem. How can affect be "consciously and deliberately engineered" when it cannot be known? There are also political limitations to work that focuses on the subject-constituting powers of affective architectures but "discourage[s] an engagement with everyday emotional subjectivities" (Thien 2005, 450). The challenge, as we see it, is to somehow link this architecture of affect to everyday emotional subjectivities—the thoughts and feelings of individual people in ordinary situations—without reverting to a discredited humanist account of the subject that "conjures up a vision of emotional authenticity" (McCormack 2006, 331).

Discursive social psychology may assist with this project because it already has a well-developed theory of meaning making that is relational, fluid, and embedded in practice (Billig 1996; Edwards 1997; Potter 1996).

Against this backdrop, Wetherell (2012) suggests that nonrepresentational geography offers an "incoherent social psychology of affect" precisely because it splits affect from thought:

> human affect is inextricably linked with meaning making and with the semiotic (broadly defined) and the discursive ... the main things that an affective practice folds or composes are bodies and meaning making. (20)

In this view, the "pipes and cables of affect" work as affective structures because they are affectively meaningful for individuals on whose participation they depend for their existence. Thinking, for Wetherell, is not something that happens silently in the mind behind the doings and sayings of people in everyday life. Rather, it is a discursive activity that deploys the shared resources of language in rhetorical contexts where the meaning of mind and world are at stake (Wetherell 1998; Edwards 2003).

Affect and thought are thus connected by ordinary people as they talk about their feelings and emotions and as they reflect on their lives. For example, when Emma, the woman interviewed by Anderson (2006, 744), described her depression as "a sort of flatness and a sort of ... lack of animation ... and a lack of any sort of sharp feelings," she was using commonsense discursive resources to construct her mental state in recognizable ways. This meaning making was designed not only to construct shared understanding but to work in the service of persuasion. Emma's mental state was invoked to justify her constructing a depressed atmosphere in her family despite the fact that her son had "been badgering me ... for cheerful music" (745). Her emotional state was connected with thoughtful meaning making, but was also connected to her actions, as she conducted herself in a depressed manner.

As this example shows, the linking of affect and thought is a concern for people as they go about their ordinary lives. Among other things, affect and thinking are linked by ties of accountability. To act in ways that are socially intelligible and defensible, people conduct themselves in ways that are appropriate to the contexts they are in, bringing their conduct under the auspices of situational norms (cf. Edwards 1997). These accountability concerns are managed by aligning two forms of conduct, meaning making and embodied practices, in the "articulation of talk and embodied practices" (Durrheim, Mtose, and Brown 2011). Emma's talk about depression expresses a mental state, but her expressions of depression are also evident in the way she conducts herself—by listening to mournful music and not responding to her son's requests despite his badgering—and for this she is accountable. One way of rendering herself accountable is to link these two expressions by constructing her actions in talk as the consequences of a depressed mental state that prevented her from acting differently. Alternatively, she can act differently, yielding to her son's requests, thereby displaying other qualities of mind (cf. Edwards 2003).

From the perspective of discursive social psychology, affect is inextricably linked to meaning making because it is "enfolded in action." Actions take place against the backdrop of normative expectation, which includes commonsense understandings of how emotions affect conduct.

> emotional displays have proper (and improper) locations in the sequences of actions to which a group of people are engaged…. These displays will have antecedents in the context of which they will make sense, and they will have consequents, which will depend on their meaning for those engaged. (Harré 1999, 55)

The mental state of depression is authentically displayed by the expressed desire to avoid cheerful music. Yet, although this mental state renders the display accountable, it is nonetheless subject to critique: the moral implications of creating a depressing environment for other family members are normatively contestable. The assemblages of depression, the practices that culminate from the channeling of conduct, the meaning of the conduct, and the mental states are inextricably interwoven in action and always open to conflicting interpretations.

In the next section, we propose an analytic concept that can assist in studying how people link affect, thought, and place in the conduct of their ordinary lives. The notion of "the vibe" is a commonsense concept that people use to account for their participation (or not) in concrete situations. It bridges the individual and the social situation both because it connects thought and affect and because it elucidates how we "experience" everyday places. By advancing this concept of the vibe, we seek to move beyond the analytics of belonging that has been of central concern in the place identity literature and also beyond both the humanist and the discursive accounts of the people-place-emotion nexus. We seek to move toward an analytics of participation that focuses squarely on the enactment of the practices/performances that constitute social life and that bring assemblages of affect into being.

The Vibe

The Oxford Dictionary defines a vibe as "A person's emotional state or the atmosphere of a place as communicated to and felt by others." The concept entered the English language in the late 1960s as a shortening of the word *vibration* which was used colloquially in American popular culture to mean an instinctive reception of feelings. Today it is in common use in everyday discourse, especially in relation to clubs, where it has attracted academic attention. For example, Sommer (2001, cited in St. John 2006) defines the vibe within underground house clubs as:

> An active communal force, a feeling, a rhythm that is created by the mix of dancers, the balance of music, the effects of darkness and light, the energy. Everything interlocks to produce a powerful sense of liberation. The vibe is an active, exhilarating feeling of "now-ness" that everything is coming together—that a good party is in the making. The vibe is constructive; it is a distinctive rhythm, the groove that carries the party psychically and physically. (11)

In the dictionary and academic definitions, it is possible to discern how the concept tries to capture the idea that affect is mobile, in flux, phenomenologically potent, and connects people to others and to places.

Several commentators have suggested that the term *vibe* is interchangeable with Victor Turner's notion of "communitas." St. John (2009) suggests that Turner's concept has become a common lens within studies of electronic dance music culture. According to Turner (1982, cited in St John 2009) spontaneous communitas may be described as a situation in which:

> individuals, often strangers to one another, in contexts that are in-between (or liminal) to their daily round, and perhaps also undergoing physical ordeals, may experience a spontaneous "flash of mutual understanding on the existential level, and a 'gut' understanding of synchronicity." (4)

Certainly, the tactility experienced in sharing an intimate space would facilitate the emergence of communitas, and, being a significant feature of the clubbing experience, it is also an important contributor to the vibe (cf. Malbon 1998).

The concept of communitas foregrounds connectedness or social insideness, but it misses two other constituent elements of the vibe, namely, its spatialization and the practices through which both subjects and spaces are formed (cf. Pile 2008). The subjects of communitas that are so profoundly connected—are so constituted—because they have plugged into the same affective currents by means of their participation in a particular form of life. This is most evident in the role that music plays in clubbing. Music has the ability to transform or create a particular kind of space, especially as it connects people, drawing them into particular trajectories and routines of activity. The crowd's response to the music creates the atmosphere of the club as an "emotionally charged space" (Malbon 1998, 271). This experience of emotionally charged connectedness was described by two of the clubbers that Rautenbach (2011) interviewed as part of our joint study of clubbing in Pietermaritzburg.[1] Although these two participants, Claire and Emma, differed significantly in terms of their personal histories and clubbing preferences, they constructed their emotional responses to the vibe in strikingly similar ways.

Claire is a twenty-nine-year-old, white female who works as a sales assistant in a jewellery store. She has been an active clubber for the past seventeen years. She goes clubbing "to lose [herself] in the music, to exercise, to be happy, and to just enjoy a fantastic … vibe that comes into the room" and describes the clubbing experience as one in which you "lose yourself, find yourself, go home, have a sleep and get back to your boring job." Interestingly, having recently become a "born again" Christian, Claire experiences music and dancing as a manifestation of the divine— a means through which she can communicate with God. In our discussions around dance music Claire argues that "there's definitely a crescendo buildup, which sometimes takes an absolute age, and there's a particular point, just before it breaks, where the entire crowd is absolutely riveted by whatever song is on." She describes the moment in which the whole clubbing crowd is "waiting for the crescendo to break," where "they're all weeping with joy and glee at precisely the same moment, and in that same moment you are carried away by that feeling and you feel buoyant and light with that energy." Interestingly, she observes that while the rest of the clubbers "could all be on drugs" she can "still feel their energy the same way they do. It is just free." For Claire, one of the main constituents of this emotionally charged sense of freedom is the music. "You lose yourself in the music. The music absolutely travels through your entire body. It has the power to change my mood and really take me on an entire journey."

Emma, on the other hand, is a twenty-four-year-old, white female, who works as a secretary at a private school in Durban. At the time of her interview, she had recently ended a long-term romantic relationship, and decided that "the best way to kind of start moving past that is to just get out … and do something different." Consequently, she decided to participate in a night of clubbing at Jacks. Describing herself as "a bit self-conscious," she spoke at length about the effects of the vibe on her subjective clubbing experiences. During her interview, Emma stressed that she "go[es] out to find a happy vibe—somewhere where people are, umm, automatically having a fun time." In Emma's experience, "if you go out to a club or to a place like Jacks you don't see anyone miserable or upset. Everyone there is laughing and chatting and dancing and drinking." She constructs these ritualized clubbing practices—and constituents of the vibe—as having the power to induce a positive emotional state, suggesting that "if you're in a bad mood, if you've had a breakup like Jane and I've just had, to go out to a place like Jacks or any club, you'll find a vibe that's very upbeat and happy and automatically you'll be made to be happy and be put in a good mood."

Both Claire and Emma's narratives demonstrate the importance of considering how the various constituents of the vibe—laughing, chatting, dancing, and drinking—combine or "interlock" in totality (St. John 2006, 11). The vibe is coconstituted by the design of the place and the way it is collectively used to produce a total social and affective situation that "amounts to much more than the sum of its parts" (Wu 2010, 70). The extracts also lend support to the idea of the vibe as a "repeatable material-ity" (Foucault 2002, cited in Ehlers 2008, 336). Although never material-izing in quite the same way, clubbers treat the vibe as a repeatable and familiar situation. Everyone has a role to play in reproducing the affective routines: the club management that maintains the space, furnishings, and so on, the waitrons and bar staff, the DJs, and the patrons who participate in the "same" party week after week.

Clubbing is a site of performativity (Butler 1990, 1993). By sharing and participating in the vibe, clubbers are produced as subjects. The extracts demonstrate the power of the vibe to produce and induce particular affec-tive states and forms of subjectivity. These affective states and processes are familiar ones for clubbers, who downplay personal agency in attribut-ing emergent forms of subjectivity to the productive powers of the vibe: Claire's expressions such as "you are carried away" and "you lose yourself," and Emma's claim that "automatically you'll be made to be happy" all por-tray the vibe as transporting the individual, who has surrendered agency, through various affective states. Subjectification—"the way a human being turns himself into a subject" (Foucault 1982, 778)—is achieved both through embodied participation in a form of life and in the language with which such practices are described, understood, and explained. With thoughts and affect connected in this way, affect can be the subject of conscious management (see especially Emma's narratives). In this sense, clubbing is a "technology of the self," a domain of knowledge and strat-egy that "permit[s] individuals to effect by their own means or with the help of others a certain number of operations on their own bodies and souls, thoughts, conduct, and way of being, so as to transform themselves in order to attain a certain state of happiness, purity, wisdom, perfection, or immortality" (Foucault 1988, 18).

In accounts such as those produced by Claire and Emma, clubbers can articulate these knowledges and strategies, but such articulations are always occasioned and oriented to accountability concerns. One of the central threads of these concerns involves issues of social inclusion and exclusion, for as Foucault (1982) explains, subjectification is premised on dividing practices which ensure that "the subject is either divided inside himself or divided from others" (Foucault 1982, 778). Thus, anthropologists of clubbing have noted that the vibe is not always a utopian, unifying and "happy" one, but may at times, "be a site for the amplification of divisions based on subculture, class, gender, ethnicity and race" (St. John 2009, 5).[2] This sentiment is conveyed in the extracts taken from our interviews with Claire, Emma, and Amy, where both belonging and accountability concerns are apparent.

For example, in defining the vibe "as a particular feeling," Claire describes how "when you walk into a room you can tell instantly whether you are welcome or unwelcome, favored or otherwise—indifference, whatever the story might be." Similarly, when describing a nightclub with multiple dance floors, Claire notes that "the top floor is definitely a very open, bit of a wishy-washy dance floor." She describes how she cannot "feel any energy from the music because … you constantly feel as though … people are just watching you dance, because they've got nothing better to do. There's not sort of joining in or feeling the music."

In recounting her experience of attending a particular club in Durban, Emma also conveys the vibe's capacity for constituting negative affective states, noting how, in one instance, it was tied up with her sense of exclusion. "I hated it because I felt like I … wasn't fitting the stereotype and, umm, I mean, it was probably my imagination, but it felt like the minute I walked in there, everyone kind of turned around and judged what I was wearing, and found it not being appropriate for the club." She then alludes to vibe again, arguing that "it's like important in terms of being included or excluded. Like I fit in here."

Similar sentiments were expressed by Amy in her interview. Amy is a twenty-four--year-old, white female, who teaches English and Drama at a local high school. For Amy, a regular on the Pietermaritzburg club scene, "to go out clubbing is to drink and to dance." Although she describes the patrons at Jacks as sometimes being "stuck up and cliquey," she spends most of her weekends in the club, describing it as "the only place to go in 'Maritzburg," with a "stylish" and "energetic" vibe. Like Emma, Amy's narratives also shed light on the complex relationship between the normative constraints of the vibe and subjectivity. "No I dunno, but, umm, you have to be like a certain—when I go to Jacks I always feel like I have to dress a certain way."

The narratives of Claire, Emma, and Amy all show that club spaces—or, more precisely, the vibe of club spaces—can be experienced as being exclusionary. The sense of not belonging is articulated in the language of feelings. The evidence for exclusion is ambiguous and tenuous at best: Claire describing a feeling that people are watching her dance or a feeling she gets when she walks in a room, Amy feels that she has to dress a certain way, and Emma experiences a feeling of not fitting a stereotype, which she concedes might simply be her imagination. The focus on feelings serves important rhetorical functions in these accounts of marginalization. Talk about feelings is not verifiable and this can be difficult to contest even though the evidence for exclusion might be lacking (cf. Edwards and Potter 1992). The rhetorical stakes are quite high in such talk about feeling unwelcome or out of place because it can imply criticism both of others and the speakers themselves, who are destroying the good vibe. As such, talk about feelings of exclusion provides self-justifying explanations that are designed to manage accountability concerns.

One way to manage these accountability concerns successfully is to act appropriately in relation to the feeling. The feelings of exclusion and talk about these feelings come as part of an elaborate embodiment of not belonging. To gain rhetorical power of authenticity (talk about) the feeling of being out of place must be written all over the body. Thus, the connecting of thought and affect happens by acting appropriately, bringing talk, feelings, and embodied practices into alignment. Such an "articulation of talk and embodied practice" then becomes constitutive of the vibe as much as it is derived from it (Durrheim and Dixon 2005a; Durrheim, Mtose, and Brown 2011). Imagine Claire on the "wishy-washy" top dance floor at the club. Likely, she is not dancing enthusiastically and joining in the feeling of the music—how could she be and still defensibly claim not being part of the vibe? To an outsider, she may appear to be one of the very people "just watching you dance" of whom she is critical. As such, her feelings and actions are partly constitutive of the vibe that she criticizes.

These extracts show that participants are concerned about inclusion and exclusion, and that their talk about feeling the vibe can be considered a localized form of place identity discourse that accomplishes effects of exclusion. In her definitive book on club cultures, Thornton (1996) argues that the club's propensity for exclusion may, in fact, be one of the main appeals of clubbing: "As a semi-private, musical environment which adapts to diverse fashions, proffers escape (sometimes with added transgressional thrills) and regulates who's in and who's out of the crowd, the dance club fulfils many youth cultural agendas" (25). Once inside the club, and temporarily attached to a community, the resultant experience of enjoyment, the "communal ethic," is derived from both the sharing of the club space, the "proximity of the act of sharing," as well as from the formation and preservation of some sense of membership or unity. The vibe makes available "feelings of membership" that work to constitute collective and individual forms of subjectivity, rendering specific affective states accessible and mediating the subject's participation in social life.

This talk about the vibe and feelings of not belonging differs from much of the discourse studied by place identity researchers in one important respect: The target is not primarily a boundary transgressing Other: Rather, it is the vibe itself. The troubling presence is the externalized assemblage of affect which pervades the place. The primary object of the discourse is a lack of fit between the speaker and the place. These first person accounts bring the analytic gaze closer to the actions of the speaker and, more specifically, to their accounts of whether or not they are able to participate in a particular form of life. The feeling of displacement is not primarily about the physical presence of persons in place as much as it is about the ability of the speaker to participate in the life of the place and thus be able to access desirable forms of subjectivity.

The vibe regulates behavior in places. It acts as a normative framework against which deviation is accountable. For example, Claire describes how "if you get deep about your problems or about what you think about the crisis in the, I don't know, in South Africa or whatever, the crime rate, whatever the story is, it destroys your vibe," which, she argues, results in the loss of "that sense of happiness." She explains that "if somebody asks you what your mental problems are or how you're dealing with the death of your mother or your recent divorce, your entire evening is ruined. That happy vibe that you have now psyched yourself up into has gone." Here, Claire provides a prescriptive account of how to behave when clubbing with friends so as to preserve a happy vibe. Talk about death and divorce is not appropriate. The vibe renders conduct in places accountable. This is apparent too when Tara—a twenty-seven-year-old, white female, and one of the primary researchers on this project—expresses a preference for places where the combination of "music and people" don't cause her to feel "judged." "I love places where you can go and just, umm, act like an idiot, which is how I usually act when I go out, and not feel like embarrassed or weird the next morning. It's like a place where you can just—do whatever you want."

The repertoire of clubbing behavior has to fit the place. The vibe should be such that it can facilitate a form of engagement with the place, the performativity and forms of subjectivity that the person is seeking from a place. If the fit is not right, if the vibe is wrong, people withdraw from the space, and thus help to preserve the character of the place. The vibe may be inaccessible to groups of clubbers from the moment they walk through the club's door. For example, Martin is a thirty-three-year-old, black Zimbabwean male, who works as a car guard in the parking lot outside Jacks, and who describes how clubbers go about deciding on which one of two adjoining clubs to attend. "Some of them, they just go. You hear them talking, but I don't answer them, I just watch them. Then they go there, they say 'ah, no, this one is not good for us,' then you see them coming out and going to Jacks. Some they go to Jacks and they don't feel comfortable."

The vibe of a place provides a sense of belonging and inclusion (or feeling disconnected or excluded) but it does this in terms of action. Does the place allow the person to behave and feel as they desire? From this perspective, the vibe can be defined as the key or entry point to participation. As such, it allows us to shift from an analytics of belonging, which has defined the place identity literature, to an analytics of participation that focuses on performance and the kinds of subjectivities that such authentic, socially connected, and spatially appropriate forms of conduct occasion.

These affects do not just happen to people as they participate in social life. The main point of our analysis has been to show that the affective potentialities of places, in their channeling of action and subjectivity, are rendered into discourse which links affect, thought, and action in ways that contribute to the constitution of places and their vibe. The notion of the vibe helps participants to explain their conduct and account for the kind of person they are being in specific situations. It allows people to accountably link affect and thought in two modalities of conduct: their embodied participation in situations and their talk about it. It is this activity, rather than the concept of "the vibe" that is of primary interest.

The Vibe and Practices of Gender Privilege at Jacks

The vibe has a gendered contour. We can detect the operations of privilege and power from the perspective of affect and subjectivity. In this section, we provide an analysis of gender privilege at Jacks, a popular cocktail bar and dance club in Pietermaritzburg. Because the vibe at Jacks is constituted from the total situation, our analysis will consider the gendered trajectories of participation from the perspective of the material design of the place, the routines of conduct that constitute social life in the club, and the forms of gendered subjectivity that the vibe constitutes.

Setting Up the Space

Jacks is an up-market cocktail bar geared toward a middle- to upper-class clientele. It is part of a franchise brand that was launched in 2004, with the Pietermaritzburg franchise opening in 2005. The company responsible for the marketing and advertising of the brand describes the "target market" as "male and female customers in the A and B income bracket within an age group of 21–35, with the emphasis being our female customers." They have a profit margin of approximately 64%, and they are one of the most costly drinking venues in the city. The establishment allocates approximately 2% of its operating budget to advertising and marketing in both electronic and print media. Indeed, the social and economic milieu in which the club is located is captured most strikingly by the following online advertisement for the establishment:

> Sometimes a pub and a beer just isn't enough. That's when you throw those heels on under your jeans (you don't want to look like you're trying too hard, after all), button up that shirt, run a comb through your hair and head on over to Jacks … This bar is crowded with the inland yuppie set, all looking each other over (discreetly, of course). So you can strike a pose by the bar with your Cookies and Cream Cocktail (but not too many if you want to stay worth looking at) or any number of yummy and colourful options, and see what's on offer. There are plenty of tables once you've caught your quarry, and a menu of light meals and other notables to keep those hands busy.

The bar doubles as a club space on Tuesday and Friday nights and as a restaurant during the day. Whilst Jacks caters to various musical genres, its website boasts that, apart from striving to bring its patrons "the best [South Africa] has to offer," one can usually expect to find its "own DJ's playing the hottest global tracks" on club nights. Specifically, these "global tracks" are drawn primarily from the genres of Top 40, dance, and rock music. Inside the club there are six large flat-screen televisions which are invariably tuned to either fashion TV or one of several sports channels. The bar is a sleek and metallic chrome, the tables and chairs also metallic and functional, giving the overall impression of a place which (when not covered with the dubious remnants of the night's excess) strives for the minimalism often associated with the contemporary, urban, middle-upper class. The privilege enacted within this space, however, is not confined to matters of economy, but also sets the stage for the performance and recitation of many daily privileges; including those of race and gender.

On club nights the large plasma screens are tuned to fashion TV. Late in the evening, the broadcasts on this channel focus predominantly on more risqué programming such as lingerie shows and fantasy segments also aimed at selling lingerie. For example, on one occasion the programming consisted of a few short sequences in which models were dressed as French maids who dusted each other in a manner similar to some genres of pornography. The women may, at times, be ethnically diverse but are all thin and selected to represent a particular ideal of attractiveness. They are presented in varying states of undress, with fantasy segments displaying models not only walking down a catwalk, but also playing to an audience by engaging in acts of striptease which range from playful to explicit.

The waitrons are exclusively female and wear outfits that are notably tight, short, and very revealing, as was frequently referenced by the patrons that we interviewed. The division of labor in the club is gendered and raced: the bartenders are all white, male, and wear smart clothes; the waitrons are all young, white attractive females who cater to the needs of the clientele; their role is to serve, flirt, and be friendly and happy. The barmen, however, are not under the same obligation and often give the impression of being too busy for such niceties. Equally as significant as these problematic gender roles is the division of labor across racial lines; all the cleaning staff and bouncers are black. Not only does the hierarchical relationship amongst staff reinforce notions of racial and gender difference in terms of their roles, but simultaneously naturalizes a particular form of white, male privilege by perpetuating the racialized and class divisions upon which the apartheid era depended.

The walls of the dance floor are adorned with large pictures of attractive, white women DJing, dancing, or gazing dreamily at an audience. These women are superimposed against colorful backgrounds and shadow-dancing figures lending an air of surrealism to the images. This surrealism in turn lends an aspect of fantasy to the pictures and the spaces which they represent.

Figure 2.1 Wallpaper image from Jacks website.

Figure 2.2 Wallpaper image from Jacks website.

In the background, shadow figures depict scenes of dance and general revelry but our eyes are drawn to the female bodies in the foreground. The model in Figure 2.2 has her head tossed back, hair flung about, with her mouth open wide and eyes partially closed but aimed toward the lens and the viewer. Her legs are parted, hips tilted to one side with her hands placed on them, raising her dress. This picture speaks to desire and it does so by deploying implicit cultural devices. Why and how these devices have come to be accepted as desirous are not germane to this study; however, what they "do" has important ramifications for the female clubber. The woman in the image is not only ideal in terms of physicality, but is also portrayed as ideal in that she welcomes the observing lens and eye. The objectifying gaze individualizes this ideal subject against a background of bodies; she stands out from the rest. Her covered collarbones, eyes, and upper thighs, in conjunction with the strong sense of movement in the picture, add a tantalizing prospect that parts of her body that are presently covered may soon not be.

These images cultivate expectations about a night of clubbing primarily by depicting an ideal female form. However, the images do not only speak to ideals of form, but also to positions which women (and men) might take up on a routine night out. They (re)produce an affective landscape of interaction and desire within the sexualized cultural and physical space of the club. They help to construct the flirty vibe of the club as an arena of heterosexual attraction, where being looked at and admired offer thrills for "beautiful" women. In addition to depicting the ideal form to which female clubbers can aspire, these images also promote very specific gendered subject positions in which individual women not only participate in their objectification, but actually enjoy it (Hollway 1984). Forms of "happiness" (and "unhappiness") are opened up to female clubbers in and through the production and reproduction of images such as those above. These affects are the outcome of regulated forms of performance and participation that are open to male and female clubbers. Enjoyment of objectification is made an explicit possibility for female clubbers and thus it implicitly shapes the performative possibilities of the space.

Conlon's (2004) work on monuments in public space can enrich our analysis of the wallpaper images at Jacks (see Figures 2.1 and 2.2). Citing Edensor (1997), Conlon (2004) argues that "monuments are a way for elites to memorialise important figures while subaltern groups are marginalised" (468). Similarly, Conlon (2004) draws on Lefebvre (1996) to argue that "monuments are representations of space wherein power relations are subsumed; they speak of a particular spatial code, which simultaneously commands bodies and orders space" (468–69). In other words, monuments serve to illustrate and provide a shared understanding of the ways in which a space might be used, and in so doing they materialize power relations. It could be argued that the models appropriated as part of the club's branding become "monuments" in this sense, serving as cultural templates for sociospatial clubbing practices such as dress, dance, drinking, and desirability. Embedded in this spatial code is a shared understanding of desirability which positions some women as elite, simultaneously rendering abject others to the realm of the subaltern. Furthermore, they serve to normalize heteronormative whiteness and the objectification of women, both by themselves and by others, whilst simultaneously setting Western standards of club culture as the ideal on which South African club culture should be modeled. These monuments to Western club culture are rendered all the more powerful by the simultaneous broadcast of Fashion TV, as discussed above.

These elements, in conjunction with other aspects such as the genre of music played and the images displayed on the club's website, menus, and walls work together to construct a vibe that is geared toward a heteronormative environment in which women are produced as objects of male consumption; their images are sexualized and displayed in a way which caters toward male sexual fantasy. By this imagery and these practices, the female body is objectified in a way that provides a framework for a particular kind of engagement with and participation in the space of the club.

Female clubbers are made more welcome insofar as they project images of sexual availability (Hutton 2006), further creating a space in which some gendered performances are privileged over others. Power operates by means of dividing practices rather than by exclusion. Women are given privileged access to the club, where they are objectified by a normalizing gaze, subjectify themselves, and are divided between and within themselves as desirable or not (cf. Foucault 1982).

Affective Practices

The form of life in the club is strongly patterned by gender in ways that reflect and exceed the gendered performances that the space itself promotes. A formal dress code applies to male clubbers, who may be refused entrance to the club if they arrive in overly casual clothing. Although no formal rules apply to female dress, powerful normative constraints regulate the way in which female clubbers dress. The female clubbers we spoke to said they "felt judged" if not dressed in accordance with other female patrons. For example, Amy stated that "when I go to Jacks I always feel like I have to dress a certain way." In general, female clubbers generally dressed in fashionable, appealing, heteronormative attire not dissimilar to that displayed in the images on the club's website and advertising media (see Figure 2.1). Men and women dressed to look good, for part of the pleasure of clubbing was to be appreciated for how one looked—as communicated through glances and comments that occasioned the joy of being desired, envied, or admired. Conversely, they sought to avoid the disappointment of disapproving looks or rejection. Dress, looking good, and the pleasures of heterosexual approval were vital elements of a happy vibe.

The space itself seemed to promote the idea of female clubbers enjoying and participating in their objectification, but the patrons we spoke to were ambivalent. Although female participants made reference to dressing up and "feeling good" about the looks they received, this was always circumscribed by the fear of evaluation. This is exemplified in our interview with Paula, where being looked at was also constructed in terms of acute displeasure. Paula, a twenty-three-year-old white female, constructed Jacks in negative terms, stating that it was a space in which she felt observed, judged, and out of place. She constructed alternative music clubs in more positive terms as places in which one could be more free.

For example, when asked by the interviewer to describe her experience of objectification, she explains that "it's like a man undressing you with his eyes, looking at you like a piece of meat that he can take home and shag. Its, ja, being looked at like, like a dildo or something." Prompted to provide a more detailed description of this look, Paula references a certain "facial expression." "It's a kind of a down the nose look and up and down your body a couple times, but like focusing on specific areas like your bum and your breasts with that jerky grihhhn." During their conversation, the interviewer also asked Paula to describe her experience of ordering drinks from the bar. For Paula, this was a stressful experience. "Oh wow, um, uhsh, I don't feel like I fit in there I, I felt like I looked different to everyone else. I probably didn't but I just felt like my dad always said, like a turd in a swimming pool, like that's not supposed to be there." This sense of awkwardness is then articulated in terms of her perceived objectification. "And so when I was at the bar I felt like the girls were judging me and the men were looking at me like a piece of meat, and like the barman wasn't giving me the attention I deserved because I wasn't dressed in a certain way or behav[ing] in a certain way."

Here, Paula describes how she feels about an unwelcome male gaze, focused on her breasts and bottom and accompanied by a "jerky grin." The objectification is experienced as being looked at like a "piece of meat" or "like a dildo or something." When she describes going to the bar, she describes feeling out of place—like a turd in a swimming pool—because her behavior and dress are not in line with the gender norm. She later explained that her dress and behavior were not provocative or flirtatious enough to allow her to feel accepted within this space. Thus, she sees her possibilities for sharing and participation in this hypersexualized vibe as being curtailed by her refusal to engage in specific practices (of dress and behavior) that promote objectification.

Hutton (2006) has observed that there is a demand on women participating in club spaces to present themselves as sexually available. By resisting male patrons' objectification of her body, and by not engaging in acts of self-objectification (by not presenting herself as sexually available), within a space predominantly oriented toward the objectification of female bodies, this participant is denied access to the "happier" affectual positions made available by the vibe. This is demonstrative of a type of affectual bias or privileging, in that the male gaze (and grab!) is so thoroughly entrenched within this arena, that one must be able to participate in self-objectification to be happy in this space and to share and participate in the vibe.

The heterosexual gendering of the club is also evident in how clubbers position themselves within and move around the space. Male clubbers typically gather around the bar, whereas female clubbers sit at tables in groups of around three to five. Although the dance floor is usually mixed, and is a prime place for socializing, female participants also express more of a preference for dancing, as Jane explained in her interview. "In my experience, the guys will stick together in one group and the girls will go out [to the dance floor] and there's always a base where you will come back to, but you will always know that your boyfriend or the group of friends is in that specific area." Jane is a twenty-six-year-old white female, who works as a secretary in a village near Pietermaritzburg. She's one of Amy's close friends, so the two often go out clubbing together. Jane enjoys Jacks because "you are bound to meet someone that you know." In her interview she spoke fondly of the space, noting that "there is a lot of festivity about it," and describing how she enjoys dancing to the "good music."

Generally the kinds of things clubbers do are referred to positively as being part of the happy vibe: sitting or standing around, chatting and having drinks with friends, dancing, or making out with a partner. However, periods of transition or movement from one space to another are open to multiple possibilities of happiness and unhappiness. These are occasions to meet friends, and have fleeting exchanges with acquaintances and strangers: glancing, flirting, touching, etc. As our interview with Peter shows, it is here that the gendered architecture of negative affect is especially manifested. Peter is a twenty-seven-year-old white man who, like Paula, constructed alternative music club scenes in a more positive light, claiming that he only went to Jacks at the behest of one of his close friends. In general, he constructed spaces such as Jacks as overtly sexual and aggressive, expressing a preference for spaces which were more relaxed.

This is particularly evident in his descriptions of negotiating the bar and bathroom spaces at Jacks. "Well, going to the bar you always gonna like, if heaven forbid you bump into some ex-rugby player from 'Maritzburg College um, get some attitude, get some looks. The barmen are really shitty, they're really surly." When asked by the interviewer to describe his experience of going to the bathroom, Peter explains that "there's a really aggressive vibe," noting that it is like "one of those places where you worried you might get punched in the mouth for no good reason." Interestingly, Peter observes that "generally if you get punched in the mouth you deserve it, but Jacks is the type of place where five or six white meatheads will beat you up for no reason."

Peter describes the walk to the bar as potentially hazardous, reflecting the aggressive vibe that male clubbers participate in. Jacks is a place where "you might get punched in the mouth for no good reason." This provides an indication of what the "specter" of the vibe may be for male patrons of the club: fear or anxiety over a physical altercation with other male patrons. His suggestion that there are occasions when male clubbers deserve getting punched in the mouth serves to underscore the currents of male aggression that are supported and channeled by the pipes and cables of affect in Jacks. Men tread a fine line between flirtation and violence. Women have other struggles.

In her interview, Paula also describes the aggressive vibe experienced in walking to the bathroom at Jacks, exclaiming that "it was pretty traumatic getting there." When asked to explain why, she draws on language similar to that used by Peter in his construction of the journey to the bathroom. "Because it's a very aggressive kind of macho place to be, and so the guys are very aggressive, so are the girls in a way, so just bumping into people—they aren't very friendly when you bump them." Paula goes on to describe how, on a particularly busy occasion, she bumped into someone on her way to the bathroom. For Paula, this incident served to cast her in an unpleasant position in which she felt objectified by the other women in the space. "I don't like being looked at like that. I'm not there for someone else's enjoyment, ah, I'm there because I want to be there kind of thing, and then the bathroom was like a whole other world."

It is important to note that the bathrooms in this club are located beyond the dance floor and can only be accessed by walking through this small, crowded space. Interestingly, although she describes Jacks as "very aggressive kind of macho place" she does this with reference to both male and female patrons whom she portrays as unfriendly rather than potentially violent. She also constructs this experience with reference to the displeasure of "being looked at" and being treated as though she is "there for someone else's enjoyment." It is the specter of unwanted or unpleasant objectification rather than violence that haunts the movement of female clubbers through the crowded space. Women in the club are the objects of (potentially) aggressive male desire, and as such need to take care of themselves. They do this by following basic rules for female clubbers, including: don't go out alone, never leave your drink unattended, and stick close to your group of friends. As Jane explained, if her boyfriend and his friends went off somewhere, "I was always left with one person, and we had to stay in that area, so I was very controlled." These practices give an indication of the ways in which the sexualized and aggressive vibe may manifest in an extremely negative manner for female clubbers. The existence of informal rules gives evidence of the dangers female clubbers may face, which take the form of unwelcome attention and, more seriously, drugging and rape.

Conclusion: Affective Geographies of Privilege

This chapter has introduced the concept of the vibe as an analytic resource for studying geographies of privilege. The vibe of a place is at once spatial and experiential. It is constituted by social interactions that produce places, and it connects people to each other and to place, governing the engagement of individual participants with the social situation. As such, circuits of power that flow though places—and the effects of power in terms of privilege, marginalization, oppression, etc.—become apparent in the vibe as it animates bodies, channeling conduct along trajectories that collectively bring privilege into being.

In drawing attention to the vibe, we have attempted to show the existence of a whole terrain of privilege that has been outside the scrutiny of the discursive approach to place identity. The discursive approach provided a useful corrective to the apolitical focus of much psychological research on individual experiences of place belonging and attachment. Place identity research foregrounded the collective, shared, and ideological nature of these feelings and emotions, and the way they were constructed and deployed to serve groups' interests. This work shifted the focus from subjectivity to talk, but in so doing, it neglected to study other kinds of embodied action by which places are constituted and the forms of subjectivity that these actions contain.

The recent literature on affective geography has attempted to recover the focus on emotions and feelings while avoiding the humanism of the earlier phenomenology-inspired work. Affect has been treated as a spatial and material practice in this work, studied in its assemblages. By drawing on the theoretical resources of Foucault and Butler, we have paid particular attention to ritualized participation in the forms of life that constitute subjects and places. This shift in focus resonates with broader developments across the social sciences, as captured by emerging work on the so-called affective turn (see Clough and Halley 2007). However, in our view, the attempt to move beyond a focus on the semiotic, textual, and discursive construction of emotional experience has limitations as well as advantages. Specifically, by focusing on embodiment and embodied action and treating affect as a nonrepresentational object, this work is in danger of disconnecting affect from thought, resulting in what Wetherell (2012) argues is an "incoherent social psychology of affect" (20).

In this chapter we have used the concept of the vibe to reconnect affect and thought, for although the vibe is embodied and spaced, it is also felt, thought, and spoken. Affect is connected with thought in discourse, and the vibe is first and foremost a discursive and commonsense object. We found nothing new or unexpected in our research at Jacks. All the participants and we ourselves were quite familiar with the gendered, sexualized, and aggressive affects that circulate in cocktail bars and dance clubs like this. Given the commonsense nature of the vibe, we should not treat affect as some mysterious prediscursive structure, something ineffable and buried deep inside the individual. Rather, as Wetherell (2012) recommends, we need to study how affective practices are rendered in talk to produce accountable conduct. The focus, then, is on the "articulation of talk and embodied practices," on how accountability is achieved by tailoring talk to embodied action in justificatory accounts, and vice versa, on how conduct is ordered and arranged by the immanent horizon of justification (Durrheim, Mtose, and Brown 2011).

Anderson (2006, 748) argues that a political geography of affect can be sensitized to the "inequalities at the heart of affective economies" by becoming attuned to "how the circulation of affect performs, and is affected by spatial and temporal distribution." This "affective cultural politics" aims to "tend to, and enact, different capacities to affect and be affected rather than correct types of representation" (Anderson 2006, 749). This political imagination exceeds that in the place identity tradition that seeks to demonstrate how talk about feelings legitimates imperatives of inclusion or exclusion. To the contrary, it shows how power may operate via the embodied production of forms of subjectivity within particular spaces, which enable the individual to achieve affective experiences that are ostensibly positive and self-affirming (yet reproduce varying forms of subjectification).

Although we appreciate the theoretical and political advances achieved by this emerging work, we would argue that practices of representation remain profoundly significant to the study of place identity relations. People use discursive constructions to frame their participation in settings and thus representations are the part of our capacities to affect and be affected. The correctness of these constructions of the vibe are participants' concerns because they are used to account for their conduct in a place.

Cocktail bars and dance clubs like the one we studied are designed to cultivate particular capacities to affect and be affected. These affective assemblages are established in the design and decor of the place, the dress codes, the conduct of staff, and the unfolding tableau of gendered practices of the patrons, which range from such mundane activities as sitting, walking, and dancing, to more risqué practices of touching, flirting, and looking. These constitute the cocktail bar as a space of heterosexual desire and male violence, a place that privileges certain ways of being and acting, certain kinds of bodies, and particular subjects. In particular, they produce female participants as sexual objects (cf. Bird and Sokolofski 2005). This provides a framework for various affective tones and forms of happiness and unhappiness. The cocktail bar is a theater of heterosexual recognition, appreciation, and adoration, but as Connolly (1999) observes, "suffering resides on the underside of agency mastery, wholeness, joy, comfort" (cited in Anderson 2006, 740). Privilege in the context of this form of life is not accomplished primarily by inclusion and exclusion but by the construction of a vibe that disqualifies certain forms of participation and renders certain bodies and forms of subjectivity abject.

Notes

1. We conducted a multisite study of clubs in Pietermaritzburg and Durban, South Africa, in 2011. This chapter reports a case study of one of those sites, which we have referred to with the pseudonym, Jacks. Research included 80 hours of fieldwork in the site and interviews with 16 clubbers.
2. What appeared to distinguish early rave and dance culture from mainstream culture was "an emphasis on social bonding, the collective dance experience, a communal state of euphoria and the 'happy vibe'" (Measham et al., 1998, cited in Goulding, Shyankar, and Elliot 2002, 266) that was opposed to aggressive vibes of other clubs and music genres.

References

Anderson, Ben. 2006. "Becoming and Being Hopeful: Towards a Theory of Affect." *Environment and Planning D: Society and Space* 24: 733–52.

———, Paul Harrison. 2006. "Questioning Affect and Emotion." *Area* 38: 333–35.

Ballard, Richard. 2004. "Assimilation, Emigration, Semigration, and Integration: 'White' Peoples' Strategies for Finding a Comfort Zone in Post-Apartheid South Africa." In *Under Construction: Race and Identity in South Africa today*, edited by Natasha Distiller and Mellissa Steyn, 51–66. Johannesburg, South Africa: Heinemann.

———. 2010. "Slaughter in the Suburbs: Livestock Slaughter and Race in Post-Apartheid Cities." *Ethnic and Racial Studies* 33: 1069–87.

Billig, Michael. 1996. *Arguing and Thinking: A Rhetorical Approach to Social Psychology* (2nd ed.). Cambridge, UK: Cambridge University Press.

Bird, Sharon R., and Leah K. Sokolofski. 2005. "Gendered Socio-Spatial Practices in Public Eating and Drinking Establishments in the Midwest United States." *Gender, Place and Culture* 12: 213–30.

Brown, Lynday. 2009. "From West Street to Dr Pixley KaSeme Street: How Contemporary Racialised Subjectivities Are (Re) Produced in the City of Durban." PhD diss., University of KwaZulu-Natal. http://dspace.ukzn.ac.za:8080/jspui/bitstream/10413/184/1/Brown-2009PHd.pdf

Butler, Judith. 1990. *Gender Trouble: Feminism and the Subversion of Identity*. New York: Routledge.

———. 1993. *Bodies that Matter: On the Discursive Limits of "Sex,"* New York: Routledge.

Cell, John. W. 1982. *Segregation: The Highest Stage of White Supremacy*. Cambridge, UK: Cambridge University Press.

Clough, Patricia, and Jean Halley, eds. 2007. *The Affective Turn: Theorizing the Social*. Durham, NC: Duke University Press.

Conlon, Deirdre. 2004. "Productive Bodies, Performative Spaces: Everyday Life in Christopher Park." *Sexualities* 7: 462–79.

Connolly, William. 1999. *Why I Am Not a Secularist*. Minneapolis, MN: University of Minnesota Press.

Dean, Mitchell. 1994. *Critical and Effective Histories: Foucault's Methods and Historical Sociology*. London: Routledge.

Di Masso, Andres, John Dixon, and Enric Pol. 2011. "On the Contested Nature of Place: Figuera's

Well, the Hole of Shame, and the Ideological Struggle over Public Space in Barcelona." *Journal of Environmental Psychology* 31: 231–44.

Dixon, John A., and Kevin Durrheim. 2000. "Displacing Place-Identity: A Discursive Approach to Locating Self and Other." *British Journal of Social Psychology* 39: 27–44.

———. Don Foster, Kevin Durrheim, and Lindy Wilbraham. 1994. "Discourse and the Politics of Space in South Africa: The 'Squatter Crisis.'" *Discourse and Society* 5: 277–96.

Durrheim, Kevin, and John A. Dixon. 2001. "The Role of Place and Metaphor in Racial Exclusion: South Africa's Beaches as Sites of Shifting Racialization." *Ethnic and Racial Studies* 24: 433–50.

———, and John A. Dixon. 2005a. "Studying Talk and Embodied Practices: Toward a Psychology of Materiality of 'Race Relations'." *Journal of Community and Applied Social Psychology* 15: 446–60.

———, and John A. Dixon. 2005b. *Racial Encounter: The Social Psychology of Contact and Desegregation.* Hove, UK: Routledge.

———, Xoliswa Mtose, and Lyndsay Brown. 2011. *Race Trouble: Race, Identity and Inequality in Post-Apartheid South Africa.* Scottsville, South Africa: University of KwaZulu-Natal Press.

Dwyer, Claire. 1999. "Contradictions of Community: Questions of Identity for Young British Muslim women." *Environment and Planning A* 31: 53–68.

Edwards, Derek. 1997. *Discourse and Cognition.* London: Sage.

———. 2003. "Analysing Racial Discourse: The Discursive Psychology of Mind-World Relationships." In *Analysing Race Talk: Multidisciplinary Approaches to the Interview,* edited by H. van den Berg, Harry, Margaret Wetherell, and Henneke Houtkoop-Steenstra. Cambridge, UK: Cambridge University Press.

———, and Jonathan Potter. 1992. *Discursive Psychology.* London: Sage.

Ehlers, Nadine. 2008. "Retroactive Phantasies: Discourses, Discipline, and the Production of Race." *Social Identities* 14: 333–47.

Foucault, Michel. 1978. *The History of Sexuality: An Introduction*, vol. 1, translated by R. Hurley. New York: Pantheon Books.

———. 1982. "The Subject and Power." *Critical Inquiry* 8: 777–95.

———. 1988. "The Political Technology of Individuals." In *Technologies of the Self,* edited by Luther H. Martin, Huck Gutman, and Patrick H. Hutton, 145–62. Boston: University of Massachusetts Press.

Goldberg, David. T. 1998. "The New Segregation." *Race and Society* 1: 15–32.

Goulding, Christina, Avi Shankar, and Richard Elliot. 2002. "Working Weeks, Rave Weekends: Identity Fragmentation and the Emergence of New Communities." *Consumption, Markets, and Culture* 5: 261–84.

Harré, Rom. 1999. "The Rediscovery of the Human Mind." *Asian Journal of Social Psychology* 2: 43–62.

Hollway, Wendy. 1984. Gender difference and the production of subjectivity. In *Changing the Subject: Psychology, Social Regulation and Subjectivity,* edited by Julian Henriques, Cathy Urwin, Wendy Holloway, Couz Venn, and Valerie Walkerdine, 227–63. London: Methuen.

Hook, Derek. 2007. *Foucault, Psychology and the Analytics of Power.* Houndmills, UK: Palgrave Macmillan.

———, and Michele Vrodljak. 2002. "Gated Communities, Heterotopia and a 'Rights'of Privilege: A 'Heterotopology' of the South African Security-Park." *Geoforum,* 33: 195–219.

Hopkins, Nick, and John Dixon. 2006. "Space, Place, and Identity: Issues for Political Psychology." *Political Psychology* 27: 173–85.

Hutton, Fiona. 2006. *Risky Pleasures? Club Cultures and Feminine Identities.* Farnham, UK: Ashgate.

Latham, Alan, and David Conradson. 2003. "The Possibilities of Performance." *Environment and Planning A* 35: 1901–1906.

Malbon, Ben. 1998. "Clubbing: Consumption, Identity and the Spatial Practices of Every-Night

Life." In *Cool Places: Geographies of Youth Cultures,* edited by Tracey Skelton, and Gill Valentine, 266–86. New York: Routledge.

Manzo, Lynne. C. 2003. "Beyond House and Haven: Toward a Revisioning of Emotional Relationships with Places." *Journal of Environmental Psychology* 23: 47–61.

Massey, Douglas, and Nancy A. Denton. 1993. *American Apartheid: Segregation and the Making of the Underclass.* Cambridge, MA: Harvard University Press.

McCormack, Derek. 2006. "For the Love of Pipes and Cables: A Response to Deborah Thien." *Area* 38: 330–32.

Pettigrew, Thomas. F. 1979. "Racial Change and Social Policy." *Annals of the American Academy of Political Social Science* 441: 114–131.

Pile, Steven. 2008. "Where Is the Subject? Geographical Imaginations and Spatializing Subjectivity." *Subjectivity* 23: 206–218.

———. 2010. "Emotions and Affect in Recent Human Geography." *Transactions of the Institute of British Geographers* 35: 5–20.

Potter, Jonathan. 1996. *Representing Reality: Discourse, Rhetoric and Social Construction.* London: Sage.

Rautenbach, Clinton L. "It's the Vibe": Race, Space, Practice and Subjectivity in South African Nightclubs. PhD diss., University of KwaZulu-Natal, Pietermaritzburg, 2011.

Rose, Gillian. 1990. "Imagining Poplar in the 1920s: Contested Concepts of Community." *Journal of Historical Geography* 16: 425–37.

Rose, Nikolas. 1990. *Governing the Soul: The Shaping of the Private Self.* London: Routledge.

Rowles, Graham. D. 1983. "Place and Personal Identity in Old Age: Observations from Appalachia." *Journal of Environmental Psychology* 3: 299–313.

Sibley, David. 1995. *Geographies of Exclusion: Society and Difference in the West.* London: Routledge.

St. John, Graham. 2006. "Electronic Dance Music Culture and Religion: An Overview." *Culture and Religion* 17: 1–25.

———. 2009. "Neotrance and the Psychedelic Festival." *Dancecult: Journal of Electronic Dance Music Culture* 1: 1–29.

Thien, Deborah. 2005. "After or Beyond Feeling? A Consideration of Affect and Emotion in Geography." *Area* 37: 450–56.

Thornton, Sarah. 1996. *Club Cultures: Music, Media and Subcultural Capital.* Middletown, CT: Wesleyan University Press.

Thrift, Nigel. 1996. *Spatial Formations.* London: Sage.

———. 2004. "Intensities of Feeling: Towards a Spatial Politics of Affect." *Geografiska Annaler, Series B: Human Geography* 86: 57–78.

Tuan, Yi-fu. 1974. *Topophilia: A Study of Environmental Perception, Attitudes, and Values.* Englewood Cliffs, NJ: Prentice-Hall.

———. 1979. *Landscapes of Fear.* New York: Pantheon.

Wetherell, Margaret. 1998. "Positioning and interpretative Repertoires: Conversation Analysis and Post-Structuralism In Dialogue." *Discourse and Society* 9: 387–412.

———. 2012. *Affect and Emotion: A New Social Science Understanding.* Thousand Oaks, CA: Sage.

Wu, Eileen M. 2010. "Memory and Nostalgia in Youth Music Cultures: Finding the Vibe in the San Francisco Bay Area Rave Scene, 2002–2004." *Dancecult: Journal of Electronic Dance Music Culture* 1: 63–78.

CHAPTER 3

Chicago's South Side Blues-Scape
Creeping Commodification and
Complex Human Response

DAVID WILSON

Introduction

Real-estate and finance capital continue their actions in the U.S. city, and with a vengeance. A stepped-up kind of elite privileging—land and blocks dramatically transformed into globally declarative, affluent play spaces—now marks many major American cities (Wyly et al. 2009). This restructuring, an affluent takeover of the urban currently moves far beyond downtown cores. In the neoliberal era, redevelopment governances (alliances of local government, prominent developers, realtors, city growth organizations) invoke a fervent rhetoric (the need for their cities to compete for resources in supposedly new global times) that elaborately rationalizes the drive to "upscale" and really expand elite patterns of consumption. In the process, condominiums and second homes supplant apartments, stores, and houses, with upper-income aesthetics, sensibilities, and recreational whims extended to new terrains. Well-coordinated landscapes of pleasure and affluent residency are cultivated, producing Gordon MacLeod's (2002) "cathedrals of consumption." To Fran Tonkiss (2005), elite privileging in current times takes many forms, but this one is particularly overt and visible.

This coordinated takeover and remaking now grips Chicago, most recently, its historically neglected South Side "blues-scape" (blues clubs and their blocks). Once consigned to policy oblivion, this two-square-mile area, encompassing nine aging blues clubs, today attracts considerable attention and looms ambiguously in a rapidly changing city (Figure 3.1). A commercialism creeps across the South Side, from an aggressive "rediscovery of the South Side" by a historically privileged redevelopment governance, remaking many of these South Side clubs. This spread of commercialism was barely imaginable 12 years ago, with most of the South Side institutionally treated as Chicago's horrific core "ghetto" (Vankatesh 2004; Wacquant 2008). But now, governance-led redevelopment pushes a restructuring by proclaiming something compelling: a rich South Side history. Beneath troubled and struggling neighborhoods, they declare, are industrious and sturdy communities whose histories and social bases need resurrection.

This chapter examines this elite-privileging transformation on Chicago's South Side as one exemplar of a national trend. Chicago, paralleling developments in cities like Cleveland, St. Louis, Boston, Washington, DC, Indianapolis, Milwaukee, and Philadelphia, now experiences this transformation that moves far beyond the downtown (Grazian 2005; Wilson 2012). An elaborate rhetoric (as important as an incipient physical and social restructuring), rooted in a race-class privilege, introduces a bold middle-class commercializing in blues blocks. These city sections, for decades systematically isolated and deemed peripheral by the City as historic storehouses for the racialized poor, are suddenly being rhetorically recast as historic, "culturally salvageable," and ripe for inclusion in deepening "go-global" resculpting efforts. A "rediscovery of the black experience" now increasingly centers "black culture," "raw blues musical performance," and "exotic black ways" as objects of bourgeois fascination. This group, it seems, has found a new playground for reverie and spectatorship. The pull to these clubs, it is suggested, is inexorably compelling for any normatively functioning person.

This chapter interrogates possible futures for these clubs and the process by which this privilege works through them. My goal is twofold: to understand how this kind of privilege (now unfolding across the vastness of urban America) operates on the ground of these clubs and to discover what this blues-scape will become. On both counts, there is far too little understanding (Brown 2006; Phillips 2010). A detailed, ethnographic analysis of one paradigmatic South Side club suggests, first, that this drive to upscale and commodify the place "hits the ground" of these venues through a complex human mediative process. In particular, I chronicle that the central decision-maker of club future, the club owner, builds a sense of self, club realities, and the world out of negotiating, internalizing, and working through three forces: neoliberal subject realities, governmentality,

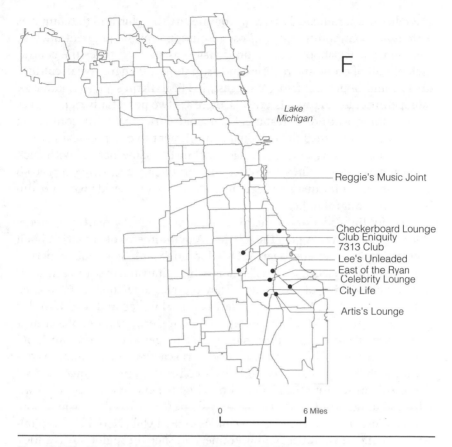

Figure 3.1 The Nine current blues clubs on Chicago's South Side.

and the constitution of class–race identities. These three forces, with deep multiscaler connections to institutions and forces outside the club, are the anchoring frames for the human production of knowledge that will determine club owner decisions about the kind and intensity of club commodifying.[1] As I show, these interconnecting, blurring forces structure the owner's production of knowledge and understandings about herself (sense of ideal identity, desires, needs, values) and her club (sense of the ideal club, sense of patrons, sense of ideal patrons, sense of ideal club practices and customs) that shapes something important: her decision about venue change. My empirical focus, Beebe's on Chicago's South Side, excavates the power and pervasiveness of these colliding forces.[2]

I chronicle, second, that the future of these blues clubs and blocks is unclear. The detailed ethnographic analysis uncovers a politically vibrant, unpredictable, and contradictory club owner. This club owner currently embodies the paradoxical drives to commodify this club and to retain it as is (to resist commodification) whose resolution is at the moment unclear. Her ambivalence about what to do is visible as she negotiates the contradictory pull of economic realities and aspirations set again social-cultural dreams and hopes. At issue, I suggest, is Nigel Thrift's (2004) notion of "competing cultural capitals"; that is, there are two potentially rich sources for obtaining a kind of resource (personal enrichment) in conflicting realms which obscures the personal commitment to one political path. A kind of double consciousness lodges within the same person with each element never superseding the other and turbulently coexisting. This club owner, at this point in an ambiguous state, has yet to decide which realm is most meaningful to her.

Both findings identify something important: agency matters in these clubs and is alive and well in the subaltern environments of our cities. But it is not a simple, unfettered agency. On Chicago's South Side, club owners as reflexive beings seize and "bear" neoliberal-capitalist drives and sensibilities in their making of knowledge. They produce a personal habitus even as they temper these to generate a desired social milieu and world. In this process, an "instantiated" three-step process (externalization, objectification, internalization) of reality-making (see Berger and Luchmann 1966) blunts the influence of a fast-acting neoliberal capitalism. Via human constituting, these drives and sensibilities become one humanly mediated set of ingredients fed into the production of highly personal stocks of knowledge and understanding that ultimately shape this person's decision about possibilities for new commercial wrinkles in their club. Neoliberal-capitalist drives and sensibilities bound, frame, and slice through their realities. But these club owners assemble and organize legible, experiential worlds that "defang" and "decolonize" these sensibilities.

I analyze club owners because they are the central decision makers of club futures. They decide the kind of social milieu that will be cultivated in the club and pursued in the future (e.g., whether it will be sold to development interests, kept but upscaled, kept and retained as is) as they poignantly live through and work through the forces that purvey this commodifying. In this process, they always operate out of a sense of their own best interest. But all is not so simple: this best interest is enormously complex and typically involves both economic concerns and social-cultural concerns (Grazian 2005). Social-cultural concerns, often extremely meaningful to club owners, involve their being able to produce pleasure and identity-nourishment for themselves and others in their clubs. To Grazian, many South Side club owners—rendered by race, class, and areal affiliation socially marginal—often feel an acute kinship for fellow South Side "subalterns" (Balkin 2002). Thus, the dominant reality made by club owners, as they engage their patrons and workers (blues wannabes, blues voyeurs, long-term local regulars, musicians), becomes crucial to determining this future. Defining a club's character, sensibilities, norms, and protocols to their satisfaction is critical when they ponder new commercial wrinkles or massive commercialization.

Beebe's, my empirical focus, like many South Side blues clubs is beginning to feel pervasive South Side commodification. On the one hand, the club has experienced little conspicuous physical change. It continues to barely subsist, located in a severely disinvested low-income economic setting. Funds to upgrade are scant (owner Jackie Smith frequently bemoans the club's economic plight). In this context, its exterior is still a gritty, industrial-looking front set within a block of seemingly abandoned buildings. A faded white sign "Beebe's" is the only evidence that a vibrant music scene lies within a seemingly falling-apart building. The interior has been the same for more than two decades (dominated by black painted walls and faded red carpeting covering all floor space). No bay windows, ample walking space for customers, or track lighting exists at Beebe's. A no-frills decorum wraps around a tiny stage which can barely accommodate five musicians at one time. Behind the stage are faded, unframed posters and photographs of South Side musicians who have played at the club. A crowded, dimly lit room with smoke wafting across the floor and tables still dominates the ambiance. Ashtrays (only occasionally cleaned) adorn the tables. Nowhere in sight is a souvenir store that sells trinkets, "authentic" barbecue sauces, or club t-shirts.

Yet, this social space now exhibits a few subtle alterations amid the South Side revitalization. Notably, Beebe's recently instituted a $5.00 cover charge for its live shows after decades of free admission (it is open and offers live music on Fridays, Saturdays, and Sundays). The owner Jackie Smith has instituted this reluctantly, with an eye to attracting more affluent customers to her club. While deeply desiring to operate a local neighborhood club, one that attracts "[her] people and [her] musicians," a competing desire is to create what Foucault (1970) would call a "total blues upgrade space." This cover charge is potentially one small step to this eventual creation. This imagined space is Smith's (2003) "smart, appreciated musical venue … with top-notch players … and a profitable, electrifying electricity [sic]." It is underwritten by "attentive, great audiences paying a fee to be at the club." Smith here imagines a place, "with thankful customers buying drinks and eating the place up … where alive, diverse people and crowds who know the music know that they are seeing some of the best blues in the world." Her club, in this idealization, would be an in-demand forum for the blues, with a wondrous producer (performer) and a consumer (customer) experience.

The Contemporary Redevelopment Governance and Its Plans

Chicago's redevelopment governance post-2000 has spurned the policy uncertainty that marked the Washington, Orr, Sawyer, and early Daley II regimes (1984–89). After 2000, a more confident governance moved into an aggressive "transform Chicago" mode. This entity, following Mayor Richard Daley, "found its druthers and mojo," and pushed harder to upscale and reaestheticize Chicago's social and cultural fabric. At the heart of this, Daley and the governance's highly effective new oratory—global-speak—now boom across Chicago. This oratory had arisen in the 1980s and spoke of the need to redevelop Chicago as an emergent global city. Post-2000, this rhetoric increasingly invoked an ominousness and foreboding city reality, and glaringly provoked the public (Koval et al. 2006; Wilson 2007). "For the first time," the *Chicago Tribune* (2000) opined, "Chicago can be a global city—if it wants to be. But does it want to be?" To the *Tribune*, "Chicago virtually symbolized the Industrial Era and was one of its big winners.... But the Global Era presents new challenges. Chicago is not meeting them.... A city that loses the world's attention will wither into a backwater, much as once-mighty cities such as Venice remain today, picturesque and ignored." It is now or never, to the *Tribune* (2004), "city eclipse is at the doorstep...."

In the post-2000 period, Chicago's redevelopment governance changed its vision of and its' relation to the South Side. This now taut, bold governance has extended its tentacles geographically and has deepened its "rediscovery" of "South Side authenticity."[3] Incorporating this terrain into their "go-global" redevelopment scheme, they have increasingly spoken of a culturally and socially recoverable part of Chicago and have inaugurated bold restructuring efforts. The governance has activated a powerful and specific discourse about the need to "reculturalize" the South Side to help the area and advance the go-global Chicago redevelopment project, which has been at the center of its restructuring efforts. It now speaks of this terrain as the city's next "cultural catch" that is deftly framed in the complexities of a contingent cultural moment—the need for Chicago to become fully global. This framing, elaborately seizing the day's concerns and anxieties, drives an ambitious restructuring.

Initially, governance efforts were concentrated in a small South Central neighborhood and were tangibly brick and mortar; they physically moved Chicago's gentrification frontier beyond the South Loop into adjoining North Bronzeville. Bronzeville gentrification began in the late 1990s fueled by a rhetoric of "an area ... seeking to re-claim its soul" (see Reardon 2000). The area, once housing primarily low- and moderate-income households in a widely disinvested terrain (Boyd 2008), came to house patches of upscale condominiums, restaurants, and shops in the early 2000s. This persisted, spurred especially by Quad Cities Development Corporation, a city-based development group that focused on the Bronzeville area. Since 2000 they have worked to attract boutique businesses to Cottage Grove Avenue (between 43rd and 47th Streets), bigger "gentry" stores to State Street, and new upscale housing along State, Cottage Grove, and Martin Luther King Drive (Wilson 2012). Mayor Daley, underscoring the area's symbolic transformation, moved into a Near Bronzeville condo and bucked a decades-old tradition of Daleys living in blue-collar Bridgeport.

The move to restructure continued. The tactic shifted, given the reality of a more restructuring-difficult middle and deep South Side. Emphasis shifted to the realm of the discursive with attempts to reengineer middle-class imaginings of South Side recreational and residential possibilities (that today is most responsible for creating the "commodification creep" across the South Side and its blues bars). To be sure, physical change picked up in some areas south of Bronzeville (south of 49th Street) post-2005. New condos, single-family homes, townhouses, and retail development came to dot blocks in the Washington Park, Chatham, and Woodlawn communities (see Bergen, 2008). But the reality has not matched the rhetoric. The *Tribune* (2007), for example, portrays a deluge of exciting, new South Side investment: "Developers are expanding out of downtown and steadily breaking ground on $300,000-plus condos and town homes.... On the South Side, public housing high-rises are nearly all demolished. And the transformation of once run-down graystones and six-flats into elegant homes is exciting. So is seeing art galleries on King Drive and cafes on 47th Street." The cherry on the topping: "A new Starbucks on the South Side has been a cause for cartwheels."

Blues bars and blues blocks have become one leading edge of this rhetorical rediscovery (see Figure 3.2 below). Offered as places of raw, authentic black culture and performance, they have been strategically sanitized as milieus for "outsider" public consumption and recreational pleasure. These clubs, in the process, have been served up as metaphors for the new South Side outsider (incoming black gentrifiers and leisure seeking North Siders and tourists) to live or recreate here. Working through the go-global rhetoric, this push has been steady and aggressive.

Yet, we should not interpret the local governance's attempt to remake Chicago's South Side blues-scape as an attempt to break down the city's long entrenched racial divisions. Chicago has a long, virulent history of segregating working-class and poor Blacks that has been personified in the systematic constructing and isolating of its South Side "Black Belt." By the early 1930s, this area, bounded by 31st Street on the north, 63rd Street on the south, and between State Street and Cottage Grove Avenue,

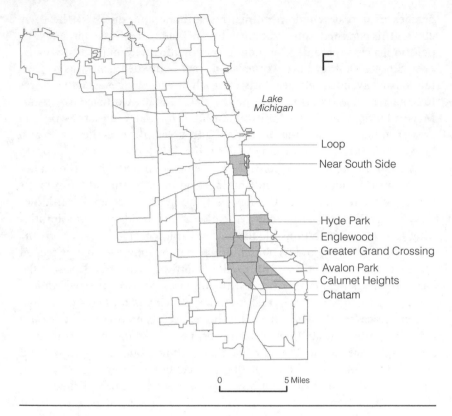

Lake
Michigan

Loop
Near South Side

Hyde Park
Englewood
Greater Grand Crossing
Avalon Park
Calumet Heights
Chatam

F

0   5 Miles

Figure 3.2 South Side communities containing the blues clubs.

housed more than 300,000 Blacks (Bennett 2006). By 1960, this number had increased to more than 750,000 (U.S. Census Bureau 1960). In this space, paraphrasing historian James Barrett (2012), black life in all its vibrancy, hopes, dreams, and despairs became confined and cordoned off. Formal government policies and informal social stigma that created and maintained this segregating persists to this day (Wilson 2007). These are overtures to remake the South Side's blues-scape and seek to extend the affluent's consumption realm to new terrain, nothing else. Today in neo-liberal Chicago, there is a heightened privileging of the upper-income's residential, commercial, and recreational desires which is manifest in this South Side "cultural rediscovery" (Wilson 2007).

Nine Dominant South Side Blues Clubs

In this context, we also need to know that the locations of these South Side blues clubs were established many decades ago and reflect this virulent segregation. As this segregation intensified over the decades and these clubs were confined especially to the South Side, Mayor Richard J. Daley's (1955–76) programs and policies systematically cemented this situation. Daley's mantra, from the outset, was to sustain an established social fabric—it was a city that supposedly worked (Bennett 2006). Adhering to this, Daley's elaborate securing and orchestrating of public housing funds turned South Side Chicago into the largest home for public housing in America. Daley's South Side was to house, confine, and separate blacks. The opening of the largest public housing project on earth, the Robert Taylor Homes in 1962 (28 high-rise buildings that contained more than 27,000 people), was flanked by "public-housing city": Hilliard Homes, Harold Ickes Homes, Dearborn Homes, Stateway Gardens, and Henry Horner Homes. By 1980, more than two-fifths of Bronzeville's population lived in public housing. Daley reinforced this segregating most directly via zoning policies, policing practices, and targeting of Section 8 vouchers (Koval et al. 2006; Greene, Bouman, & Grammenos 2006). Against this backdrop, there have been precious few locations outside of this area that blues clubs interested in serving their dominant patron—African Americans—could locate.

Thus outlined, a brief mention of the South Side's ever-evolving blues-cape post-2000 is important. After 2000, circumstances in the clubs diverged, reflected in the "Big Nine" of venues (Lee's Unleaded, Checkerboard Lounge, Celebrity Lounge, 7313 Club, Artis's Lounge, City Life, Club Eniquity, Reggie's Music Joint, East of the Ryan). On the one hand, clubs in the South 20s up to the 50s—Reggie's Music Joint, Club Eniquity, Checkerboard Lounge—experienced sustained economic stability. Bronzeville's gentrifying was at the heart of this. Growing numbers of middle-class "clubbers" (tourists, gentrifiers, university students-professionals) meant greater gate sales and more spending on drinks and food. Owner L.C. Thurmond of Checkerboard Lounge called his club "a renewed place by 2007 or so financially from what existed in the 1990s—the place was just doing better." Owner Kal P. of Reggie's Music Joint noted that "by 2003 we had squarely become a South Loop phenomenon—the South Loopers put us on their schedule and they were massing at the door on weekends to come in ... I had no complaints about that."

On the other hand, the clubs south of 53rd (Lee's Unleaded, Celebrity Lounge, 7313 Club, Artis's Lounge, City Life, East of the Ryan) continued an economic struggle. The core of this: The post-2000 economic fortunes of many far South Side Chicago areas (beyond Bronzeville) continued to slide. Physical and social change that had gripped large portions of Bronzeville proceeded highly unevenly south of Hyde Park. Thus, select blocks in Chatham, Avalon Park, and South Shore experienced physical upgrading and new "urban pioneers" (Moberg 2006). In 2008 the official unemployment rate for four large South Side communities—Englewood, Auburn Gresham, Washington Heights, and West Englewood—was a staggering 23.2 percent (*Chicago Reporter* 2009; see Figure 3.3). Among all of urban America's neighborhood groupings, only Northeast Detroit had a higher rate of unemployment in 2008 (*Chicago Reporter* 2009). In and around these four Chicago neighborhoods, most clubs simply fought to survive. Some adventurous clubbers—Dennis Grammenos's (2011) "courageous-voyeuristic" music lovers—journeyed south from places like the Loop and Hyde Park to visit these clubs, but most customers lived in South Side neighborhoods. As owner Stanley Davis of Lee's Unleaded (South 74th) noted, "Yeah, we saw at this time some clubbers, but they had not yet really discovered us—we continued to service mainly the nearby neighborhoods ... and typically they didn't have a lot of money."

South Side Community Areas that Contain Blues Clubs

Yet, in these Big Nine clubs, business and attendance has been typically excellent, particularly on weekends. Today throngs of people today populate these venues on Friday and Saturday evenings. Social relations also seem unduly rich and fulfilling (compared to other music clubs I have visited across urban America). In the social milieu, social links seamlessly extend across the clubs; drinks are frequently bought for friends across tables in gestures of sharing and camaraderie; and many also openly enjoy and sing along with the music. The ongoing dramaturgy also involves patrons frequently engaging in dialogue with performers on stage. As many patrons across these clubs have told me, the venue is important to them. Some say the music and social order is a needed release from their daily round of work and tedium. Others note that instead of bridge clubs, foreign legion halls, or bowling venues, their social life revolves around a blues club. As one 61-year-old man at Artis's Lounge told me, "I am at home here ... it's where I most wanna be. I hook up here regularly with my war buddies so to speak [laughter] ... My wife and kids know where to find me."

Five Weeks at Beebe's

It's 10 p.m. on a Sunday evening, and the lights dim in Beebe's Lounge on South 78th Street. Like other South Side blues clubs I have visited this month, people quickly hush, hear the introduction of the evening's first band, and let out a thunderous clapping. The crowd has steadily grown, anticipating a club favorite, Tommy Ariva and His Band of Blues, who play here nearly every Sunday night. Few seem to care that Beebe's sits on a decrepit corner of disinvested buildings and stores. People seem to easily erase the reality of a drab interior and the trappings of a decayed block and side of town forgotten by the middle class. Enthusiasm for the music and for being in this social milieu overwhelms the décor of drab orange curtains draping a few dirty windows. The bulk of the audience is regulars; many have been coming to Beebe's for years. Small groups of inquisitive nonregulars dot the room. Some are men and women who live nearby and are out for good music, others offer themselves as intrigued, voyeuristic outsiders intent on immersing themselves in their sense of a mysterious world of black blues. In all cases, bodies, mannerisms, and social conduct unmistakably signal a sense of self, values, ideals, and expectations for the evening.

The Complex Club Owner and Sense of Beebe's

Throughout this evening, club owner Jackie Smith scurries around Beebe's to ensure a social orderliness. She continually multitasks: She checks and replenishes the alcohol stock, spot scrubs the floors, receives the cover charge at the door from early arrivals, makes and serves drinks at the bar and at tables, supervises the two waitresses/bartenders, and cleans up tables and counters. These occur all the while that she participates in a splintered banter with new arrivals as they saunter in and look for seating. Both Jackie and the patrons seem to relish the talk. A bond between these parties is obvious; each deftly plays off against each other. As she tells me in a semiexasperated tone while I sit at the bar, "I'm glad the customers are coming on time, with some of these people, you just never know ... some of them would get lost in their own homes!"

Jackie cuts a distinctive stroke into the club's social space. With the power to hire, fire, and dictate club rules, this whirlwind is a powerful club force and a central producer of club knowledge. Her truths shoot across the club and are negotiated by others (to help define club norms and protocols) as she deftly wields her body and partakes in social relationships. Through this production and allocation of knowledge, Jackie both accepts and renounces the commodification of Beebe's that reflects her distinctive positionality and reality making as a local and societal being. At the core of this reality making is a guiding template: her sense of the club's value and utility.

Tonight Jackie demonstrates that she constitutes Beebe's in a dominant way: as an economic space to thwart a nagging fear of economic failure and material collapse. She, like many at Beebe's, worries about her economic future, and emotively vacillates between economic disillusionment

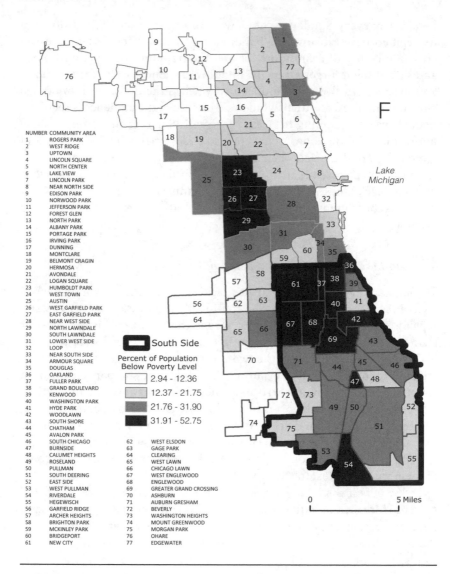

Figure 3.3 Chicago's impoverished neighborhoods: Proportion of population below poverty level by neighborhood areas, 2010.

and economic hope. In her darkest moments, Jackie comes close to invoking a dystopic futility: A trace of potential economic collapse haunts her. It, in her words, "is felt throughout the day; when I'm cleaning tables, serving drinks, talking to customers, and dealing with the bands." She has had first-hand knowledge of hunger, homelessness, and deprivation, having lived these over her life. She grew up poor on Chicago's South Side, at the height of Chicago's second regime of "black ghetto building" (1945–65) where low income Black households were systematically stashed and isolated (see Hirsch 2005). The South Side at this time was profoundly segregated, disproportionally poor, and aptly characterized by William Tabb's (1970) moniker "labor plantation economy." Job opportunities for locals were largely confined to arduous assembly-line and laboring work, with wages overwhelmingly paltry (Osofsky 1967; Hirsch 2005). As a South Side kid who went to a local public high school, she almost never ventured outside of the area.

Jackie's recent history further illuminates this worry. Twelve years ago, desperate to move her and her husband out of poverty, Jackie cobought Beebe's as the solution to her fears. Her husband, a Chicago police officer, pushed the undertaking with great enthusiasm and hope. As she put it to me, "this was our decision [buying the club] … it was our way to confront the demons that were plaguing us … an opportunity to once and for all, make life for us more certain … and to build a satisfying life." Previously, a work life of odd jobs, stay-at-home raising kids, and bartending had raised the materialist fear to a haunt. Throughout, food insecurity, shelter worries, and materialist survival gripped her. South Side Chicago, then and now, was her home, it has always been, in her words, "the love and hate of [her] life, a place of "strong [intense] symbolic attachment" and a place of perceived ensnaring and material insecurity. These twelve years, as Susan Berger's (2008) "neo-citizen" of Chicago, have been tough and trying.

One day, she hopes, Beebe's will be remarkably successful, beyond her wildest dreams. Jackie hopes for a lucrative club that features the best known blues bands in America. "I would one day love to bring the best here—ya know, B.B. King, Buddy Guy, Albert King, Stevie Wonder—but I'm not there yet … but a girl can dream!" In her words, "to bring this talent and inspiration to the South Side folk around here would be the ideal." But she also knows that making this a reality in current neoliberalized Chicago will be extremely difficult. Jackie understands current race-class relations and political times, noting to me the discursive and material obstacles Black South Siders now face. "We are not particularly liked, or tended to by the city, it's pretty obvious … we are seen outside the area [South Side]—by many—as threatening and scary … you know … we are made to be that way." To Jackie, "the politics and the laws are stacked against us … there used to be more concern for poor black folk than there is today … the focus today is building up the downtown, building those skyscrapers, not helping our neighborhoods or families."

Jackie is a self-identified "grower" of the club, initially having a muted enthusiasm for the club's possibilities when her husband (now deceased) owned and managed the facility. But with his death in 2010, she says, her interest in and ambitions for Beebe's skyrocketed. There is, in her words, now a "thrill of the hunt" involved, that is, to see how far she can make the club a thriving and successful entity. "For a black girl from the South Side to make it in business, let alone in the rough-and-tumble music world, would be quite a story … something to be cherished," she says to me. Jackie knows that black women face enormous obstacles to being successful business people. "The sex, the race, the lack of money, these things work against black women, especially from the South Side," she notes. But Jackie never seems to forget her difficult past and the club's role in potentially alleviating her materialist worries. This is at the core of her "drive to therapeutize" the self, what Dennis Mumby (1993) calls "the human construction of the self-therapeutic motif." Beebe's, in this sense, is a direct pipeline to her deepest aspirations and her darkest fears.

But Jackie also desires something else for Beebe's: a space of self-happiness and self-affirmation. Club interiority and exteriority, using Miranda Joseph's (2002) terms, is intricately linked in a life. This kind of microspace, to Joseph, becomes an imagining inseparable from society's realities. Thus, Jackie, as a societally formed subject, desires a vibrant and sustaining cultural life that the club could help provide. The economic struggle to subsist and deal with her past preoccupies her, but she is also a self-identified "black blues women" and proudly wears this appellation. "I'm a black woman … and I'm proud of myself and this club … the stuff it provides me and my customers," she says to me. "This club is me … and it's my baby," she adds. This is the side to her that wants to resist the commercial creep into her club. Commercialization, in this trace, should only go so far, the club's integrity could be lost forever. This, like a chill, seems to tug at her, entering her thoughts at a moment's notice. In this parallel track of thinking, one vision of club success—large crowds relishing the music, throngs of people enjoying themselves at the bar, happy social relations resonating across the club—are moments when personal possibility and potentiality are at their brightest.

Not surprisingly, then, Jackie continually etches hope across the club's vastness: in faces, bodies, musical instruments, social relations, frayed pictures and posters on the wall. People are engaged and understood this way: musicians, club owners, waitresses, club outsiders, strangers, and casual acquaintances. "We're all [everyone in the club] doing fine when we're in Beebe's," Jackie says to me, "it may be different out there [waving outside the club], but it's all good when we're assembled [here]." Positive meanings (nostalgic remembrances, current social recollections) are continuously infused in the sociospatial fabric of a place's objects (the bar, the stage, the bands, pictures draped on the stage). Jackie, for example, identifies the stage as "a place of history ... where some of the best musicians in Chicago have stepped foot on [sic] and blown the place away. It's a historical treasure." A space of identity nourishment and social contentment will be produced here: unmasking possibility, potentiality, and current pleasure is vital to her. Beebe's becomes a space of elaborate constructing and choreographing attuned and refined to a person's social desires.

In this vein, Jackie desires to have a club that upholds her notion of "a black blues tradition." "I've always loved the blues," she tells me, "as a little girl this is what my father would listen to, this is what I listened to ... it [the blues] was in my psyche at an early age." Race and class interconnect in Jackie's conception of "black blues." It, to Jackie, was borne out of black people's struggles for dignity and decent lives. This music is seemingly reflective of a people's age-old tussle to transplant, adapt, socially and economically struggle, and heal. Jackie here draws on both the sense of past and present, identifying a legacy of slavery and racism, oppressive gendering, coping with ghettoization and racism, struggles to keep a sense of positive racial affiliation intact, and the malleability to inaugurate individual and group repair and rehabilitation. "Blues music," Jackie tells me, "is a history! We've face a bitter history to survive ... we were official slaves and unofficial slaves. Today, poor black women are as much as before unofficial slaves.... It ain't goin' away, but I'm gonna fight and try to make a club that preserves the integrity of black culture, black women, and black men."

Jackie attaches a sense of moral nobility to this notion of protecting "black blues." She declares she will not compromise her quest to establish a vital, pleasurable, and profitable blues space for herself and others. Moral nobleness becomes one central form of cultural–moral capital captured in her club actions. "People may put me off, or not understand me ... but I'm gonna stay with it [club actions]," she says to me this evening.... I like the money, it's not much, but I also like the sense of duty and purpose ... I always think god has directed me to do this [own and operate Beebe's]." In this sense, Jackie too (like many others in the club) revels in an ethos of being a kind of battle-scarred survivor intent on sustaining the club. As she repeatedly noted to me, she constantly battles difficult and sometimes tawdry circumstances, but can see her personal growth and strength. Yet, one more time (see next section), epic struggles of personal strength are only peripherally directed against the forces that structure her difficult life circumstances. Instead, she targets most fervently for removal of the feelings that these forces create. In conversation with me this evening, she continually pits her heroic struggles to survive against the afflicting feelings that supposedly must be confronted. Forces and processes that structure her haunts, obliterated from interrogation, enable an overtly less politicized life.

The Demographic Attachment

Jackie also has remarkably strong feelings for the long-term regulars who come into Beebe's, a loyalty rooted in years of informal interactions with these clubbers. This is the population that flows into the club every Sunday evening just before Tommy and band begin, and surges in numbers as the music begins. Immediately upon arrival, they too become central producers of knowledge in the club's flow of activities. Arrivals, often eye-catching and audacious, provide greetings, hugs, handshakes, and banter across the club. Visible displays of bodies and ritualized engagements reverberate across Beebe's for all to digest. Some serve up long, symbolically rich strolls across the club floor, others offer brief but semiotically poignant cuts through club space. Less colorful walkers rely on other body elements—garb, facial expressions, subtle body movements, to do their communicating. In all cases, modes of social conduct, faces, torsos, hands, arms, and styles of dress are mobilized, meaning-rich signifiers.

Jackie knows that these club regulars so conduct themselves amid constructing Beebe's in a dominant way: as an escape from the dull trace of an entrenched, unshakable trauma. As she told me in different terms, club interiority and exteriority are intricately linked in their lives, one seamlessly structures the other. At the core of this, a tough, gritty life outside the club sears a haunt into them which is intact Sunday evenings at Beebe's. Many are low-wage workers, and material standings are often unstable and afflicting. Many toil in the new burgeoning service economy and workfare economy of Chicago as fast-food workers, phone solicitors, grounds keepers, burger flippers, postal workers, retail sellers, and the like. Some are retired or semi-retired but struggle to produce a livable income. As proof, an elderly man, in discussion with me this evening, touches upon the haunt and the problem of minimal opportunity: "my life ain't great … it's hard … it's a real challenge … yeah, I feel it all the time, it stays with me … and it's tough for my kids too, there's just not a lot of opportunities around anymore, lots of marginal stuff—fast food jobs, doin' some repair, ya know, the usual thing." More curtly, another elderly man says to me: "It's hard to shake, this crazy life … where you don't have much money … but ya know, ya gotta keep going…." Their most poignant struggle, Jackie realizes, is to economically subsist. As she told me, this population has daily struggles and fears around food insecurity, housing insecurity, low wages, growing debt, and fear of job termination.

Perhaps unsurprisingly, then, Jackie permits long-term regulars to support an active shadow economy at Beebe's. This subgroup seeks to capitalize on their skills, abilities, and social acceptance at Beebe's to supplement frequently meager incomes. This economy flourishes in an informal, mouth-to-mouth way. An informalized peddling of childcare services, home maintenance care, video and CD sales, haircut services, gardening care, plumbing services, and car fixing occurs throughout the evenings. Sellers eye the crowd, identify a best spot for intervention, and go from table to table, bar stool to bar stool. This evening, I was approached at the bar by two amiable sellers, hawking blues CDs and lawn care maintenance. Both encounters were friendly, direct, and brief. With sellers told that I had no interest, they quickly withdrew from the interaction. As other clubbers later told me, many at Beebe's are, in their words, "survivors ... foragers." "It is," one person told me, "the way the club operates ... everyone accepts it, even Jackie [the owner], she looks the other way ... the battle is to haul in that dollar ... that almighty thing [laughter]."

Jackie's Body and Social Relations

In addition to offering club rules and regulations, Jackie produces Beebe's social character through something transparent: her body and styles of engagement. Jackie, in this way, seeks to create her ideal Beebe's by affixing in the club her values, beliefs, and desires. Jackie thus strives to construct an ideal Beebe's by locating and activating power through mundane, ritualized activities and practices; that is, "the capillar[ies] ... the extremities ... the 'outer limits' of societal formation" (Foucault 1970). This complex deployment of power is important to this study: it fundamentally shapes Jackie's concrete thoughts about the desirability of club commodification; that is, the degree to which this kind of change should be pursued. For, Jackie's desire to induce change in the club will be a response to her sense of club strengths and deficiencies, the degree to which her ideals can be met. If she cannot forge a Beebe's that fulfills her social desires, economic dreams, and cultural aspirations, club change would appear as an attractive possibility.

This evening, Jackie bodily and stylistically locates herself and her club as South Side blues insiders. On the one hand, a bodying and social style works to retain the current social space of Beebe's and to resist excessive commercialization. Most poignantly, she nonstop performs as a weary, overworked attendant to the club's veracities. All are to see a person strikingly dedicated to an important task: serving the club's and community's blues tradition. Thus, in her daily round, Jackie theatrically hurries, gyrates, and gesticulates the difficulties of nurturing this club. In one moment, an exhaustive body and face cringes at having to clean up messy tables. In the next moment, she unveils a tired but courageous whirl across the club to take drink orders from customers. Moments later, Jackie displays a weary patience for customers who take their time ordering drinks. Her message, that she is engaged in an elaborate self-sacrifice to keep Beebe's vibrant, reverberates across the club. Throughout these rhythmic movements, Jackie's bodily assemblage—face, arms, legs, gait, hands—becomes a perfectly synchronized text for all to read.

I am not exempt from this treatment, tonight being greeted with a visibly tired hello and query about having my usual (a beer). "Hey, you, welcome back, what will you have, the usual," Jackie says to me with a slight, tired smile. She stands stooped and seems to have difficulty supporting her body weight. Upon my receiving the beer, we make small-talk for five minutes. We talk about the music, the latest poster mounted near the stage, and the whims of trying to manage a South Side blues club. Then, Jackie abruptly cuts off the interaction, and moves deftly across the bar to talk with other customers. She, again, brings out the sly, weary smile and uneven stance. Always shooting quick glances across the club, the gait quickly becomes a bold, confident trek as she moves hurriedly across the club floor to service newly arrived customers. Throughout this microcircuitry of embodied practices, Jackie cuts a visible swath through the club. She, in her own words, "is constantly hustling to make ends meet … to keep this place going." Her body, projecting a martyrdom, asks the clubbers not to feel for her, but to feel for her club—a supposedly struggling venue that needs customers and loyalty to club ways.

In another way, Jackie activates her body and style of engagement to nourish the sense of a proud, struggling blues club. This evening, Jackie engages customers in a shifting, strategic offering of emotions and behaviors: She is at once friendly, terse, demanding, theatrical, calm, disciplining, and fawning. Engaging customers—taking drink orders, seating parties, running drink tabs—typically involves usage of this entirety. Thus, three tables from me, Jackie pressures a middle-aged man to have another drink during Tommy's intermission. An initial benevolent suggestion, turned down, quickly becomes a tersely worded imploring for him to buy another drink (an unwritten rule in the club is that patrons should always be drinking). When he balks, she turns to a disciplining tactic of suggesting and gesticulating that all club customers should constantly "work" drinks. As he softens his stance, the stone-cold aesthetic becomes supplanted by a benevolent coaxing. Finally, he orders the drink and Jackie—in this engagement—returns to the persona of the tired, overworked servant of the blues club and local blues ways. A seductive coercion—using diverse emotions, behaviors, and sensibilities—proves successful. Throughout the evening, Jackie repeats this recipe in her engagements with customers, but never displays the identical sequence of personal transformations.

At the same time, this bodying and style of engagement works within the club's coda and signals a reverence for its current social milieu; that is, an engagement style draws on established styles of socializing within Beebe's. In this process, Jackie uses what Kobeena Mercer (1997) calls "a bebop blues" style of engagement which mixes humor, sarcasm, sternness, revulsion, teasing, and joyousness. To Mercer, this bebop blues style of interaction is common in working-class blues clubs and blues settings. It pays tribute to these milieus while being immensely respected as an engagement style by its observers. This style, to Mercer, provides a kind of sliding easiness and conviviality to transactions—business and nonbusiness—that lessens tensions and edginess. Human negotiation, through this form, is infused with a comfort and an easy respectability. But also, this style used by Jackie massages and elevates the club's "code" and the identities of her customers. Asked about this kind of engagement, Jackie said to me, "Oh yeah, it's how I relate to customers ... everyone talks this way to everyone else, it's just the way it's done." One more time, the ritualized order of the club is enriched. Every instance of this strokes the club's dominant social contours, seizing them, demarcating them, and elevating them.

But, Jackie's bodying and engagements also signal something quite different: an openness to accepting a more commercialized club in certain ways (i.e., the influx of more affluent customers, bar offerings that cater to this population). At the core of this, Jackie engages "club outsiders" in a distinctive way. For all to see, she is upfront friendly, vivacious, and ultra-accommodating to them. Spurning the interactive style deployed for club regulars, she is flagrantly engaging, and at times, unduly obedient and solicitous (compared to her style of engagement with club regulars). She strikes a stance here that reverberates across the club. Club regulars tend to take notice immediately, and some ascribe an ominousness to this. "I know what she's doing," one club regular told me, with people like that she's cozyin' up, making nice, you know what I'm saying ... I hope it's not a sign of things to come ... but those dudes are being given the green light to be here and could one day take the place over." Another club regular called it, "Weird, man, a playin' up, it's kind of puzzling."

This evening, for example, Jackie continuously tends to a white middle-aged man sitting at the bar's corner. Here is Gertz, Valsoner, and Breaux's (2007) notion of a strategic trope: "semiotically traveling friendliness." This kind of friendliness, to Gertz et al. is a hermeneutic instrument to communicate alliances, allegiances, and shared values for all to digest. Beneath the friendliness, then, is a deliberate politics of communication. Thus, waves of friendliness sweep across this man and Jackie as she makes frequent stops at his location to ensure that all is well. His drink this evening (martinis) is constantly refreshed and accompanied by friendly banter. When he is joined by a friend later on, he receives the same treatment. Jackie lets these people and everyone in the club know that Beebe's welcomes "outsiders." If there is a hint of discomfort that they ["outsiders"] feel, she tells me, "I am going to try and chase it away and make these people feel at home ... hey, I'm the owner, it's my place, and everyone should know that all that can pay their tab are welcome." There is no "peculiarizing" of them, she does not cast them as objects of Otherness. Rather, there is a message being sent: anyone who can pay and respect club practices is welcome.

Jackie sees this population as a potential gateway to something promising: possibilities to upgrade the purchasing power of her customer base at Beebe's. This possibility, she tells me, would be welcome provided the club does not lose its blues ways and aesthetic. "These other folk, you know the North Siders, the tourists, if they come, I am okay with that, as long as they pay and respect the place.... In fact, I don't give a damn where they're from, they're welcome as long as they can add to the place." Jackie acknowledges a tension between keeping the club as is and throwing open the gates for tourists to come en masse and transform the club. She is quick to note that Beebe's would never be a place of unfettered "North Side takeover" and become "one more supposed blues club." In discussion, her commitment to retaining Beebe's current character is strong: "Nothing is going to change in a major way what we have here. I won't let it ... I am open to everyone, this is a public club, we now have a cover, I know why people want to come to Beebe's ... but god willing we keep it as is ... no ands, ifs, or buts."

Jackie admits to creating confusion in the club in embracing both the club's current content and the signifiers for a potential demographic upheaval. She terms this "an irony that everyone's just got to figure out." She also acknowledges that some club regulars—herself described "bread-and butter of club operations"—are concerned about the club's future. Yet, she proceeds on encouraging both, living and working through a recognized paradox that for the moment creates confusion about the club's future. Jackie is unwilling to give up on either front; retaining the club's current content and moving it into a more lucrative reality are equally compelling ideals to her. In her daily round, there is never a slippage in either ideal. At the moment, her luminous bodying and styles of engagement continue to boldly embrace this paradox.

Discussion and Conclusion

A new kind of elite privileging—land and blocks transformed into globally declarative, affluent play spaces—now marks many major American cities (Wilson 2004, 2007; Wyly et al. 2009). This remaking now moves far beyond downtown cores to engage a new terrain: once flagrantly marginalized black communities and their blues-scapes. In Chicago, its South Side blues-scape (a scatter of nine aging blues clubs) experiences this, attracting intense media attention after being consigned to policy oblivion for decades. Chicago's redevelopment governance, one more time, harnesses the power of the state and planning apparatus to achieve its objectives. A mobile, quick acting capitalism strikes out to expand this class's "city consumption field" that works through productions of elaborate imaginaries and city need. At a rhetoric's core, a supposed new hypercompetitive reality makes Chicago easily discardable as a place for investment, production, and business. Against this supposed reality, Chicago is now a threatened, but still historically resilient locale that once again must act innovatively to survive.

Multiple scenarios exist for how this commodification will proceed and what this blues-scape will become. A dominant vision, one that needs interrogating, suggests that power is overtly and bluntly applied in a hegemonic process and these clubs will simply be overwhelmed by capital's creeping, infiltrating prowess (Martin 1998; Koval et al. 2006). Blues clubs, in this vision, will soon be one more gentrified city element that will be normalized under a creative destruction ethos (spatially extending the go-global restructuring project). A powerful streak of determinism, but also a sense of intense realism and reference to on-the-ground history, cuts through this vision. Yet, this vision may be too simple; that is, it ignores the fact that these core South Side clubs have defied the odds before and have been remarkably resilient in the face of different kinds of economic pressures (from both intense commodification and economic decline). Moreover, there is evidence that these clubs contain a potent mixture of vibrant human agency, unpredictable human vision and social constructing, and intense personal striving for pleasure and meaning that make the operation of this commodification influence unduly complex.

My findings corroborate this idea of a complex commodification process and unpredictable club futures. At the core of this, the present study suggests that club owners, the central decision-makers of club futures, are reflexive people who engage, internalize, and work through three central forces: new neoliberal subject realities, governmentality, and class–race identity constituting. These multiscaler, worked-through "templates" guide a multitextured, complex club owner production of knowledge about the club and its relation to personal goals, values, and desires. These interconnections are crucial: they intermix the owners' drive to commodify the club with desires to embolden their identities, upgrade their enriching as cultural beings, and service fellow "subaltern" people. The results are contradictory, conflicting desires that tear at the consciousness of club owners. The process of club commodification, I conclude, is anything but

a dominant, hegemonic imposition on agency-bereft people. The interconnections of neoliberal subject realities, governmentality, and class–race
identity ultimately embed the drive to commodify in produced stocks of
knowledge that also carry other ideals, aspirations, and "imperatives" in
them.

Finally, why do I take on the issues of how commodification operates
on this floor space and blues club survivability in their present forms?
These blues clubs and communities face, one more time, turbulent times.
In their currently formation, the core group of clubs, thinned by economic
attrition over time and also now a focus for affluent upscaling, may soon
disappear or be substantially altered. This would prove damaging to these
South Side neighborhoods; these clubs are a substantive social and cultural resource. Whether "authentic" or not, these clubs continue to be an
important social glue in their communities. Yet, I am not convinced that
stepped-up attempts to commodify them will be successful, the forces of
resistance may prove stronger. The remarkable survivability of these nine
Blues clubs, with their staunch club owners and dominant club populations, may be sufficient to thwart capital's overtures. The power of capital
to transform all places in our cities to their specifications, in the final analysis, continues to meet deft and adroit opposition in unlikely places and in
unlikely ways. Predicting these clubs' evolution, then, is difficult, and we
must re-examine this deepened interface of capital and community in the
upcoming months and years.

Acknowledgments

My sincere thanks to France Winddance Twine and Bradley Gardener
for offering important, constructive comments on earlier versions of this
manuscript. Special thanks to Matt Wilson for making the figures that
accompany this chapter.

Notes

1. Neoliberal subject realities references the intensification of post 1980 societal values—commodified social relations, market solutions to individual and societal ills, atomized and
individually causative beings—that have become imperceptibly internalized by many (Wilson 2004; England and Ward 2007). Governmentality references the Foucaultian notion of
power being exercised by current power regimes in the mundane every day (Larner 2003).
This "government from afar" notion identifies a meaning-rich everyday—modes of dress,
manner, gesticulation, body movement, and human imagining—as influential political
acts. Finally, class–race constituting identifies the continuous human act of constituting
selves in daily actions that bolsters the creation of proud, competent class–race beings
(hooks 1993; Mercer 1997).

2. The name and address of the club has been changed to preserve the identity of respondents. I offered this to respondents as a way to ensure more candid discussions.

3. It is important to briefly note that this South Side governance rediscovery is not entirely new: it had a predecessor of a different kind. In the late 1990s and early 2000s, banks and lenders eyed new markets here in a "bodily rediscovery." A speculative wave of mortgage lending inundated many South Side blocks amid banks and lending institution "subpriming." A 1990s steady stream turned into a post-2000 tidal wave as banks sought to upgrade stagnant profits (Wyly et al. 2009; Crump 2002). Previously, this area had been ruthlessly delinked from circuitries of housing finance consumption for decades (see Flammer 2010). But between 1999 and 2005, this changed: more than 10,000 subprime loans were granted to South Chicago households. By 2008, more than 60 percent of households in Chicago's African American neighborhoods relied upon credit provided by subprime lenders (Tweh 2010). Multinational Wells Fargo, Citi Bank, and Superior Bank were particularly egregious lenders (see Pallasch 2008). A calculated process to entrap economically vulnerable households in debt proved immensely lucrative (much of the mortgages were securitized by the secondary mortgage market) (Fishbein and Bunce 2002; Wyly et al. 2009).

References

Balkin, Steven. 2002. Discussion with professor, Department of Economics, Roosevelt University, Chicago, June 3.

Barrett, James. 2012. Discussion with historian, University of Illinois at Urbana-Champaign, January 13.

Bennett, Larry. 2006. "Chicago's New Politics of Growth." In *The New Chicago: A Social and Cultural Analysis*, edited by J. P. Koval, L. Bennett, et al., 44–56. Philadelphia: Temple.

Bergen, Kathy. 2008. "Community's Promise Attracting Money, Faith." *Chicago Tribune*, March 16, p. 5:1.

Berger, Peter, and Thomas Luckmann. 1966. *The Social Construction of Reality*. New York: Basic.

Berger, Susan., 2008. *Global Feminism*. Minneapolis: University of Minnesota.

Boyd, Michelle R. 2008. *Jim Crow Nostalgia*. Minneapolis: University of Minnesota.

Brown, Steve 2006. "House of Blues Sert for Gig at Victory." *Knight Ridder Tribune Business News*, June 1, 1.

Chicago Reporter. 2009. "Chicago's South Side Has the Nation's Second Highest Unemployment Rate." www.chciagoreporter.typepad.com/Chicago-reporter/2009

Chicago Tribune. 2000. "Here's Our Chance to Be Global." April 23, 2:1.

———. 2004. "21st Century Chicago: Transformed Windy City Has a Truly Global Reach." October 17, 2:1.

———. 2007. "Language and Perception: Selling the South Side," February 11, 1.

Crump, Jeff. 2002. "Deconcentration by Demolition: Public Housing, Poverty, and Urban Policy." *Society and Space: Environment and Planning D* 20: 581–596.

England, Kim, and Kevin Ward. 2007. *Neoliberalism: States, Networks, Peoples*. Oxford, UK: Blackwell.

Fishbein, Allen, and Harold Bunce. 2000. "Subprime Market Growth and Predatory Lending." www.huduser.org/publication.

Flammer. 2010. Discussion with Planner, City of Chicago, 11 June.

Foucault, Michel. 1972. *The Archaeology of Knowledge*. New York: Pantheon.

Gertz, Sun Hee Kim, Jaen Valsoner, and Jean-Paul Breaux. 2007. *Semiotic Rotations: Modes of Meaning in Cultural Worlds*. New York: Information Age.

Goodrich, P. 1987. *Legal Discourse: Studies in Linguistics, Rhetoric, and Legal Analysis*. New York: St. Martin's.

Grammenos, Dennis. 2011. Discussion with professor, Department of Geography, Northeastern Illinois University, October 17.

Grazian, David, 2005. *Blue Chicago: The Search for Authenticity.* Chicago: University of Chicago.

Greene, Richard, Mark Bauman, and Dennis Grammenos. 2006. *Chicago's Geography: Understanding the Chicago Region.* Washington, DC: Association of American Geographers.

Hirsh, Arnold. 2005. *Making the Second Ghetto: Race and Housing in Chicago 1940–60.* Chicago: University of Chicago.

hooks, bell. 1993. *Outlaw Culture.* London: Routledge.

Joseph, Miranda. 2002. *Against the Romance of Community.* Minneapolis: University of Minnesota.

Koval, J. P., Larry Bennett, Michael Bennett, Fassil Demissie, Roberta Garner, and Kiljoang Kijm, eds. 2006. *The New Chicago.* Philadelphia: Temple University.

Larner, Wendy. 2003. "Neoliberalism?" *Environment and Planning D: Society and Space* 21: 509–12.

MacLeod, Gordon. 2002. "From Urban Entrepreneurialism to a Revanchist City? On the Spatial Injustices of Glasgow's Renaissance." In *Spaces of Neoliberalism*, edited by N. Brenner and N. Theodore, 531–554. Oxford: Blackwell.

Martin, Andrew. 1998. "Blues District Plan Off-Key, Critics Say." *Chicago Tribune*, February 22, p. 2:1.

Mercer, Kobeena. 1997. *Welcome to the Jungle.* London: Routledge.

Moberg, D. 2006. "Economic Restructuring: Chicago's Precarious Balance." In *The New Chicago*, edited by J. P. Koval, Larry Bennett, Michael Bennett, Fassil Demissie, Roberta Garner, and Kiljoang Kijm. Philadelphia: Temple University.

Mumby, Dennis. 1993. *Narrative and Social Control: Critical Perspectives.* Newbury Park, CA: Sage Publications.

Osofsky, Gilbert. 1967. *Harlem: the Making of the Negro Ghetto.* New York: St. Martin's Press.

Pallasch, Abdan. 2008. "Obama's Subprime Pal." *Chicago Sun-Times,* April 28, p. 13.

Phillips, Michael. 2010. "Chess Records Story Still Untold: Like Cadillac Records, Who Do You Love Feels Inauthentic." *Chicago Tribune*, April 30, p. 6.

Reardon, Patrick. 2000. "Can Bronzeville Reclaim Its Soul?" *Chicago Tribune*, May 21, 10.

Smith, Neil. 2003. "Ashes and Aftermath." *Studies in Political Economy* 67 (Spring): 7–12.

Tabb, William. 1970. *Political Economy of Black Ghetto.* New York: W.W. Norton.

Thrift, Nigel. 2004. "Intensities of Feeling: Towards a Spatial Politics of Affect." *Geografiska Annaler. Series B, Human Geography* 86: 57–78.

Tonkiss, Fran. 2005. *Space, the City, and Social Theory.* Cambridge, MA: Polity.

Tweh, Bowdeya. 2010. "Underemployed Are Unseen Face of Recession." *New York Times.* www.nytimes.com/business/local/article_714eo89c.

U.S. Census Bureau. 1960. *Statistical Data on Housing, Economic and Population Trends.* Washington, DC: U.S. Department of Commerce.

Vanketesh, Sudhir. 2004. "Tearing Down the Community." *Shelterforce,* 138, Nov/Dec .

Wacquant, Loic. 2008. *Urban Outcasts.* Cambridge, MA: Polity.

Wilson, David. 2004. "Toward A Contingent Urban Neoliberalism." *Urban Geography* 25: 771–783.

———. 2007. *Cities and Race: America's New Black Ghetto.* London: Routledge.

———. 2012. "Chicago's South Side Blues Clubs: The Latest Struggle." Unpublished manuscript, available from author.

Wyly, Elvin, Marcus Moos, Daniel Hammel, and Emanuel Kabahizi. 2009. "Cartographies of Race and Class: Mapping the Class Monopoly Rents of American Subprime Mortgage Capital." *International Journal of Urban and Regional Research* 33 (2): 332–25.

PART II

Privileged Migrants and Post-Colonial Racism

Africans, Europeans, and Transnational Movement

CHAPTER 4

Landscaping Privilege
Being British in South Africa

PAULINE LEONARD

Privilege etches the landscape of South Africa. Racialized advantage is produced through multiple social mechanisms of South African life, but it is the materiality of space that makes their daily operations starkly visible. Exploring such questions as who owns what, who goes where, how this or that person travels and why, helps to expose the texture of privilege and its corollaries: inequality and discrimination. In South Africa, the geographical lens is particularly significant because the management of the spatial has long been the key means by which racialized positions have been constructed and privilege secured. From the early days of colonialism, and particularly since the introduction of the apartheid regime in 1948, whiteness has sought to construct superiority through the establishment of partitioned and privileged white spaces. However, it is now nearly twenty years since the post-apartheid government in South Africa came into office with a mandate of universal democracy and racial equality. It is therefore important to explore the extent to which the landscape of South Africa, and the position of bodies within it, has changed in accordance with the new ideological climate of egalitarianism and multiracialism. In short, what does the transition away from apartheid tell us about privilege, its positions and its possibilities?

Colonial settler elites of Dutch and British immigrants first introduced a racialized inscription onto the spatial landscape of South Africa in the mid-seventeenth century. However, it was the system of white minority rule known as apartheid which particularly consolidated racially exclusive places of work, residence, and leisure as policy (Murray 2011). Indeed, the racial demarcation and management of space was a fundamental tenet of apartheid, and Johannesburg, one of the nation's largest and most powerful cities, was a quintessential example of how the urban environment was used as a resource to segregate people by race and establish white privilege. For most of the twentieth century, land management philosophy was to eliminate racial diversity and construct racially distinct and single-use zones in the city landscape. The fundamental ideology behind the design of its commercial districts and residential neighborhoods was to prevent any possibility of racial mixing: "to keep apart rather than bring together" (Murray 2011, 177). As a result, everyday life was conducted within luxurious and cocooned enclaves for the whites, whilst for the blacks, this life took place "in ramshackle townships on the urban fringe, blighted inner-city ghettoes or featureless squatter settlements" (Murray 2011, 148).

However, as the twentieth century came to an end, a progressive breach in and disintegration of a racially exclusive metropolitan area started to emerge in cities such as Johannesburg. Certain groups of people: a few liberal whites as well as blacks, started to challenge the racialized exclusivity of certain spaces within the city, constituting a profound crisis for apartheid governance (Conway 2009). Yet since the eventual abolition of apartheid in 1994, this early promise of changing the positions and identities of people/space has only been very partially delivered. Many white people have resisted the full democratization of space in a number of ways (e.g. Ballard 2005; Lemanski 2007), such that, in short, space continues to be a key resource by which privilege is constructed and maintained (Leonard 2010).

In this chapter, I draw on new ethnographic and biographical research to explore this issue further. I examine how one particular group of South African residents, white British expatriates in South Africa, draw on the spatial landscape to negotiate their identities and social relations in this changing political context. "The British" or, as they are now more commonly known in South Africa, "English-speaking whites"[1] (Lambert 2009, 601) are a group that has clearly lost much of its political power in contemporary South Africa, but by and large they continue to enjoy a privileged lifestyle economically, socially, and geographically (Conway and Leonard forthcoming). Space, in the material ways in which it is managed and lived, as well as through its cultural imaginings, is a key resource in the making and maintaining of this privilege (Hughes 2010). The ways in which this process is further marked by nationality is explored here by examining the everyday lives of British residents living in Johannesburg. Not only does

Johannesburg have a significant history of segregated white presence, but it has also maintained transnational connections with Western Europe. The ways in which British residents locate themselves within this dynamic context reveals a diversity of positions but, for all, the geographies of privilege are a continuing accomplishment, forged both locally and through transnational connections. This chapter argues that landscape undoubtedly still provides a powerful means by which whiteness sustains its privileges in the new South Africa. It also hints that other possibilities may exist (Merleau-Ponty 2002).

The Changing Context of South Africa

South Africa has a unique history of raced relations, produced through periods of colonization, racial segregation, and democratization. Between 1948 and 1994, the system of racial discrimination known as "apartheid" was established. The word comes from the Dutch word "apartness" or "separateness," by which the country was framed both politically and materially (Butler 2009). Yet even before this time, the country was far from integrated. There had been continuous skirmishing for power, since the first European migrants arrived in the mid-seventeenth century. In the period from the 1870s onwards, three groups of people emerged as particularly significant in the battles over resources and power: the African farmers known as the Xhosa and Zulu, the Dutch immigrants, known as Afrikaners or Boers, and the British imperialists. The Boers, the descendants of the early Dutch colonists from the Cape, had supplied the Dutch East India Company and had later spread north and east into African land. They had grasped seemingly "empty" stretches of land resulting from the divisions between different African peoples (Butler 2009). Meanwhile the British, who had acquired the Dutch East India Company in 1802, took control of the Cape Colony and started to take possession of the coastal regions. They did this by force and without the consent of its indigenous peoples.

The two white communities were divided. The period after 1870 was marked by a particularly dramatic disintegration of their relationships. Diamonds, and then gold, were discovered in the Transvaal region, which is now known as Johannesburg, "City of Gold." This fueled the British desire to gain control of the whole of South Africa, culminating in the Boer War of 1899 to 1902. After the "defeat" of the Afrikaners, the country was unified as a British colony through the 1910 Act of Union and became a leading place of settlement for British migrants. As a British Dominion, it shared the racial and governmental features of the British Empire; namely that whiteness and a British nationality delivered substantial social mobility, power, and privilege. Indeed, it was the racialized political machinery developed at this time which laid the economic, political, and institutional foundations of the later apartheid system (Butler 2009).

After 1910, emerging systems of racial segregation deepened the need for migrant labor in the British owned mines and farms. A flexible migrant labor system required mobility, and to this end the Natives Land Act 1913 squeezed African access to land by allocating 87 percent of land to Whites and prohibiting land purchase and non-labor-based tenure by Africans. Although there were some successful pockets of resistance, with some successfully buying land and establishing "black spots" in "white" South Africa (Sparks 1997), this Act, combined with a complex set of pass laws which prevented blacks from moving around the countryside to sell their labor, meant that many had little choice but to migrate toward cities. However, at this time, the 1923 Urban Areas Act entrenched spatial segregation practices as well as acting to control the "influxes" of the black and coloured[2] population. Through a complex system of "pass laws" the movement of Africans and coloureds in the urban areas was highly regulated, preventing their entry into designated "white" spaces.

At the same time, however, conflict within the white community intensified. Compared to the Afrikaners, many of whom were unskilled and poor, the British were prosperous, and an emerging middle class soon developed which scorned its neighbors, whilst the Afrikaners in turn still resented the outcome of the Boer War which had been unfavourable to them. In the 1930's, an Afrikaner National Party emerged which developed ideologies of racial purity and even more racial segregation. These ideas became increasingly popular amongst the white population, which associated black urbanization with fears of being "swamped" (Butler 2009). In 1948, the Afrikaner National Party (NP) won an election victory under the mandate of apartheid, a system of governance that remained in place until the first universally democratic elections of 1994.

Whilst the NP immediately introduced the Population Registration Act, which enforced the classification of people into four strict racial categories: White, Coloured, Indian/Asiatic, and Native (later Bantu or African), it wasn't until the 1960s that apartheid really reached its zenith. The 1950s were marked by a series of acts which consolidated the ways in which space was drawn upon to underpin the apartheid regime. The Group Areas Act of 1950 enforced residential segregation by race across the country, whilst the Registration of Separate Amenities Act of 1953 segregated transport, cinemas, restaurants, sporting facilities, and, later, all educational institutions. In the "European" cities such as Johannesburg, black squatter camps were destroyed and replaced by segregated satellite "townships" adjacent to the main urban conurbations. The Native Laws Amendment Act of 1952 limited permanent residency in urban areas to blacks who had lived there for fifteen years and who had worked for the same employer for ten years (Sparks 1997). Residential details like these were stamped into a pass book which black people had to carry with them at all times on pain of instant arrest. It was through such ratcheting up of the pass law system that white areas were increasingly "purified." This was not without substantial costs, however, as within a few years pass law arrests were amounting to two thousand a day (Sparks 1997).

Up until the 1960s, however, the racial segregation in South Africa was not so different from other parts of colonial Africa, or indeed the world.[3] After South Africa declared itself a Republic in 1961, apartheid entered a second phase, and a period began in which space was drawn upon still more invidiously as a fundamental resource for racism and discrimination. The new policy of "separate development," engineered system of "retribalization" under which black people were forcibly removed from "incorrect locations" to the ethnic-based developments of newly created Homelands or Bantustans.[4]

In 1970, homeland citizenship was forced upon all Africans, who had to be assigned to an ethnic group according to rules of descent. By 1989, 3.5 million black Africans, Coloureds, and Indians had been forcibly removed after being judged to be of the incorrect ethnicity for their location (Thompson 2001; Butler 2009). The primary aim of the homeland policy was to remove Black African access to any area other than their homelands, unless they were needed by white employers to work. In 1967, the Government strengthened this position by prohibiting Africans from visiting any urban area for more than 72 hours without a special permit. Under this law the number of African arrests rose still further, peaking in 1975 and 1976 at nearly 400,000 (Thompson 2001).

The system was unsustainable. In the decade between 1960 and 1970, the black population in white urban areas fell by over 200,000, but it grew in the reserves by almost a million, resulting in substantial overcrowding and impoverishment (Butler 2009). As the black population rose, so did their political power, making it increasingly difficult to maintain spatial control. This, together with the rising power of the predominantly, but not exclusively, black African National Congress (ANC), as well as the growing global antagonism to the South African regime, started the gradual erosion of the NP.

The 1970s and 1980s witnessed a series of anti-apartheid resistance efforts including the boycotting of commuter buses, strikes, and demonstrations against the school system. These incidents, which included the renowned Soweto Uprising in 1976, were met by the militarized Afrikaner regime with increasing levels of brutality. Ordinary black people, including school children, were injured or killed in the riots. These eventd provoked international condemnation and strong disapproval by Afrikaner intellectuals. With the eyes of the world upon them, the government realized that changes would have to be made.

By the mid-1980s, some segregation laws had been eliminated and black people had limited access to public facilities and transport. The government was also "turning a blind eye" (Thompson 2001, 221) to black occupation of some of the white residential areas of Johannesburg, such as Hillbrow. However, the reform process had its limits: the Land and the Group Areas Acts still excluded Africans from land ownership outside the homelands, and African communities were still being forcibly relocated. Consequently, anti-apartheid resistance was escalating. In a desperate attempt to maintain control over the black population, the government declared a national state of emergency in 1986. These attempts at control proved to be unsuccessful. The writing was on the wall: things had to change. With the presidential appointment of F. W. de Klerk in 1989, dialogue was at last opened with the ANC, culminating in the cancelation of the state of emergency, the repeal of the remaining apartheid laws, and eventually, the release of Nelson Mandela in 1990. On April 27, 1994 the country held its first universal franchise democratic elections (Sparks 1997; Thompson 2001; Butler 2009).

Since 1994, however, land reform has been slow. Although white farmers agree land ownership patterns are unequal, little has been done to change them in any systematic way. There have been some "heart-warming cases of land restored to communities from which it had, effectively been stolen" (Johnson 2009, 585–86) but in practice, this has almost invariably meant a return to subsistence agriculture. The landscape has changed little in urban areas as well: the blacks still live predominantly in the townships and squatter camps on the urban fringe, and the whites remain nestled in luxurious accommodation behind high walls and barbed wire fences. However, the rise of a black middle class has started a slow process of change in the residential and commercial spaces of Johannesburg. As I will show, multiracial environments are increasing, offering new spatial resources to their residents.

The British in South Africa

What of the white British residents in South Africa over this time? How do we understand their position during this long period of racial and spatial segregation which has so blighted South African history? It can be argued that during the period when the country was governed by the (Afrikaner) National Party, British immigrants and the wider English-speaking white community (who are largely of British and Irish descent) occupied a politically marginalized and socially ambivalent position (Conway and Leonard, forthcoming). Indeed, as the central political relationship was between Afrikaans-speaking whites and black Africans, British migrants have been described as playing a "curious role in a drama cast for two" (Sparks 1997, 46).

On their side, the British were accused by the Afrikaners of being uncommitted to the nation, as "soutpiel": having one foot in South Africa, one foot in Britain, and a penis dangling in the Atlantic. However, the declaration of a Republic in 1961, and the expulsion of South Africa from the Commonwealth because of its apartheid regime, marked the beginning of a rapprochement between the National Party government and English-speaking whites. The Afrikaners now needed all the white support they could muster. South Africa's rapid economic growth in the 1960s and 1970s coincided with the reintroduction of the assisted passage scheme for skilled white migrants and the active recruitment by the South African government of British people belonging to certain professions and having certain skills. British citizens who settled in the country did not have any significant political power, but they were rewarded significantly in terms of lifestyle and social status. Between 1946 and 1961, 115,394 British emigrants settled in the country and at the height of white immigration (1961–77), 243,000 British-born citizens settled in the country (Republic of South Africa [RSA] 1989, 101). Between the 1960s and 1975, South Africa gained between 20,000 and 35,000 immigrants a year, which accounted for no less than 46% of white population growth (RSA 1989, 85).

Of all white immigrant nationalities, British immigrants are consistently and by far the largest community, comprising between 45.6% and 30.2% of annual immigrant arrivals between 1946 and 1987 (Conway and Leonard forthcoming). Similarly, the UK was also the leading destination for emigration between these years (RSA 1989, 101). However, unpalatable political events such as the 1976 Soweto Uprising and the declaration of the national state of emergency in 1986 contributed to further net white emigration in 1977 and from 1986 onwards (RSA 1989, 98; Conway and Leonard forthcoming).

Since 1994, and the shift from an authoritarian white minority regime to a multiracial democracy, South Africa has come to be viewed more positively by the outside world more generally and British migrants in particular. Its full readmittance to international flows of trade, finance, and cultural exchange has been accompanied by significant increases in British tourism, second home ownership, and retirement migration to the country, along with continued professional and other forms of labor migration. Between 2005 and 2009, South Africa was the seventh most popular destination for British emigrating retirees and now has the eighth largest British-born community in permanent residence: 219,000 people in 2008 (Finch, Andrew, and Latorre 2010, 29, 37). However, divisions within the country remain, not only between blacks and whites, but also amongst whites. In particular, the different position of English speakers continued to be revealed after 1994, where, interestingly, "both conservative and liberal English-speaking South Africans seem wary of accepting the new dispensation and are accused by Africans of being less prepared to adapt than are Afrikaners" (Lambert 2009, 611). This differentiation within the white community occurs amidst the wider crisis in white identity after apartheid, as there is now "an acute sense of loss of the familiar, loss of certainty, loss of comfort, loss of privilege, loss of well-known roles ... a delusional home now collapsed" (Steyn 2001, 150). Although the crisis of whiteness has led to significant white emigration from South Africa, it is not necessarily accompanied by a loss of discursive confidence or insistence that South African whites have no right to live in and define the country (Conway and Leonard forthcoming). Indeed, Steyn and Foster argue that "In this new context, the central question for whiteness, as the orientation which takes its privilege as normal and appropriate, can be put simply: *how to maintain its advantages in a situation in which black people have legally and legitimately achieved political power?*" (Steyn and Foster 2008, 26, italics added). As this chapter aims to show, the use of space and the construction of place provide key answers to this question.

The most popular places of British settlement remain as they have been since the nineteenth century: Johannesburg, Cape Town and the Western Cape, and Durban and Pietermaritzburg in Kwazulu-Natal. Yet Johannesburg is a very different sort of place from Cape Town or Durban. It lacks the dramatic beauty of Cape Town or the cosy Britishness of Kwazulu-Natal, which is often called "the last outpost of the British Empire" (Lambert 2010, 150), but it is certainly not constructed by British residents as in any way a poor relation. On the contrary, it too is seen to offer very specific and even attractive resources for identity construction and, in the process, race making.

Two competing discourses currently dominate the representation of Johannesburg's space (Lefebvre 1991). The first of these is national and global: this is often how the city of Johannesburg and often South Africa as a nation (and sometimes the whole nation) tend to be represented in much of the (Western) world. This is asa an infamous "arena for violence, crime and shocking inequality" (Holland and Roberts 2002, 1); summed up through the discourse of "Jo'burg." Jo'burg is constructed as a deeply segregated city, where everyday lives are organized into racially distinct spaces and places, and white and black residents in the main live and work in very different representations of space. As such, Jo'burg is a city of deep contrasts: downtown, central Johannesburg was deserted in the 1980s by industry, business and finance, entertainment and leisure, and is now physically deteriorating and tarnished by white people as a tense, danger- ous, and litter-ridden place of crime, drugs, violence, homelessness, and fear (Murray 2011). However it is, simultaneously, a vibrant and cosmo- politan African space (Simone 2004; Tomlinson, Beauregard, Bremner, & Mangcu, 2003).

To the south, southeast, and southwest lie the townships and informal settlements, often described as "squatter camps" stretching out toward Soweto, where the bulk of black residents were forced to live under apart- heid and still remain to this day. Many of these areas lack social amenities and in certain cases even the most rudimentary of services (Murray 2011). To the north, white South Africans, British and Afrikaners intermingle in the white dominated and luxurious suburbs. The standard of living here is high, with large houses in extensive grounds, often in residential gated communities or (due to intense security) quiet, tree-lined streets.

The contrast between the suburbs and the townships is vast, and this fuels the dominant subdiscourse which frames the landscapes of privilege: "safety and security." This is a key white fear into which British migrants are quickly socialized, such that the norm is that houses are surrounded by heavy duty fortification: high concrete walls topped by curling barbed wire, with security cameras and electric gates. Everyone has a big dog, and (black) security guards oversee comings and goings. Sadly, the large and beautiful parks with which these suburbs were historically landscaped are often completely deserted.

In contrast to the Jo'burg discourse, however, a new and competing dis- course is emerging. This is Jozi, the "cool cousin" of Cape Town, which has grown up since 1994. Jozi is a city of "urban vibe", an "infused mixture of Africa and the west" with a "cultural and cosmopolitan buzz, a youthful energy and edge" (Holland and Roberts 2002, 4). As such it draws new arrivals from across the continent and beyond; a far cry from the Johan- nesburg of old, with its history as an exploitative white mining city or even the more recent crime-ridden Jo'burg. For some, as the seat of the attack against apartheid, chiefly by black residents, but also by some whites, Jozi is now seen by some to be making a real attempt to be a city representa- tive of the "Rainbow Nation." Its representations of space reveal how town planners and property developers are attempting at one level to construct a modern multicultural and egalitarian city through vast new shopping malls, cosmopolitan entertainment and eating areas, all of which attempt to give a substantial nod to black African inclusion. Chief cultural attrac- tions such as the Apartheid Museum, the Hector Peiterson Museum, and

Mandela House in Soweto, and Soccer City in Nasrec (between Soweto and Johannesburg) forward Jozi's struggle history in movingly uncompromising ways.

Yet in spite of the emergence of this more optimistic discourse, Johannesburg remains substantially a racially excluding and divided city, just as it was in the apartheid era. Clearly this claim is nothing new, and as such the purpose of looking at this nearly twenty years after the fall of apartheid must be to explore critically whether there has been any change in the context by which space is conceptualized and drawn upon in the making of privilege. This paper begins answering this question by focusing on the everyday lives of Johannesburg residents.

Conceptualizing Place

> The identity of a place is formed out of social interrelations, and a proportion of those interrelations—larger or smaller, depending on the time and on the place—will stretch beyond that "place" itself. (Massey 1994, 115)

Contemporary geographical understandings of place stress how the grounded locales of everyday life are continuously produced by a range of social, economic, and cultural processes which range from the very local to the global (Lefebvre 1991; Massey 1994; Cresswell 2004). Identities of places are far from fixed, but are continuously constructed by social interactions and relations which intersect at that particular location. I have argued elsewhere that places are where encounters happen, and through these encounters, important connections are made between the identity of place and constructions of personal subjectivities (Leonard 2010). As we are "always multiple and contradictory subjects, inhabitants of a diversity of communities ... constructed by a variety of discourses, and precariously and temporarily sutured at the intersection of those positions" (Mouffe 1988, 44), we bring multiplicity to places and with this help in turn to produce the multiplicity of place (Massey 1994). These processes cannot be understood therefore by considering the local context in isolation. As Massey (1994) argues, the diversity of people's biographies and transnational connections mean that the global world is always constituted in and through the local, and as such a local place is made distinctive by its particular set of interrelationships with the global.

This conceptualization of space as active and alive has its legacy in Lefebvre's (1991) influential geography, which views space as simultaneously socially producing and socially produced. Lefebvre constructs space as mutually created by and creating social actors, through both discourse and the senses, and as necessarily involving issues of identity, politics, and power (Merrifield 2000). These notions are brought together by Lefebvre into an analytical framework which I suggest can offer a particularly useful point of access to exploring the relationships between space, race, and (privileged) migration.

Migration involves multiple processes: at one end is the packing up of homes and lives and the leaving of the familiar. Then, after traveling to a new country and landscape, there is, at the other end, the choosing of a place to live and the establishing of a new home and life. In most situations this involves, at the very least, a multiplicity of emotional, sensory, social, and political processes. In the case of British migrants to South Africa, with its diverse and complex history of race/national relations, this has also always involved decision making on how to position oneself within these relations. Lefebvre's attempt to capture the complexity of space, and its connections with everyday life, offers a conceptual framework by which to understand the multiple processes involved here.

Lefebvre conceptualizes space through three key aspects. The first of these, spatial practice, makes clear links with Merleau-Ponty (1962) and Bourdieu (1984) by recognizing that space is a phenomenological experience, taken for granted through the habits or practical knowhow of the body. This describes how we develop everyday routines through and in space, doing so in regular, habitual, and even prereflective ways. The paths and journeys we make, whether short or long, whether walking, jogging, cycling, or driving, require a combination of sensory and spatialized activities which not only constitute the phenomenological ground of "doing everyday life" but are also useful in revealing the embodied ways in which this is accomplished, both individually and collectively, within specific social structures and relations (Hockey and Allen-Collinson 2009).

The conceptualization of the second aspect, representations of space, is particularly useful in capturing the planned nature of space, and how this may be strategically redesigned in the management of cultural change. Since 1994, much of urban South Africa has been subject to a new generation of property developers, town planning professionals, and land speculators who, as I have discussed above, have set their sights on constructing world-class cities and residential developments (Murray 2011). The energy marshaled by these professionals in redesigning the material conditions of work, consumption, leisure, and home bear witness to the fact that space is viewed as an integral means by which to represent relations and practices not only materially, but also socially, politically, culturally, and psychologically. However, Lefebvre's triadic framework challenges us to develop a more heterogeneous or even heterotopian perspective; one that complicates the relations of power between planners, developers, and citizens, and represents space as simultaneously controlling and enabling (Foucault 1980).

What people do with and in space is not always what was intended. Pertinent here, is the third aspect, the notion of representational space, which enables the conceptualization of space as something imagined and discursively constructed by everyone through symbols and language. It is thus not only planners and architects who have the power to interpret space; we all do, whether this be through decorating our homes, managing our plots of land (or "stands" as these are called in South Africa), or selecting our neighbors. Further, this aspect makes important connections with recent geographical work which explores the relationships between space, place, and emotion (Sibley 1995; Davidson, Bondi, and Smith 2005; Smith, Cameron, and Bondi 2009). This perspective highlights how different environments can evoke complex emotions, and that attending to such feelings as fear, anxiety, longing, anger, envy, and hatred may be essential if we are to understand fully how space is integral to processes of racialized inclusion and exclusion.

White Spaces

> We must be consistently aware of how space can be made to hide consequences from us, how relations of power and discipline are inscribed into the apparently innocent spatiality of social life. (Soja 1989, 6)

Taking a multiple analytic approach, which incorporates embodied and emotional responses as well as social and political action and imagination, is thus particularly important in contexts where space is highly racially segregated and emotionally charged, such as South Africa. Space and place are integral to the production and performance of white privilege here, and the Lefebvrian framework helps to reveal how this is concatenated through embodied activity, the management of space as well as language and symbols. Part of learning to be white in South Africa is to learn the specific places of whites, where these are and what these look like, as well as how to perform within these in ways that produce and maintain power, distance, and authority over other people in other places (Frankenberg 1993; Kothari 2006).

The social category of whiteness, as well as the individual, inscribes race further by making material and imagined connections between spaces and places, such that, for example, Britain becomes an important symbol to British expatriates. For example, to represent their transnational connections, I have often seen living rooms belonging to British families in

South Africa decorated in "the English style": paintings of English land-scapes, chintz-covered sofas, Victorian antiques, with English magazines on the footstool. In this way whiteness and nationality (as well as class) are constituted materially and imaginatively in the ways particular spaces and places, and the things within them, are conceived. In addition, through the performance of daily routines and habits, these places and spaces are further constructed as white: cups of tea are made, dogs are cuddled, and British soap operas are watched. As Tuan describes, "what begins as an undifferentiated space becomes place as we get to know it better and endow it with value" (1977, 6). The inscription of meaning in places is therefore intertwined with the embodied performances which take place there, the people who are making these, as well as the connections these people make with other spaces, both local and global.

Place and space do not therefore merely provide a backdrop for the negotiation of raced and national identities, but are central resources in the construction of these (Halford and Leonard 2006). Further, and perhaps more critically, space is also implicated in the construction and structuring of our relations with others, and, as Gregory and Urry put it: "Spatial structure is now seen not merely as an arena in which social life unfolds, but rather as a medium through which social relations are pro-duced and reproduced" (1985, 3). Space is thus central to the production, organization, and distribution of identity, race, and also power (Foucault 1980; Shome 2003).

It was to explore the relationships between identity, race, and place that research was conducted in South Africa between 2009 and 2011.[5] The research aimed to look at the lives and experiences of a broad variety of British residents and to investigate the extent and manner to which they were accommodating themselves to the changing political and social regime. The research was primarily based in Johannesburg, Cape Town, and Pietermaritzburg near Durban, three key sites of British dwelling, and a multimethod, ethnographic, and biographical approach was taken. This included visual methods and unstructured interviews, but also, cru-cially, mobile methods. As a key aim was to explore the spatial, attach-ment to place, and how people draw on space and place in the production of their identities, everyday practices, and senses of social networks, the "mobile interview" was chosen in addition to more conventional, static, typically room-based interviews conducted in my hotel as well as people's homes and workplaces (Clark and Emmel 2010). I thus accompanied par-ticipants as they went about their daily lives, and joined them on drives around the city, walks through gated communities, horseback rides, and even safaris through privately owned game parks (Conway and Leonard forthcoming).[6]

In the remaining sections of this chapter, I draw on the Lefebvrian analysis discussed above to return to explore the two competing discourses that I identified as framing contemporary Johannesburg. These discourses by no means encapsulated the total diversity of lifestyles amongst my research participants, but it was clear that they were powerful in framing experience and understandings, and as such were actively drawn and used in different ways by participants to situate themselves in relation to white privilege in the changing political context.

Jo'burg

Many of my participants represented Johannesburg as an inescapably divided city, but this view was then drawn upon in diverse ways. Stephen, a wealthy professional in his fifties, drew on difference—race, class, and nationality—as a desirable resource to produce and maintain his extremely privileged lifestyle. Having lived in the city for thirty years, coming out in the early 1980s via the assisted passage route, he describes himself as "not a great Johannesburg fan." However, Stephen was very keen to pick me up from my hotel and spend several hours driving me in his large and luxurious car around the greater Johannesburg area in order to give me his guided tour. As we drove, it was clear that what animated Stephen were indeed the landscapes of privilege. His language was shot through with social structure, so as I was invited to look at this house or that township, I was able to see the representations of Johannesburg's space, as well as to gain an insight into Stephen's own representational space and spatial practices. Leaving Sandton behind, we drove over The Ridge toward

> the old town, which is where we're going; when the mine bosses, you call them Randlords, chose to build a house they picked the best location, and at that time it was outside of the city. So there's some marvellous houses that I can point out as we travel along here.

Passing the mine dumps which punctuate Johannesburg's landscape as a living reminder of its gold mining past, our ultimate destination was The Rand Club in the old central district. Once the thriving haven of Johannesburg's business and finance community, this is now for many whites a completely "no-go" area. As such, the Club is on its last legs, struggling for membership. However, Stephen still comes here often, loving its colonial past, what this represented, and what this can still deliver:

The Rand Club is very interesting, it was started in about 1890 by Cecil Rhodes. And he began the club to my knowledge really as a bit of one upmanship. The club was intended to appeal to people like me. White, male, Anglo Saxons. The people that we don't want would effectively be blacks, Jews, women. Anybody nonwhite. You'll be pleased to know that the club voted to admit women members only just before I arrived! And I can now use my reciprocal membership to get into a club that wouldn't have me as a member in the UK. That's the joy of colonialism, a bit of class hopping!

Stephen tells me that he has indeed class hopped—he has made a great deal of money by setting up his own business in Johannesburg, and is very pleased he came to South Africa because of this:

This to me is one of the things that you can do in a place like this that you cannot do in a place like London. So occasionally I ask why am I still here, I know the answer, it's because my kids go to fantastic schools and it's because I'm now fifty something, and it'd be very difficult to adjust back to working in London.

However, in spite of this, and the fact that he has a white South African wife and his children have been born and brought up here, nationality remains very important to him as a marker of his difference. He remains resolutely British:

I am British, and I will always be British. And the reason for that is that people like to identify you, to each part of the community, the racial group, the economic group. And so you're pigeon holed without even being asked. And I'm pigeon holed into British South African, and there's an element of me in there obviously I don't want to let go. I quite like being seen as the English fellow. I think when I was doing my business that was an asset. Because I like to think I'm very straight. So when you get an insurance deal it's done right and if somebody expects to get their finger in the pie, well, sorry, that isn't going to work here. So I sort of styled myself and quite enjoyed the concept of the Rand Club. I'm a member of the Rolls Royce and Bentley club. I have ten cars, I have three Bentleys, so I can choose which one I want to use. You can't do that in England. So what's happened here is that for me I've enjoyed moving into a *space that is clearly the space that I fit into.* (emphasis added).

It is clear that this is very much a "white space" and Stephen is unabashed at the continued segregated nature of his life:

> I can't relate to these people. So, the gardener is from Zimbabwe, the maid is from Lesotho. Lovely people, but they're in completely different space to where I'm at. So I'm in the privileged white, you know, monied [space], my kids go to the best schools.

Stephen's wealth clearly enables him to occupy only the spaces of privilege. He connects these with his car journeys around the city, sweeping through, observing the landscape and lives of his fellow citizens but remaining spatially distanced from them, both materially and imaginatively. However, for other, less well-remunerated British, Johannesburg's divisions require less comfortable negotiation. Neil, a computer programmer in his late twenties, has been in the city for six years. Married to an Afrikaner woman, they have just had their first child, and this, and the fact that they position themselves within the Jo'burg subdiscourse of crime and security, is prompting them to think about returning to the UK.

They live in a smallish flat in a middle-income white neighborhood, on the corners of which cluster groups of black men waiting for offers of work or chances to sell things through car windows. Driving past them on a daily basis makes Neil nervous: his representational space is full of danger and crime, and as such he positions himself as ever on the brink of victimhood. This defines his spatial practice: he has never been to Soweto, for example, and his pathways around the city are confined to car journeys between his house, his workplace, the shop, and a British style pub where we meet for lunch. As he explains: "normally the most you would walk is from your car to the shop, or car to work, or car to the garage. That's all you do. Nothing else, don't do walking—I can't even think of a place you would walk without worrying about it."

At home, Neil enjoys the "luxuries you have behind the barbed wire fence—swimming pool, greenery, somewhere to park my truck…" and he is willing to defend these privileges:

> No-one's going to get in my house. I mean I have weapons as well and I'll use them if anyone does get in the house, I mean not a gun and stuff but I've got an axe and I've got a knife, and they're strategically placed. Because all the horror stories that I hear, it's unbelievable.

Yet, whilst his daily life is largely produced in some comfort behind these defenses, he resents what this does to the representation of space as well as his own representational space:

> There's no freedom, where do the children play? Well she can go round the corner there, but it's all within security fences, it's all

electrified you know. Then you'll worry about them, you know. We've got a sliding door to the back garden and there's a gate that anyone can get through and I just keep saying "keep the door shut!" and my wife's like "yeah but it's not dangerous," and I say "it just takes once. It just takes once, that's all, then it's very, very unpleasant...."

As we talked, it was clear that Neil is not happy with the confined nature of his life in South Africa. He recognizes his privileges, but the ways in which these are achieved sit uneasily with him. He worries that he is being changed personally by the raced representations of space in the city, and the ways these play out in spatial practice at a range of scales. This not only affects his relationship with the geography of the city, but also he can see how it affects the embodied, microspatial interactions of everyday life:

It turns you into a racial thing ... for example: service. This is another reason I want to go to the UK, we're so spoilt in this country, you know, just snap your fingers and you've got a beer on the table, and I see the worse side of it as well. I've seen a bloke come in, he'll sit down and he won't say his please, thank you and he'll complain that his glass is slightly warm and then "can you take my beer back" and "don't you bother us." I mean that's not me, that's not my lifestyle.

Albeit in contrasting ways, Stephen and Neil both demonstrate in their constant references to the UK how the grounded locales of everyday life are continuously produced by a range of social, economic, cultural, and embodied processes that draw on both the local and the global (Lefebvre 1994; Massey 1994; Cresswell 2004). Thus as they both position themselves within the Jo'burg discourse, this plays out differently for each of them. Stephen's sense of belonging to/longing for both South Africa and the UK is produced through stereotypical constructions of what it means to be white/male/middle-class/British. He has no desire to return to Britain, however, enjoying its imaginative reach but fearing a substantial material impact on the privileged lifestyle he so enjoys in South Africa. But of course he can if, at any time, he finds he wants to; and this may explain why, in spite of the political changes he has witnessed in the past thirty years, he remains "soutpiel" and largely untouched by these, and untroubled by the social costs involved in the production of his everyday life.

In contrast, Neil's occupation of spatial privilege is more complex. Whilst he feels trapped and confined, and lives in fear for himself and his family, he is troubled by the continued racial divisions which mark life in the city and his engagement with it. At the same time he is rendered immobile by his fears, and these prevent him from taking up alternative positions within South Africa. For Neil, escaping back to what he sees are the privileges of the UK is the only answer; and for him these are primarily a life which lacks the constant fear of crime and, consequently for Neil, a less anxious relationship with the black Other.

Jozi

For other participants, however, Johannesburg represents the "real South Africa," offering new and exciting opportunities for social relationships and the performance of everyday lives. Although these too are seen as "privileges," these advantages are not so much understood in material terms as in cultural ones. *Jozi* is the name given by some to represent Johannesburg as a city of hope, and some British prefer to position themselves by this metaphor. To illustrate, Lauren and Matt are a young couple in their thirties who have lived in the city for six years, having come from Britain so that Matt could take up a position as a Christian minister. In fact, Matt had been offered two positions—one in Cape Town and one in Johannesburg. Lauren explained how they made their choice:

Lauren: They're very different, yes. So, at one level, everything in me wanted to go to Cape Town, because it's like, "I don't really want to emigrate, I don't really want to go to South Africa (laughter)."

P: Oh, you had mixed feelings?

L: Yeah, I had very mixed feelings because I'm quite English really (laughter). Cape Town just feels like, "I could do that." But at the same time I also felt it was almost too English. If you're actually going to make a difference, really engage in South Africa, Jo'burg is—it feels much more—so I guess there was that tension of—Cape Town's nicer, but Jo'burg feels more, this is where South Africa is really changing. And in the same way in terms of the demographics of the college where my husband teaches, it's 75% black and 25% white. Whereas the college in Cape Town would be much more the other way round. So, that ability to be transformed can happen much quicker up in Jo'burg whereas I think Cape Town is much more pedestrian in its change.

For Lauren and Matt, Johannesburg's attraction was its racial dynamic, and the ways in which they felt they would be able to engage with this. They live close to a religious college, where Matt trains black ministers as well as preaching in the church. The college is based in the south west of the city which, as Lauren explains is: "a nice area but it's not normal suburbs."

By this she means several things. First, in terms of the representations of space, it is a racially mixed community, unusual in Johannesburg:

> Down the road is Sophiatown which was the classic place in the '50s where all the black people were thrown out of the township. Sophiatown is definitely multicultural whereas Auckland Park would still be more white than that. But it still feels very mixed.

Second, in terms of spatial practice, Lauren and Matt walk and cycle around the suburb. As I have shown above, this is also unusual in any space other than inside a whites-only gated community. Yet Lauren pushes their young baby in her stroller to the shops or to see friends and Matt cycles to the college. Third, in terms of representational space, it feels safer than Lauren had expected: "the security didn't feel as anxious as I thought it would and part of that's where we live it's not such a big issue—you could walk round the area and get out and exercise."

Seeing Johannesburg as a contemporary and multicultural space is important to the couple. They were keen to avoid the cosy easiness of Cape Town which just felt:

> [A]lmost too English. If you're actually going to make a difference, really engage in South Africa! Cape Town is nicer but Jo'burg feels more real—this is where South Africa is really changing. Our word for it is intense—Cape Town is like second gear—whereas in Jo'burg you're in fourth gear!

In contrast, Lauren and Matt are excited by the possibilities which Jozi offers:

> In Jo'burg the walls are high but the thresholds are low, whereas in Cape Town, the walls are lower but the thresholds are higher. Jo'burg's this place where everybody's looking for a network, everybody's looking to know people and there's less of an old boy's network and that sort of thing going on. There's just this high energy to everybody that's willing to engage and connect ... that's the fun thing about it—the first year we were here, there's just an advert in the paper saying it's Helen Suzman's memorial service, the public are invited. So we go along and Nelson Mandela's wife's there and the old president's there, the great and the good are there. We wouldn't be able to go to this in the UK—but here there's a sense that everybody's invited to join in the history—you're very close to history being made here because it's in the making. When Jacob Zuma won the election, our church was meeting in a big shopping mall

in Soweto and so Zuma was doing a rally going along to the city thanking people for voting for him. So he comes into the shopping mall, he goes up the escalator so we know he's going to come down at some point, so my husband stands at the bottom of the escalator, sticks his hand out, and shakes hands with the president and we'd never—no, actually, I did meet John Major when I was very little (laughter) but there's that whole—you can taste it in your—that edge of meeting people. Everybody's making an effort and moving forwards—it's an opportunity—everyone says the opportunity is here to be grabbed and you're quite close to the people who are trying to grab the opportunities.

Lauren and Matt's production of space in Johannesburg is quite different to Stephen's and Neil's. For them Jozi is a space of quite differently imagined opportunities, social and cultural rather than material. Their landscapes of privilege are those that enable them to mix freely in a black community and make new friends. Lauren says: "I'm grateful that a lot of our friends are different to us and I feel really enriched by that." Having actively chosen the neighborhoods and social circles which most white people in South Africa avoid, Lauren and Matt thus position themselves as "other" to what are perceived as normative white attitudes and behavior. However, whilst they are keen to put a moral distance between themselves and the white majority, Lauren's narratives reveal that the couple is still enmeshed in a colonial sense of entitlement to what Johannesburg has to offer (Reay et al. 2007, 1043).

Being British in South Africa

In this chapter I have drawn on a spatial analysis to explore the everyday lives of a small selection of the British community in Johannesburg. I argue that the different ways in which Stephen, Neil, and Lauren draw on space in the production of their identities and everyday lives, and their talk to me about these, are highly revealing: showing both how they make themselves and their social relationships. The minutiae of their spatial practices, and their language to describe these, offer a point of access to understanding how this very small group of people is positioning themselves in the post-1994 regime, as well as how privilege itself may be changing. The complexity and multiplicity of their narratives reflect that there is by no means a unilinear response within the British community to the social and political changes: some still cling to the wreckage of separated existences, others are consumed by fear of the Other, while still others look forward to the opening up of opportunities which new metaphors of Johannesburg attempt to encapsulate in built and symbolic form.

In its various interpretations, however, it is clear that for the British participants featured in this chapter race is still central to their South African existence. It is deeply embedded in representations of space, in spatial practice, and in representations of space. The point at issue here is that: "Space is not the setting in which things are arranged, but the means whereby the position of things becomes possible" (Merleau-Ponty 2002, 284). Whilst for some Johannesburg space offers the possibility to arrange differently raced people in very different spaces, and, in the process, to use geography to produce and maintain the privileges whiteness has always enjoyed in South Africa, others, like Lauren, articulate a changing relationship to and imagination of space.

Clearly this is a complex amalgam: on the one hand, space offers Lauren an important resource for the construction of the liberal identity she desires, and in her ability to negotiate this to her own ends, it can be argued that, albeit in a different form, her position is still undoubtedly one of privilege. On the other hand, however, it must be acknowledged that Lauren recognizes this. And, in the making of such identities, there is a hint that the position of things may also be changing, and perhaps in positive ways. Whilst the Jozi discourse can be critiqued for offering no more than a superficial nod to multiculturalism, it is a small step toward imagining a more twenty-first century sense of citizenship in which British and Afrikaner, black and white South Africans practice a cospatial existence. It is in the recognition that it is this very cospatiality itself which is now the privilege for its white peoples that the South African landscape is so revealing.

Acknowledgments

The project "The British in South Africa: Continuity or Change?" was funded by The British Academy and my Coinvestigator is Daniel Conway, University of Loughborough, UK. I am very grateful to Daniel for all our inspiring discussions, and to France Winndance Twine and Bradley Gardener for their helpful and insightful advice and support.

Notes

1. I will call this group British in this paper to emphasize that the research includes both long- and short-term expatriates.
2. South Africa developed a rigid set of racial classifications. People who did not fit into a precisely definable ethnic group were lumped together into a hold-all category, "coloured."

According to the Population Registration Act 1950 this included people from the Cape, Malays, Griqua, Chinese, Indian, Other Asiatic, and Other Coloured (Sparks 1997, 85).

3. In the United States, for example, this period was also marked by substantial racial and spatial segregation. In the Jim Crow era (1877–1960s), a series of laws and customs were introduced in the Southern states of the former Confederacy designed to segregate public facilities such as schools, public places (e.g., toilets), transport, restaurants, and drinking fountains, albeit with a supposed "separate but equal" ideology. This legalized racial discrimination took place in the South, but in the North segregatory practices were more covertly institutionalized through, for example, job and housing discrimination (Hoelscher 2003).

4. In the United States, reservations were also introduced for American Indians from the 1860s onwards, after tensions over land possession between white settlers and Native Americans. These still exist to this day, and some reservations have different laws from the surrounding areas. Not all tribes have reservations, and some tribes were forcibly relocated to areas to which they had no connection (Castle and Bee 1992).

5. This research was conducted with Daniel Conway and was funded by the British Academy.

6. More than twenty interviews were conducted in the Johannesburg area. These included a mixture of long-term residents, who had lived in the country since the 1960s and 1970s as beneficiaries of assisted passages, as well as others who had arrived since 1994, and some who had only been in residence for a year or so. Interviewees were a mixture of self-selected people who had responded to newspaper articles about the research as well as participants identified through personal contacts and the snowball method. As the concept of space was of particular interest, variety was sought in the places in which people lived and worked, as well as their connections with the United Kingdom.

References

Ballard, R. 2005. "When in Rome: Claiming the Right to Define Neighbourhood Character in South Africa's Suburbs." *Transformation* 57: 64–87.

Bourdieu, Pierre. 1984. *Distinction*. London: Routledge, Kegan & Paul.

Butler, Anthony. 2009. *Contemporary South Africa* (2nd ed.) Basingstoke, UK: Palgrave Macmillan.

Castle, George, and Robert Bee, eds. 1992. *State and Reservation: New Perspectives on Federal Indian Policy*. Tucson: University of Arizona Press.

Clark, A., & N. Emmel. 2010. "Using Walking Interviews." *Realities* 13: 1–6.

Conway, Daniel. 2009. "Queering Apartheid: The National Party's 1987 'Gay Rights' Election Campaign in Hillbrow." *Journal of Southern African Studies* 35 (4): 849–63.

———, and Pauline Leonard. (Forthcoming). *Migration, Space and Transnational Identities: The British in South Africa*. Basingstoke, UK: Palgrave.

Creswell, Tim. 2004. *Place: A Short Introduction*. Oxford, UK: Blackwell.

Davidson Joyce, Liz Bondi, and Mick Smith. 2005. *Emotional Geographies*. Aldershot, UK: Ashgate.

Finch, Tim, Holly Andrew, and Maria Latorre. 2010. *Global Brit: Making the Most of the British Diaspora*. London: IPPR.

Foucault, Michel. 1980. *Power/Knowledge*. Brighton, UK: Harvester Press.

Frankenberg, Ruth. 1993. *White Women, Race Matters: The Social Construction of Whiteness*. London: Routledge.

Gregory, Derek, and John Urry. 1985. *Social Relations and Spatial Structures*. New York: St. Martin's Press.

Halford Susan, and Pauline Leonard. 2006. *Negotiating Gendered Identities at Work: Place, Space and Time*. Basingstoke, UK: Palgrave.

Hockey, John, and Jacqui Allen-Collinson. 2009. "The Sensorium at Work: The Sensory Phenomenology of the Working Body." *The Sociological Review* 2: 217–39.

Hoelscher, Steven. 2003. "Making Place, Making Race: Performances of Whiteness in the Jim Crow South." *Annals of the Association of American Geographers* 93(3): 657–86.

Holland, Heidi, and Adam Roberts, eds. 2002. *From Jo'burg to Jozi: Stories about Africa's Infamous City Johannesburg.* Johannesburg, South Africa: Penguin.

Hughes, David. 2010. *Whiteness in Zimbabwe: Race, Landscape and the Problem of Belonging.* New York: Palgrave.

Johnson, R. W. (2009). *South Africa's Brave New World: The Beloved Country Since the End of Apartheid.* London: Penguin.

Kothari, Uma. 2006. "Spatial Practices and Imaginaries: Experiences of Colonial Officers and Development Professionals." *Singapore Journal of Tropical Geography* 27: 235–53.

Kriel, Kallie. 2004. "The Revival of Racial Classification in Post-Apartheid South Africa." *Business Day* August 10, 2.

Lambert, John. 2009. "An Unknown People: Reconstructing British South African Identity." *Journal of Imperial and Commonwealth History* 37 (4): 599–617.

———. 2010 "The Last Outpost": The Natalians, South Africa, and the British Empire." In *Settlers and Expatriates*, edited by R. Bickers, 167–182. Oxford, UK: Oxford University Press.

Lefebvre, Henri. 1991. *The Production of Space.* Oxford, UK: Blackwell.

Lemanski, Charlotte. 2007. "Global Cities in the South: Deepening Social and Spatial Polarisation in Cape Town." *Cities* 24 (6): 448–61.

Leonard, Pauline. 2010. *Expatriate Identities in Postcolonial Organizations.* Farnham, UK: Ashgate.

Massey, Doreen. 1994. "Double Articulation: A Place in the World." In *Displacements: Cultural Identities in Question*, edited by Angelika Bammer, 110–122. Bloomington: Indiana University Press.

Merleau-Ponty, Maurice. 1962. *Phenomenology of Perception.* London: Routledge and Kegan Paul.

Merrifield, A. 2000. "Henri Lefebvre: A Socialist in Space." In *Thinking Space*, edited by Mike Crang and Nigel Thrift, 167–182. London: Routledge.

Mouffe, Chantal. 1988. "Radical Democracy: Modern or Post Modern?" In *Universal Abandon? The Politics of Postmodernism*, edited by A. Ross. Minneapolis, MN: University of Minneapolis Press.

Murray, Martin. 2011. *City of Extremes: The Spatial Politics of Johannesburg.* Durham, NC: Duke University Press.

Reay, Diane, Sumi Hollingworth, Katya Williams, Gill Crozier, Fiona Jameson, David James, and Phoebe Bedell. 2007. "'A Darker Shade of Pale?' Whiteness, the Middle Classes and Multi-Ethnic Inner City Schooling." *Sociology*, 41(6): 1041–60.

Republic of South Africa Bureau for Information (RSA). 1989. *South Africa 1988–89: Official Yearbook.* Pretoria: Government Printer.

Shome, Raka. 2003. "Space Matters: The Power and Practice of Space." *Communication Theory* 13 (1): 39–56.

Sibley, David. 1995. *Geographies of Exclusion.* New York: Routledge.

Simone, Abdoumaliq. 2004. People as Infrastructure: Intersecting Fragments in Johannesburg. *Public Culture* 16 (3): 407–429.

Smith, Mick, Joyce Davidson, Laura Cameron, and Liz Bondi. 2009. *Emotion, Place and Culture.* Farnham, UK: Ashgate.

Soja, Edward. 1989. *Post-Modern Geographies: The Reassertion of Space in Critical Social Theory.* London: Verso.

Sparks, Allister. 1997. *The Mind of South Africa: The Story of the Rise and Fall of Apartheid.* London: Arrow Books.

Steyn, Melissa. 2001. *Whiteness Just Isn't What it Used to Be: White Identity in a Changing South Africa.* Albany, NY: SUNY Press.

———, and Don Foster. 2008. "Repertoires for Talking White: Resistant Whiteness in Post-Apartheid South Africa." *Ethnic and Racial Studies* 31(1): 25–51.

Thompson, Leonard. 2001. *A History of South Africa.* Jeppestown, South Africa: Jonathan Ball.

Tomlinson, R., R. Beauregard, L. Bremner, and X. Mangcu. (Eds.). 2003. *Emerging Johannesburg: Perspectives on the postapartheid city.* New York Routledge.

Tuan, Yi-fu. 1977. *Space and Place: The Perspectives of Experience.* Minneapolis, MN: University of Minnesota Press.

CHAPTER 5

The Visa Whiteness Machine
Transnational Motility in Post-Apartheid South Africa

MAX J. ANDRUCKI

Introduction

In the autumn of 2006, the South African Institute of Race Relations (SAIRR) reported that the white population of South Africa had shrunk by over 16 percent between 1995 and 2005; that is, in the post-apartheid era (SAIRR 2006). More recent data indicate that roughly half of all South Africans living overseas are in the UK, and that those living in the UK have the most interest in and are the most likely to return to South Africa. Keeping this mass migration in mind (though by no means one-directional), in this article I bring into conversations current debates within literatures on geographies of race and geographies of transnational mobility using the case of white South African migration. This article examines mobilities—the mobile practices of the white, English-speaking South Africans from KwaZulu-Natal. Beginning with a critique of approaches to the study of race that privilege discourse and a brief review of materialist approaches to understanding whiteness, I move on to discuss the visa regimes that facilitate access of white South Africans to the UK and Europe, and then I draw on interview data to argue that whiteness can be understood as a material racial formation through its contingent coconstitution, at a variety of scales, with mobilities both past and present, or what I call the "visa whiteness machine."

More than Representation: Race, Mobility, and the Visa Whiteness Machine

Within social science and the humanities, whiteness has been portrayed as primarily a socially constructed, discursively mediated identity (Bonnett 2000; Dwyer and Jones 2000; Hoelscher 2003; Jackson 1998; Kobayashi and Peake 1994; Pred 1997; Vanderbeck 2006, 2008). It is argued that race in general, and whiteness in particular do not have an ontology, but rather an epistemology, or a way of knowing and interacting with the world. It is not a material property of bodies with objective existence in the world but a means by which bodies are represented and understood, and variously valued and devalued. Whiteness is entwined with particular power relations at a variety of scales, and depends on political authority and spatial separation in order to maintain itself as hegemonic and not reveal itself as relationally constituted through the abjection of blackness. In post-apartheid South Africa, whiteness, shorn of its politically enforced authority, is seen to be under threat and thus in need of defense and shoring up. Thus, scholars of whiteness in post-apartheid South African society (Ballard 2004a, 2004b; Steyn 2005; Steyn and Foster 2007) have primarily focused on discursive techniques such as "white talk" to argue that "the dominant white representations of contemporary South Africa attempt to 'fix' groups relative to each other, reproducing and extending the power structures of whiteness into post-apartheid South Africa society" (Steyn and Foster 2007, 27).

I would like to suggest that these ways of thinking about whiteness are unsatisfactory. If "whiteness" is used to refer to an epistemology of power, how does it make sense for both Ballard and Steyn, among others, to refer to whites that are progressive, cosmopolitan, antiracist, and comfortable with diversity and democracy in the post-apartheid period as "whites" at all? Through the persistence of this unacknowledged slippage, I would like to add to arguments that whiteness can be understood as more than an epistemology. I would therefore like to shift the focus somewhat from thinking about whiteness as only or primarily a mode of representation, a way of seeing, or an epistemology, in order to open up space for thinking more specifically about whiteness as an embodied and material accomplishment. Arun Saldanha (2006, 2007; see also Slocum 2008) has attempted the ambitious project of moving away from a social scientific obsession with the discursive construction of race to a project of reontologizing race as allowing for the potential of the body to create effects, for materiality to, in a sense, speak for itself. As Saldanha puts it, he sees "race as a heterogeneous process of differentiation involving the materiality of bodies and spaces" (2007, 9). He goes on: "race is a shifting amalgamation of human bodies and their appearance, genetic material, artefacts, landscapes, music, language, money, and states of mind" (2007, 9).

I want to follow Saldanha in asserting that race exists and is closely related to phenotype, generated relationally through the body's interactions with other bodies, the environment, as well as a product of those discursive relationships to space and place so much more familiar to geographers. I contend that we cannot speak of "whiteness" without reference to the actual bodies of white people and how, in particular, those bodies are shaped through spatial practice.

In making this move I want to highlight transnational mobility as one means through which whiteness-as-materiality can be understood. Through mobility, the virtual capacities of bodies are mediated and directed toward, and away from, certain places. As Sara Ahmed writes, "bodies are shaped by motility and may take the shape of that motility" (2007, 159). In terms of thinking through the prism of South Africa's post-apartheid, transnationalizing moment, and in tandem with the new "mobilities turn" (Sheller and Urry 2006), which has attempted to displace the hegemony of sedentarism from social scientific analysis, I suggest that transnational mobility is not incidental to, or an epiphenomenon of, whiteness in South Africa, but is immanent in it. In the contemporary period, the formulation of whiteness as a "passport of privilege" (Kalra, Kaur, and Hutnyk 2005) cannot only stand abstractly for the transcendent power consistently bestowed on and associated with whiteness across the globe, but must also be stretched to indicate the emergence of whiteness as a congeries of bodies characterized by their capacity to move across borders, and how this is linked both to earlier histories of movement and the current globalizing era. Sherene Razack's (2002) notion of unmapping and Alistair Bonnett's (2000) discussion of the global history of white identities, among others, can help situate this. Razack argues that unmapping the fait accompli of whiteness in settler societies allows us to understand that white countries came to be that way for a reason; in other words, that social construction is material (cf. Nayak 2006). The demographic profile of a country, even if those demographic categories are contingent constructions, is still the outcome of often violent material processes. This includes genocide and disease spread as well as immigration regulations that have constructed the phenotypic constitution of various settler countries (e.g., the White Australia policy or the regulation of Chinese immigration in the United States). Whitening is a material, biopolitical process, as illustrated by, for instance, Australia's stolen generation and the policy of whitening in Venezuela (Bonnett 2000), and this highlights the central role of the state in mediating transnational flows of bodies in a globalizing world economy.

Similarly, McDonald's (2008) discussion of the whitening of the Cape Town landscape through removal of African bodies from central areas highlights the importance to the symbolic hegemony of whiteness in the landscape of the sorting of bodies as much as the discursive scripting of space. This again demonstrates the centrality of the materiality of the body to formations of racialized geographies. The complex regulation of transnational (and internal) migration on the part of states as well as suprastate networks works as part of an ensemble out of which race emerges. By attending to ancestry we can argue that through histories of the movement of certain kinds of bodies into certain national spaces, the presence of white bodies has been materially constituted in particular places. And it is those white bodies that, through material privilege to move between South Africa and the UK offered by ancestral regimes of movement, are now also partially constitutive of the face of elite transnational mobility as we have come to know it today. I want to argue that the UK's suite of visa and passport arrangements on offer to South Africans constitutes a machine that attracts and repels bodies, and that whiteness emerges out of the workings of this visa whiteness machine.

Saldanha writes, "From a machinic perspective, race is not something inscribed upon or referring to bodies, but a particular spatiotemporal disciplining and charging of those bodies themselves" (2007, 190). Thus the material arrangement of where bodies can be is as important, if not more so, than how racialized identity is mediated through discourse. Valerie here illustrates well the way in which she and her boyfriend (later husband) ended up in London because it happened to be a path open to her, by virtue of her ancestry, a path that exerted a financial pull of its own:

Valerie: For us, it was never really about living in London. It was just about living somewhere and earning an income. We didn't choose to go to London because we liked living there, or particular experience. I mean, we always talk about the weather in the UK.

Max: It was just the path that was available?

Valerie: Yes, ja, ja. I would say from, a salary point of view, money got us there in the first place.

Valerie and her partner moved to London not in order to "shore up" their whiteness in some abstract sense by returning to the imperial center. In fact they didn't even really like London. The draw of London's economy and the cultural capital afforded to them as beneficiaries of apartheid were central to their decision to migrate transnationally, but, in the final analysis, Valerie and her partner moved to the UK because, thanks to the visa whiteness machine, they could.

Context

This research is part of a wider project on the transnational practices of white South Africans. A series of in-depth, semistructured interviews were conducted in and around Durban with white South Africans who had experience living overseas at some point in their lives but were currently residing in South Africa. Durban is an industrial city of approximately 3 million, and its hinterland, the former British colony of Natal, is the only region of South Africa where English speakers constitute a majority amongst whites (as well as Coloureds). The white population of the former province of Natal (since 1994 merged with the former homeland into the province of KwaZulu-Natal) is renowned for its staunch history of loyalism, royalism, and even separatism before and during the apartheid period. Even after South Africa became a republic in 1961, Natal was often dubbed "The Last Outpost of the British Empire" (Thompson 1990). Roughly half of all South Africans living overseas are in the UK (and those living in the UK have the most interest in and are the most likely to return to South Africa).

Although people have moved back and forth between Britain and South Africa for the whole of the latter's history as a European colony, the period since the end of apartheid, which took place between 1990 and 1994, is the focus of this article. This is particularly important because, since the early 1990s, South Africa has reinserted itself into the international community through the repeal of apartheid-era sanctions, its reentry into the Commonwealth, and the dramatic liberalization of its economy, and there are now roughly 1 million fewer whites in South Africa than in the mid-1990s. Thus the juridical ability, the desire, and the economic pathways enabling and encouraging white South Africans to move overseas have all drastically increased during South Africa's postcolonial period.

Scales of Availability

In Kalra et al.'s (2005) assessment of what they call white diasporas, these authors discuss whiteness as a "passport of privilege" that enables privileged ease of movement for white bodies around the globe. The notion of a passport of privilege can, however, be deepened and extended by attending to the ways in which white bodies themselves emerge as products of this very mobility. In this phrase, privilege shouldn't be understood as some sort of transcendent advantage universally accrued to whiteness through the structures of the contemporary episteme. Instead, it makes more sense to turn to the "passport" half of the phrase, which must be taken, in fact, at face value, as real, with material effects that accrue contingently to some bodies by virtue of overlapping historical layers of access to economic and social capital. As Neumayer indicates, there is a "great degree of inequality of access to foreign spaces" (2006, 78). The visa and overseas citizenship regimes of rich countries not only partly explain the inequality of transnational motility but also constitute a means for states to engage diaspora populations in particular projects of governance (see Dickinson and Bailey 2007), such as filling gaps in the labor market with bodies that appear less foreign, or promoting investment from overseas citizens.

There are a variety of avenues, embedded in South Africa's colonial history with Britain, available to South Africans, and particularly to whites, to enter the UK and work. The Working Holiday Visa, though recently scrapped for South Africans, was available between 1994 and 2009 to Commonwealth citizens aged seventeen to thirty who planned an extended holiday in the UK for up to two years. Recipients could work but the holiday needed to be the primary reason for entering the country; as many as 17,000 South Africans took part annually. Working holiday visas could not be extended but an opportunity was offered for South African citizens to find employers who would sponsor them for a work visa. Candidates for this visa scheme, however, were expected to have a substantial sum of money in the bank in order to be granted the visa, which in effect closed this option off to most black South Africans. Ancestral visas are offered to Commonwealth citizens aged seventeen or over with a grandparent and in some cases great-grandparent born in the UK and they allow the bearer to work for five years in the UK, followed by the opportunity to gain citizenship. British nationality is available to anyone with a British-born parent if it is claimed by the age of seventeen. Because of the UK's membership of the European Union (EU), since the Maastricht Treaty became law in 1993, any South African in possession of citizenship of any EU country is also eligible to reside in the UK (this has been the case for Irish citizens since the UK Parliament passed the Ireland Act 1949).

In addition, until 2009 South Africans benefited from visa-free access to the UK as tourists (visa-free access was revoked because of security concerns about the illegal possession of South African passports by non-South African nationals). There are other avenues through which South Africans can enter the UK on a permanent or temporary basis, but these are the three most common routes, and are the ones that arise directly out of the historical relationship between South Africa and the UK, and have flowed through family trees via previous histories of transnational migration.

These three categories of legal access to UK employment encircle South African bodies like a Venn diagram, in increasingly smaller scales, from less to more contingent on sociocultural factors such as class and education. The working holiday visa thus encompasses all South Africans without British parentage—especially Afrikaans speakers who constitute the majority of South African whites, and who through colonial- and apartheid-era privilege would be more likely than blacks to have access to the financial means required, while the ancestral visa includes South Africans of British descent with longer family histories in the country, and the availability of UK nationality includes the not insubstantial numbers (perhaps 600,000) with at least one British parent.

UK Passports

In the following quotations respondents with British parents, such as Gary, Maureen, Daniel, and Greg, all of whom therefore possess UK nationality, repeatedly indicate the ease of moving to and working in the UK for South Africans with access to UK passports. Not coincidentally it is striking how respondents draw on family histories of migration from the UK to South Africa:

Gary: My father was English. He grew up in Bristol, and he emigrated to initially Zambia I think in the 1970s, and then he moved down to South Africa where he met my mother, so I had a British passport. It was easy to go to the UK.

Greg: I managed to get British ancestry through my mother who was born over there. And I'd been thinking about going overseas mostly through my 20s. Finally got round to doing so when I was twenty-seven. Quite late. Probably prompted by a girl who I worked with here, who went to London in advance.

Daniel: My father was English, he was born in Cornwall....

Max: So you already had a British passport, by nature of descent?

Daniel: Already had a British passport, ja, that was from my father. My wife [is] South African and South African passports on both kids as well. Ja, so I just basically packed up and left.

Maureen, whose Scottish-born parents emigrated to Rhodesia (now Zimbabwe) in the 1950s, illustrates just how easy it was for her, along with her British-born partner, to move to London from South Africa:

Maureen: Well, I went with my partner. Um, and, um... and we bought our tickets [laughs].

Max: He was from the UK?

Maureen: He was from the UK, he's got a British passport. So he didn't have any visa, whatever, issues, and neither did I. So, we could ... we didn't really need to make ... formal plans.... We could just buy our tickets and go, which is what we did.

The possession of British nationality through descent thus enables whites who have it to freely move between the UK and South Africa, fueling a transnational culture of mobility in which the body's occupation of any given space can always be contingent, temporary, and voluntary. As Daniel indicates, and unlike Maureen, this marked him out as significantly more motile than his partner and children—who were eventually able to join him in London, but not right away.

Ancestral Visas

The possession of relatively close UK ancestry also clearly functions to enact whiteness machinically through motility:

Francine: Well because of my grandfather being born in the UK, I'm allowed to get an ancestral visa. So that's what I'm working on at the moment, and I intend to do caring work, once I get there.

Max: OK, and why are you planning to leave?

Francine: Because of my financial situation. I can't really see myself lasting here financially. Because I don't have the income.

Francine has been recruited as a locum providing semicasualized home health care to seniors in the UK. So we can see here how visa arrangements have allowed for the import of low-cost social reproductive labor (see Misra, Woodring, and Merz 2006), but, in addition, for Francine, attaining access to the UK through her ancestry has become a crucial mechanism through which she hopes to be able to maintain a middle-class standard of living that she implicitly associates with her whiteness.

In this way we can see how, in contrast to much recent work on transnationalism, especially of the "middling" variety (Conradson and Latham 2005), mobility associated with the visa whiteness machine is not confined to elites but applies equally to all who can prove UK descent and thus allows South Africans to negotiate the spaces between very different political and economic conjectures in the north and south. South Africans who stay in the UK for the full four years on their ancestral visa can then apply for indefinite leave to remain and, if they choose, shortly thereafter, a British passport, which would enable complete ease of movement between the two countries:

Cicely: I have ancestry to the United Kingdom, that was how I landed up in the UK. Through my paternal grandmother.

Max: OK, so you used an ancestral visa.

Cicely: I went on an ancestral visa, which was four years. I stayed for four and a half years, because at the end of four years I wasn't ready to come home yet, so I asked for indefinite leave to remain. So I have an indefinite leave to remain in my passport.

Max: So you can go back anytime?

Cicely: Born and bred South African.... I wouldn't change my South African passport for an English one.

Cicely thus demonstrates how the need to make emotional decisions such as the acquisition of foreign citizenship is obviated as the attainment of indefinite leave to remain means a passport is not even required to facilitate continuous mobility between South Africa and the UK.

Working Holiday Visas

Though an English-speaker living in Durban, Peg has primarily Afrikaans heritage and does not qualify for an ancestral visa—and again she makes explicit mention of her heritage when describing how she had to resort to using the working holiday visa to enter the UK to work:

Peg: The whole plan in going was basically just a change. I was twenty-six, and I could only be in London up to the age of twenty-seven, because you can't get a working holiday visa [after that age], so....

Max: OK, so that's what you used?

Peg: Ja, so I used a working holiday visa to go.

Max: Were you eligible for an ancestral visa? Did you try?

Peg: No, because I don't have any grandparents living there, that are close. It's more, further down the tree.

As Randi illustrates, meeting the eligibility requirements for securing a working holiday visa as her means of last resort (despite the fact that she would have been eligible for an ancestral visa), was not difficult:

Max: Were you on the working holiday [visa]?

Randi: Ja, I just took that out ... quick and easy.

Meeting the requirements of age, South African citizenship, and, crucially, the ability to prove they had the means to support themselves, Randi and Peg did not encounter much difficulty in attaining working holiday visas, the means used by many white youth of Afrikaans and Jewish extraction and those with only very distant roots in the UK.

Scales of Motility

Scale is also relevant in the way in which transnational South Africans are able to deploy various levels of membership in order to enhance their motility. Suzette, whose father immigrated to South Africa from Italy, was able to use the scaled-up citizenship regime of the EU to achieve easy motility into the UK. She explicitly recognizes that this embodied motility places her in a different spatially inflected subject position to other South Africans without EU or other foreign passports. Speaking of the persistent fear of crime that stimulates much emigration, she notes that:

Suzette: I do kind of feel that … touch wood, there's not been anything really violent happen to anyone I know, but if something were to happen, I don't know how I would react. I don't know if I would turn tail and just say, phew, that's it, boy, I'm out of here, if it's close family or something, or whether I would stick it out and fight. And I wonder if because of my Italian link, … I don't know how [a] 100% South African person would think, who had a South African passport and whose only option was to go through a full immigration process somewhere. And I do sometimes wonder if because of the European link, I sort of…not that I feel I have an out, but it's kind of … ja, sometimes I don't feel 100% South African, if that makes sense….

Suzette here acknowledges how the possession of a foreign passport allows her to feel differently about living in South Africa—in this case, easily able to flee if she felt threatened by crime. In this way, the pull of the UK, in particular, becomes evident. Despite Suzette's ability to move anywhere in the EU, it is the economic lure of the global city of London, as well as the cultural status of the city and the embodied fact of Suzette's monolingual anglophonism that directs her mobility.

Misty used the same scaled-up European citizenship regime in reverse. The daughter of English emigrants, she used her EU passport to go with her husband to Ireland to work:

Max: When you and your husband first tried to go abroad, why was it Ireland?

Misty: Just because it would be easier for him to find work there, really.

Max: Did he have Irish …

Misty: No it's because I'm British …

Max: … because of your British citizenship.

Misty: Ja, ja.

Greg is aware of his ability to use his UK passport to move himself and his wife to Sweden—thus also displaying his awareness of the ability to deploy the heterosexist mechanism of marriage-based privilege to bestow motility on his female partner, scaling up the unit of his motility from individual body to household unit:

Max: Does [your wife] have another passport, or just South African?

Greg: No, she's just South African, but, me being British, we're on an EU passport. That's how we'd look to arrange getting her over.

Max: OK, so you can go into Sweden with no fuss at all.

Greg: No fuss. Same as going to England or Greece or anywhere....

Max: Or would you also be interested looking at other countries— North America or Australia?

Greg: Well, we'd be very interested in North America, but the passport issues are difficult, and I think to get into North America is difficult. So, for that reason it's easier for us to try and get into Europe.

Greg here clearly demonstrates the interaction of ability and choice in his discussion of possible emigration destinations. He and his wife would like to live in North America and not Australia. However, the easiest path is into the EU. Having lived in the UK previously, Greg, despite his possession of a British passport, has no desire to move back there, but would be able to use that passport to move to Sweden, a country to which neither he nor his wife have ancestral ties.

Jane's decision to bestow future motility to her family was quite strategic, in that she intentionally planned on having her baby in the UK before returning to South Africa so that, unlike in Daniel's family, he would in future have a UK passport and thus ease the possibility of migration at the scale of the family:

Max: So how did you come to decide that it was actually, now was the time to go home?

Jane: Well we had planned it that I wanted my child to have a British passport. So I fell pregnant and we planned that we were gonna come back after he was born.

Max: Was it a planned pregnancy?

Jane: Ja.

Max: How come you wanted him to have a British passport?

Jane: So that he had an opportunity to go back.

Through her own reproductive decision making Jane is thus creating embodied migration histories of the present in which her British lineage is reaffirmed as a whiteness privileged with motility, and highlighting the role of individual agency in reproducing the privileges associated with the visa whiteness machine.

Conclusion

In this article, I have engaged with the literature on whiteness in geography and South African studies, bodies of work that primarily posit race as just that—a socially constructed and fictitious epistemology of power relations framed through discourse and language. Drawing insights from Saldanha's materialist theory of race, I have argued that motility is a particularly instructive prism through which to demonstrate the materiality of whiteness for a particular, though representative, set of white English-speaking South Africans. Transnational motility, I have argued, is not merely an epiphenomenon of lingering white privilege in post-apartheid South Africa, but is embedded within the white South African body through its material origins, at a variety of temporal and spatial scales, in ancestral histories of migration. Through what I call the visa whiteness machine, motility is an immanent but unequally distributed property of South African whiteness, located in the body by nature of that body's relation to ancestry. I have argued that motility is a set of capacities that are unevenly distributed, even amongst white South Africans. Many white South Africans are eligible for UK passports, many more for ancestral visas, and those who aren't could participate in the working holiday visa scheme. I have also argued that motility, as a property, can move between bodies and change scales. Through recent European citizenship law, South African holders of other EU passports have gained the right to move to the UK and other EU states. Meanwhile, those in possession of white motility can choose to share it and pass it on to officially recognized family members.

All the same, I am keen to be clear that I am not pursuing an either–or approach to the debate around race and social construction, but am more interested in an approach best characterized as both-and. Thus I am keen to emphasize that the transnational motility embedded in white bodies involves only capacities that are mobilized and activated by discourses, cultural norms, and the material circumstances of everyday life and in particular emerges as a means of reconciling the possession of a white body with its emplacement in postcolonial, newly third world space. Not only does transnational motility demonstrate the materiality of whiteness, but, I would suggest, it is part of the very ontology of South African whiteness itself, as it emerges machanically out of the movement of white bodies through transnational space.

References

Ahmed, S. 2007. "The Phenomenology of Whiteness." *Feminist Theory* 8(2): 149–68.

Ballard, R. 2004a. "Assimilation, Emigration, Semigration, and Integration: 'White' People's Strategies for Finding a Comfort Zone in Post-Apartheid South Africa." In: *Under Construction: "Race" and Identity in South Africa Today,* edited by N. Distiller and M. Steyn, 51–66. Sandton, SA: Heinemann.

———.2004b. "Middle Class Neighbourhoods or 'African Kraals'? The Impact of Informal Settlements and Vagrants on Post-Apartheid White Identity." *Urban Forum* 15 (1): 48–73.

Bonnett, A. 2000. *White Identities: Historical and International Perspectives.* Harlow, UK: Prentice-Hall.

Conradson, D., and A. Latham. 2005. "Friendship, Networks and Transnationality in a World City: Antipodean Transmigrants in London." *Journal of Ethnic and Migration Studies* 30 (2): 287–305.

Dickinson, J., and A. Bailey. 2007. "(Re)membering Diaspora: Uneven Geographies of Indian Dual Citizenship." *Political Geography* 26: 757–74.

Dwyer, O. J., and J. P. Jones, III. 2000. White Socio-Spatial Epistemology." *Social and Cultural Geography* 1: 209–22.

Hoelscher, S. 2003. "Making (P)lace, Making Race: Performances of Whiteness in the Jim Crow South." *Annals of the Association of American Geographers* 93: 657–86.

Jackson, P. 1998. "Constructions of 'Whiteness' in the Geographical Imagination." *Area* 30: 99–106.

Kalra, V. S., R. Kaur, and J. Hutnyk. 2005. *Diaspora and Hybridity.* London: Sage.

Kobayashi, A., and L. Peake. 1994. "Unnatural Discourse: 'Race' and Gender in Geography." *Gender, Place and Culture* 1: 225–43.

McDonald, D. A. 2008. *World City Syndrome: Neoliberalism and Inequality in Cape Town.* New York: Routledge.

Misra, J., J. Woodring, and S. Merz. 2006. "The Globalization of Care Work: Neoliberal Economic Restructuring and Migration Police." *Globalizations* 3(3): 317–32.

Nayak, A. 2006. "After Race: Ethnography, Race and Post-Race theory." *Ethnic and Racial Studies* 29 (3): 411–30.

Neumayer, E. 2006. "Unequal Access to foreign Spaces: How States Use Visa Restrictions to Regulate Mobility in a Globalized World." *Transactions of the Institute of British Geographers* NS31: 72–84.

Pred, A. 1997. "Somebody Else, Somewhere Else: Racisms, Racialized Spaces and the Popular Geographical Imagination in Sweden." *Antipode* 29: 383–416.

Razack, S. H. 2002. "Introduction: When Place Becomes Race." In *Race, Space, and the Law: Unmapping a White Settler Society,* edited by S. H. Razack, 1–20. Toronto: Between the Lines.

Saldanha, A. 2006. "Re-ontologising Race: The Machinic Geography of Photype." *Environment and Planning D: Society and Space* 24 (1): 9–24.

———. 2007. *Psychedelic White: Goa Trance and the Viscosity of Race.* Minneapolis: University of Minnesota Press.

Sheller, M., and J. Urry. 2006. "The New Mobilities Paradigm." *Environment and Planning: A* 38: 207–26.

Slocum, R. 2008. "Thinking Race through Corporeal Feminist Theory: Divisions and Intimacies at the Minneapolis Farmers Market." *Social and Cultural Geography* 9 (8): 849–69.

South African Institute of Race Relations (SAIRR). 2006. "More Jobs Less Work." Fast Facts no. 8–9. http://www.sairr.org.za/research-and-publications/fast-stats-online/fast-facts-2006/.

Steyn, M. 2005. "'White Talk': White South Africans and the Management of Diasporic Whiteness." In: *Postcolonial Whiteness: A Critical Reader on Race and Empire,* edited by A. J. Lopez, 119–35. Albany, NY: SUNY Press.

———, and D. Foster. 2007. "Repertoires for Talking White: Resistant Whiteness in Postapartheid South Africa." *Ethnic and Racial Studies* 31 (1): 25–51.

Thompson, P. S. 1990. *Natalians First: Separatism in South Africa, 1909–1961*. Johannesburg: Southern Book.

Vanderbeck, R. 2006. "Vermont and the Imaginative Geographies of American Whiteness." *Annals of the Association of American Geographers* 96 (3): 641–59.

———. 2008. "Inner-City Children, Country Summers: Narrating American Childhood and the Geographies of Whiteness. *Environment and Planning A* 40: 1132–50.

CHAPTER 6

Who Gets to Be Italian?

Black Life Worlds and White Spatial Imaginaries

HEATHER MERRILL

From 1876 to the early 1980s, approximately 26 million Italians princi-pally from the south and northeast emigrated to industrialized parts of Europe, the United States, and other parts of the globe where they fre-quently encountered a version of racism. This is poignantly portrayed in the 1974 film, *Bread and Chocolate* in which Franco Brusati uses humor to tell the painful story of an Italian guest worker who colors his hair blonde in a desperate attempt to be treated with respect as he seeks to build a life in Switzerland. In European spatial imaginaries, Italians have frequently been perceived as of a different shade of whiteness, closer to the Global South. Until recently seen predominantly as transgressors in other parts of Europe, Italian migrants were excluded from the privileges of whiteness associated with the Western and Northern European captains of moder-nity. However, Northern Italian political and corporate leaders have long sought alliances and cultural identifications with Europe. The Italian pub-lic and elites alike were among the most enthusiastic supporters of Euro-pean integration and have been regarded as the most Europhile in Europe.[1]

In the 1990s, Italy transformed from a country of immigrant export to a key immigrant destination for people from Africa, Latin America, Cen-tral, and Eastern Europe. Since 1990 the shift in Italian demographics has been spectacular. There has been a fourteen-fold increase in the foreign resident population from roughly 330,000 in 1990 to almost 5 million in

2011 (ISTAT n.d.) representing some 7.5 percent of the population, not including the undocumented (Bonifazi et al. 2009). The bodies of immigrants are not evenly distributed, with 87 percent residing in the densely populated northern and central industrialized zones of the country (Contini 2011). This includes the north and northeastern regions, home to the Northern League, a populist central-right, anti-immigrant, and frequently anti-Southern Italian political party. Although the Piedmont province, whose seat is in Turin has historically been center-left, it has not been unaffected by the Northern League, which has had considerable influence on immigration policies and popular perceptions of immigrants as threats to regional identities in the North.

Although immigrants from North and Sub-Saharan Africa currently comprise only about 20 percent of foreign residents, Black and Arab migration hold considerable symbolic valence within the logic of Italian North–South relations. The border between Italy and the African continent remains a focal point in an intense and enduring debate over space and identity. Reconstituted as the signifier of immigration, the Southern maritime border is portrayed as a site of moral panic, where boat people clandestinely enter Italian territory from North and Sub-Saharan Africa.[2] This border space has been partnered with earlier dominant tropes of itinerant African street peddlers and prostitutes as representations of an immigrant threat to the purity of public and private spaces where native Italians live and work. Such hyperbolic images signal a deep anxiety toward immigrants that can be observed in routine (quotidian) interactions in which individuals are analytically associated with entire ethnic groups believed not to belong in Italy (see Pred 2000).

The imagined border between Italy and Africa is, in fact, somewhat fictional. There has been a constant flow and exchange between Europe and Africa beginning with medieval 5th to the 15th centuries trans-Mediterranean trade routes and the interpenetration of ideas, people, values, and commodities. Colonial and postcolonial investments have set the stage for the current immigration. North African and Sub-Saharan African cultures have played a forgotten but constitutive role in shaping the heterogeneous cultures of contemporary Italy (Pugliese 2008). Furthermore, today's migrants comprise a surplus population whose labor has been vital to the country's economic prosperity (Merrill 2011). However, over the past two decades, the Italian State has fortified the material borders between Europe and Africa in a number of ways. In accordance with European Union guidelines on immigration and refugee policies, and most potential migrants enter via air or land routes (Carter and Merrill 2007; Carter 2010). However, the perception of an invasion of Italian territory by desperate Africans and Arabs seeking illegal entry via porous maritime borders and for whom there can be no appropriate employment or housing accommodations, remains constant. This is fueled in some measure by the Northern League whose political narratives are drawn from old racialized spatial imaginaries of Southern Italy as an extension of Arab and African worlds.

While each of Italy's twenty regions maintains its own distinct cultural and historical particularities, the Northern region of the Italian industrial triangle of Piedmont, Genoa, and Lombardy and more recently from Valle d'Aosta to Veneto and into Central Italy has been encouraged to perceive a common identity as fused into a "Northern Italy" distinct from the "South" (Mezzogiorno) beginning in Rome. This North–South division is perhaps more imagined than material, as thousands of southern Italians migrated for work and settled in the northern industrial zones after the Second World War where they encountered substantial prejudice and discrimination from the local populations. Their children and grandchildren now constitute noteworthy, if not always fully integrated members of northern cultures.

The idea that Northern and Southern Italy are incommensurable places dates back to national unification, when the campaign by the Kingdom of Piedmont to incorporate the South involved both a repressive military campaign and conceptual operationalization via linguistic references to the South as a distinct moral space. As Allan Pred suggested, it is in part through language that individual consciousness is given expression and differentiated perceptions of the world are produced and retained (Pred 1990). In the North, a racialized, derogatory terminology was employed to describe Southerners as *cafone*, meaning *primitive, barbaric, uncivilized, vulgar,* and *backward* (Pugliese 2008). The signifier "Africa" has also been used in the North as a lens through which to make sense of the South, as if the peninsula and its islands were split along a Black/white axis. As Joseph Pugliese suggests, "the whiteness of the North operated as a priori, in contradistinction to the problematic racialized status of the South, with its dubious African and Oriental histories and cultures" (Pugliese 2008, 3).

During the 1950s and 1960s period of mass migration to Northern industrial cities Southerners were targeted as *terrone*, a racialized slur meaning "people of dirt, the dirt beneath one's feet." This cultural, economic, and social othering of the South by the North has persisted in the contemporary period. But since the arrival of immigrants from the Global South two decades ago, Southern Italians have moved up the white supremacist racial hierarchy and what Pugliese refers to as Italy's "caucacentric fantasies of a pure white/European nation" toward what he calls "proximate whiteness" (Pugliese 2009). As compared with non-European immigrants,

Southern Italians who may not appear white are brought into the fold of whiteness. Several neologisms have recently emerged to describe migrants from Africa and the Arab world, including *sottoterrone*, or the "subdirt beneath one's feet" and *Marocchini*, an umbrella term that refers to people of Sub-Saharan and Arab origin, thereby lumping together a diverse group of people with a name that negatively signifies "Blackness" and "African" (De Maio 2009).

Blackness is such a pivotal trope of Otherness in Italian society that even those with the most unequivocally culturally Italian identities may be associated with the "dark continent" and an imminent threat to national geographies of whiteness. The soccer player, Mario Balotelli recently became a symbol of the country's apparent resistance to embracing its growing heterogeneity. Born to Ghanaian parents but adopted by an Italian family and raised in the northern town of Brescia, Balotelli's identity has been seen by many Italian soccer fans as a provocation. When he was a rising star of the Inter Milan club, supporters of Turin's Juventus team held up banners with the words, "A Negro cannot be Italian." Yet Balotelli speaks with a regional Italian accent and an intimate description by his adoptive sister suggests that he is a quintessentially Italian son, who as she put it, "Wouldn't go to sleep without his mother holding his hand."[3]

These distance producing images and discourses seek to deny and make unintelligible the participation and vital contributions that African and Arab populations are making to Italian civic life. They also obfuscate the transcultural crossings that have been taking place for centuries, most notably via Italy's colonial and neocolonial relationships with Libya, Eritrea, Ethiopia, and Somalia. Italian colonial history has only recently begun to be critically examined by scholars,[4] and among the Italian public the continuing silence about this history is deafening. The rigid silences that surround colonial atrocities perpetrated by Italy and other European countries in Africa, the relations of force, cultural imposition, and racialized exclusion serves not only to reproduce relations of power but also to remove from view the interwoven histories and identities of people of African descent, European histories and identities.[5] As Neil Smith and Cindi Katz have argued, there is a need to challenge the presumed homogeneity of identities. Postcolonial migrants are in Europe because Europe was in Africa, and from their perspective, "We are here because you were there" (Smith and Katz 1993, 77). Today, the production and transformation of Turin, its becoming as a place, is intertwined with the embodied practices and biographies of people of African descent who daily negotiate their sense of belonging.

The African Diaspora in Postcolonial Europe

There are few studies of African diasporic experiences in relation to place and identity in postcolonial Europe. The racially essentializing logic of Western Modernity continues "to project a nightmarish shadow over the formations of Black cultural and political identities" (Hesse 1993, 166), demands that critical scholarship on the Black Diaspora must directly engage with issues of power, race, and racial inequality. In this chapter I bring geographical perspectives on place into dialogue with critical race scholarship focused on the African Diaspora. I do this by analyzing place and belonging through the prism of race and the lived experiences of first generation Africans in Turin, Italy. Exploring contemporary meanings of place and belonging from the vantage point of black experiences or what Michael Hanchard (2006) refers to as "Black life worlds" provides insights into the intersections of place and belonging without neglecting the enduring legacies and rearticulations of modern racial hierarchies (cf. Malkki 1992; see Gilmore 2004; Puwar 2004). Hanchard defines Black life worlds as Black subjectivities constructed through experiential knowledge and practiced in everyday lives, and I use the concept here in a somewhat revised form to refer to the distinctive ways that Italo-Africans perceive the world as it has been generated through ongoing experiences in racialized spaces that link Europe inextricably with Africa (Hanchard 2006). Afro-Italians experience place in Italy through what Thomas and David have called the "long durée" of colonial history, in which the transcolonial national, ethnic, and racial borders between Africa and Europe are porous, overlapping, and ambiguous (Thomas and David 2006).

Among people from former European colonies, the meanings of place and belonging are particularly fraught. They are connected with interlocking and conflictual histories around collective identities dominated, or at least strongly influenced by, and continually bound together with European political and cultural institutions and modern European racialized formations (Winant 1994; Hall 1991a, 1991b, 2003). This is not to suggest that there has not been a great deal of resistance or that African political and cultural institutions were erased; on the contrary, African cosmologies and practices have been reproduced within colonial ruptures and forms of displacement in what Stuart Hall, borrowing Leopold Senghor and Aimée Césaire's metaphor, describes as a continuous "Présence Africaine" that is a source of inspiration, agency, and creation. Yet there is also always in African Diasporic formations a "Présence Européenne," a troubling aspect of identity because the European presence has been so overwhelming, introducing the issue of power through imposition, exclusion, force, and appropriation. Hall cautions that movements among former colonized people to locate the Présence Européenne as external, and to separate all that it represents from their cultural identities rooted in Africa is problematic, for the many dimensions of the European influence are irreversible and its presence also continues (Hall 2003). In their everyday practices, these postcolonial immigrants embody both Africa and Europe. This can be applied more widely to all Africans whose lives have been touched in varying degrees by European colonization, and it takes on some unique and compelling dimensions for those who have recently migrated to Europe (Brown 2005; Keaton 2006; Carter 1997, 2010; Hine, Keaton, and Small 2009).

That intersections of identity and place become more complex in a world of increasing and routine mobility and displacement is not a new area of theoretical inquiry. The first wave of path breaking reflections on the topic appeared in the early 1990s (Appadurai 1990; Gupta and Ferguson 1992; Basch, Glick Schiller, and Szanton Blanc 1994; Malkki 1992). Much of this work argued that displaced social actors formed multiple transnational attachments to geographically distant places through daily communication, memory, and communication technologies. These approaches tended to undertheorize or elide analyses of the ways that the long durée of colonial and neocolonial power relations grounded in Eurocentric racial hierarchies have remained pivotal antagonisms for social actors who are part of the African Diaspora (Marable 2008).

Stuart Hall and Paul Gilroy, Black British cultural theorists, have offered early noteworthy exceptions, focusing on how people from the Caribbean and African countries strove to carve out places of belonging in England in opposition to monolithic and absolutist conceptions of British identity as white, male, and upper class. Where exclusionary constructions of place have been addressed, there has been a tendency to conceive of these problems in generalized terms influenced by color-blind ideologies in the United States. Scholars have skirted around issues of race by discussing categories of difference broadly conceived in a language of "intolerance," "xenophobia," or even "cultural racism" toward immigrants whom local populations perceive as threatening to their ways of life (Taguieff 1990; Miles 1993; Stolke 1995). As important as these studies have been, they have fostered approaches that tend to underestimate or erase the continuing impact of colonial histories, as well as the specific and ongoing weight of European power, and struggles over recognition, place, and belonging among descendents of Africa.

The flip side of this obfuscation of the significance of racialized identities and racism to place can be found in studies which tend to conceive the lives of people in the African Diaspora as though they operated in self-contained social worlds, where social relations appear to exist in autonomous third dimensional spaces unconnected with wide social, cultural, political, and economic processes (Gregory 1997; Brown 2005). Even in Paul Gilroy's seminal work, *The Black Atlantic*, arguably the most influential work of African Diasporic studies over the past two decades in which he problematized common struggles across African Diasporic spaces and places in the North Atlantic, there is a tendency to reify diasporic space as a type of separate and distinct, closed cultural place.

Rediscovering the significance of African histories and the contributions of people of African descent to the making of the contemporary world is extremely important, yet there is, as Jacqueline Nassy Brown has pointed, out some danger in conceiving of diaspora as itself a place where one is by definition bounded off from European society. As Brown suggests, race is not autonomous from place (Brown 2005). Diasporic identities aren't typically produced by communities that are suspended in-between national territories—even if they sometimes feel that way. Black experiences are situated in places that are products of interconnected power relations and meanings, the long durée of colonial histories, and the reworkings of the present.

I offer an analysis of the negotiations, and meanings of place, identity, and belonging among diverse first generation Africans in Turin with whom I have conducted extensive field research for two decades (Merrill 2006). These Italo-Africans and their descendents are as Stuart Hall put it, "taking back the Empire" as they make their presence increasingly felt in the territories of former European colonial powers. They are part of a renewed cycle of African Diasporic formation in which increased flows of migrants and displaced peoples are forced to move from war or in search of work, what Achille Mbembe described as an "unprecedented revival of the imaginaries of long distance" (Mbembe 2001, 6).

Scholars of Africana Studies have begun to note that the cultural fabric of Europe is being transformed as first and second generations of Africans challenge monolithic, Eurocentric definitions of belonging, racialized logic, and exclusionary practices (Gilroy 1987; Hall 1991a, 1991b; Keaton 2006: Carter 2010). Their experiences in Europe are different from those of other immigrant populations whose presence may also be contested. As Barnor Hesse suggested in the only article to discuss race in a seminal volume on place and identity politics edited by Keith and Pile, immigration is distinctive for Blacks whose settlement in Europe is always enmeshed in racial antagonisms that affirm "ambivalences and equivocations in the conditions for settling" (Hesse 1993, 167). Settlement is not a discrete moment for these Africans from countries profoundly intermeshed with Europe. Overturning simple teleologies, Italo-Africans claim place in a Europe whose history is their own, and partake in the making of new histories.

The Spatial Contours of White Privilege and Belonging in Turin

Maria Abbebu Viarengo spent the first twenty years of her life in Ethiopia and Sudan before her father brought her to Turin, Italy in 1969. Italy was no stranger to Maria who had previously visited the country not only in actual terms but through her imagination as a young person schooled in Italian language and history while growing up in a place briefly part of the Italian colonial empire. In her partially published autobiography, Maria describes the gradual reawakening of the African dimensions of her identity she had felt forced to repress until the late 1980s when a growing number of Africans appeared in the Piedmont region. Her memories of Africa had always been present, yet she could seldom express them. Compelled to assimilate and conform to Italian cultural identities, she never quite experienced a sense of belonging in spite of the fact that her father was Italian, she spoke the official and regional languages better than many Italians, and she too was an Italian citizen. Maria wrestled with her multiply textured identity, her early life in Africa and relationship with her African mother, her Italianness, and the way she was perceived by Italian society. Of her experiences as a perceived outsider she writes:

> I have heard people call me, hanfez, klls, meticcia, mulatta, cafelatte, half-cast, ciuculatin, colored, armusch. I have learned the art of pretence; I have always looked like whomever others wanted me to look like. I have been Indian, Arab, Latin American, and Sicilian. (74, Quoted in Ponzanesi 2004, 161)

Maria's predicament is reminiscent of Frantz Fanon who described being caught between his own self-understanding as part of French society and experiences of erasure in France because of his appearance and designation as someone from a European colonial territory. Fanon and Maria are, as he put it, "over-determined from without" in European society, perceived through a binary racial gaze that demarcates nonwhites as absolute others against privileged and well established social identities. Both spent the better part of their lives acquiring the knowledge, cultural codes, and habits of a colonizing culture they had believed their own but then moved to Europe where they experienced a rupture as their "sisters and brothers" did not to recognize their existence. Maria describes in her autobiography what we might characterize as another rupture because both her self-identification as belonging in Turin was denied by the surrounding world, and the parts of her identity that were Oromo, Ethiopian, and the histories of Italy's relationships with Africa were forced into hiding and effaced by her Piedmontese, Italian identity (Ponzanesi 2004).

Maria represents a particular variant on the experience of people who are part of African Diasporic belonging in Italy. She is part of a broad group of first generation Africans who have lived in Italy for twenty to forty years and experience place in Italy as integrally connected with Africa. Maria is from a former Italian colony, while many others living in Italy today spent their youths in diverse parts of Africa colonized by other European nations. They share diverse yet overlapping African cultural histories and common histories of colonization and racialization that unite them across the multiple spaces and places of the Diaspora.

As Stuart Hall argued, the identities of subjects of African descent are always in the process of being produced as part of struggles over representation and belonging in relation to exclusionary national and racialized frameworks that have sought to erase their histories and participation in European Modernity. Hall's observations suggest that while united by shared experiences of powerlessness and the pursuit of freedom and inclusion, highly diverse members of the African or Black Diaspora always also speak from somewhere, from material and discursive positions and places (Hall 2003). Maria Abbebu Viarengo struggles to be recognized in Turin as Italian and Oromo in a context that links her transnationally with Africa and other spaces of the Diaspora, but she also very importantly awakens each morning and falls asleep in Turin, and the truth of her experience coincides with where it takes place.

As Allan Pred argued, identities and places are made through lived geographies and bodily engagements in particular locally situated practices (Pred 1990, 2000). And in Turin, where the number of officially registered immigrants has grown from 41,665 in 2001 to 129,767 in 2010, and where Africans constitute some two-thirds of non-European immigrants, place and Black life worlds are indeed being irreversibly remade. The Eurocentric and caucacentric frames of Northern Italian citizens and political figures of which Pugliese writes belie a growing heteroglossia (in this sense, contestatory practices) and polyculturality.

During the past two decades I have listened to and observed people of African origin negotiating, contesting, and contributing to the transformation of Turin.[6] The initial period was marked by dramatic precarity when some of the most common problems included their being in highly vulnerable positions without residence papers, being rejected time and again for jobs they were qualified to do, and paying exorbitant rents for substandard housing. During later visits I sometimes caught them breathing sighs of relief, for instance as they or members of their families found work after having been unemployed for many months, their cooperatives were awarded grants from the municipal, regional governments or the European Union for various work and intercultural projects, their residency permits were renewed, or they had managed to find a landlord to rent them a reasonable apartment. At other junctures I found them upset, anxious, frustrated, and talking about how their family members were dying in African conflicts while the Italian and other European governments did nothing to help, they'd lost a job or hadn't been paid by an employer, weren't making enough money to pay their rent, were experiencing *and* being blamed for crime, were losing jobs to competition from Eastern Europeans, or they were not being heard by anyone with authority in the Italian government, trade unions, or political parties. But I have to say that until the summer of 2010 I had never heard from my African and Italian informants such a converging and encompassing sense of despair and desperation. The *crisi* or crises of unemployment, precarity of work, and vulnerability to job loss, rising costs and lower salaries, high taxes, and cutbacks to or erasure of government supports were constant refrains among my Italian informants. Almost all of my African informants were either unemployed or working part time with temporary and low paying contracts, usually in the informal economic sector. Some talked about leaving Turin.

These stories were also expressed in the ways that people in Turin inhabited and experienced place, in what Allan Pred referred to as the "situated practices" of everyday life that intersect with what I believe are some very dramatic transformations in Turin's political culture (Pred 1990, 2000). Labor historian, Francesco Ciafaloni described what was happening in Turin as "I think the worst situation in two hundred and fifty years," typified by the *rovesciamento* or capsizing of the partnership of trade unions and government that had worked to represent workers and protect them from exploitation. By 2010, most of the trade union leadership had become professionalized, following middle-class habits and ways of life, modeling themselves after managers of large firms or heads of offices in public administration and using their positions as stepping stones for positions of greater authority, for instance in politics (Ciafaloni 2011) These leaders had bargained away almost fifty years of labor gains and agreements. Worker traditions were so degraded and labor so debased that there was little if any difference by 2010 between the working conditions for those with trade union representation and those working in *Lavoro Nero* or the informal economy where the most egregious forms of exploitation are well documented (Ciafaloni 2011). And perhaps the worst part of all of this, according to many of my Italian informants, was the loss of culture, which as one complained bitterly, "Once you kill a culture, you can't revive it." There was an overwhelming sense that the world had forever changed, but not for the better. Vanishing were the shared desires for equality, trust in leadership, and general regard and responsibility for each other, including those who owned little or nothing. Perhaps most disconcerting was the fading away of collective consciousness, political and social participation, and the rise of political apathy, especially among youth who either did not vote or supported political parties that promoted highly localist and binary ideologies in defense only of the rights of those who appeared to be Italian citizens, and against "foreigners."

Turin has long had a localist culture based on closely knit social and political networks along with a global vision of itself not only as part of a broader Europe but of the world of workers. That the Northern League recently won the regional elections in Piedmont is therefore somewhat of a paradox. It is a party with a divisive, tightly communitarian, and anti-immigrant ideology promoting images of a closed territory under threat of invasion and pollution by people that follow "inferior" ethnocultural beliefs and practices.[7] The Italian Communist party subscribed to an inclusive ideology that incorporated many Catholics and internal migrants from agricultural zones in the South and Veneto. Gramsci, founder of the party, was from Sardinia. An industrial city, home of the Fiat automobile company, and one of the principal engines of Italian economic expansion and also of the Royal House of Savoy, the city was until recently both provincial and expansive. And on the surface of it, this expansive, global sense of itself has been nurtured over the past two decades as municipal and regional governments have embraced economic and cultural union with Europe and supported the construction of several multicultural sites such as the Alma Terra, the Gate, the Centro Interculturale and the planned construction of the second mosque in Italy (the other is in Rome).

Officials have promoted an image of Turin as a cosmopolitan city, and on the outside it does appear this way more than it did in the past. Investments in urban renewal in preparation for the 2006 Winter Olympics improved many of the roadways, lending to the city's more urban feeling with amplified traffic and more people driving Fiats and other automobiles manufactured in Europe than the noisy *motos* that had only recently rivaled cars for domination. One of the foremost symbols of Turin's transformation from a predominantly industrial to a city of research, services, and tourism was the conversion of the old Fiat Lingotto plant into a massive shopping complex with a grocery, movie theater, and hotel. In recent years this site has picked up considerably in popularity with the addition of Turin's Eataly grocery store, cooking school, and restaurant with a series of kitchens specializing in single course meals, all featuring locally produced Slow Food products.[8] This has become, along with the shopping complex, a favorite site for dinner among young, fitness, and health conscious professionals who don't have time to cook, yet still have very well trained palates and high standards of consumption and are now willing to frequent a restaurant that in spite of its claims to being part of the Slow Food movement might be characterized as serving impersonal, albeit healthier and authentically Italian fast food. In late 2010 an Eataly site opened in Manhattan near the historic Flatiron Building on Twenty-Third Street and it's even more popular than the original Turin location, attracting millions of New Yorkers and tourists for a rather expensive taste of Italian cuisine. Turin has also recently exported a Gelato site, Grom, which like Eataly promises consumers healthy, Slow Food, rooted in the cultural and territorial traditions of Piedmontese gastronomy. In July 2007, Fiat relaunched in Turin with great ceremonial display along the River Po and culminating in the grand Piazza San Carlo its iconic automobile, the "500" or "Cinquecento." The Cinquecento was released in the United States in 2011, promoted by the international pop star, Jennifer Lopez. The expansion of Eataly, Grom, and the Cinquecento seem to provide evidence that Turinese are becoming more globally minded and open to cultural differences, but these developments may instead point more strongly to the emergence and exportation of an ethnoregionalist culinary identity and consumerist culture.[9]

Another noteworthy development is that every warm night of the week until early in the morning, except for Sunday, bars with tables covering sidewalks and in piazzas are packed with young Italians. The Italian press refers to these youth soirees as "La Movida," actually a Spanish term for the end of the Black Satanic Mills of industry and the culture of tourism and consumerism. Yet as much as it is tempting to characterize this in uplifting terms as evidence of globalization and expanded wealth, many of these consuming youth are unemployed. Like the Eataly phenomenon, this spectacle of contented consumerism and sociality hides the ugly underbelly of growing poverty, unemployment, poor working conditions, very low birth rates, intolerance, and anti-Islamic, anti-Black racism hidden from the nonanalyst. Like much of Northern Italy, Turin of Piedmont is struggling to contain social transformation within the logic of its own inwardly directed and spatially inscribed notions of ontologically pure, traditional, and authentic ways of being.

As Italy seeks to grapple with its new identity as part of the European Union and as a country of immigration, some effort has been made by local governments and NGOs to promote acceptance of cultural differences. But in general the country has relapsed into localism and nationalism, while multiculturalism has been countered by racism (Di Maio 2009). As the International Labour Organization (ILO) has suggested, in the past two decades in Italy there has been a sort of involution in terms of antiracism and egalitarian norms (ILO 2010). The Italian zeitgeist has changed, and a significant portion of the population rejects antiracist norms. Populist rhetoric, often based on old prejudices and stereotypes, has returned to characterize public debates. Many no longer believe they need to be tolerant of or open to people who appear different from mainstream Italians (Volpato et al. 2010). These attitudes are promoted by politicians currently in power, as demonstrated in remarks made by the Italian Foreign Minister and member of the European Parliament, Mario Borghezio, who following the July 2011 tragedies in Norway said that the antimulticultural positions of Breivik, the perpetrator of the mass murders, "Could certainly be agreed with," and that the Oslo killings were "The fault of multiracial society," which he described as "disgusting" (*New York Times* July 28, 2011).[10] Borghezio's Northern League (la Lega) promotes the idea of a pure and culturally homogenous territory under attack by ethnic and cultural pluralism.

As Tim Creswell has suggested, in the creation of place the definition of what lies "outside" plays a critical role in defining what is "inside" (Creswell 2004). The Lega, which has achieved growing influence, redefines Northern Italy as a culturally and territorially distinct space where out of place foreigners are destroying local Italian identity. People from Northern and Sub-Saharan Africa in particular are perceived as belonging elsewhere, in the culturally and geographically separate and backward territories of their origins, "South of the South" (Huyseeune 2006). The Lega sees the northern River Po basin of an imagined Padania as belonging to a Celtic-Germanic culture and European Italy as opposed to the Greek-Latin culture of African Italy; that is, the Mezzogiorno and beyond (Cachafeiro 2002). The party has responded to transformations in the Italian economy by self-consciously inventing a newly imagined community and manipulating territorial imagery to create a sense of cultural and economic distinctiveness, reifying its claims with definite borders. This discourse of ethnic absolutism has gained increasing traction in replacing the Left/Right and class oppositions that dominated Italian politics until the early 1990s with a strong sense of Insider or "Us" identity (Agnew and Brusa 1999). The Lega gained strength in the early 1990s in the wake of the political collapse of the parties that had for decades been seen to defend industrial workers, the erosion of racialized communitarian ways of life, and the tertiarization of the economy as against what was seen as the corruption of the state and its Southern Italian public sector representatives. But the party also endorses and promotes widespread prejudices against "colored immigrants" (Cento Bull 1996, 179). Their exclusivist discourse is currently aimed particularly toward "Arabs" and those with darker skin whom Umberto Bossi, leader of the Lega depicts as the least assimilable among foreigners or those perceived as the most culturally and ethnically distant from the host population (Cento Bull 1996).[11]

Political representations of a unified Italian identity (in this case Northern Italian) and the cultural borders between Italy and Africa have been widely interpreted by scholars as fabricated, contradictory, and fleeting. But the Lega's electoral triumphs and growing influence on political discourse and culture are hard to dispute. Moreover, the exclusionary discourses and images of Africans and Arabs used to reinvent Italian identities currently circulating in the media did not appear out of an historical vacuum. As part of the fascist regime's campaign to create national unity, it delegitimized Africans and Jews, introducing Italians to anti-Semitism and recirculating old narratives that European culture had used for centuries to dehumanize Africans. And today, Lega narratives and posters bear a striking resemblance to those that circulated during the fascist regime. The targets have changed; the strategies have remained the same (Volpato et al. 2010). Thus, many Italians today respond to the growing presence of Africans and other migrants through the optics of old ideas. Indeed, the fact that there has been an ongoing effort to suppress from Italian collective memory and consciousness any negative features of the colonial experience and especially the crimes perpetrated in the African colonies explains in part the current redirection of old ideas and attitudes toward immigrants.

Italian colonial amnesia and the myth that Italian colonialism was benign are deeply embedded in popular consciousness in spite of a recent flourish of critical historiography.[12] There is widespread resistance to acknowledging and even wishing to know about Italy's colonial past, so it remains hidden in the shadows where it guides current ideas and practices (Labanca 2005). The legacy of Italian colonialism includes some atrocious acts of containment and extermination as well as racial segregation and preoccupation with hierarchy and differentiation between Italians and colonial subjects. Moreover, as Italy expanded into Africa it projected an image of a distinct national identity in opposition to Black people, marked as other (Ponzanesi 2004). Such patterns of hierarchy and distinction do more than linger in the Italian collective unconscious; they permeate current perceptions and practices and are reinforced through a variety of legislative and institutional mechanisms. One Lega official recently proposed washing down the buses that "Blacks" had ridden and creating segregated compartments. According to my informants as well as those of Jacqueline Andall, Italians are most hostile to people with dark skin and perceived to be from Africa (including Egypt) whom they perceive as belonging to "unacceptable" immigrant groups (Andall 2005b).

The Lega's expanding influence on and resonance with popular sentiment regarding the exclusive place of Northern Italy in modern racial hierarchies seems to now permeate quotidian practices in Turin. Over the past decade, there has been a gradual removal of identifiable foreigners from central locations to the shadows of common spaces. In the 1990s the city appeared to have been becoming culturally diverse, as one would frequently travel or shop next to people of color, some culturally identifiable because dressed in colorful flowing or white robes or African print shirts and dresses and caps or hair coverings. Once highly visible in the city and particularly in the residential areas around the Porta Nuovo train station, shops in the San Salvario neighborhood, on the streets in the retail arcades along Via Po, and in the Sunday "balon" or multiethnic market, people of African descent are now seen much less frequently in public places. They are there, but less visibly in their flats and workplaces or the "black spaces" of occupied buildings, detention centers, and homeless shelters. Informants speak of the heightened and frequently chilly reception they often experience while going through everyday activities.

Place politics can be exclusionary and reactionary, and groups such as the Northern League define themselves with a monolithic, territorial sense of belonging as against outsiders (Keith and Pile 1993; Creswell 2004; Adams, Hoelscher, and Till 2001; Till 2001). Confirming long-standing Northern anxieties about securing whiteness as against Southern Italians, Italo-Africans are positioned as permanent interlopers, unwanted visitors who can occupy only a temporary or provisional status as workers, not citizens with attendant privileges and rights. As Pugliese has argued, there is a fear in Northern Italy that "whites are at risk of being overthrown by people of colour," and there's a "paranoic sense of white people under siege and facing the possibility of extinction due to the increasing presence in the Italian peninsula of people of colour ..." (Pugliese 2008, 27). The Italian white spatial imaginary is articulated in the sentiment that if the piazzas, parks, markets, and streets are not swept clear of *extracommunitari* (especially people of color), the urban spaces and very social fabric of Italy will be polluted, rendered nonwhite, and lose its identity (and real or imagined privilege) as part of the European citadel. As Umberto Bossi, the Northern League's leader has argued explicitly, "'it is impossible to assimilate' these immigrants because the cultural differences are too great. The difference in skin colour is detrimental to social peace. Imagine if your street, your public square, was full of people of colour, you would feel no longer part of your own world" (quoted in Pugliese, 30).

However, as Doreen Massey suggested, from an analytical perspective places can be conceived as products of interconnecting flows and routes of people, ideas, and things (Massey 1993). And the transformation of Turin's public spaces as Italian-African-Arab sites should be seen as embodied instantiations of the transcolonial interweavings of Europe and Africa. Instead of conceiving of Turin, Italy, or Europe as a distinct, geographically bounded discursive place, I think it crucial to reimagine its cartography through the ontology of people in the African Diaspora with air, water, and virtual arteries to and from Africa in a single, hierarchical social configuration produced through the continuing legacies of colonialism, cultural exchange, capitalist expansion, and human movement. The life experiences of many people born in Africa and living in Italy are far from simply and singularly "African" any more than they are simply and only "Italian." For them, Italy and Africa constitute overlapping worlds. As Achille Mbembe has suggested, "African identities" are not monolithic, they are multiple, straddling several different cultural, local, and regional identities (Mbembe 2001). In Heideggerian terms, the Being-in-the-world of these African-Euros is what I call a polymorphic being, a Being-in-Polymorphic places (Heidegger 1962). This being in the world has to be grasped as simultaneously African and European. African-Italian multiple subject positions contest and displace the Lega's monocultural perspectives, suggesting different ways of belonging in the contemporary world.

Polymorphic Place and Being

In her pathbreaking ethnography of race, identity, and the French educational system, Tricia Keaton suggests that a second generation of African Muslim high school students are perceived and spatially marginalized in France as Other, even though the French state doesn't officially recognize racial and ethnic minorities. According to an absolutist and color-blind political philosophy and state policy the French educational system equalizes by sublimating all differences to "common cultural" norms. Nevertheless, teenagers from the Maghreb and West Africa who live in urban projects located on the urban peripheries, are treated as less than fully "French." Socialized in French public schools, the young women practice and inhabit a French cultural habitus or learned dispositions and taken for granted practices, and when in public spaces are forced to conceal the portions of themselves that participate in the cultural and religious habitus of their parents. Their subjectivity is shaped by a sense of not being recognized as truly French along with identification with the African and Arab worlds that are perceived in France as alien, Other, and dangerous. Even though they are perceived as outsiders, these young women challenge the dominant discourses of belonging by self-classifying as "French" and with hyphenated Afro-French or Arab-French identities. These acts are part of a process in which these young Black women insist they belong in France by positioning themselves as part of overlapping, polymorphic cultural worlds. Keaton suggests that material practices contradict myths of national (racial) identity and cultural boundaries:

The world, including France, belongs to no single people—despite popular perception to the contrary—and the cry of *je suis français (e)*, *'c'est mon pays* now opens the gates of fortress France to its children of various African (and Asian) origins; opens the doors, that is, to these "being perceived." (88–89)

First generation Italo-Africans tend to express some resentment in relation to taken for granted assumptions that they couldn't possibly be Italian, and they negotiate white spatial imaginaries in their quotidian practices. Saba, one of my informants of Somali origin who works as a cultural mediator at an interethnic association for immigrant women, jokingly recounts her interchanges with Italian women who phone her office asking for immigrant domestic workers and qualify their requests with comments like, "But, Signora, I don't really want to have a 'Black' woman, Not that I'm racist or anything." The potential clients address Saba formally and assume she's Italian because of her impeccable command of the language (see Merrill 2006). In one instance Saba asks an Italian client to come to the office, and she describes with enormous satisfaction the client's embarrassment upon seeing that Saba is herself a Black woman. Other Italo-Africans (the majority) who speak Italian with an accent not identifiable as internal to the peninsula also experience offensive slights on a daily basis. Many seek to take these interactions in relative stride by developing a Teflon skin and focusing on the Italians and other Italo-Africans or more recently arrived African who are friendly and appear accepting of their presence.

With less self-consciousness than the subjects of Keaton's ethnography, these Italo-Africans instantiate their belonging culturally and aesthetically through for example their knowledge of and adoption of local cultural manners, customs, and tastes as well as the incorporation in daily social spaces of a variety of African clothing and hair styles, foodstuffs, musical instruments and music, art work, books, religious practices, and forms of sociality that are not as dissimilar from Italian forms of sociality as is commonly supposed. In addition, and perhaps of most significance politically in a context in which a conscious and participatory cultural politics influenced by workerism is being diluted by neoliberal and technocratic philosophies and policies, Italo-Africans and other immigrant populations are vital social actors in the rearticulation of a disappearing civic consciousness. In collaboration with a variety of local activist and social advocacy organizations including the trade unions, Casa della Donna, Catholic associations, and youth social centers these people not born on Italian soil are revitalizing the grassroots political climate (Ciafaloni 2011).

As a place, Turin is being made by embodied practices, and biographical formation is interwoven with the becoming of this place (Pred 2000).

Among the most strikingly visible features of Turin's transformation are the La Movida or youth soirees that have become standard sites of nightly youth gatherings at bar-restaurants whose tables blanket sidewalks and piazzas. Businesses compete for customers with high quality appetizers, service, and music. In a neighborhood with a high concentration of North Africans, one restaurant-bar in a gentrified zone off one of the most exclusive shopping areas in Turin is particularly well regarded and popular. Until at least 2 a.m. each night customers hang about to nibble, drink, and chat. The enterprise regularly hires young women from other parts of Europe, but for years the owner has had a man from Dakar in his employment. His contribution to the smooth functioning of this restaurant-bar and the manager's reliance on his expertise is an example of the pivotal yet frequently concealed role played by immigrants in contemporary Italy. In this instance, there is a startling contrast between the polymorphic life world of the Italo-African and the burgeoning consumerist night life that dramatically signals Turin's transformation.

I met Malik, who is originally from Senegal in 1990, shortly after he arrived in Turin. He speaks Italian quite fluently, moving easily between that language, French, and Wolof. He has at least one Italian friend with whom he worked at the Fiat firm. A native Wolof speaker who attended schools where the instruction was in French, he couldn't find gainful employment in Senegal and moved initially to France where he found himself under so much scrutiny as an "illegal" without hope of regularization that he decided to seek a livelihood in Turin. He arrived at a moment of ferment when the first real immigration legislation was established (The Martelli Law).[13] Early on, Malik secured limited term contract work cleaning machine components for a Fiat firm. When the contracts expired, he worked with his compatriots as an itinerant trader for which he traveled throughout the country and to France or Switzerland. Eventually accorded a longer-term contract with the Fiat firm he worked extended hours including Sundays, but joined a trade union and received wages according to standard union rates for the job he performed.

As the restructuring of Fiat and its subsidiaries and contractors in Turin has held pace with global industrial patterns and moved many of its manufacturing firms to rural areas and parts of the less economically developed world, including Eastern Europe, Malik worked less regularly and assumed a second position at the popular bar-restaurant as a busboy and handyman. After many years Fiat closed its local shop, and he lost his job. As industrial work has increasingly vanished or become unstable, consumer and professional service positions have expanded and Malik was fortunate to be working for a bar-restaurant thriving during the economic downturn. He works in the kitchen where customers don't see him and yet appears crucial to the success of the business, fiercely relied upon by the owner who phones him at all hours of the night.

Malik was also fortunate to have acquired subsidized housing via the municipal government. He lives in a tiny one bedroom flat on the top floor of a building that he has at various times shared with as many as five compatriots, sisters, and their spouses. His apartment is located off a cobble-stoned street and above several upscale bar-restaurants. For the past twenty years his wife and children have remained in Senegal. He sends most of his earnings to support them and his mother. As the eldest surviving son, he has been responsible for the family since the death of his father. His wife and mother have also earned income through trade, but are increasingly dependent on Malik to cover the rising costs of living in Dakar.

Malik's two younger sisters and maternal aunt also live in Turin. His aunt arrived with him in 1989 and initially lived with him in a flat with other Senegalese men for whom she did most of the cooking. She currently lives alone in a tiny flat paid for by her husband who spends most of his time traveling for work or in Senegal. Malik has a brother in Southern Italy married to an Italian woman and they recently had a child. His sisters speak Italian fluently. Both sisters have moved in and out of apartments, some subsidized and some not. One sister, Fatima, lost her home because it was designated as a space for a family with children and although she has tried for many years, her face scarred from fertility medications, she has never been able to conceive. There is a long list of families in need of subsidized housing in Turin, so the municipal government took the one bedroom flat and sent Fatima and her spouse packing. The couple has moved in and out of stable employment for over twenty years.

The other sister in Turin, Ama, earned a university degree in information technology and formerly held a job working for a firm that made resin for yachts. Shortly after the trade unions organized the majority female and immigrant employees to strike against toxic working conditions, the company moved out of the country. She told me that her advanced degree meant nothing in Italy because she was "solo una colonizzata" (only a colonized). Fatima, once opened a phone calling/Western Union site where she feared for her safety in a neighborhood with growing crime rates and struggled to keep it afloat during the economic downturn but was unable to keep up with rent payments. She has since traveled for trade in African clothing, handbags, and other items while searching for waged employment.

In the summer of 2010 Fatima was in deep despair about conditions in Turin and the virtual impossibility of an African over thirty-five finding work, particularly when up against competition from Eastern Europeans who for a number of reasons were preferred. She had finally been offered a job for a few weeks paying well under union standards watching an eighty-two-year-old woman, the mother-in-law of a Senegalese acquaintance married to a wealthy Italian. The family was going on vacation and the grandmother didn't want to stay alone. Fatima's husband had been unemployed for a very long time but had just found temporary and part-time low paying work as a security guard for a Chinese operated gambling casino in Turin. Fatima worried about his safety walking back from work late at night as public transportation was unavailable.

When we first began talking with this Senegalese family over twenty years ago we communicated in French and they were struggling to navigate the local social and political landscape with the help of mediators with knowledge and connections to representative organizations in the local government, church, and trade unions. After an initial period of uncertainty when they struggled for basic housing, residence documents, and health care, they became more settled in Turin, making connections with Italian advocates and Senegalese in leadership positions with the trade unions or associations. They learned to follow national and local political developments in Italy and in Senegal, and to identify local political leaders whom they pass on the street. Their cooking now combines elements of Senegalese and Italian cuisine, although they are able to obtain many of the ingredients they use for Senegalese cooking from a local Chinese owned grocery. They follow Italian soap operas, American television shows dubbed in French or Italian, and Senegalese sports competitions and music videos in French or Wolof. The Présence Africaine is of course very strong for these members of the new African Diaspora who lived in Senegal for some twenty years and maintain continual exchanges with their countries of origin via television, telephone, networks with other Senegalese in Europe, and deliveries via family and compatriots. Yet during the past several years coolness and even hostility toward the visibly non-Italian and non-European sanctioned by the nativist rhetoric of the Lega and white spatial imaginary now generated throughout the country has become acceptable practice. In this context, they don't really choose to distance themselves from Italian society. When asked about their national identities, they have for some time readily self-identified as both "Italian" and "Senegalese." Malik had already defined himself in part as European prior to his arrival in Italy, having been educated in French language, history, and culture and from a country where the long durée of French colonialism permeates many domains of quotidian life. Yet today, when they walk out the door of their apartment and through Italian streets, piazzas, and markets, and use public transportation, they frequently experience microaggressions (Merrill 2004). They are often glared at, especially when wearing African clothing. In these racialized, Italianized spaces where there is tremendous anxiety about the loss of a distinctive cultural identity, difference is not allowed. Sadly, these Senegalese have turned increasingly inward, focusing on Muslim religious rituals and speaking regularly of their wish to return to Senegal where life is so much better than in Italy because people treat them with respect and hospitality. They focus even more today than in the past on gaining status via Senegalese networks.

Conclusions

Italy is widely represented by Europeans as the birthplace of Western Civilization, the epicenter from which intellectual, artistic, political, and economic leadership flourished and expanded throughout Africa, the Atlantic World, and eventually all over the globe. Every year over 43 million people visit the country to discover a little of their own histories instantiated in architectural and artistic achievements and to experience a sense of unity with humanity through Italian cooking and the warm and friendly people whom they expect will welcome them.[14] These images and expectations were as salient among a first generation of transcolonial Africans when they first arrived in Italy as they are to the continuing flow of visitors who claim diverse European descent. All identify in varying measure with an Italy of creativity, achievement, and human warmth. And arriving on national soil most visitors discover this, in various degrees. However, visitors who remain in the country permanently and do not demonstrate biological or hereditary roots are far less warmly welcomed than those without them[15] They are "overdetermined from without" (Fanon 1967), or perceived via their physical appearance, speech, and association with the Italian South or Africa, and they may be treated with suspicion and as out of place, kept at a social distance, and quite possibly ruthlessly exploited in the labor market.

Over the past two decades, the refashioning of racial hierarchies have effectively repositioned racialized subjects so that the South is no longer the absolute Other to the North that Africa has come to signify. The dominant images for instance of boatloads of nameless people landing on Lampedusa, an island off the coast of Sicily proliferate the idea of Africa as the cradle of unwanted and illegal immigration. These and other dominant tropes have worked as images of mass distraction (see Pred 2006), diverting attention from the growing militarization of the Italian borders and urban spaces, and the ongoing weakening of worker rights (Merrill 2011). The climate of insecurity and uncertainty that foments anxiety about newcomers blamed for the country's social ills and the emergence of a zeitgeist that rejects the antiracist norms established after fascism doesn't make it easy for people like Maria, Malik, Fatima, Amu, Saba, and many others to express openly the multiple dimensions of their identities, their polymorphic being as participants in an ongoing transcolonial histories. The binary narratives that divide Italy from Africa don't even begin to describe the complexity of Black life worlds, situated practices and self-understandings.

Europe's frayed narrative of itself as the closed space of phenotypical ethnic and cultural whiteness is being protested and transformed. In Italy itself there have been numerous demonstrations over the past two years demanding social and legal recognition for Africans and other immigrants (Merrill 2006). The assassination in December 2011 of two Senegalese street vendors and the wounding of two others in Florence by a member of the neofascist social center, Casa Pound, triggered a national outcry as Senegalese leaders called for mass antiracist protests all over the country. A flyer distributed by the Senegalese Association in Pavia in the northern region of Lombardy, called for "Unity against racism" and suggested that "The murder is the result of prejudice and racial hatred cultivated by many organizations, not only Casa Pound, but diffused and nourished also by the newspapers and television." And in a statement quoted in the national newspaper, *La Repubblica*, a migrant leader in Bologna, Sene Basir, stated, "We feel Italian and instead we're called illegals."[16] These are expressions of Black subjectivities, forms of experience and knowledge about who is or ought to be classified as a legitimate "insider" with the attendant rights and privileges.

In spite of drastic measures that include contracting with the Libyan coast guard to patrol the Southern coasts or erecting more detention centers both on and off-shore, Italy has over the past two decades been irrevocably transformed into a country of immigration. Taking demographic trends as just one indication, it's evident that the nation is rapidly becoming more ethnically diverse. This country that until at least the late 1980s was solely a sender of Italian migrants who now comprise a vast Italian Diaspora, and not a receiver of immigrants is ever more heterogeneous, and its future includes Italo-Africans and their children.

Acknowledgments

I would like to thank France Winddance Twine and Bradley Gardener for their incisive and insightful comments and suggestions on earlier versions of this chapter.

Notes

1. See Michelle Comelli (2011).
2. The would-be immigrants and refugees seeking entry to Europe via the Southern Mediterranean borders hail from Sub-Saharan, East, North Africa, the Middle East, and South Asia.
3. "Italy's Culture of Racism Exposed By Fans' Abuse of Black Football Star," *The Observer*, December 12, 2009.
4. See the pathbreaking work of Angelo Del Boca (e.g., 2002, 2005).
5. See McIntyre and Nast (2011).
6. My research in Turin began in 1990 when the first wave of the political battles over immigration crested. I have regularly returned to Turin, every two or three years to conduct field research.
7. The 2010 elections saw a surge in support of the anti-immigrant right. Thirteen percent of the national vote went to the Northern League. Bossi's party won governorship of Piedmont and Veneto, and expanded outside its Po valley homeland into "red" Emiglio Romagno winning 14 percent of the vote. League policies include turning back would-be immigrants at sea (which is a violation of the Geneva Convention), and setting up centers for identification and expulsion—policies that have already been implemented.
8. Turin is the birthplace of Eataly, founded by Oscar Farinetti and the Slow Food movement which is a consultant for Eataly.
9. See the outstanding undergraduate honors thesis by Luke McKinley, "Yes to Polenta, No to Couscous!: Constructed Identities and Contested Boundaries Between Local and Global in Northern Italy's Gastronomic Landscape," Henry M. Jackson School of International Studies, University of Washington, 2010.
10. Another telling example comes from the former Italian Prime Minister himself. When Silvio Berlusconi remarked that Barack Obama was "Young, handsome and even has a good tan" the conventional wisdom in Italy seemed to be that Berlusconi was just being Berlusconi. But as Jeff Israely suggested,"In many ways, mainstream Italian society is several generations behind the rest of the West when it comes to race. In supposedly polite company, one can still hear the word, Negro (pronounced neh-grow) which essentially translates to the N word." He added that Northern Italians joke that dark-skinned Southerners are "Moroccans" (*Time World,* Oct. 1, 2002).
11. The Northern League is a regionalist party that created an imaginary of its own pseudo Northern Italian culture based on differences from an underdeveloped Southern Italy, symbol of a corrupt and parasitic state. Yet discourses of race and racialized science in Italy were formulated around distinctions between Northern and Southern Italians, the latter allegedly born with atavistic "primitive" traits found among African "savages." Cesare Lombroso wrote *L'Uomo delinquente* in Turin, postulating that Southern Italians and Africans were genetically predisposed to criminality. One of Umberto Bossi's slogans is, "Africa begins at Rome" (Agnew and Brusa 1999; Huysseune 2006; Giordano 2000; Cento-Bull 1996; Saint-Blancat and Schmidt di Friedberg 2005).
12. A growing literature grapples with the myths and realities of Italian colonialism: Del Boca (1984, 1988); Labanca (2000); in English: Ben-Ghiat and Fuller (2005), Palumbo (2003).
13. The political party structure (PCI or Italian Communist Party, the DC or Christian Democrats, and the Socialists) in power since World War II had not yet collapsed. Bossi's Lega Nord and Fini's neofascist party (MSI or Italian Social Movement currently called the People of Freedom Party) had very little influence, and the trade unions (still connected with political parties in Turin) held some legitimacy and authority.
14. These figures are from 2009, compiled by the World Tourism Organization (UNWTO).
15. Italian citizenship is awarded to people with maternal or paternal grandparents with Italian citizenship, and for others reviewed after living in the country for ten years. Refugees may apply after five years, but refugee status is seldom granted in Italy.

16. Simona Poli, "La Marcia dell'Italia antirazzista: In ventimilia a Firenze per ricordare Samb e Diop. Cortei da Milano a Napoli" [The Italian antiracist march in Florence to remember Samb and Diop: Marches from Milan to Naples]. *La Repubblica, Domenica* December 18, 2011, 13.

References

Adams, Paul C., Steven Hoelscher, and Karen E. Till, eds. 2001. *Textures of Place: Exploring Humanist Geographies.* Minneapolis: University of Minnesota Press.

Agnew, John A. 2002. *Place and Politics in Modern Italy.* Chicago: University of Chicago Press.

Agnew, John, and Carlo Brusa. 1999. "New Rules for National Identity? The Northern League and Political Identity in Contemporary Northern Italy." *National Identities* 1 (2): 117–133.

Andall, Jacqueline. 2005. "Immigration and the Legacy of Colonialism: The Eritrean Diaspora in Italy." In *Italian Colonialism: Legacy and Memory*, edited by Jacqueline Andall and Derek Duncan, 171-87. Bern Switzerland: Peter Lang.

—— and Derek Duncan, eds. 2005. *Italian Colonialism: Legacy and Memory.* Bern, Switzerland: Peter Lang.

——, eds. 2010. *National Belongings: Hybridity in Italian Colonial and Postcolonial Cultures.* Bern, Switzerland: Peter Lang.

Appadurai, Arjun.1990. "Disjuncture and Difference in the Global Cultural Economy." *Public Culture* 2 (2) 1–24.

Basch, Linda G., Nina Glick Schiller, and Cristina Szanton Blanc. 1994. *Nations Unbound: Transnational Projects, Postcolonial Predicaments, and Deterritorialized Nation States.* London: Routledge.

Ben-Ghiat, Ruth, and Mia Fuller. 2005. *Italian Colonialism.* New York: Palgrave Macmillan.

Bonifazi, Corrado F., Frank Heins, Salvatore Strozza, and Mattia Vitiello. 2009. "Italy: The Italian Transition from Emigration to Immigration." IDEA Working Papers. http://www.idea-a6fp.uw.edu.pl/pliki/WP5_Italy.pdf

Brown, Jacqueline Nassy. 2005. *Dropping Anchor, Setting Sail: Geographies of Race in Black Liverpool.* Princeton, NJ: Princeton University Press.

Cachafiero, Margarita Gomez-Reino. 2002. *Ethnicity and Nationalism in Italian Politics: Inventing The Padania: Lega Nord and the Northern Question.* Hampshire: Ashgate Press.

Carter, Donald. 1997. *States of Grace: Senegalese in Italy and the New European Immigration.* Minneapolis: University of Minnesota Press.

——. 2010. *Navigating the African Diaspora: The Anthropology of Invisibility.* Minneapolis: University of Minnesota Press.

——. Heather Merrill. 2007. "Bordering Humanism: Life and Death on the Margins of Europe." Geopolitics 12 (2) 248–64.

Ciafaloni, Francesco. 2011. *Destino della Classe Operaia.*[Fate of the working class]. Rome, Italy: Edizioni dell'asino.

Cento Bull, Anna. 1996. "Ethnicity, Racism and the Northern League." In *Italian Regionalism: History, Identity and Politics,* edited by Carl Levy. Oxford, UK: Berg Press.

Comelli Michelle. 2011. "Italy's Love Affair with the EU: Between Continuity and Change." (Working Paper No. 57). Rome, Italy: Istituto Affari Internazionale.

Contini, Dalit. 2011. "Immigrant Background Peer Effects in Italian Schools" (Working Paper No. 14). Department of Economics, University of Turin.

Creswell, Timothy. 2004. *Place: A Short Introduction.* Oxford, UK: Blackwell.

Del Boca, Angelo. 1984. *Gli Italiani in Africa orientale: Nostalgia delle colonie* [Italians in East Africa: Colonial nostalgia]. Roma-Bari: Laterza.

——. 1988. *L'Africa nella conscienza degli italiani Miti, memorie, errori, sconfitte* [The conscience of the Italians in Africa: Myths, memories, mistakes, failures]. Bari, Italy: Laterza.

————. 2005. *Italiani, brava gente?* [The Italians, a brave people?]. Vicenza, Italy: Neri Pozza.

Di Maio, Alessandra. 2009. "Black Italia: Contemporary Migrant Writers from Africa." In *Black Europe and the African Diaspora,* edited by Darlene Clark Hine, Tricia C. Keaton, and Stephen Small. Champagne-Urbana: University of Illinois Press.

Fanon, Frantz. 1967. *Black Skin, White Masks.* New York: Grove Press.

Gilmore, Ruth Wilson. 2002. "Fatal Couplings of Power and Difference: Notes on Racism and Geography." *Professional Geographer* 54 (1): 15–24.

Gilroy, Paul. 1991. *"There Ain't No Black in the Union Jack": The Cultural Politics of Race and Nation.* Chicago: University of Chicago Press.

Giordano, Benito. 2000. "Italian Regionalism or 'Padanian' Nationalism—The Political Project of the Lega Nord in Italian Politics." *Political Geography* 19: 445–71.

Goldberg, David Theo. 1993. *Racist Culture, Philosophy, and the Politics of Meaning.* Oxford, UK: Wiley Blackwell.

Guillamin, Colette. 1995. *Racism, Sexism, Power and Ideology.* New York: Routledge.

Gregory, Steven. 1998. *Black Corona: Race and the politics of place in an urban community.* Princeton, NJ: Princeton University Press.

Gupta, Akhil, and James Ferguson. 1992. "Beyond 'Culture': Space, Identity, and the Politics of Difference." *Cultural Anthropology* 7 (1) 6–23.

Hall, Stuart. 1991a. "The Local and the Global: Globalization and Ethnicity." In *Culture, Globalization and the World System* edited by Anthony D. King. London: Macmillan.

————. 1991b. "Old and New Identities, Old and New Ethnicities." In *Culture, Globalization and the World System,* edited by Anthony D. King. London: Macmillan.

Hall, Stuart. 2003. "Cultural Identity and Diaspora." In *Theorizing Diaspora,* edited by Jana Evans and Anita Mannur, 233–46. Oxford, UK: Blackwell.

Hanchard, Michael. 2006. *Party/Politics: Horizons in Black Political Thought.* New York: Oxford University Press.

Heidegger, Martin. (1962) 2008. *Being and Time.* New York: Harper Row Publishers.

Hesse, Barnor. 1993. "Black to Front and Black Again: Racialization through Contested Times and Spaces." In *Place and the Politics of Identity,* edited by Michael Keith and Steven Pile. London: Routledge.

Hine, Darlene Clarke, Tricia Danielle Keaton, and Steven Small, eds. 2009. *Black Europe and the African Diaspora.* Urbana: University of Illinois Press.

Huysseune, Michel. 2006. *Modernity and Secession: The Social Sciences and the Political Discourse of the Lega Nord in Italy.* New York: Berghahn Books.

International Labour Organization. 2010. *Report of the Committee of Experts on the Application of Conventions and Recommendations.* Geneva, Switzerland: Author.

ISTAT. n.d. http://www.demo.istat.it/index_e.html

Keaton, Tricia Danielle. 2006. *Muslim Girls and the Other France: Race, Identity Politics, and Social Exclusion.* Bloomington: Indiana University Press.

Keith, Michael, and Steven Pile, eds. 1993. *Place and the Politics of Identity.* London: Routledge.

Labanca, Nicola. 2000. *Storia dell'Italia colonial* [History of colonial Italy]. Milan, Italy: Fenice.

————. 2005. "History and Memory of Italian Colonialism Today." In *Italian Colonialism: Legacy and Memory,* edited by Jacqueline Andall and Derek Duncan. Bern, Switzerland: Peter Lang.

Malkki, Liisa. 1992. "National Geographic: The Rooting of Peoples and the Territorialization of National Identity among Scholars and Refugees." *Cultural Anthropology* 7 (1): 24–44.

Marable, Manning. 2008. "Introduction: Blackness Beyond Boundaries: Navigating the Political Economies of Global Inequality." In *Transnational Blackness: Navigating the Global Color Line.* New York: Palgrave Macmillan.

Massey, Doreen. 1993. "Power-Geometry and a Progressive Sense of Place." In *Mapping the Futures: Local Cultures, Global Change,* edited by John Bird, Barry Curtis, Tim Putnam, and Lisa Tickner, 59–69. London: Routledge.

Mbembe, Achille, 2001, "Ways of Seeing: Beyond the New Nativism. Introduction" *African Studies Review* 44 (2) 1–14.

McIntyre, Michael, and Heidi J. Nast. 2011. "Bio(necro)polis: Marx, Surplus Population and the Marxist Theory of Imperialism." *Antipode* 43 (5): 1465–1572.

Merrill, Heather. 2004. "Space Agents: Anti-Racist Feminism and the Politics of Scale." *Gender, Culture, and Space* 11 (2): 189–204.

———. 2006. *An Alliance of Women: Immigration and the Politics of Race.* Minneapolis: University of Minnesota Press.

———. 2011. "Immigration and Surplus Populations: Race and Deindustrialization in Northern Italy." *Antipode* 43 (3): 1542–72.

Miles. Robert. 1993. *Racism after "Race Relations."* London: Routledge.

Orton, Marie, and Graziella Parati. 2007. *Multicultural Literature in Contemporary Italy.* Madison, NJ: Farleigh Dickinson University Press.

Palumbo, Patricia, ed. 2003. *A Place in the Sun: Africa in Italian Colonial Culture from Post-Unification to the Present.* Berkeley: University of California Press.

Parati, Graziella, ed. 1999. *Mediterranean Crossroads: Migration Literature in Italy.* Madison, NJ: Farleigh Dickinson University Press.

Ponzanesi, Sandra. 2004. *Paradoxes of Postcolonial Culture: Contemporary Women Writers of the Indian and Afro-Italian Diaspora.* New York: State University of New York Press.

Pred, Allan. 1990. *Lost Words and Lost Worlds: Modernity and the Language of Everyday Life in Late Nineteenth Century Stockholm.* Cambridge, UK: Cambridge University Press.

———. 2000. *Even In Sweden: Racisms, Racialized Spaces, and the Popular Geographical Imagination.* Berkeley: University of California Press.

———. 2006. "Situated Ignorance: State Terrorism, Silences, W.M.D., Collective Amnesia, and the Manufacture of Fear." In *Violent Geographies: Fear, Terror, and Political Violence,* edited by Derek Gregory and Allan Pred. London: Routledge.

Pugliese, Joseph. 2008. "Whiteness and the Blackening of Italy: La Guerra cafona, Extracomunitari and Provisional Street Justice." *Journal of Multidisciplinary International Studies,* 5 (2).

Puwar, Nirmal. 2004. *Space Invaders: Race, Gender and Bodies Out of Place.* London: Berg.

Saint-Blancat, Chantal, and Ottavia Schmidt di Friedberg. 2005. "Why are Mosques a Problem? Local Politics and Fear of Islam in Northern Italy." *Journal of Ethnic and Migration Studies* 31 (6) 1083–1104.

Smith, Neil, and Cindi Katz. 1993. "Grounding Metaphor: Towards a Spatialized Politics." In *Place and the Politics of Identity,* edited by Michael Keith and Steve Pile. London: Routledge.

Stolcke, Verena. 1995. "Talking Culture: New Boundaries, New Rhetorics of Exclusion in Europe." *Current Anthropology* 36 (1) 1–24.

Taguieff, Pierre A. 1990. "The New Cultural Racism in France." *Telos* 83: 109–122.

Till, Karen. 2001. "Reimagining National Identity: 'Chapters of Life' at the German Historical Museum in Berlin." In *Textures of Place: Exploring Humanist Geographies,* edited by Paul C. Adams, Steven Hoelscher, and Karen Till. Minneapolis: University of Minnesota Press.

Thomas, Dominic, and Richard David. 2006. *Black France: Colonialism, Immigration, and Transnationalism: African Expressive Cultures.* Bloomington: Indiana University Press.

Volpato, Chiara, Federica Durante, Alessandro Gabbiadini, Luca Andrighetto L, and Silvia Mari. 2010. "Picturing the Other: Targets of Delegimization across Time." *International Journal of Conflict and Violence* 4 (92): 269–87.

Winant, Howard. 1994. *Racial Conditions: Political Theory Comparisons.* Minneapolis: University of Minnesota Press.

———. 2008. "The Modern World Racial System." In *Transnational Blackness: Navigating the Global Color Line,* edited by Manning Marable and Vanessa Agard-Jones. New York: Palgrave Macmillan.

CHAPTER 7

Human Blacklisting

The Global Apartheid of the EU's External Border Regime

HENK VAN HOUTUM

Opening

> And now what shall become of us without any barbarians?
> Those people were some kind of solution.
>
> —Konstantinos Petrou Kavafis (1904)

In 1992, in her beautiful essay on boundaries, Dagmar Reichert posed the following intriguing question: The limit, the frontier, the boundary, time-series of boundaries, or ditches, the void, or *differance*, they are all modifications of the line, the form of topological thinking. Can we escape this thinking in terms of spatial metaphors (Reichert 1992)? The spirit of openness and opening borders that Reichert was after has perhaps been grounded to some extent in the topological thinking inherent in the cross-border mobility policies of one of the significant global borderlands, a unity of countries that increasingly sees itself as a soft empire—the European Union. Yet, at the same time, the internal opening of the borders has led to the rise of new fears and new walls in its external peripheries as a manifestation of its increasingly divisionary view of countries. For a decade or so now, and especially after 9/11, the Zeitgeist of global freedom and opening borders—that special moment in Europe after 1989 in which a change in the wall-inspired logic that dominated Europe for so many decades was truly believed in—has become a ghost that haunts EU external border politics today. The desire to control and reclaim space, power, and national identity has found new populist political adherents and partisans. As a result, rather than focusing on maximal inclusion, cross-border mobility, and harmonious integration into the rapidly grown container of the EU that has dominated the debate in the EU over the past decades, the emphasis has now shifted towards a constitutive "management" of exclusion of the "Other" inhabitants of the world. Some speak of the three global wars that have become dominant—the war on drugs; the war on terror; and, increasingly dubiously intertwined with the latter, the war on "illegal" migration (see also Inda 2006). For some this renewed focus on (preemptive and often military) protection and territorial identity is an illustration that the world is not borderless. Rather, it consists of global borderlands (Duffield 2001; Rumford 2007, 2008) or "planetary frontier lands" (Bauman 2002a, 2002b) in which power, identity, and sovereignty are being disconnected from territorial nation-state politics yet are not becoming institutionalised in a new global territorial order. Hence, what we see is a constant border-work trying to separate the wanted from the unwanted, the barbarians from the civilised, and the global rich from the global poor in the territorial society. In so doing the EU increasingly is not only defining itself via its internal affairs, its ordering practices, but also by the production of new border rules and legislation towards its incoming migrants. The migration of the undocumented paradoxically, therefore, also induces and evokes a stronger political community and new bordering legislation of the EU, thereby reinforcing that which the migrants wish to escape or cross, fierce borders (see also Zapata-Barrero 2009). Obviously, these practices of geopolitical and biopolitical control—this carving up of territorial containers and purified "dreamlands" of identity—have a counterpart, the other face of the Janus border (van Houtum 2010): the generation of (a dreamland of) escape into far-reaching openness and freedom, into a world of global cosmopolitan development and global distributive justice (see also Rumford 2007, 2008). But it seems that this latter development is currently much less on the political agenda now. In so doing, the ontological multidimensionality, which is intrinsic to any border, is increasingly being deprived and depressed to make place for only the tightening and filtering dimension of a border. The border, which is more a necessary and unfixable continuum between openness and closure than it is a line, is being reinterpreted into a super position of lines of security and protection, often coinciding with an inward-looking reproduction and canonisation of its self-constructed history and culture (see also

Balibar 2004a, 2004b). The global course towards stronger protectionist and identity politics has gained considerable momentum again in today's global geopolitics (see also Bigo and Guild 2005). The desire to open the border, to seize the spirit of the fall of that Ur-border and the Berlin Wall and to escape topological thinking seems rather far removed from us.

So somewhat less than two decennia after Reichert's intriguing article, the quest that her imaginary questions embrace is still most inspiring; that is, the quest for the justification for and the way we draw borders in society and space. In this paper I will take up the quest to understand in more depth and detail how the EU is currently bordering itself by focusing on the current topological practices we endorse, manifest, and legitimise in the drawing of borders for people. More particularly, I will focus on the often tacit or implicit justification and modus operandi of our border regimes that should prevent, select, and prioritise the movement of certain people across borders in the world of today. In order to complement existing efforts that seek to understand the desires and fears expressed in the current moral choreography of the (future) external borders from a conceptual point of view, this article scrutinises the visions and long-term EU strategies with regard to the external border regime vis-à-vis the so-called unwanted migrants. To gain insight into these power geopolitics of the EU expressed through its external border regime, I direct my attention to the border ideology, the "borderology," the EU is developing. Next, I critically scrutinise the everyday institutional practices recently enforced at the external border proper. In particular, I will navigate my way through a new, explicitly moral landscape that has been built at the external borders of the EU that consists of waiting zones, camps, new fences, and new biometric methods of patrol. Hence, an EUscape with increasingly defensive external borders is being erected. Building on the theoretical insights that have been gained, uttered, and brought forward already on various elements of the external border of the EU, this article could be read as a theoretically inspired conceptual protest, a counternarrative against what I see as an off beam and increasingly mechanic external border choreography of the EU.

B/ordering and Othering

The act of bordering is critical to understanding the building or transformation of a specific sociospatial entity. To quote geographer Anssi Paasi: "through the institutionalisation process and the struggles inherent in it, the territorial units in question 'receive' their boundaries and their symbols which distinguish them from other regions" (1996, 33). The EU's external border regime and immigration policy towards the outer borders touch the heart of the EU as a macroborderland. When desiring to understand the importance of borders for a given entity, in this case the EU, it is not enough to study the line, the limit, the border itself; there is a need to also study the transformation process, the genealogy of that line: the bordering (e.g., van Houtum and Naerssen 2002; van Houtum, Kramsch, and Zierhofer 2005). A border should first and foremost be understood as a process, as a verb (van Houtum 2011). Analytically, three different dimensions can be seen to play a role in this process of border production acting in close cooperation and simultaneously, yet in different nuances and degrees for different contexts—bordering, ordering, and othering (van Houtum and Naerssen 2002). Together these dimensions of the border process can be seen as a generic lens through which the building or transformation of a specific sociospatial entity can be analysed. Obviously, one has to bear in mind that any schematic description of the multidimensional border-production processes can offer nothing more than an abstracted frame of mind that needs to be enriched and mutated for the specific historical and geographical context and contingency of a certain border production. What is more, the internalisation of and subjection to a certain border regime, through which the border regime gains or sustains its power, will be different over time, space, and people.

The first dimension of the border-production process, bordering, implies the continuous (search for the) legitimisation and justification of the location and demarcation of a border, which is seen as a manifestation of one's own claimed, distinct, and exclusive territory/identity/sovereignty. In doing so, the spatial containerisation and unification of the people, and hence implicitly the silencing of the internal differences, are reproduced (see also Sibley 1995). This is not a once-and-for-all event. Critical for border production is that all possible social and spatial dynamics that might occur are given meaning and a vision by looking through the eyes of the self-defined territory/identity/sovereignty.

In this production of meaning and vision the second dimension, ordering, is crucially important (cf. Schmitt's Ortung und Ordnung 1950). The process of making and remaking a sociospatial order, the ordering, implies that in its beginning the sociospatial container is emptied and purified from its past despotic codes and occupants and, to use the words of Deleuze and Guattari ([1980]2004), despotically recoded with the codes and people of the now owner. If not militarily, this is done symbolically through the production of belonging and nostalgia through the selective invention and narration of communality and tradition via common rituals, memories, and history. In doing so, the self-constructed sociospatial code and order is normalised, it becomes the norm against which exceptions and aberrations are defined. The process of normalisation involves such mechanisms as internalisation, subjection, and the taming of resistance through the use of, for example, language politics, education politics, and labour politics, which are all territorially defined and demarcated as the norm (e.g., Foucault 1975). Moreover, what further characterises this process of ordering is the statistical biopolitical registration and territorial surveillance of the population in terms of the birth, skills, ethnicity, age, health, fertility, productivity, and death of every body into the machinery of the Order (Deleuze and Guattari 2004; Foucault 2007; Salter 2006).

The third dimension of border production that I distinguish here is the making of borders via the making of others, othering. This implies the production of categorical difference between ours and theirs, here and there, and natives versus nonnatives, so important for the realist topological thinking still. It involves the now so often critically engaged and, in academic circles, so often deconstructed dichotomous and antagonising production of socioeconomic and sociocultural competition, for which thinkers like Jacques Derrida and Edward Said have become dominant and well-known sources of academic inspiration. The discrimination between what is imagined to be ours in terms of identity/territory/sovereignty, as many insightful academic studies on this have shown us, is often done through the use of geopolitics (the politicisation and discrimination of spatial differences) and chronopolitics (the politicisation and consequent discrimination of time differences), expressed by terms like *development, underdevelopment, lagging behind, speed, race, modernity, postmodernity,* and *a-modernity.* What is also critical in this process of othering, and of much significance to the understanding of the modes of border control of a certain sociospatial container, is the regime of access—the dominant beliefs or ideology by which a sociospatial order manifests itself in a certain configuration of the biopolitical, geopolitical, and chronopolitical regime of access at hand. The configuration of this regime in turn shapes how access to the order is sustained and hence how, through which border tactics, the other is stratified, immobilised, and dislocated at borderlines that are no longer, as has been argued by many scholars now, necessarily found at the territorial end or beginning of nation-states but can be found increasingly everywhere, such as in airports, public spaces, and traffic roads: the omnipresence of a diffused border (see Parker and Vaughan-Williams 2009).

B/ordering and Othering the EU

How then can the EU's current border regime be understood keeping the above generic approach on b/ordering and othering in mind? If we look at the entity of the EU then through this border lens, what is most significant perhaps is the rapid change of the bordering, ordering, and othering developments. After the opening of the internal borders of the EU, the political and policy attention shifted more and more, and swiftly so, to the protection of the external borders of the EU. Because of the new and heavy emphasis on the external borders, many argue that the EU is also changing how it is or should be perceived and understood. In this context, early commentators optimistically pointed to the many faces the external border of the EU had in terms of its distinct and noncongruent geopolitical, institutional/legal, transactional, and cultural spaces (Friis and Murphy 1999; Hudson 2000; Smith 1996). To wit, some have argued that the external borders of the EU are to be understood as "fuzzy" (Christiansen and Jorgensen 2000; Zielonka 2001) and that the EU as a bordered entity will resemble a "maze" or "sieve" (Brown 2002; Christiansen and Jorgensen 2000). Yet, over the last few years, and especially with various authors within the constructionist and postcolonial wings of the research front, the discourse has become dominant that the EU is increasingly constructing colonial-like lines or frontiers, boundaries of a self-perceived superior imperial power, often then seen as the soft imperial sister of the United States.

At the frontiers of the EU then, which are often defined as Europe and not the EU, these authors typically claim that the EU sees for itself a civilisational mission, often typified as othering, to Europeanise or at least downscale the "radicalisation" of perceived inferiors or others (the "Barbarians") in both the East and the South (Anderson and Armstrong 2007; Boedeltje 2007; Tunander 1997; Walters 2002, 2004; Zielonka 2001). For some, this latter neocolonial, empire style is most visible in one of the most striking extraterritorial development plans of the EU of the recent years; that is, the development of a New Neighbourhood and Partnership Instrument destined to implement the Commission's European Neighbourhood Policy as laid down in the Wider Europe Communication and the Strategy document on this European Neighbourhood Policy (ENP). The goal of the ENP is, according to the EU, to share the advantages of the 2004 enlargement of the EU by fostering stability, security, and prosperity among all parties. The Neighbourhood Policy is said to be developed to prevent new lines of division between the enlarged EU and its neighbours and to offer new possibilities to engage in the diverse activities of the EU by means of enlarged political, security, economical, and cultural cooperation (see also Emerson 2004). The EU Commission sees the border "management" as one of the core goals of the ENP:

> Border management is likely to be a priority in most Action Plans as it is only by working together that the EU and its neighbours

can manage common borders more efficiently in order to facilitate legitimate movements. The Action Plans should thus include
measures to improve the efficiency of border management, such as
support for the creation and training corps of professional non-mil-
itary border guards and measures to make travel documents more
secure. The goal should be to facilitate movement of persons, whilst
maintaining or improving a high level of security. (European Commission 2004, 16f; see also Apap and Tchorbadjiyska 2004)

For some, in contrast to nation-states and ideological blocs, adjoining
empires are imagined to have blurred and underenergised borders at the
frontiers in the periphery where their power "fades out" (Waever 1997;
Zielonka 2001). These peripheral "grey," intermediate, or transit zones
between empires such as Russia and the United States then would rub
against each other and would be the new potential zones of global conflict. The recent conflict in Georgia is often mentioned as a case in point.
Convincing as this may be, at the same time such euphemisms of fading
grey zones, transition zones, and neighbourhood policies fail to capture
the rather fierce and increasingly militaristic inclusionary–exclusionary
logic of the current external border regime of the EU that is also increasingly apparent. More than a crossing border policy, the ENP clearly is a
border policy—since when one defines their *neighbours*, one defines one's
own borders. It is a hegemonic *buffer zone geopolitics*, the installation of a
cordon sanitaire. For, although the neighbourhood policies may be a clear
sign of politics of good intentions, they are also an unambiguous form
of excluding some countries from the arbitrary and self-made category
"Europe" and from membership of the EU. So, to the world the EU shows a
Janus-face, one face of development aid and humanitarian assistance and
another of a security-obsessed economic and cultural comfort zone. And
both faces are related, especially in the ENP, for the aid to the neighbours
is quid pro quo. The EU is transparent in its aims; it promises neighbours
to develop and become more democratic and economically strong (mea-
sured by the EU with "European standards") in order to help protect the
EU from what is often defined as spill-over threats from imagined unstable
neighbouring countries, by which largely irregular immigration and terrorism is meant. EU values are "exported" in exchange for monetary assistance and the promise of the vague terminology of a "stake" in the internal
market. Increasingly, the imagined buffer states of the EU are also being
asked or ordered, again in exchange for development aid, to tighten their
border control for the sake of the EU. In addition, the EU is subsiding anti-
migration campaigns in the neighbouring countries. In other words, apart
from the erection of a tighter border control at the external borders of the

EU itself, the control is, as will be shown below, outsourced to its neighbours in what the EU calls a "new global approach to border management" and "global approach to migration." So the EU is not merely defending its borders; it is expanding its perimeter. This inclusionary–exclusionary mechanism—and thereby attack on the dignity of others beyond self-defined borders, so significant for the ontology of any b/ordering and othering process—has explicitly, via immigration and security control, and also implicitly, via neighbourhood policies, become an essential feature within the rebordering process of the EU. Most clearly perhaps, this can be testified by the increasingly machine-like bordering of certain categories of migrants to which I now turn.

The Border Machine

Apart from the interesting and rich debates on how the imperial external border of Europe should best be understood, there is a still marginal but growing academic debate on the degree of moral (in)justice of the increasingly fierce external border regime that coincides with the development of extraterritorial European civilisational politics. Over recent years, the EU has been deploying a rapidly increasing active global engagement with regard to the battle against irregular migration, terrorism, and the proliferation of weapons of mass destruction and the fulfilment of international law as well as the effort to prevent conflicts. The geopolitical objectives range from fighting transnational crime and terrorism to nourishing local cultural ties across the external border. Gradually, the EU's external border regime is transforming into a digital and selective border machine (see also Walters 2002, 2006). It seems that the neoliberal logic of maximum efficiency is also transferred to the logic and rationale of the border control, which is illustratively termed border management (see van Houtum and Boedeltje 2009). This border machine produces new products of border control all the time. Yet, this machine does not run by itself. Let me explain this further.

The Global Migrant Black List

At the front door of the EU a rather powerful and security-obsessed distinction between travellers is increasingly being constructed between the travellers who "belong to" the EU and those who do not. Illustrating this is the EU's common risk-analysis model, which was set up in order to achieve a common and integrated risk analysis on immigration issues. It is the word *risk* that is politically related to immigration which is perhaps the most crucial and worrying aspect in understanding the recent development of the EU's external border regime. With risk, the EU largely means practices that are defined as "illegal" (see also Samers 2004). For its border management, as the EU calls it, and to mitigate the "risks," the DG Justice and Home Affairs has released a whole range of proposals in the last few years addressing the development of a common policy on irregular immigration, human trafficking, and the security of external borders.

What is perhaps most illustrative in the makeup of this external difference-producing border regime in the world of today is that the EU has composed a so-called white Schengen list and a black Schengen list (European Council, Common List, Annex 1, Council Regulation 539/2001; European Council Regulation No 851/2005 of 2 June 2005 amending Regulation No 539/2001). This list includes citizens from countries that require a visa; that is, an individual permission for entrance during a given period of time and for certain purposes (see also Salter 2006). As such, in contrast to a passport, a visa is not issued by the sovereignty of destination, in this case the EU. For the EU a visa is, therefore, a way to grant (or deny) admission before leaving a country and a way to control when someone enters and leaves the EU. The "white" list represents the countries whose citizens do not need to apply for a visa for a visit or transit in Schengen countries. This list contains 60 countries of the world. The rest, the "black" list, consists of 135 states out of a total of 195 states in today's world whose inhabitants require a visa for entrance into EU-space.[1] Figure 7.1 gives a cartographic overview of the listing of visa-obliged countries by the EU. Of all possible geographical visions on the world, the EU thus inscribes an unambiguous divisionary borderline on the planet. It has made a division into black and white list countries, into countries whose inhabitants are in principle unwelcome (the black list) and whose inhabitants are welcome (the white list). It is a form of chronopolitics as it slows down, illegalises, or immobilises the mobility of a significant part of the world population and prioritises and mobilises the travelling speed of a select human segment. One suspects that the criteria used for a state to be put on the visa list relate to the perceived possibility of irregular residence after entering EU space, the perceived influence on public security, and the international relations existing between the EU and the third country in question (Guild 2001; Guild, Groenendijk, and Carrera 2009). Yet, strikingly, no information can be found in the otherwise rather transparent communication channels of the EU on why and how this list was made, despite its obvious far-reaching consequences. Nor is it clear what criteria are being used to move from the black to the white list. Recently, the EU changed the wording of this di-visionary view of the world, from a black/white list to a positive/negative list. The wording may be less racial, but this does not alter the intentions and the discriminatory effects of this apartheid geopolitics (see also

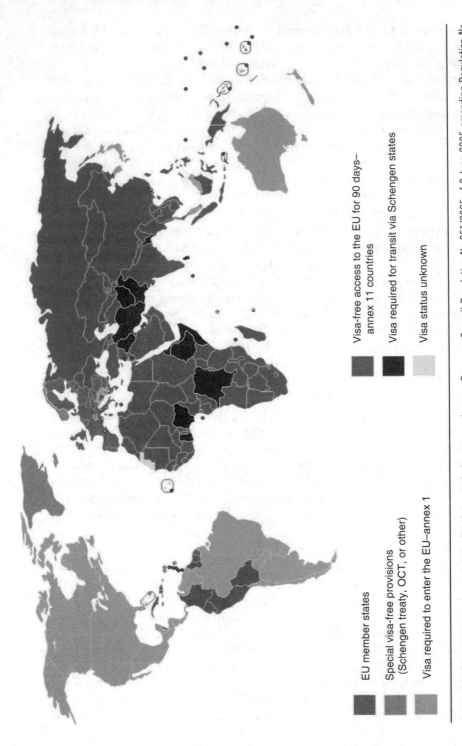

Figure 7.1 EU's divisionary borderland by EU (Schengen) visa access (source: European Council Regulation No 851/2005 of 2 June 2005 amending Regulation No 539/2001. Map from http://www.upload.wikimedia.org/wikipedia/common/6/61/EUvisallsts.png)..

Legend:

- EU member states
- Special visa-free provisions (Schengen treaty, OCT, or other)
- Visa required to enter the EU–annex 1

- Visa-free access to the EU for 90 days–annex 11 countries
- Visa required for transit via Schengen states
- Visa status unknown

Hansen 2004). With this list, the EU has created a dichotomous border of in–out, a digital 1–0. In so doing, the biopolitical border that is constructed selects and prioritises people and social relations in the world. The EU thus, in terms of access, unjustly discriminates against people by their country of origin. To base a territorial politics in this time and age on one's place of birth is not only archaic, as we increasingly live in a transnational world, but also immoral, as it regulates and thereby destines the lives of humans on the mere fate of where they were born. Such nativist geopolitics has perhaps most powerfully and influentially been criticised by Joseph Carens in his well-cited 1987 article in which he convincingly argued against a politics based on the lottery of birth.

It is clear that in the discriminative biopolitical and geopolitical border regime of the EU there is no outside; the globe is the playing field of the EU's border regime. The EU border decides what and especially who is to be included and excluded, what the territorial grouping and the discipline of the EU will look like, and what the global border wishes to communicate. The EU regulates who is considered legal input and who is considered unwanted input—a threat to the system, hence redundant and deportable people, or in the words of Bauman (2004) "wasted lives"—to the border machine.

What is telling when analysing the negative list is that there are a significantly high number of Muslim states listed. Another important portion of countries that are listed are developing countries. Hence, there is an implicit and strong inclination to use this list not only as a tool to guarantee security in physical terms or in terms of Western identity protection but also as a means of keeping the world's poorest out. The scapegoating is done on the valuation of the Other's god and economy. So, again, to put it sharply, as in former colonial times, it is the EU that selects people on the basis of their imagined added value for the EU and their imagined potential (security) risk for the EU. Alongside the execution of this new external border policy that is implicit in this negative list, there is a growing anxiety about people coming from these countries. Some literally fear an invasion of poor or Muslim migrants, who en masse threaten to flood "our" territory. A Dutch extreme right-wing politician, Geert Wilders, often even speaks of a "tsunami" of Muslim migrants in this respect, as if the mobility of some people could be compared to a natural disaster. The discriminatory place on this list for non-EU people is not a self-chosen option. Every society creates its own strangers, and so does the political particularity of the EU. It is the inequality of a politics of difference of which the migrants are victim. The migrants are pushed in the non-self-chosen category of the immigrant with no legal name and seen as a "burden" that needs to be shared among the various states of the EU. It has reached a point that a decrease in the numbers of (undocumented) asylum seekers is now viewed as a success. The consequences of this production of the eternally desired "We" and the eternally undesired "They" is a vicious circle between the self-produced increase of irregular travellers, as the regular routes of the citizens of the black-list countries are foreclosed, and the increase of moral panic about precisely that, the increase of irregular migrants, which nationalistic politicians thankfully seize upon in their competition for more votes.

Invasion Maps

One of the most important and striking representations of this moral panic is seen in the construction and use of maps. On many of the dominant and often used "official" maps, stemming from media as well as political institutions, thick arrows, lines, and dots indicate the routes and main hubs of the trajectories of undocumented migrants. These lines and arrows represent migration flows without in any way reflecting the heterogeneity of those who move, without reflecting on the possibly active role of the "receiving" countries, and without adequately reflecting possible shuttle or circular movement migrants may have already made. What defines undocumented migration processes is invisibility, as most migrants without papers obviously fear getting caught—hence their strategy is to stay invisible and intractable for the biopolitical gaze of the border control. For, in the EU border machine, the life as a migrant is controlled as in a Foucauldian panopticon. The controlling eye of the Camera we live in is omnipresent and internalised on the penalty of being considered an outlaw, an illegal. The watching connects to the double function of the word *border guard*. They guard the border, the entrance to their domain, their law, but they also stand guard; they wait for your coming and watch your moves to check for possible threats to the sustenance of the law. This also implies that how what is undocumented, irregular, and out of sight is made visible can be a determining factor in shaping the public opinion. Many of the current maps present migration as massive, unaffected, unidirectional, and unstoppable flows towards imaginatively reactive and vulnerable states (see, for instance, Figure 7.2, made by FRONTEX that aims to identify and map the routes).

Maps like this do not only represent moral panics; they also coconstruct them (van Schendel 2005). As Denis Wood (1993) has famously argued, the map's effectiveness lies in the selectivity with which it is produced. The fear

Figure 7.2 The representation of an invasion (source: Frontex, 2009).

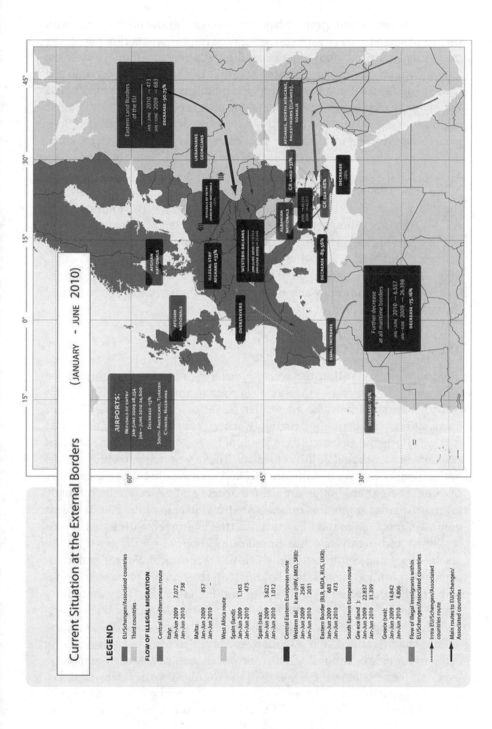

Current Situation at the External Borders (JANUARY – JUNE 2010)

of undocumented immigrants across the EU is generally not grounded in a thorough awareness of contemporary global migration developments. The maps suggesting invasions of people omit that a very small minority of the global population flees or migrates and that the EU is only "receiving" a fraction of this total number of refugees and migrants (Walters 2007). And the majority of migrants is staying in the geographical proximity of their regions of origin; only few have the possibility or will to travel over longer, intercontinental distances. What is more, the reality of undocumented migration is often more dispersed, dynamic, fluid, and more of a transitory and zig-zag nature. The often taken for granted notion of migration as one of linear movement leading to a final destination—and often illustrated by the use of straight arrows, lines, and dots—is flawed (van Houtum 2012). A few inspiring, although still fragmented, attempts to alternatively represent migration into the EU have been made already, mainly by NGOs (e.g., Migmap, IndyMedia, and Migreurop). Until now, these detailed accounts of when and why migrants migrate as well as these alternative representations of migration are washed away in the highly influential mediated image of the "invasion" of unwanted migrants.

The EU as a Gated Community

The geopolitical result of the fiercer b/ordering of the EU is a bifurcated policy of immigration in which a strong selection among non-EU migrants is made between those who are wanted (investors, tourists, some IT managers, nurses, cleaners, construction workers, etc.) and who are unwanted (the rest), largely based on the net result of their migration for the national economy and national cultural identity. Those who wish to enter the EU and fall outside the nationally defined and continually changing category of "wanted migrants" often are denied access and hence are increasingly taking irregular migration routes (see also Carrera 2007a, 2009). In this context, Roos Pijpers and I have argued that by implementing such a protectionist and highly selective immigration policy, the EU has come to resemble a gated community in which the biopolitical control and management of immigration is, to a large extent, the product of fear (van Houtum and Boedeltje 2009; van Houtum and Pijpers 2007). The community thereby defines itself to be the good life, thereby reifying figures of societal difference and danger, such as the criminal, the terrorist, the invading enemy, the migrant. Often fear manifests itself in terms of fear of losing economic welfare, cultural identity, or public security. More often, however, this fear relates to the entrance of the immigrant, the stranger, and is, as such, associated with a fear of losing comfort and a community's self-defined identity. These perceived threats to a community's comfort lead to the politicisation of protection, whereby the terra incognita beyond the border is justifiably neglected due to the indifference shown and the intentional blindness to the outside. Over land and sea this fear manifests itself physically in the installation of a barbed-wired gate, making it difficult to apply for entrance into the EU factory. Over time, the dissolution of the internal barbed wire in the EU and the Iron Curtain between West and East Europe has been replaced by new barbed wire and what some define as a new Golden Curtain between EU and non-EU. Regardless of whether that metaphor is appropriate or not, it does allude to the commercialisation of politics, what Slavoj Žižek has called the postpolitical society that the EU has become (Žižek 1999).

Death at the Border

To guard the newly installed barbed wire, the European Agency for the Management of Operational Cooperation at External Borders of the Member States of the European Union (FRONTEX), which was installed a few years ago, has become increasingly important. The Agency's mission is defined as:

> FRONTEX coordinates operational cooperation between Member States in the field of management of external borders; assists Member States in the training of national border guards, including the establishment of common training standards; carries out risk analyses; follows up the development of research relevant for the control and surveillance of external borders; assists Member States in circumstances requiring increased technical and operational assistance at external borders; and provides Member States with the necessary support in organising joint return operations.... FRONTEX strengthens border security by ensuring the coordination of Member States' actions in the implementation of Community measures relating to the management of the external borders.

Hence, the goal of FRONTEX is to strive for an overall enhanced common effectiveness and efficiency in controlling the EU's external border; the goal is to come to a pan-European model of integrated border security. To this end, FRONTEX also works with what they call RABITs, an acronym for Rapid Border Intervention Teams. The analogy with the term *rabbits* is striking. Such an implicit (or explicit) animalisation and dehumanisation of border control is worrying, yet not uncommon (see also Papadopoulos, Stephenson, and Tsianos 2008). The empowerment of state power through animal representations and metaphors has long been used by nation-states. Most of the nation-states would have an animal (e.g., a bear, eagle, cock, lion) as their national animalistic representation, to make their nation-state (and hence their sovereignty and border control) border animated, bodily present, and potent. But, increasingly, the animalisation of the state is extended to migrants who are to be seen as wild or untamed animals that run and need to be stopped by quick and potent border guard predators of the state. Illustratively, often one reads or hears about the cat and mouse game between border guards and irregular migrants. And along the U.S.-Mexico border one often hears the terms coyotes or *polleros* (the smugglers) and pollos (the undocumented migrants), and along the Chinese borders the term *shetou* (snakehead) is commonly used to typify migration brokers and smugglers. Hence though not new, the EU's use of RABITs is no less sarcastic and worrying.

As of 2004, FRONTEX has been employing various boats, helicopters, and planes coming from various EU members in the Mediterranean and along the northern and western African coast to prevent boats with migrants from entering into the territorial waters of the EU, creating a whole new EU-landscape of defence and fences (see also Carrera, 2007b). What is more, the detection phase of the border machine that has been developed has increasingly become a lethal phase. Over the years, as the securitisation and patrolling of the border control has grown, attempts to remain unseen or to escape from border guards has led to the death of many would-be immigrants who are trying to get into the EU. Obviously, the closing of the gate has not stopped migrants from coming. It has only made it more dangerous. In the words of Bauman (2002b, 85):

> The doors may be locked; but the problem won't go away, however tight the locks. Locks do nothing to tame or weaken the forces that cause displacement and make humans into refugees. The locks may help to keep the problem out of sight and out of mind, but not to force it out of existence.

With the construction of a gated isle of wealth, and with the conscious denial of regular access to citizens from 135 countries, the EU widens the gap globally and regulates mortality of people on a global scale. It produces a segment of the world population willing to risk their lives to get into the EU. Hideously, the deaths of those who do try to cross the border without permission are implicitly seen as the "collateral damage" of a combat against irregular migration (Albahari 2006; Bauman 2004). Illustratively, neither the number of deaths nor their names or cause of death is even counted or registered officially (see also Spijkerboer 2007). They are made absent, unrepresented, and invisible. As a protest of this silencing the deaths of undocumented migrants who have died in their attempt to get into or stay in the EU, the counting of the number of "deaths at the border" is done by alternative organisations, like United Against Racism and No Borders. Rough estimates indicate that the number of deaths is somewhere in the 13,000s now (see Figure 7.3). Other sources, however, speak of many more deaths, especially among those who have tried to enter the EU by boat,[2] for instance, through the Canary Islands. The question that begs our moral attention is how many deaths does this politics of fear bear?

Bioborder Politics

In the global borderland we live in an officially stamped passport is the state proof that you exist as a citizen. By birth, a human being is thus seen not only as an individual but as a political subject subjected to the polity. For those who are subjected to the political order that is mostly seen as comforting, as it provides a state home, but it is equally discomforting as the political order thereby also decides who you are. For the political order in its turn, there is also discomforting uncertainty, for an officer of a state never completely knows with 100 percent certainty that the person in the passport is indeed the person standing in front of him or her. The more fear society has for the stranger, the more the political order wants to be certain of his or her identity. Especially in the moral panic that emerged after 9/11, the measurement and determination of one's civic identity through iris scanning, facial recognition, bone-age checking, and fingerprints has entered more and more the actual corpus of the stranger (see also e.g., Broeders 2007; Dijstelbloem and Meijer 2009; Epstein 2007; Muller 2005; Salter and Zureik 2005; van der Ploeg 1999). Increasingly, the civic identity of the European is carried and manifested by his or her body: the body as a passport. As a result of such metrical biopolitics, border control can be exercised on multiple subjectifications within the same individual. For those who do make it into the EU-factory, be it irregularly or regularly as a refugee who is asking for asylum, they enter into the increasingly digital test-room, which increasingly is an apparatus designed for hearing, checking, biometrical scanning, photographing, fingerprinting, and evaluating every moving body. The external border increasingly should, hence, be understood as a digital firewall protecting the machine (see also Walters 2006). This border machine scans, registers, profiles, filters, selects, and categorises people on the basis of our desires and fears (see also Amoore 2006). Whether you will be stopped as a non-EU citizen or seen as an interesting added value for the EU is dependent on your code. This code is made by the EU and loaded in the mechanic machinery of the border, the computers of Schengen. As argued above, this border code is

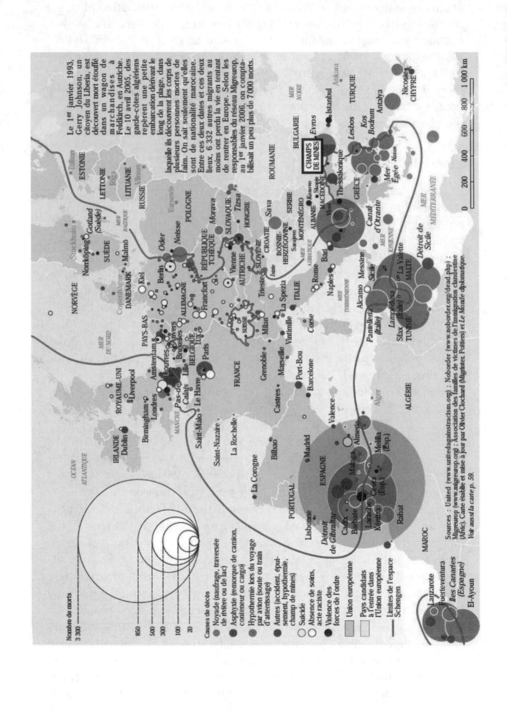

Le 1er janvier 1993, un citoyen du Liberia, Gerry Johnson, est découvert mort étouffé dans un wagon de marchandises à Feldkirch, en Autriche. Le 10 avril 2005, des garde-côtes algériens repèrent une petite embarcation dérivant le long de la plage, dans laquelle ils découvrent les corps de plusieurs personnes mortes de faim. On sait seulement qu'elles sont de nationalité marocaine. Entre ces deux dates et ces deux lieux, 6 332 autres migrants au moins ont perdu la vie en tentant de rentrer en Europe. Selon les responsables du réseau Migreurop, au 1er janvier 2006, on comptabilisait un peu plus de 7 000 morts.

Nombre de morts

3 300
850
500
300
100
20

Causes de décès

○ Noyade (naufrage, traversée de rivière ou de lac)
● Asphyxie (remorque de camion, conteneur ou cargo)
● Hypothermie hors du voyage par avion (soute ou train d'atterrissage)
● Autres (accident, épuisement, hypothermie, champ de mines)
○ Suicide
○ Absence de soins, acte raciste
● Violence des forces de l'ordre

Union européenne
Pays candidats à l'entrée dans l'Union européenne
Limites de l'espace Schengen

Sources : United (www.unitedagainstracism.org) ; Noborder (www.noborder.org/dead.php) ; Migreurop (www.migreurop.org) ; Association des familles de victimes de l'immigration clandestine (Afvic). Carte établie et mise à jour par Olivier Clochard (Migrinter, Poitiers) et Le Monde diplomatique.
Voir aussi la carte p. 59.

currently based on the black and white list by which the EU divides the world. What this means is that the EU perceives people less as individual human beings than as subjects of a political order. People are coded by their country of birth and/or country of origin before they are individuals. Such classical ground-politics has major moral consequences. The migrants from a black-list country are listed as a hit by the digital border machine and are refused entry as undesirables—thus resulting in the dangerous attempts of the people of black-list countries to remain unseen, to remain uncoded. The irregular migrants are hence made into a faceless, depoliticised subclass excepted from the territorial sovereignty, or what Agamben (1998) famously termed the "homo sacer." Not registering the death, as argued above, further illustrates this. Such EU-depoliticisation and dehumanisation not only suppresses the humanitarian value of people outside the codes of what the EU sees as added value but also misrecognises the social entrepreneurship, the creative way of escaping their fate and future in their native country.

Para-Sites

The above-described machine-like apparatus for decision making is constantly working to finally be able to make a binary decision: stay or go. For many the actual bureaucratic production of the final decision is taking a long time. As a result, over time, the migration to the EU for those migrants who are seen as a burden and for whom a "decision" has to be made, has led, as argued above, to a buffer zone geopolitics with a new landscape of asylum camps that act as—taking Michel Serres (2007) word *pests* for the host body literally—parasites, within the state borders yet outside in a space where EU citizenship is placed in suspension. In the words of the scholar who is most often used these days when it comes to camps, Agamben, these camps are dislocated localisations (Agamben 1997). In these camps the category of "citizen" is not, not yet, or no longer operative for the figure of the refugee (Perera 2002). If, usually after considerable waiting time, the outcome of the asylum procedure is not a yes (which would mean the road to national integration of the migrant) but a no, then the purification machinery orders the migrant to go back to the future outside the EU. Over the years this has led to the creation of a landscape of expel apparatuses and deportation centres as a semipermanent state of emergency, what could be called, to use Zygmunt

Figure 7.3 The immigration death atlas in Europe (source: http://www.unitedagainstracism.org). Human blacklisting: the global apartheid of the EU's external border regime.

Bauman's linguistic metaphor of waste, a form of social dumping via waste sites. Although the word *prison* is carefully being avoided in the bureaucratic jargon of the border machine, it is difficult to perceive the bodily registration and locking up of migrants—who have committed no other crime than not having the right documents—in detention centres or expel centres differently. These camps, these spatial para-sites, which famously Agamben identified as "the fundamental biopolitical paradigm of the West" (1998, 181), are for those who have to go but have refused to do so. This is neither the time nor the place to analyse in all its absorbing details the ontological function or sociology of the camp. Others have done that in a compelling way already (see e.g., Diken and Laustsen 2005; Fassin 2001; Minca 2006, 2007; Schinkel 2009; Ticktin 2005). The point that I wish to make is that over the years, as a result of the tightening border regime of the EU, we have witnessed an exponential growth in the number and size not only of asylum centres, the beginning of the border machine, but also of detention or expel centres, the end of the production chain of migrants. For people without papers the constant monitoring and spatial control of their whereabouts have become a practice of daily life. For the EU, then, the installation of camps is a form of concentration and containment, of "stocking" the people without papers in order to facilitate and manage more efficiently the daily biopolitical control of their whereabouts. (Interestingly enough, apart from these formal camps other more informal anti-camps are increasingly being constructed in and at the borders of the EU in the form of migrant camps made by migrants themselves often in the woods or other sites out of sight and in the form of temporary No Border Camps, made by activists protesting against the border control and camps for undocumented migrants.) For the EU the camp has become a way of managing the legality of the labour market as well as preventing the misuse of the channel of asylum of political refugees. More concrete, politically then a camp represents chronopolitics, the politics of time, represented by waiting time that is used to control, manage, and slow or even immobilise all together the travelling speed of the mobile yet unwelcome others, as well geopolitics, the politics of space, morphologically represented in terms of walls and gates of a constructed dis-place (see also Papadopoulos et al. 2008). Hence, time and space are used as tools in the camp machinery to refabricate the illegalised "input" into politically acceptable codes, as legal "output" for the EU, that is, as new labourers, political refugees, or waste that can be dumped. Figure 7.4 provides an overview of the various migrant camps in the EU, be it asylum "waiting rooms" or detention centres.

Figure 7.4 The immigration camp atlas in Europe (source: http://www.mlgreurop.org/).

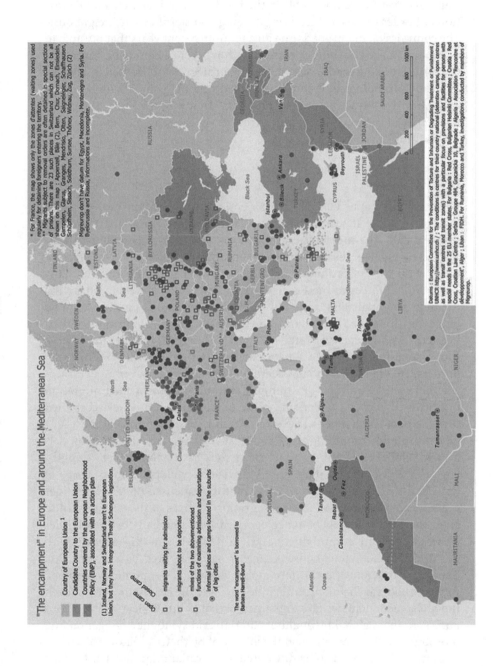

As can be seen in Figure 7.4, and as argued above, in the context of the European Neighbourhood Policy, the border control, as well as the erection of border camps, is increasingly being transferred to the neighbours. The commission has argued time and again in recent years that it wants to "share the burden" of border control with respective countries. Countries of origin are being made complicit to the protection of the system, the law of the EU. In doing so, it could be argued, the EU is increasingly selling and morally contracting out its "problem." In a way, therefore, the external border of the EU is becoming a frontier, in the sense of the shifted EU "civilization" in space.

Ending

I started this paper with Reichert's enticing provocation on our topological thinking. It seems that her plea to be wary about and to scrutinise critically the topologics of borders is now as timely as it ever was. An increasing liberalisation of border control inside the EU is being combined with an increasingly machine-like external border control. Current political forces in the EU have expressed a key interest in attracting the high potentials and some low-cost labour migrants on the one hand and controlling the "redundant" and allegedly difficult to integrate "non-Western" immigrants and refugees on the other hand in order to preserve social cohesion and protect national labour markets within European borders. In addition, although there is no proof whatsoever of a connection between labour-market immigration and undocumented migration on the one hand and terrorism on the other hand, it can be ascertained that the post-9/11 (attacks in New York and Washington, DC), post-3/11 (attacks in and around Madrid), and post-7/7 (attacks in London) anxieties over global terrorism and security issues have only further strengthened the restrictive and increasingly di-visionary global border regime of the EU. This has resulted in a policy that is so focused on a strict border regime and assimilation that the migration motives of those who want to enter the EU are merely being categorised into a globally defined border between productive/unproductive, friendly/fiendish, and good/bad, with the direct dichotomous consequence of being allowed entrance or not. The restrictive and increasingly global apartheid geopolitics combined with a neoliberal cherry-picking policy outside the EU is unjust from both the global economic welfare and a normative point of view, as it sustains and reproduces global inequality, material, and symbolic segregation and reproduces a discrimination on the lottery of birth. In addition, this newly engaged global "war" against unwanted or irregular migration has become falsely and illegitimately intertwined with the global "war" against terrorism. Such a climate in itself is not helpful, to say the least, either in destroying any possible seedbed for discriminatory practices and attitudes toward the Stranger inside the EU or in diminishing the global inequality. This b/ordering and othering machine of the EU is co-constructing more not less "illegality," xenophobia, and fear. The politics of desire for comfort, identity, and security and of fear for the invading other, as it is currently framed, is mutually constitutive and hence continuous: without the identification and targeting of "waste" there is no clean(s)ing desire and vice versa. The self-declared "combat" is being fought with increasingly higher fences, bigger army tools, and a growing number of detention and expel centres.

The current largely exclusionary character of the global world vision of the EU makes the borders between the EU and its (Near) Abroad(s) spatially extremely pressing and edgy. A new landscape of control has come into existence. The migrants for whom this new landscape of border politics concerns often creatively use the new frames of control such as biometrical body controls, boat patrol, and camps to their own advantage. No matter how high the wall may be, there is no wall high enough to block off migration. Migrants adapt to the new rules, invent personalities, disidentify themselves by throwing away their papers, or even crudely erase their finger reliefs in order to avoid finger printing, zigzag their shadow ways into the EU, use migrant camps as a stopover on their way to the next station. In short, they constantly multiply and construct new liminal becomings (Papadopoulos et al. 2008). As a result, with the tightening of legal entry into the EU, the EU is only expanding the "illegal" escape routes and entries into the EU.

The EU started as a means to an end, no more war between states through the construction of a framework of reciprocity, a union, in which states would be included as much as possible. Now the means of the Union has become the end itself. Using an analytical framework of bordering, ordering, and othering in studying the external border production of the EU, we can ascertain that we are currently witnessing the making of a new border ideology, a new borderology in the EU. The absence of a global union, a striking global political void, has provided a constant invitation to an extraterritorial bargain-by-force by the EU (Bauman 2002b). The EU consciously recodes, narrates, and canonises a common past; creates an exclusionary military external front; and buys the imagined security of these external borders by developing an imperial development aid that is based on "European values" for its neighbouring states (see also Balibar 2004a, 2004b). It seems that the EU has become a global borderland, indeed.

Acknowledgements

I wish to thank James Scott, Roald Plug, Freerk Boedeltje, Roos Pijpers, Olivier Kramsch, Thomas Geisen, Virginie Mamadouh, Chiara Brambilla, Giuseppe Sciortino, Ellie Vasta, and Olga Lafazani for their helpful suggestions, collaborative reflections, or reviews of earlier versions of this paper. I wish to thank participants of the NORFACE-funded seminar on global borders at Royal Holloway organised by Chris Rumford, as well as the participants of the border seminar at the University of Bergamo co-organised by Chiara Brambilla for interesting comments and discussions on older versions of this paper. Needless to say, I am responsible for any errors made in the text.

Notes

1. Afghanistan, Albania, Algeria, Angola, Antigua and Barbuda, Armenia, Azerbaijan, Bahamas, Bahrain, Bangladesh, Barbados, Belarus, Belize, Benin, Bhutan, Bosnia and Herzegovina, Botswana, Burkina Faso, Burundi, Cambodia, Cameroon, Cape Verde, Central Africa, Chad, China, Colombia, Comoro Islands, Congo, Congo (Democratic Republic), Coote d'Ivoire, Cuba, Djibouti, Dominica, Dominican (Republic), East Timor, Ecuador, Egypt, Equatorial Guinea, Eritrea, Ethiopia, Federal Republic of Yugoslavia (Serbia-Montenegro), Fiji, Former Yugoslav Republic of Macedonia, Gabon, Georgia, Ghana, Grenada, Guinea, Guinea Bissau, Guyana, Haiti, India, Indonesia, Iran, Iraq, Jamaica, Jordan, Kazakhstan, Kenya, Kiribati, Kuwait, Kyrgyzstan, Laos, Lebanon, Lesotho, Liberia, Libya, Madagascar, Malawi, Maldives, Mali, Marshall Islands, Mauritania, Mauritius, Micronesia, Moldova, Mongolia, Morocco, Mozambique, Myanmar, Namibia, Nauru, Nepal, Niger, Nigeria, North Korea, Northern Marianas, Oman, Pakistan, Palau, Palestinian National Authority, Papua-New Guinea, Peru, Qatar, Russia, Rwanda, St Kitts and Nevis, St Lucia, St Vincent and the Grenadines, Solomon Islands, Sao Tome and Principe, Saudi Arabia, Senegal, Serbia and Montenegro, Seychelles, Sierra Leone, Somalia, South Africa, Sri Lanka, Sudan, Suriname, Swaziland, Syria, Tajikistan, Tanzania, Thailand, The Gambia, The Philippines, Togo, Tonga, Trinidad and Tobago, Tunisia, Turkey, Turkmenistan, Tuvalu, Uganda, Ukraine, United Arab Emirates, Uzbekistan, Vanuatu, Vietnam, Western Samoa, Yemen, Zambia, Zimbabwe.
2. Interestingly, in his genealogy on madness Foucault analysed the use of the *Narrenschif* (boat for the crazy people) in medieval times. To spatially and socially except and exclude people, those who were believed to be crazy were put on a boat, as society did not know how to deal with them otherwise. Hence, the people were treated as pariahs. It could be argued that a boat containing irregular migrants is also treated and perceived by the EU as pariahs on a *Narrenschiff*.

References

Agamben, G. 1997. "The Camp as Nomos of the Modern." In *Violence, Identity and Self-Determination,* edited by H. de Vries and S. Weber, translated by D. Heller-Roazen, 106–18. Stanford, CA: Stanford University Press.

———. 1998. *Homo Sacer, Sovereign Power and Bare Life,* translated by D. Heller-Roazen. Stanford, CA: Stanford University Press.

Albahari, M. 2006. "Death and the Modern State: Making Borders and Sovereignty at the Southern Edges of Europe." CCIS Working Paper No. 137.

Amoore L, 2006. "Biometric Borders: Governing Mobilities in the War on Terror." *Political Geography* 25: 336–51.

Anderson, J., and W. Armstrong, eds. 2007. *Geopolitics of European Union Enlargement, the Fortress Empire.* New York: Routledge.

Apap, J., and A. Tchorbadjiyska. 2004. "What about the Neighbours? The Impact of Schengen along the EU's External Borders." Working Document No. 210, Centre for European Policy Studies, Brussels.

Balibar, E,. 2004a. "Europe as Borderland." The Alexander von Humboldt Lecture in Human Geography, University of Nijmegen.

———. 2004b. *We, the People of Europe? Reflections on Transnational Citizenship,* Princeton, NJ: Princeton University Press.

Bauman Z, 2002a. *Society under Siege.* Cambridge, UK: Polity Press.

———. 2002b. "ReconnaissanceWars of the Planetary Frontier Land." *Theory, Culture and Society* 19: 81–90.

———. 2004. *Wasted Lives: Modernity and Its Outcasts.* Cambridge, UK: Polity Press.

Bigo, D., and E. Guild, eds. 2005. *Controlling Frontiers: Free Movement into and within Europe,* Aldershot, UK: Ashgate.

Boedeltje, F., O. T. Kramsch, H. van Houtum, and R. Plug. 2007. "The Fallacious Imperial Geo politics of EU Enlargement: The Case of Cyprus." *Tijdschrift voor Economische en Sociale Geografie* 98: 130–35.

Broeders, D. 2007. "The New Digital Borders of Europe: EU Databases and the Surveillance of Irregular Migrants." *International Sociology* 22: 71–92.

Brown, D. 2002. "Storming the Fortress: The External Border Regime in an Enlarged Europe." In EU *Expansion to the East: Prospects and Problems,* edited by H. Ingham and M. Ingham, 89–109. Cheltenham, UK: Edward Elgar.

Carens, J. H. 1987. "Aliens and 'Citizens': The Case for Open Borders. *Review of Politics* 49: 251–73.

Carrera, S. 2007a. "Building a Common Policy on Labour Immigration: Towards a Comprehensive and Global Approach in the EU?" Working Document No. 256, Centre for European Policy Studies.

———. 2007b. "The EU Border Management Strategy: FRONTEX and the Challenges of Irregular Immigration in the Canary Islands." Working Document No. 261, Centre for European Policy Studies.

———. 2009. "The Externalisation of the EU's Labour Immigration Policy: Towards Mobility or Insecurity Partnerships?" Working Document No. 321, Centre for European Policy Studies.

Christiansen, T., and K. E. Jorgensen. 2000. "Transnational Governance 'Above' and 'Below' the State: The Changing Nature of Borders in the New Europe." *Regional and Federal Studies* 10: 62–77.

Deleuze, G., and F. Guattari. (1980) 2004. *A Thousand Plateaus.* London: Continuum.

Dijstelbloem, H., and A. Meijer, eds. 2009. *De Migratiemachine: OverTechnologisering en Informatisering in het Migratiebeleid* [The migration machine: Overuse of technology and information gathering in the migratory world]. Amsterdam, Netherlands: Van Gennep.

Diken, B., and C. B. Laustsen. 2005. *The Culture of Exception-Sociology Facing the Camp.* London: Routledge.

Duffield, M. 2001. *Global Governance and the New Wars: The Merging of Development and Security.* London: Zed Books.

Emerson, M. 2004. "European Neighbourhood Policy: Strategy of Placebo?" Working Document No. 215, Centre for European Policy Studies.

Epstein, C. 2007. "Guilty Bodies, Productive Bodies, Destructive Bodies: Crossing the Biometric Borders." *International Political Sociology* 1: 149–64.

European Commission. 2004. "European Neighbourhood Policy Strategy Paper 373." Communication from the Commission.

Fassin, D. 2001. "The Biopolitics of Otherness: Undocumented Migrants and Racial Discrimination in The French Public Debate." *Anthropology Today* 12: 3–7.

Foucault, M.1975. *Surveiller et Punir* [Surveillance and punishment]. Paris: Gallimard.

———. 2007. *Security, Territory, Population.* New York: Palgrave Macmillan.

Friis, L., and A. Murphy. 1999. "The European Union and Central and Eastern Europe: Governance and Boundaries." *Journal of Common Market Studies* 37: 211–32.

Guild, E. 2001. "Moving the Borders of Europe." Inaugural Lecture, University of Nijmegen, Netherlands.

———. K. Groenendijk, and S. Carrera. 2009. *Illiberal Liberal States, Immigration, Citizenship and Integration in the EU.* Farnham, UK: Ashgate.

Hansen, P. 2004. "In the Name of Europe." *Race and Class* 45: 49–62.

Hudson, R. 2000. "One Europe or Many? Reflections on Becoming European." *Transactions of the Institute of British Geographers, New Series* 25: 409–26.

Inda, J. X. 2006. *Targeting Immigrants, Government, Technology and Ethics.* Oxford, UK: Blackwell.

Kavafis, K. P. 1904. "Waiting for the Barbarians." http//users.h0l.gr/barbanls/cavafuy/barbar lans.html

Minca, C, 2006. "Giorgio Agamben and the New Biopolitical Nomos." *Geografiska Annaler, Series B* 88: 387–403.

———. 2007. "Agamben's Geographies of Modernity." *Political Geography* 25: 78–97.

Muller, B. 2005. "Borders, Bodies and Biometrics: Towards Identity Management." In: *Global Surveillance and Policing: Borders, Security, Identity,* edited by E. Zureik and M. B. Salter, 83–96. Cullompton, UK: Willan.

Paasi, A. 1996. *Territories, Boundaries and Consciousness: The Changing Geographies of the Finnish-Russian Boundary.* New York: Wiley.

Papadopoulos, D., N. Stephenson, and V. Tsianos. 2008. *Escape Routes, Control and Subversion in the 21st Century.* London: Pluto Press.

Parker, N., and N. Vaughan-Williams. 2009. ''Lines in the Sand? Towards an Agenda for Critical Border Studies." *Geopolitics* 14: 582–87.

Perera, S. 2002. "What Is a Camp? Border Phobias: The Politics of Insecurity Post 9/11." *Borderlands ejournal* 1(1). http://www.borderlands.net.au/vol1n012002/perera camp.html

Reichert, D. 1992. "On Boundaries." *Environment and Planning D: Society and Space* 10: 87–98.

Rumford, C., ed. 2007. *Cosmopolitanism and Europe.* Liverpool, UK: Liverpool University Press.

———. 2008. *Cosmopolitan Spaces; Europe, Globalization, Theory.* London: Routledge.

Salter, M. 2006. "The Global Visa Regime and the Political Technologies of the International Self." *Alternatives: Global, Local, Political* 31: 167–89.

———. E. Zureik, eds. 2005. *Global Surveillance and Policing: Borders, Security, Identity.* Cullompton, Devon: Willan.

Samers, M. 2004. "An Emerging Geopolitics of 'Illegal' Immigration in the European Union." *European Journal of Migration and Law* 6: 23–41.

Schinkel, W. 2009. ''Illegal Aliens' and the State, Or: Bare Bodies vs the Zombie." *International Sociology* 24: 779–806.

Schmitt, C. 1950. Der Nomos der Erde im Völkerrecht des Jus Publicum Europaeum [The Nomos of the Earth in the International Law of the Jus Publicum Europaeum]. Berlin, Germany: Duncker and Humblot.

Serres, M. (1980) 2007. *The Parasite.* Minneapolis: University of Minnesota Press.

Sibley, D. 1995. *Geographies of Exclusion: Society and Difference in the West.* London: Routledge.

Smith, M. 1996, "The European Union and a Changing Europe: Establishing the Boundaries of Order." *Journal of Common Market Studies* 34: 5–28.

Spijkerboer, T. 2007, "The Human Costs of Border Control." *European Journal of Migration and Law* 9: 127–39.

Ticktin, M. 2005, "Policing and Humanitarianism in France: Immigration and the Turn to Law as State of Exception." *Interventions* 7: 347–68.

Tunander, O. 1997. "Post-Cold War Europe: A Synthesis of a Bipolar Friend–Foe Structure and a Hierarchic Cosmos-Chaos Structure?" In *Geopolitics in Postwall Europe. Security, Territory and Identity*, 17–44. London: PRIO/Sage.

van der Ploeg, I. 1999. "Written on the Body: Biometrics and Identity." *ACM SIGCAS Computers and Society* 29: 37–44

van Houtum, H. 2010. "Waiting before the Law: Kafka on the Border." *Social and Legal Studies* 19 (3): 285–297.

van Houtum, H. 2011. The Mask of the Border. In *Companion to Border Studies*, edited by D. Wastl-Walter, 49–62. Aldershot, UK: Ashgate.

van Houtman, H. 2012. Remapping Borders. In *A Companion to Border Studies*, edited by H. Donnan and T. Wilson, 405–418.

van Houtum, H., and F. Boedeltje. 2009. "Europe's Shame, Death at the BORDERS of the EU." *Antipode* 41: 226–30.

———. O. Kramsch, and W. Zierhofer. 2005. *B/ordering Space*. Aldershot, UK: Ashgate.

———. R. Pijpers. 2007. "The European Union as a Gated Community: The Two-Faced Border and Immigration Regime of the EU." *Antipode* 39: 291–309.

———. T. van Naerssen. 2002. "Bordering, Ordering and Othering." *Tijdschrift voor Economische en Sociale Geografie* 93: 125–36.

van Schendel, W. 2005. "Spaces of Engagement: How Borderlands, Illegal Flows, and Territorial States Interlock." In: *Illicit Flows and Criminal Things: States, Borders and the Other Side of Globalization*, edited by W. van Schendel and I. Abraham, 38–68. Bloomington: Indiana University Press.

Waever, O. 1997. "Imperial Metaphors: Emerging European Analogies to Pre-Nation-State Imperial Systems." In *Geopolitics in Postwall Europe. Security, Territory and Identity*, edited by O. Tunander, P. Baev, and I. Einagel, 59–93. London: PRIO/Sage.

Walters, W. 2002. "Mapping Schengenland: Denaturalizing the Border." *Environment and Planning D: Society and Space* 20: 561–80

———. 2004. "The Frontiers of the European Union: A Geostrategic Perspective." *Geopolitics* 9: 674–98

———. 2006. "Border/Control." *European Journal of Social Theory* 9: 187–204.

———. 2007. "The Contested Cartography of 'Illegal Immigration,'" paper presented at Royal Holloway, University of London.

Wood, D. 1993. *The Power of Maps*. London: Guilford Press.

Zapata-Barrero, R. 2009. "Political Discourses about Borders: On the Emergence of a European Political Community." In *A Right to Inclusion and Exclusion: Normative Fault Lines of the EU's Area of Freedom, Security and Justice*, edited by H. Lindahl, 15–33. Oxford, UK: Hart.

Zielonka, J. 2001. "How New Enlarged Borders Will Reshape the European Union." *Journal of Common Market Studies* 39: 507–36.

Žižek, S, 1999. "Carl Schmitt in the Age of Post-Politics." In *The Challenge of Carl Schmitt* , edited by C. Mouffe, 18–37. London: Verso.

PART III

Unstable Privileges
Class Inequality, Residential Mobility, and Whiteness

CHAPTER 8

Swedish Whiteness in Southern Spain

CATRIN LUNDSTRÖM

Southern Spain is one of the most attractive places in Europe for so-called lifestyle migrants to live and retire. Most of them come to the Spanish Sunbelt from Great Britain and the Scandinavian countries. The presence of Northern European migration is striking in the coastal towns of Fuengirola, Marbella, and Málaga. Stores or bars such as the London Pub, O'Hara's Irish Pub, Nordic Video, and Casa Nórdica, or organizations such as the Swedish Church, Club Nórdico, and the Swedish School, give a glimpse of the institutionalization of migrants' national identities. Along with the thousands of British, Norwegian, Danish, or Dutch migrants, about 65,000 Swedes spend part of the year, generally during the winter, on the Costa del Sol.

This chapter analyzes the various expressions of national identity among Swedish migrant women, and their institutionalization in a foreign context. It draws on in-depth interviews and visual network analysis conducted in 2010 with 20 Swedish migrant women between 27 and 72 years of age, and field research in the Swedish community in Andalucía located in a region in southern Spain, popularly known as the Costa del Sol. Most of my fieldwork took place in Fuengirola, which was characterized by a predominantly lower-middle-class Swedish community that is more vulnerable economically in Spain than in Sweden. Migrants of upper-middle-class background, like their homologues of other national origins, settled in the area of Nueva Andalucía outside Marbella, close to Puerto Banús, a resort for international celebrities. These upper-middle-class migrants retained their class positions in Spain more effectively than those who belonged to the lower middle-class. For the lower middle classes, migration to Spain could include a sense of downward class mobility in terms of economic capital, and a higher orientation toward national organizations and institutions. This tendency was most obvious among those living in the coastal town of Fuengirola. According to the women interviewed, the loss of their former class position was compensated for by the gentle climate and a higher quality of life, defined as a shift from a materialistic lifestyle in Sweden to a more enjoyable one in Spain. This sense of downward class mobility shows how whiteness as a site of privilege intersects with other forms of disadvantage (Frankenberg 1993).

The participants were mainly lifestyle migrants who moved to Spain after retirement for part of the year, or who sought a different lifestyle from the one they had in Sweden. Both Spain and Sweden are part of the European Union, so with EU citizenship it is possible to work or retire in member countries other than one's own. This study details how the women were integrated into these exclusive communities through the identifications of whiteness among diverse Northwest European communities of lifestyle migrants.

Through an analysis of intra-European migrations, the idea of a common, culturally homogeneous European identity is dissected. What appears is a South-North divide built upon a deep Swedish postcolonial identification with Anglo-Saxon countries and cultures and parallel disidentification with the former colonial powers in Southern Europe. As the chapter will show, the Swedish women interviewed mainly socialized with other North(west) European migrants from similar social segments who shared the embodiment of white "structured invisibility," thus separating them from non-European migrants, but also from the native Spanish.

White Migrations: An Outline

The concept of white migration could be read as an oxymoron, since a migrant is not expected to be white and a white person is not seen as a migrant but rather as a tourist or an expatriate. Conceptually, the term *migrant* tends to be used as a marker for people excluded from the "white" social category and non-Western-ness, indirectly linked to experiences of discrimination. Subsequently, racialized bodies not qualified for whiteness, are often conflated with being migrants, despite their citizenship (Lundström 2007). Migrants seen as white tend, on the contrary, to be excluded from the category of migrants and fall into the category of "expatriates," "tourists," or simply Europeans.

It is argued here that different examples of migration constitute new forms of mobility that we need to understand as part of the contemporary world in order to not reserve the concept of migration for the idea of underprivileged migrants moving from South to North, since these images only show parts of these global processes. This raises the social and conceptual relationship of white affluent migrants who migrate between their home and host countries as new aspects of transnational migration. Some of these migrants retain a home in more than one place, others seek a different way of life from the one they have at home, while still others work or study for a limited period in a given country but may not intend to return "home" but rather migrate to a third country, or some may choose to retire in a different country. These forms of white migrations illustrate current trends as well as historical patterns and conditions that may be on a continuum of old themes, such as colonialism, raising new questions about the processes of transnational migration.

In this chapter, I am concerned with the relation between migration and whiteness and the institutionalization of white migrants' national identities in Southern Spain. How are racial logics of whiteness lived and negotiated in this particular migratory context? Who feels close to whom? Why do some nationalities live in close proximity to one another and avoid certain groups and areas? Why are some being included in a particular community while others are excluded from the same communities because they are read as migrants?

Here I analyze the lived experiences of white migrants when they reinstall themselves in a different geopolitical context. I look also at the varying ways in which migrating national identities and social networks are expressed and communicated to other white diasporic communities, and their interaction with the local dynamics of racialized systems and "racial formations" (Winant 1994). Being a migrant is, as Seyla Benhabib and Judith Resnik (2009) put it, to be in transit. Migrants migrate from one place to another, rendering every migrant both an emigrant and an immigrant. I call this group of women *transmigrants*, using Nina Glick Schiller's (1995, 48) concept, in that their "daily lives depend on multiple and constant interconnections across international borders and [their] public identities are configured in relation to more than one nation-state." The women maintained close contact with friends and family in Sweden, read Swedish newspapers, owned property here (and elsewhere). In short, their lives spanned multiple national borders. By examining the postmigration experiences of this group of European women, and using an empirically grounded ethnography, the study contributes to the literature on racism, whiteness, gender, class, and migration, which has focused primarily on disadvantaged groups in migration.

The analysis is grounded in the interdisciplinary fields of whiteness studies and transnational migration, aiming at broadening and deepening debates about the experiences of migration and the continuous racial production that shapes our positions in a global arena (Ahmed 2007; Bonilla-Silva 2012; Frankenberg 1993; Hübinette and Lundström 2011; Hughey 2010; Lipsitz 1995; Leonard 2008; Omi and Winant 1994; Steyn and Conway 2010; Twine and Gallagher 2008; Ware 2010; Weiss 2005). The goal is to provide a theoretically founded analysis of the ways in which whiteness as a product social is embodied, lived, and experienced differently through processes of migration. Migration, can alter migrants' ideas of self and identity.

By dislocating whiteness and white national identity, this study is an example of what Twine and Gallagher described as "third wave whiteness studies": an analysis that "takes as its starting [point] the understanding that whiteness is not now, nor has it ever been, a static, uniform category of social identification." Thus, as Twine and Gallagher argue, avoiding "the tendency towards essentializing accounts of whiteness by locating race as one of many social relations that shape individual and group identity.... A third wave perspective sees whiteness as a multiplicity of identities that are historically grounded, class specific, politically manipulated and gendered social locations that inhabit local custom and national sentiments within the context of the new 'global village'" (Twine and Gallagher 2008, 6).

In order to understand how white migrants reinstall themselves as privileged subjects in a global arena, I use the concept of "white capital," which is elaborated through Pierre Bourdieu's (1994) forms of capital (social, economic, cultural, and symbolic), and is here employed as a form of cultural capital that is convertible into other forms of capital. White capital is interlinked with (transnational) institutions, citizenships, a white (Western) *habitus,* and other resources that are transferable cross-nationally. Following the feminist scholar Sara Ahmed (2007), I discuss whiteness as a form of *habit,* as second nature, that defines what bodies do, how they are repeated, and also shapes what bodies *can do,* and, I would add, what they *choose* to do.

The women's specific migratory experiences are used as a point of departure to understand how gender- and nation-specific forms of white capital are upheld, converted, or challenged through migration, and further how embodied privileges travel, as well as how people may invest in whiteness as a form of identity politics (Lipsitz 1995). White privileges are experienced in many ways, but they often remain normalized and invisible to the subjects that embody them. In this sense, the complexities of "white capital" as a cultural resource that may be transferred to different contexts as well as being converted into new forms of capital, is experienced intersectionally with other axes of power, such as gender and class, as the boundaries of these categories are drawn in the local contexts (Skeggs 1997; Twine 2010).

Transnational (White) Migration

As feminist research shows, transnational migration constitutes a deeply gendered phenomenon that organizes and (trans)forms the lives of women and men in different ways. Women and men inhabit different social spaces and networks as migrants, and their social locations are reconstructed in different national and regional contexts and in relation to the labor market, the household, and the community. Research on white migration, referring broadly to migration from or within the Western world, shows that gender, as well as race and class restructure white migrant women's positions in the new society, a situation that is negotiated through national ideologies of gender, sexuality, and race (Leonard 2008).

By including white European migrants in the analytical frame of transnational migration, my aim is to broaden and deepen debates about migrating experiences and focus on the continuous racial production that shapes migrants' diverse positions in a global context. From the racially privileged Swedish women who often experienced upward class mobility, I argue that we need to understand migration as a racialized, classed, and gendered phenomenon. The German sociologist Anja Weiss (2005) argues that depending on migrants' positions in the transnationalization of social inequality, we must ask what "quality of space" different groups have access to in order to understand how privileged migrants view themselves through the frame of migration.

Migration as a concept is fundamentally linked to the incentive to increase one's opportunities in life, but Swedish women who migrated to Spain, whether they did so on a permanent or temporary basis, could either increase their prosperity by taking part in global privileges reserved for white migrants abroad, or in some cases experience downward class mobility. Yet, they did not experience the negative social costs of discrimination and racism encountered by darker skinned migrants, who may not qualify for whiteness, but they did have to adjust to Spanish income levels, which were described as being generally lower than those in Sweden.

Being a White Migrant—An Oxymoron

From the informants' viewpoint, the conceptualization of a migrant (immigrant or emigrant) was not one that included them. Their understanding of the term, and its discursive context involved discrimination, borders, and racism, elements that they did not experience from an under-privileged position. The sense of not fitting into the dominant discourse of a migrant was obvious in an interview with Rakel, a 53-year-old Swedish woman who has lived in Spain with her husband for four years. Her two adult children still live in Sweden, but Rakel studies Spanish and plans to stay in Spain for the foreseeable future even though she has not continued to work here. Despite experiencing a deeper economic dependency on her husband, she says she is satisfied with her life.

Catrin: Do you feel like an immigrant in Spain, living like this for the foreseeable future, or ... in some way. What are you?

Rakel: Yeah, that's a really good question. What am I? Yeah, well what I have been thinking about many times is that you are incredibly privileged as white, Swedish, because wherever you go there is no one who is critical toward you. I mean, you can go all over the whole world, and well, I have never met anything negative, and it is the same thing here. I mean, we're really immigrants, if you say so, foreigners, immigrants, okay we are not foreigner in a negative sense. I have never been confronted with anything like that from Spaniards; it's such a difference being Moroc-can or Swedish.... I mean, it is so easy in a way when you ask me what I am, well I actually am an immigrant in their view I guess, but it doesn't feel negative but rather in a positive way.... So what the heck am I?

What the heck am I, asks Rakel? For Rakel, from her privileged position, the situation of an immigrant is not available to her. Since the concept of the (im)migrant is inherently related to negative discrimination, she cannot "be" an immigrant, even though she "actually is one," as she puts it. Thus, here migration is not associated with mobility, but to certain negative experiences and discrimination in the "host country" which Rakel doesn't share, and thus she cannot see herself through the discursive frame of migration. Yet, her (white) privileges enable her to "go all over the whole world" without problems. But migration as such made her conscious of her privileges in relation to other migrants, in this region primarily those from North Africa.

"International Communities" and Institutionalized Whiteness

In Spain, the identification of whiteness was in my analysis not experienced through the identification or disidentification with Spaniards, but in relation to the institutionalization of a particular whiteness juxtaposed with social experiences in the local population. Swedes living in Spain related themselves, socially and culturally, first and foremost to other migrants from Northern Europe, producing a local privileged position outside the Spanish definition of whiteness. This identification was upheld by investing in various forms of capital, such as housing, social networks, private clubs, and private insurance. The women described themselves as being part of an international community consisting of mainly British or Scandinavians in the region of Andalucía, but they seldom had personal relations with Spaniards.

Britt-Marie is 50 years old and moved to Spain seven years ago, after having lived and worked abroad for several years. She has her own business and is living with her son outside Marbella. For her, the most important aspect of moving to Spain was the sunny weather, but also the international atmosphere and way of life here. She describes herself as a person with great social skills with a "fantastic social life," but she cannot identify herself as being an immigrant in Spain.

Britt-Marie: I feel very Swedish ... I have always felt very Swedish. Maybe even more so after moving abroad. When you live in Sweden you don't think about that. Of course you're Swedish.
Catrin: What does that mean more precisely?
Britt-Marie: To be Swedish? Well yes, that you are not by a long way integrated in the Spanish society. Which maybe could be good or bad. But if you settle here. This is not Spain! This is a North-European colony! That's what I think. I think so.
Catrin: Swedes, Brits...
Britt-Marie: ... Dutch, Germans, Russians. It is incredibly international. It is as international as London. And it is probably not a coincidence that I live in these places, because I want an international milieu. That's where I feel most happy. If I'd lived in Sevilla or Jerez it would have been a totally different thing. Then you would have had to confront yourself with the Spanish culture in a different way.

Like Britt-Marie, the women interviewed living in the Spanish Sunbelt socialized primarily with other Northern European migrants from similar social segments who shared the embodiment of "structured invisibility," thus separating them from "visual" migrants, but also from Spaniards. These networks were not defined as migrant communities but as international communities that consist of overlapping and connecting relations between British, French, Scandinavian, and Dutch migrants in this particular part of Andalucía, but less so with Spaniards. "There are no Spaniards here," Britt-Marie says.

> Of course, it is a bit boring, but on the other hand, that wasn't the reason for moving to Spain, to become a Spanish woman, it was rather a question of lifestyle. And then I think the cultures are very different. You have more in common with English people than Spanish people.

Why does Britt-Marie feel she has more in common with English people than Spanish people? Why do some people feel close to each other but distant from others? When analyzing how different nationalities, such as Swedish, Norwegian, Dutch, and British lifestyle migrants tend to cluster in southern Spain, I use Sara Ahmed's (2007) concept of orientations toward whiteness, likeness, and institutions as meeting points where some bodies tend to feel comfortable as they *already belong here*. Whiteness is a position created by "likeness" and "shared attributes" that bring some people together in a foreign context. As Ahmed (2007: 157) puts it, "[w]hen we describe institutions as 'being' white (institutional whiteness), we are pointing to how institutional spaces are shaped by the proximity of some bodies and not others: white bodies gather, and cohere to form the edges of such spaces." Following Ahmed, I argue that the "institutionalization of whiteness" in southern Spain recruits subjects who feel they are part of an international community, but that results in a division between migrants from Northern Europe, other migrants from North Africa, as well as locals from Spain or Andalucía. Being part of an international community is not associated with (demands for) integration into Spanish society, but rather with retaining one's cultural and social norms (and privileges) inside/outside Spain. Migrants carrying white capital can institutionalize this and convert it into other forms of capital, such as social or economic capital.

These social divisions were most often explained by cultural differences between Spanish people and Northern Europeans. Ursula, a woman in her seventies, who has lived outside Marbella with her husband for 20 years, identifies a common cultural ground between Nordic people and parallel distinct cultural features among Spanish people in particular. In a discussion about the similarities and divergences between Brits and Scandinavians living in the Sunbelt, I asked her:

Catrin: Do you socialize with Brits or do you know Brits?
Ursula: Well, I know the ones in the [golf] club. They are a majority. The Spaniards are a minority. Englishmen are the majority and after that come the Scandinavians and then there are some Germans. Maybe some French. Very occasionally Italians.
Catrin: Do you know Spaniards otherwise?
Ursula: Yes! Oh, yes we do! Absolutely! But they are so damn difficult to invite to one's home, I think. For one thing they would like

to come between nine and ten, half past ten. For dinner. But at that time I think we finished dinner. It's too late. And even so in the summer, we think. And then you invite them at nine o'clock, let's say. Well, then they may show up at ten. They are … they are not very orderly. Well then, however nice they may be, you have to speak Spanish with them. And then, if there are other guests here who perhaps do not do that, it often ends up with Englishmen socializing with Englishmen and Northerners socializing with each other. That's how it is! We have sort of a different common culture.

For Ursula, groups are divided along social and cultural lines. Even though she knows Spaniards, it becomes difficult for her to socialize with them, due to different cultural habits, language, and other circumstances. As her statement makes clear, the local golf club—and its costly entrance fees—creates the (class-based) selection of people in her everyday life. In these clubs, the British constitute the majority and Spaniards are in the minority, which allows to Ursula and her husband to socialize with the British despite the cultural difference that exists between Continental Europeans and British Islanders.

National Identity and the "Problem" of Integration

In the coastal town of Fuengirola, the institutionalization of whiteness looked slightly different. Fuengirola constituted a prime destination for Swedish migrants so it was, I was often told, possible to "live an entirely Swedish life" here, which included social networks, food, language, music, as well as professional contacts with insurance companies, dentists, housing, and other needs. At the same time, this view was challenged by the informants as being "stereotypical" and giving a negative picture of Swedes who in fact tried to learn Spanish and to be a part of Spanish society. Yet, during my fieldwork, I learned that most Swedish activities that one could take part in in Fuengirola were on the one hand considerably more inclusive to people with diverse class backgrounds, but on the other hand excluded nationalities other than Swedish. The Swedish women who identified as "upper class"—yet who lived in Fuengirola—were more oriented toward the activities in Marbella than in Fuengirola. The Swedish activities in Fuengirola included genealogical research, the Swedish Church choir, the local sewing circle (informally called "la junta"), a quiz night, and the weekly Swedish dance orchestra night at Hotel Florida, in addition to a variety of Swedish restaurants that organized special activities, clubs for Nordic people, food at Swedish grocery stores, a local Swedish radio station "for Coastal Swedes," and magazines in Swedish, such as *En Sueco*, the *South Coast*, and the *Swedish Magazine*. This also implied that the discourse of an "international community" was not as strong in Fuengirola as in Marbella. Instead Swedes in Fuengirola had to negotiate a discourse of disintegration, the widespread idea that Swedish migrants have no relation to Spanish people or Spanish society.

Freja, 55, has lived with her husband outside Fuengirola for more than 10 years. In light of her experiences in Spain, she has lost her belief in integration.

Freja:	To live in this culture. Even if we are not ... Andalusian people, never will be. We will always be foreigners to them, Andalusian people and Spaniards who live in Andalucía, naturally. Integration ... is something I always fought for, this thing with integration. But it is not easy. And I have taught Swedish to immigrants and things like that.
Catrin:	So how do you think about that in relation to yourself?
Freja:	For my part I must say that the idea of integration is not a valid one. Then you have to be in a mixed marriage, I think. Then you can become integrated. Or that you have lived here for a very long time, like some women and men have done, and they had their children here, that's more Spanish. They have been here for a long time, they came when they were young, they had their children here, the children have become more Spanish than Swedish, even if they can speak Swedish. They have grandchildren, they have sons- and daughters-in-law. That's different. But if you move here when you are older, and do not become part of this thing with schools and children and so on, then it is, then you should get married to someone or have a girlfriend here who is married to a Spanish man.... You know, one always believed in that, oh integration, which is so debated in Sweden, which you have opinions about yourself, but I have to say that I now understand the fact that Chinatown, Rosengård, and what's the name of that place in Stockholm ... Rinkeby, Hammarkullen, and Angered outside Göteborg [different segregated areas in Sweden] exist. I do understand that.... I have a very different view on that today.

For Freja, it is the institutions in a society; schools and marriages that provide integration, and since she is not part of these, integration is not possible for her. In the discussion on integration, Freja compares her own situation to marginalized migrants in Sweden and elsewhere. Due to her experiences in Spain, not only can she now understand the processes of disintegration, but accept them as well. From her migrant position, she has got new experiences, which for her shed new light upon migrants' comparable situation in Sweden. Despite this idea of parallel marginalization with migrants in Sweden, or elsewhere (which was rather common among the informants), this idea was not carried into effect in the local context by socializing with marginalized migrants here, such as Northern Africans or Latin Americans. Instead, the Swedish migrants were integrated into parallel communities of Swedish or Northern European whitenesses.

White Divisions

An analysis of intra-European migrations illuminates how social practices create the idea of a common, culturally homogeneous European (white) identity. What appears to be a South-North divide is built upon a deep intra-Nordic postcolonial identification and identification with Anglo-Saxon countries and cultures—and parallel disidentification with the former colonial powers in Southern Europe. In this way, the idea of a homogeneous whiteness—often interchangeable with "the idea of the West" (Bonnett 2004)—is disentangled. Through an analysis of Swedish women as migrants, the chapter strives to destabilize the idea of whiteness as a homogeneous entity. Ruth Frankenberg has argued that whiteness "is a complexly constructed product of local, regional, national and global relations, past and present. Thus the range of possible ways of living whiteness, for an individual white woman in a particular time and place, is delimited by the relations of racism at that moment and in that place" (1993: 236). Reinstalling whiteness in different national racial systems could either improve one's feeling of opportunities in life, but as well involve a sense of being deprived of one's normative and structurally invisible position. Yet, for Swedish women, these forms of mobility and reorientations are not elaborated through the discursive frame of migration, because the concept of migration is deeply interrelated with racialized groups and bodies, negative discrimination and borders. This chapter shows how this division is lived, negotiated, and reinscribed by Swedish migrants who mark a cultural distance toward Spaniards, which draws the line for the institutionalization of a certain migrant community, to some extent separated from the local Spanish society. As privileged migrants they identify as being part of an international community outside the discursive boundaries of "locals" and "migrants." Beverley Skeggs (2004: 49) puts it this way: "[m]obility and control over mobility both reflect and reinforce power."

The chapter illustrates how while whiteness constitutes a form of structural privilege that is convertible to local forms of privilege transnationally, it is not a static global position. Rather, it takes various shapes in shifting social and racial national and regional logics, as whitenesses have always done. Ramón Grosfoguel (2003) suggests that the map of whiteness changed during "the second modernity" 1650–1945 when Europe's "heart" moved from Spain and Portugal to the Northern parts of Europe and further to the United States. As a result of this shift, the previously "white" Southern Europe was partly excluded from the discursive field of whiteness (a tendency which is currently reinforced by the economic crisis in Europe). Grosfoguel (2003, 45) argues that "'Hispanics' were constructed as part of the inferior others excluded from the superior 'white' 'European' 'races'."

Nevertheless, the fact that the imagining of "the white Europe" is deconstructed does not imply that European privileges in relation to mobility, accessibility, and (global) rights are dissolved. Privileges of whiteness connected to institutions, passports, or bodies, are still contingent forms of white capital for migrants socially classified as white, which are transferrable to other contexts, being relocated and renegotiated in relation to local formations of class, gender, race, and sexuality in different geographical spaces. Thus, we need to be sensitive to the fragmented constructions of contemporary whitenesses, yet remain alert to the forms of "white privilege that are not undone, and may even be repeated and intensified, through declarations of whiteness, or though the recognition of privilege as privilege," as Ahmed (2004: 58) points out.

Acknowledgments

I would like to thank the women who shared their time and stories with me during my field work. This research would not have been possible without the support from the foundation of Helge Axison Johnson. Thanks to Umeá Ientre for Gender Studies and the participants at Images of Whiteness in Oxford 2012, for important comments on this research.

References

Ahmed, Sara. 2004. "Declarations of Whiteness: The Non-Performativity of Anti-Racism." *Borderlands*, 3(2).
———. 2007. "The Phenomenology of Whiteness." *Feminist Theory* 8: 149–68.
Benhabib, Seyla, and Judith Resnik. 2009. "Introduction: Citizenship and Migration: Theory Engendered." In *Migration and Mobilities: Citizenship, Borders and Gender*, edited by Seyla Benhabib and Judith Resnik, 1–44. New York: New York University Press.
Bonilla-Silva Eduardo. 2012. "The Invisible Weight of Whiteness: The Racial Grammar of Everyday Life in Contemporary America." *Ethnic and Racial Studies* 35(2): 173–194.
Bonnett, Alastair. 2004. *The Idea of the West: Culture, Politics and History*. Basingstoke, UK: Palgrave Macmillan.

Bourdieu, Pierre. 1984. *Distinction: A social Critique of the Judgment of Taste*. London: Routledge.

Frankenberg, Ruth. 1993. *White Women, Race Matters: The Social Constructions of Whiteness*. Minneapolis: University of Minnesota Press.

Glick Schiller, Nina, Lisa Basch, and Cristina Szanton Blanc. 1995. "From Immigrant to Transmigrant: Theorizing Transnational Migration." *Anthropological Quarterly* 68(1): 48–63.

Grosfoguel, Ramon. 2003. *Colonial Subjects: Puerto Ricans in a Global Perspective*. Berkeley: University of California Press.

Hübinette, Tobias, and Catrin Lundström. 2011. "Sweden after the Recent Election: The Double-Binding Power of Swedish Whiteness through the Mourning of the Loss of 'Old Sweden' and the Passing of 'Good Sweden.'" *NORA: Nordic Journal of Feminist and Gender Research* 19(1): 42–52.

Hughey, Matthew W. 2010. "The (Dis)Similarities of White Racial Identities: The Conceptual Framework of 'Hegemonic Whiteness.'" *Ethnic and Racial Studies* 33(8): 1289–1309.

Leonard, Pauline. 2008. "Migrating Identities: Gender, Whiteness and Britishness in Post-Colonial Hong Kong." *Gender, Place and Culture* 15(1): 45–60.

Lipsitz, George. 1995. *The Possessive Investment in Whiteness: How White People Profit from Identity Politics*. Philadelphia: Temple University Press.

Lundström, Catrin. 2007. *Svenska latinas. Ras, klass och kön i svenskhetens geografi* [Swedish Latinas: Race, class and gender in geographic Swedishness]. Stockholm/Göteborg: Makadam.

Omi, Michael, and Howard Winant. 1994. *Racial Formation in the United States: From the 1960s to the 1990s*. New York: Routledge.

Skeggs, Beverley. 1997. *Formations of Class and Gender: Becoming Respectable*. London: Sage.

———. 2004. *Class, Self, Culture*. New York: Routledge.

Steyn, Melissa, and Daniel Conway. 2010. "Introduction: Intersecting Whiteness, Interdisciplinary Debates." *Ethnicities* 10(3): 283–91.

Twine, France Winddance. 2010. *A White Side of Black Britain: Interracial Intimacy and Racial Literacy*. Durham, NC: Duke University Press.

———, and Charles Gallagher. 2008. "The Future of Whiteness: A Map of the 'Third Wave,'" in "Whiteness and White Identities," special issue, *Ethnic and Racial Studies* 31(1): 4–24.

Ware, Vron. 2010. "Whiteness in the Glare of War: Soldiers, Migrants and Citizenship." *Ethnicities* 10(3): 313–330.

Weiss, Anja. 2005. "The Transnationalization of Social Inequality: Conceptualizing Social Positions on a World Scale." *Current Sociology* 53(4): 707–728.

CHAPTER 9

Residential Mobility and the Market Value of Whiteness in Boston

MELISSA MacDONALD AND FRANCE WINDDANCE TWINE

Between 1998 and 2001 Becca, a thirty-two-year-old single mother and former welfare recipient, lived in a series of homeless shelters as well as in a homeless community under a bridge with her boyfriend, a Native American (American Indian) from California. Their daughter was born in October of 2001. After her daughter's birth she applied for welfare assistance and was assigned to Section 8 housing. Her Section 8 housing voucher provided her with the opportunity to move outside of Boston, Massachusetts to the suburb of Norfolk, Massachusetts.

How do individual, welfare dependent white women, like Becca, negotiate the structures of institutional racism in the housing market? What benefits do they gain by employing their whiteness as a form of capital in this context? Describing her ability to move into her previous town of residence, Norfolk, Massachusetts, Becca states, "I knew what public housing had done to my mother. It was hellish, so Section 8 would be my best chance because I knew I wanted to live in a suburb." She goes on:

> Without a question there is a stereotype and fortunately I did use white privilege. I could pass in a certain way. I did present myself well. I do speak well. I'm using that privilege … and it was something I needed to do in order to get where I needed to be—I had to use my white privilege to get in [to her apartment].

Today Becca and her daughter live in a two-bedroom, Section 8[1] apartment in Newton, Massachusetts. Newton is a predominantly white upper middle-class residential community. The median income in Newton, Massachusetts is $107,696 and the media home cost is $692,000. White people comprise 82.3% of the local residential population while Asians make up 11.5%, blacks make up 2.5%, and Hispanics are 4.1%; 72.8% of the population has earned a bachelor's degree. Only 5.9% of the population, compared to 10.5% of the population in the state of Massachusetts, lives below the poverty line. What we learn from Becca is that being white is a form of capital that one can employ to gain access to residential communities that are racially segregated as well as class segregated.

In 1968 the U.S. Congress passed the Fair Housing Act. This legislation criminalized what had previously been state-sanctioned segregation by race in the U.S. rental and real estate markets. After more than four decades, residential segregation by race and class continues as a durable form of inequality and a stable feature of the U.S. rental market.

Residential segregation is associated with life-long disadvantages that include limited access to friendship networks, limited access to quality public education, and limited access to affordable housing, as well as exposure to higher rates of violence and crime. This form of residential segregation has been described by the sociologists Douglas Massey and Nancy Denton (1993) as a form of "American apartheid." Their research has revealed that blacks in particular, are hypersegregated from other

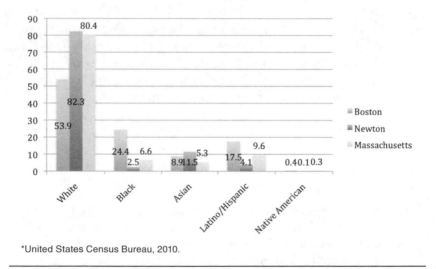

*United States Census Bureau, 2010.

Figure 9.1 Percentage of the population by race and ethnicity, 2010.

groups and this has very harmful consequences for single and married mothers of African ancestry.

Boston, like Chicago, is representative of this hypersegregation and its consequences. In this chapter we contribute to and expand the literature on white privilege and residential mobility by providing a nuanced analysis of the ways that whiteness can be deployed as a form of privilege and converted into economic and social capital in specific local and regional contexts by welfare dependent women. Drawing upon a field research project we show how women deploy racial privilege as part of a larger strategy to facilitate movement out of impoverished residential neighborhoods and into racially exclusive and class segregated white, middle-class communities. This strategic use of whiteness as a mobility strategy provides welfare dependent white women and their families with access to a number of financial, material, social, and symbolic resources unavailable to black and Latina welfare recipients.

Drawing from twenty-five interviews with twenty former and current welfare dependent white women,[2] we identify six potential benefits white welfare dependent women gain from concealing their welfare status in a racially segregated housing market. First, it enabled them to secure access to Section 8 housing located in middle- and upper middle-class suburban communities where there was less demand for social services for low-income families. Second, it provided access to material resources due to reduced competition for donated food, clothing, gifts, and in-kind services provided by local philanthropists. Third, these neighborhoods provided access to safety by reducing exposure to physical violence and theft. Fourth, the children of welfare dependent women gained access to superior public education services, especially for those children with special needs. Fifth, concealing one's welfare status provided access to privileged social networks and social capital. Finally, concealing one's welfare status mediated welfare stigma and provided welfare dependent white women with a form of respectability.

Welfare Stigma Management

Erving Goffman (1963) defines social stigma as a discrepancy between an individual's virtual social identity and an individual's actual social identity. Three types of social stigma exist: physical defects or deformities, character flaws and "tribal stigmas of race, nation, and religion" (Goffman 1963, 4). Using Goffman's framework, the poor, especially welfare recipients, are stigmatized due to their "blemishes of individual character." Elaborating further, Goffman argues that all stigmatized individuals fall between two categories: the discredited or the discreditable. A stigmatized individual is characterized as discredited when his or his stigma is readily apparent or has been previously exposed to others. "Covering up" is the process by which a discredited individual manages and reduces tension in mixed social interactions. Covering-up strategies primarily involve efforts "to restrict the display of those failings most centrally identified with the stigma" (Goffman 1963, 103), which is an essential component of assimilative techniques. For example, changes in name or physical appearance are not merely about passing as nondeviant but function to minimize the presence of one's stigma in social interactions.

Conversely, discreditable individuals are those whose stigma is unknown to others. In order to manage personal information, the discreditable use of "passing" as normal is a stigma management strategy. One critical passing strategy "is to conceal or obliterate signs that have come to be stigma symbols" (Goffman 1963, 92) which often occurs along with the use of disidentifiers. Furthermore, those who pass strategically maintain physical and social distance with others in order to ensure the concealment of their stigma. Goffman identifies different levels of passing activities. The discreditable individual may unintentionally engage in passing; engage in passing "for fun"; engage in passing for nonroutine or routine daily occasions; or "completely pass … in all areas of life, the secret being known to the passer himself" (Goffman 1963, 79). Given the nature of passing, a discreditable individual can experience an act of discrediting, which reassigns the individual as discredited. According to Goffman, however, the means by which one employs passing or covering-up strategies "are quite similar … and in some cases identical" (Goffman 1963, 102).

The literature on welfare stigma and management has illuminated the various ways welfare dependent women have negotiated welfare stigma. Drawing upon Goffman's (1963) foundational work on social stigma, numerous research studies have explored the depth to which welfare recipients internalize the social stigma associated with welfare dependency and the range of stigma coping strategies that welfare recipient's employ to manage, resist, and challenge the stereotypes they face (Briar 1966; Goodban 1985; Rank 1994; Roger-Dillons 1995; Jarret 1996; Kaplan 1997; McCormack 2004, 2005; Latimer 2006; Cleaveland 2008; Reutter et al. 2009).[3] These studies found that stigmatized individuals employed collective or individual responses for managing stigmatizing labels, perceptions, and treatment. In particular, welfare recipients "respond[ed] to [social] stigma with a variety of cognitive and behavioral strategies that reflect[ed] their efforts to reconcile their "social" and "personal" identities" (Reutter et. al. 2009, 297). The literature highlights five stigma management strategies: avoidance, passing, seeking social support, self-promotion, and social distancing. In this chapter we focus on passing, concealment, and covering-up stigma management strategies utilized to facilitate social class mobility into racially exclusive and class segregated white, middle-class communities. These strategies enable mothers to access resources denied to whites and ethnic minorities living in lower-income communities.

The welfare stigma management literature (Roger-Dillons 1995; Kaplan 1997; Seccombe 1998; Latimer 2006; Reutter et al. 2009) indicates that welfare recipients attempt to improve their interpersonal experiences by passing as nondeviants. Welfare recipients, along with other economically disadvantaged groups, "can minimize their poverty status by convincing others that they are not poor" (Latimer 2006, 91). For example, Seccombe's (1998) research found that some welfare recipients attempted to pass as part of the middle class by not identifying their welfare use. These women often used clothes and other social status markers to signify their status as part of the middle class. In her study of black teenage motherhood, Kaplan (1997) found that teen mothers used "covering-up" strategies to mask their welfare recipient status. In particular, welfare recipients "dressed up" or didn't "carry themselves as poor" in order to avoid recognition and "to make [themselves] less vulnerable to the stigma associated with [black] welfare mothers" (Kaplan 1997, 149). Other impoverished individuals worked to conceal their stigmatized status by changing personal biographies (Kaplan 1997) or by withholding key personal information (Reutter et al. 2009) For example, in Kaplan's study, black teenage mothers often omitted their welfare dependency status or prior history. These individuals frequently "used nondisclosure to protect themselves from overt discrimination" (Reutter et al. 2009, 305). None of these research studies, however, critically addressed the ways in which the intersection of race and social class status mitigated welfare recipients' ability to pass as middle-class women and within which social, geographic contexts such passing or covering up strategies were employed.

Goffman and Whiteness Studies

Although Erving Goffman (1963) and Pierre Bourdieu (1984), in contrast to Franz Fanon and Albert Memmi, do not explicitly address race, racism, or postcoloniality, their concepts can be applied to white women who are perceived as socially transgressive (Twine 2010). Critical race scholars can employ Goffman's concept of covering to theorize the ways that white women who are poor negotiate respectability and stigma. In the United States, black women, regardless of welfare dependency status, already have a "spoiled identity." Due to their blackness, they occupy a discredited social position and are often assumed to be welfare dependent by virtue of their blackness. Thus black welfare dependent women are often unable to employ passing or concealment as a stigma management strategy. White women, however, by virtue of their race privilege, are always creditable until they are proven otherwise. White welfare dependent women can conceal their welfare dependency and pass for middle class, thereby obtaining social mobility for their children, because their whiteness serves as a flexible form of capital.

Cheryl Harris (1993) theorizes that whiteness, as the basis of racialized privilege, was constructed and legitimated in law as a type of property. Property and whiteness share a common premise: "a right to exclude" (Harris 1993, 1714). Those who legally qualified for whiteness were granted "the legal right to exclude others from the privileges inhering in whiteness; whiteness became an exclusive club whose membership was closely and grudgingly guarded" (1736). Drawing from the legal history of *Plessy v. Ferguson*[4] (1896) and *Brown v. Board of Education*[5] (1954), Harris illustrates the transition of whiteness as a form of status property to a form of modern property. One of the primary property functions of whiteness is the right to use and enjoyment. Whiteness, as the embodiment of white privilege, can be deployed as a resource or usable property, maintained by the law's regard and protection (1734). Thus, for white women, being legally and socially classified as white "meant gaining access to a whole set of public and private privileges that materially and permanently guaranteed basic subsistence needs and, therefore, survival" (1713).

Drawing from Bourdieu's (1984) groundbreaking work, France Winddance Twine in *A White Side of Black Britain: Interracial Intimacy and Racial Literacy* (2010) identifies "the ways white members of interracial families in Britain negotiate race, racism and racialization and acquire racial literacy" (4). Her longitudinal study illustrates how various forms of capital (economic, cultural, social, symbolic, and ethnic) possessed by white mothers parenting children fathered by black men structured their transracial lives and mediated their experiences of race, racism, and their whiteness. For white mothers, whiteness was a form of embodied capital that could be traded for social, cultural, or economic capital in specific contexts. In particular, Twine notes that white women who were positioned as working class or poor were not able to leverage their whiteness in ways that middle-class white women were able to do and were disciplined and subjected to various forms of "rebound racism." In other words, they symbolically stood in for their black partners.

Like Hartigan (1999) and McDermott (2005), Twine argues that locality is crucial in the ways that whiteness is interpreted, managed, and deployed strategically. In postcolonial and multicultural cities in the Midlands of England, "whiteness has multiple meanings and its value can vary depending on the family dynamics, the local community, and the resources available to the family" (Twine 2010, 220). In particular, value of whiteness for working-class white women who possess little economic, social, or cultural capital and sexually partner with black men is diminished. Twine argues, "Their whiteness, rather than becoming a source of status or social resources, can become a stigma, and in some cases a liability" (Twine 2010, 222). Similarly, white women who find themselves welfare dependent (TAFDC or AFDC) may find the value of their whiteness enhanced or diminished based upon the local context.

Today whiteness continues to be a resource that can be deployed to provide greater access to desirable housing, even among the poorest families. While poverty and class inequality restricts the type of housing that welfare-dependent white women can afford, nevertheless, white women possess forms of embodied capital that black women and brown skinned Latina women lack. These forms of capital can provide them with material, social, and psychological privileges that are not available to women who are not perceived as white in the U.S. context (Du Bois [1935]1999; Roediger 1991; Frank 1998). In other words, racism and white supremacy continues to structure access to the housing market at all income levels in the post-Civil Rights era.

Research Setting: The Greater Boston Area

McCormack (2005) expressed difficulty in locating white welfare recipients for her research on welfare stigma management. McCormack theorized that, "white recipients may have more at stake in protecting their identity and concealing their welfare status as they are not already marked [by their skin color]" (McCormack 2005, 665). These women may be more likely to pass as middle-class and as a result, would be reluctant to be identified as a welfare recipient in any context (research or otherwise). The Greater Boston area was chosen as a field location because it contains a range of neighborhood types, including predominantly white lower working class, predominantly black lower working class, multiethnic lower working class, predominantly white and middle class, in close proximity in which white women on welfare may theoretically reside.

The "Greater Boston," area, comprised of Essex, Middlesex, Suffolk, and Norfolk counties, has a population of over 4.9 million residents and is the tenth largest metropolitan area in the United States.[6] Greater Boston includes Boston city proper, which has a population of 617,594.[7] The city has a population density of 11,900 people per square mile, ranking just behind New York City, Chicago, and San Francisco.[8] There are twenty-one official neighborhoods in the city of Boston: Allston/Brighton, Back Bay, Bay Village, Beacon Hill, Charlestown, Chinatown/Leather District,

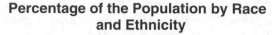

Percentage of the Population by Race and Ethnicity

■ White   ■ Black   ■ Asian   ■ Latino/Hispanic   ■ Native American

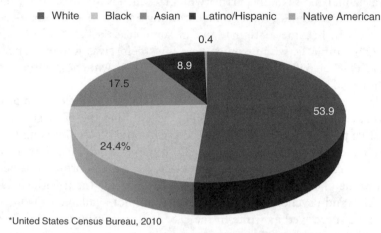

*United States Census Bureau, 2010

Figure 9.2 Racial and ethnic breakdown of the city of Boston, Massachusetts.

Dorchester, Downtown/Financial District, East Boston, Fenway/Kenmore, Hyde Park, Jamaica Plain, Mattapan, Mission Hill, North End, Roslindale, Roxbury, South Boston, South End, West End, and West Roxbury.

Boston's overall racial demographics are 53.9% white, 17.5% Latino or Hispanic, 24.4% black, 8.9% Asian, 5.0% mixed raced and less than 1% Native American and Pacific Islander.[9] The city's overall ethnic population includes 15.8% Irish, 8.3% Italian, and 6.4% West Indian.[10] In 2010 the median household income was $50,683[11] compared to Massachusetts' median household income of $64,509.[12] In 2000, Boston was ranked 13th and 20th for the most racially segregated metropolitan area for blacks and Hispanics.[13] The Boston Indicators Project found that "almost one in five African Americans in Massachusetts—19%—live in the area of Boston spanning Roxbury, Mission Hill, Mattapan and South Dorchester, while 14% reside in Jamaica Plain, Roslindale, West Roxbury, and North Dorchester."[14] Boston city proper remains highly racially and ethnically segregated. For example, while Boston city proper's Black population was 25.3%,[15] Dorchester and Mattapan's black population was 36.0%[16] and 77.0%[17] respectively.

Numerous racially, ethnically, and class segregated suburban communities border Boston. For example, Newton, Massachusetts' racial demographics are 81.1% white, 2.7% black, 11.5% Asian, 0.1% Native American, and 3.5% Hispanic.[18] The city has a median household income of $107,696 per year. In 2010, the median home cost $692,000 and 72.5% of the

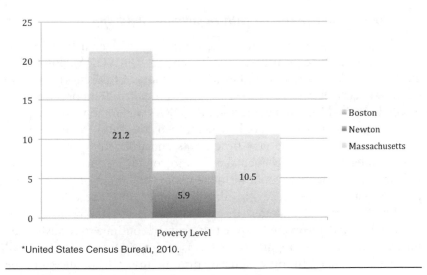

*United States Census Bureau, 2010.

Figure 9.3 Percentage of the population below the poverty line, 2000.

population owned their own home; only 4.5% of the population resided below the federal poverty line; 96.1% of Newton held a high school diploma, and 72.0% held a bachelor's degree or higher.[19] Brookline, Massachusetts' racial demographics are 81.1% white, 2.7% black, 12.8% Asian, 0.1% Native American, and 3.5% Hispanic. In 2000, the median family income was $92,993 per year. The median family home was worth $599,500; 96.3% of the Brookline population held a high school diploma; and 76.9% of the population held a bachelor's degree or higher; 4.5% of Brookline families lived below the federal poverty line.[20] Franklin, Massachusetts' racial demographics are 96.0% white, 1.1% black, 1.1% Hispanic, 1.7% Asian, and less than 1% Native American. The median family income was $71, 174 per year; 92.9% of the Franklin population held a high school diploma; and 42.7% of the population held a bachelor's degree or higher; 2.8% of Franklin families lived below the federal poverty line. Dedham, Massachusetts' racial demographics are 94.51% white, 1.54% black, 1.87% Asian, and 2.42% Hispanic. Dedham's median household income is $61,699 per year; 87.9% of the population has a high school diploma; 33.0% of the population has a bachelor's degree or higher; 3.2% of the Dedham families live below the poverty line. Finally, Canton, Massachusetts' racial demographics are 92.5% white, 2.9% black, 1.4% Hispanic, and less than 1% Asian. The median household income is $69,260; 93.2% of the population has a high school diploma; 44.7% of the population has a bachelor's degree or higher; 2.2% of Canton families live below the poverty line.

Transitional Aid to Families with Dependent Children

On August 22, 1996 President Clinton signed the Personal Responsibility Work and Opportunity Reconciliation Act (PRWORA). PRWORA effectively replaced Aid to Families with Dependent Children with a more decentralized and restrictive welfare program called Temporary Aid to Needy Families (TANF). Furthering PRWORA's welfare to workfare goal, new provisions limited welfare benefits to two consecutive years and five years cumulatively. These new time limits and work first policies effectively hindered welfare recipients' efforts to complete educational or job training programs that would ultimately move them out of poverty and public assistance dependency (Mink and Solinger 2003; Reese 2005).

PRWORA radically altered the welfare landscape for impoverished welfare dependent women. Despite this, women continue to receive some forms of government support. These forms of support have different social and material values. In this chapter we draw on research conducted in the Greater Boston Area to argue that women who are physically qualified for whiteness, meaning that they are socially classified as "white" in the U.S. racial system, are often able to access housing benefits that are unavailable to women who are classified as "black" or are brown skinned Latinas. In a context in which impoverished women are demonized, criminalized, and defined as a social problem for taxpayers, race structures how women negotiate gaining access to housing when they are welfare dependent.

Section 8 Housing in Massachusetts

Massachusetts's Section 8 housing, a federally funded program, provides low-income residents with the opportunity to rent housing that meets the program's health and safety requirements, through housing vouchers in an area of their choice. Massachusetts has three different types of housing vouchers: Federal Section 8 Housing Choice Voucher Program, Massachusetts Rental Voucher Program (MRVP), and Alternative Housing Voucher Program (AHVP). Eligible candidates for Section 8, MRVP, and AHVP vouchers must meet the following requirements: (1) the candidate's household must have limited income (i.e., a household's net income [after deductions] no greater than 200% of the federal poverty guidelines); and (2) at least one member of the household must be a U.S. citizen or eligible noncitizen. For the state-funded MRVP and AHVP programs, all noncitizens are eligible.[21] For the federally funded Section 8 program, only some noncitizens are eligible. In general, you must be in one of these categories to be eligible: U.S. citizen, permanent resident, refugee or asylum seeker, withholding grantee, conditional, entrant, or parolee, registered alien or

1986 amnesty status, and victim of trafficking. Undocumented noncitizens are allowed to live with an eligible family member who has a voucher.
Individuals are ineligible for housing vouchers if: (1) they have a recent
history of illegal drug use, alcohol abuse, or violent criminal behavior; (2)
have committed fraud in connection with a housing assistance program
in the past (for example, lying on an application); or (3) the apartment
an individual plans to rent is owned by a family member or other close
relative.

The waiting lists for rent vouchers in Massachusetts are very long. The
majority of housing voucher candidates, who meet the eligibility requirements, may wait several years before receiving a voucher. One's place on a
waiting list depends on the preference category he or she is in, and when
the individual applied. Individuals who are listed in one of the high preference categories move ahead of nonpreference category individuals on the
waiting list. For MRVP and AHVP vouchers, preference is given to people
in these categories, in this order: (1) people who are homeless due to fire,
earthquake, flood, or other disaster; (2) people who are homeless or will
be made homeless due to public action such as urban renewal or other
public improvement; (3) people who are homeless or will be made homeless due to public action related to sanitary code violations; (4) people in
emergency situations, whose life or safety is threatened by a lack of suitable housing, such as victims of domestic abuse or those with medical
emergencies; (5) people with disabilities who are living in nonpermanent

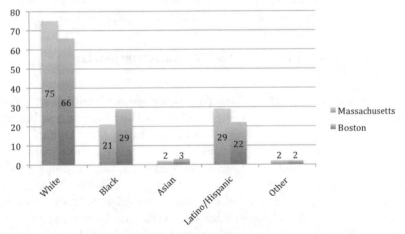

*Massachusetts Tenant Based Voucher U.S. Department of Housing and Urban Development
Resident Characteristics Report, October, 2011.

Figure 9.4 Percentage of tenant based housing vouchers by race/ethnicity, 2011.

transitional AHVP housing; (6) people who are already in public housing who must move; (7) standard applicants not in any of the above categories. For MRVP and AHVP vouchers, within each preference category, veterans or families of deceased veterans whose death was service-related, get priority. Local residents who live and work in the community receive housing vouchers next.[22]

Between July 1, 2010 and October 31, 2011, the state of Massachusetts had 52,206 individuals receiving tenant vouchers, 12,311 of whom resided in the Boston metropolitan area. The average annual income of Massachusetts tenant voucher recipients was $15,443 and $16,009 for Boston tenant voucher recipients. Thirty-nine percent of Massachusetts' tenant voucher recipients receive some form of welfare benefits. Thirty-four percent of Boston area tenant voucher recipients receive some form of welfare benefits. Female-headed households with children constituted 41% of Massachusetts tenant voucher recipients and 38% of Boston tenant recipients. The majority of tenant voucher recipients in Massachusetts are white. Seventy-five percent of Massachusetts tenant voucher recipients were white, 21% were black/African American only, 2% were Asian only, 1% were Native Hawaiian or Pacific Islander only; and 1% were any other combination. Twenty-nine percent of Massachusetts tenant voucher recipients were Hispanic or Latino; 66% of Boston tenant voucher recipients were white only; more than 10% higher than Boston's white resident population overall. Twenty-nine percent of tenant voucher recipients were black/African American only, 3% were Asian only, 1% were Native Hawaiian or Pacific Islander only; and 1% was any other racial combination. Twenty-two percent of Boston tenant voucher recipients were Hispanic or Latino.[23]

The Class Closet: The Benefits of Camouflaging Welfare Dependency

Using four cases of welfare dependent white women residing in suburban communities, we identify six material, social, and symbolic benefits white welfare dependent women gain by concealing their welfare status in a racially and class-segregated housing market. First, it enabled them to secure access to Section 8 housing located in middle- and upper middle-class suburban communities where there was less demand for social services for low-income families. Second, it provided access to material resources due to reduced competition for donated food, clothing, gifts, and in-kind services provided by local philanthropists. Third, these neighborhoods provided access to safety by reducing the women's exposure to physical violence and theft. Fourth, the children of welfare dependent women gained access to superior public education services, especially for those children with special needs. Fifth, concealing one's welfare status provided access to privileged social networks and social capital. Sixth, concealing one's welfare status mediated welfare stigma by providing respectability.

Theresa: Respectability and the Class Closet

Theresa is a forty-nine-year-old, white woman and former welfare recipient. Theresa is the twice divorced mother of four children. In 1981, at age eighteen, she married her first husband, a white man. Shortly after she became pregnant with her son David, her husband, was incarcerated and would remain in and out of the criminal justice system for the next thirty years. She gave birth to her eldest son, David, in August 1982 and her daughter, Krissy, in December 1983. Theresa eventually divorced her first husband in 1985 and left her two children in the care of paternal relatives in Portland, Maine. Her second husband, who is socially classified as a black American, is the father of her two youngest children. Her third son, Mark, was born in September 1992 and her youngest son, Sean, in April 1994. Her children, however, can be socially classified as olive skinned white ethnics, which protects them from the overt racism that children being parented by women (mothers) classified as black and of visible African ancestry, routinely encounter in the Boston area.

Theresa and her second husband were married in 1995 in order to qualify for Section 8 housing together. After discovering used needles outside of her East Boston apartment in the summer of 1998, Theresa made the decision to move her family into one of Boston's suburbs. One of the strategies that Theresa employed in order to secure housing in a residentially segregated community, was to lie about her biography and conceal her welfare status. In her view she had no other choice after being denied housing several times. Describing the difficulty of trying to access housing reserved for middle-class employed families, she explains why she began to conceal (or lie) about her employment status. She states,

> I remember when I was looking for places when my kids were little and me and my ex had the Section 8. I ran into a lot of deterrents.... Once ... like you know, you can feel ... you know how you can feel ... I went to one apartment. I went to go look at it. It was in Swampscott. It was really nice. It was up on the hill.... It's very wealthy. It's a lot of real ritzy people. I didn't say I had Section 8 because I never bring that up when I go to an interview for an apartment. I wait until after I get accepted from them, but with this one ... I got the impression. He says to me, "I got like twenty applications. I don't know if you even want to bother." I don't know if he sensed by my

appearance that I wasn't of money. But he kind of deterred me. It took me three months to find a place. I looked at places every single day. A lot of them were like, "Oh yeah. You're like the tenth person. We've got a lot of applications. We'll put you on file. We'll run your references." You know what I mean?

After being rejected so many times, she realized she needed to change her biography. Theresa states,

So then I felt I had to lie. I had to say I was working. I had to say that I was who I wasn't. I had to pretend to be someone else. I had to put up a façade that wasn't really comfortable.

Altering one's personal biography to conceal welfare status was not enough to secure affordable housing in Boston's white, middle class suburbs. Theresa also had to alter her physical presentation to match her new class performance. She describes her new style:

I always made sure that I was very … you know, pressed clothes and dressed very decent and had my makeup on, had my hair done. You know, I wouldn't go with you know, holey jeans. You know, choose your words wisely. Think before you talk. Not say too much. It's nerve wracking looking for an apartment and trying to sell yourself to a landlord to rent their place.

For Theresa, and many other white women on welfare in this study, performing respectable white femininity meant passing as middle class and this became a critical strategy to secure privileged housing opportunities.

Once Theresa began to conceal her welfare history, she found an apartment in Dedham. She settled, however, for the worst apartment she could find in this residential community. Describing her prospects in Dedham, Massachusetts she states,

And when I moved out of East Boston to Dedham I settled for less. [What was that place like?] It was a really a … I looked at it. I didn't like it. It was a rundown townhouse that was very drafty. There was only one place where heat came up from downstairs. And then if you didn't block the downstairs, you had no heat upstairs. The pipes used to freeze every winter. The kitchen pipe and the bathroom pipe would freeze every winter. The basement was like a cave. It was really bad but I was so desperate to move out of East Boston. I took it.

Despite these challenges, Theresa and her family remained in Dedham for five years for the safety, educational, and social resources it provided.

Like many women, Theresa chose the suburbs because it would provide a better life for her children. Quality public education was critical to achieving this goal. Theresa states,

> I didn't want to raise them in any of the Boston schools so we moved to Dedham. [Why not Boston Public Schools?] Because Boston Schools is no education.... I went to Boston Schools and I never finished. You know, there is just so much that goes on that it's hard for a kid to focus on their learning when you've gotta go through a metal detector just to get into school. You have to worry about the next person jumping you. You have to worry about gangs. There is so much to worry about in Boston schools where in the suburbs you don't have that.

Describing the educational services her son, Mark, receives as a special needs student, Theresa states,

> He was in a very tiny class. There might have been twelve or fourteen kids. They had a teacher, an assistant teacher, plus three aids. So he had one on one a lot. Also they allowed him, because he couldn't sit still, to stand up by the window if he wanted to as long as he wasn't disturbing the class. As long as he wasn't disrupting the class, he was allowed to do things that the Boston public schools wouldn't have never allowed him to do. So it made it a little easier for him in school.

Unlike most special needs students in the Boston Public School system, Theresa's son receives superior educational and emotional resources through her suburban public school system. Access to these services would not have been possible if Theresa was unable to capitalize on her whiteness to gain entrée into a highly racially segregated housing market.

Becca: Safety and High Quality Education as Privileged Emotional Resources

Becca, a low-income, welfare dependent mother, gains access to a variety of material benefits from residing in a white suburban, middle class community. These benefits included physical safety and improved educational resources. Describing her current safety level in Newton, Massachusetts, Becca states,

Well my safety is not a concern. Um, I'm not worried about getting robbed. I'm driving a Hyundai you know, no one is going to rifle through my Hyundai [laughs]. I do feel safe. I don't feel like I'm going to get shot. All of those basic safety concerns and safety needs are there which is awesome. Um, for me, I don't feel like [pauses] I don't feel like, I feel really safe and I think that is important because I've slept under bridges before. That wasn't there for me....

I don't feel scared when I walk out of my house at 9 o'clock at night. I can go to the store and I can do things and not worry about my physical safety. I'm not worried about being attacked. That is lovely.

Like several women interviewed for this study, Becca had a history of domestic violence and had endured abuse in her relationship with the father of her daughter. As a result of her history of domestic violence and homelessness, Becca perceived safety as a precious resource and did not take it for granted.

For many white welfare mothers, ensuring that their children had access to quality public school systems meant moving to middle- and upper middle-class, white suburbs. Becca's daughter, Taylor, was diagnosed with a generalized anxiety disorder and a global development delay, placing her academically three years behind grade level. In order to support her daughter's special needs, Becca sought out communities with exceptional public school systems. She states,

I knew my daughter had extraordinary needs. So I told myself I need to get myself into a community that has what she needs. Newton, right now, has what she needs. Um, I know I don't pay taxes but my landlord does and you know? I'm going to take advantage of it. I'm going to get those services for her. So she has, you know, has access to more services, more scholarships. If I need to get her into a tutoring program, I have a scholarship for that.... The only reason why I'm here is for that outside placement. If I don't get the outside placement, I'm out of here. I don't like it here. I'm here for the school system. It's the best school system in the country. I will exploit it. Absolutely....

I got a tutoring scholarship for somewhere in Needham, which is also another community that's affluent. Being around affluence sort of helps you access more things when there's not so many hands in the pot. You know, that expanded access is really important to me. They have funds for my priorities: special needs education. That's important to me.

Affluent suburban neighborhoods provide high quality public education and access to additional educational services such as tutoring, that welfare dependent children residing in low-income, urban neighborhoods often do not. For instance, in the Newton public school system Taylor is provided with an inclusion classroom with scaffold instruction from a general education teacher, a special education teacher, and two classroom paraprofessionals. In addition, Taylor receives weekly sessions of cognitive behavioral therapy and social skills building groups with the school psychologist. Thus, educating one's child in middle-class, white neighborhoods and suburbs allowed white women on welfare, like Becca, the possibility of class mobility for their children.

Leanne: Access to Privileged Residential Housing and Material Resources

Leanne is a thirty-year-old mother of four children and a current welfare recipient. Although currently receiving welfare and social security disability assistance, she struggles to provide for her children. Leanne and her family resided in a shelter care program in Chelsea, Massachusetts, a low-income city adjacent to Boston, Massachusetts, for over two years while awaiting her Section 8 housing voucher. Describing the time she spent living in Chelsea, Leanne states,

> What a nightmare! I ended up moving out of there. I had someone murdered on my front doorstep. That was probably one of the biggest mistakes of my life: moving back there. I had previously stayed there, before I got my Section 8, I was in one of their shelters. I had my own apartment and everything. It was nice. But moving back was probably one of the biggest mistakes of my life. After I moved in, I found out that I had gang members on the second floor. I couldn't send my kids outside. The neighbors were dealing drugs out of…. The house was raided by the feds. The whole building was raided by the feds. It was…. It was one of the biggest mistakes of my life moving there.

Once Leanne was granted her Section 8 housing voucher, she decided to move out of the city to one of Boston's suburban areas. Leanne described wanting a safer, more stable environment for her children to grow up in. She explains,

> I thought to myself I had to move somewhere where nobody would least suspect me. So I moved to Franklin…. It's a very quiet area.

> Nobody would expect me to be [a welfare mother]. It's quiet. Um,
> it's actually been one of the best moves in my life that I've ever done.
> I mean I have this gorgeous two-floor apartment. I have a yard for
> my kids to play in. My ten-year-old son can go bike riding ... I don't
> have to worry about any of it [violence].

Leanne currently lives with her children in a two-bedroom, Section 8 apartment in Franklin, Massachusetts. Franklin is a predominantly white community. According to the U.S. Census data the racial demographics of the population are: 85.9% white, 7.1% black, 5.1% Asian, 8.8% Hispanic. The median home price is $185,700. The median household income is $65,304.

What does Leanne gain by living in a white middle-class community as a single mother who is dependent upon welfare from the government in order to support her family? According to Leanne, she receives a number of resources that black, Latina, and other women who cannot pass as white would not have access to if they live in poorer, urban, and racially diverse residential neighborhoods. This includes holiday meals and expensive Christmas presents that she could not afford on her income alone. For example, the Friends of Franklin organize the gift drive for low-income families within the community. The process is completely anonymous. In addition, Leanne gets to choose the presents she desires for her family. She states,

> Well before Thanksgiving they sent me a letter saying, "Do you
> want a free meal?" When they bring me my Thanksgiving meal
> they give me this paper to sign up for my Christmas meal. With
> my Christmas meal, they gave me a paper to sign up for toys for my
> kids. And [pauses] they bring me at Christmas time, three garbage
> bags full of toys for my kids. And then last year, the school called
> me, actually I've gotten it for the last two years [laughs] ... I think
> I'm one of the only families. It's a lot of people helping people out
> here.... I mean you got less people here on free lunch.

She goes on to describe the gift drive process:

> So my son wanted roller-blades so I wrote down roller blades (on
> the wish list that she gave to the social workers). I couldn't believe
> it. These people gave me receipts for things. I mean they bought
> my son a $50 sweater, $100 roller-blades; they bought my daughter
> a $150 dollhouse.... now that's just the gifts, never mind the $100
> gift card to Target—between Target, Wal-Mart, Stop and Shop, and
> Shaws (grocery stores) I got $400 worth of gift cards.

As a woman living in a community with a small number of welfare recipients, there was less demand for these resources. During the Thanksgiving and Christmas holidays, Leanne does not have to worry about how she will pay for holiday meals because once again, she benefits from the generosity of the middle- and upper middle-class donors who provide dinners.

These donated dinners, combined with the free holiday gifts, enable Leanne's children to not feel deprived and to have the same material comforts as their middle-class peers. Leanne states,

> They don't stand out from the other kids that do have the stuff. They don't know who I am and I don't know who they are. That's the thing: they get boy age ten with a list. They don't know who I am. The only person who knows who I am is the school nurse. Nobody else knows who I am. You know ... You know, it's good because my kids can go to school and wear what their friends are wearing. They can do what their friends are doing. It's really, really good.

Access to these material resources enables Leanne to shield her children from the stigma of being welfare dependent because their class status remains hidden due to the fact that they have the same clothes, toys, and nutritional experiences as their friends. In other words they can pass as middle class or at least as not welfare dependent.

Joy: Upward Social Mobility and Privileged Networks

Joy is a fifty-eight-year-old, Jewish lesbian mother of two daughters and self-described "loud mouth Dorchester woman." Joy grew up in a working-class to lower middle class Jewish community in Mattapan, Massachusetts. After graduating high school, she earned her bachelor's in education at the University of Massachusetts Amherst. Unlike the other women in this study, Joy purposefully chose single motherhood. Using a sperm donor, Joy became pregnant with her first child in 1985. After losing her teaching position, shortly after becoming pregnant, she applied for welfare, food stamps, and Section 8 housing assistance. While receiving these benefits, she earned her master's degree in community organizing at the University of Massachusetts at Boston. She eventually worked at several nonprofit and grass roots organizations in the Greater Boston area. In 1999, Joy, using another sperm donor, gave birth to her second daughter and reapplied for welfare assistance. Shortly after, Joy was hired by a local welfare rights organization as an executive manager. Although funding for the position disappeared a few years later, Joy continues to volunteer her services as a grant writer.

Joy raised her first daughter primarily in Newton, Massachusetts and her second daughter in Brookline, Massachusetts. When asked why she decided to move out of Jamaica Plain, a neighborhood in Boston, Massachusetts with vibrant queer, working-class, and multiethnic communities, she explains,

> [Jamaica Plain]'s where I want to live. That's where my people are. [Laughs]. It's all mixed in a way: racially, economically, and queer. Lots of activists there. It really is my community but the school system there is Boston Schools, you know? I tried for a long time, for years, trying to find a place. When my older daughter was little we lived in JP and when she became school age I found a place in Newton. I was open to a place in either Brookline or Newton but this time I found one in Brookline, which is even better for her I think.

Later Joy expands upon her decision to move to a predominantly, white upper middle-class suburb:

> I know housing [Section 8] is a big deal for me. I like to testify about housing because I don't want them to take it away. You know it's critical for me. It has to do with me being here and educating my kid in Brookline, which is important to me. Education is important to me.

Like the other welfare dependent white women mentioned, educational access was a primary motivator. Joy understood that while she may never have wealth or upward social mobility for herself, raising her children in a white, upper middle-class community with a superior public education system would provide her children with upward social, economic, and cultural mobility. In fact, her elder daughter graduated with honors from the University of Massachusetts at Amherst and currently works as a Montessori teacher in Hawaii.

Despite being a welfare recipient and welfare rights activist, for the past few decades Joy has been able to use her whiteness, specifically her Jewish ethnic identity, to gain access to racially segregated and class exclusive communities. She states,

> This is a Section 8 apartment. I am *very* resourceful. There are no people in Newton or Brookline that really want to rent to "us" [poor] people. You know.... Even though it's multicultural, the money part, the class part is actually worse because they [Brookline] are starving everyone who wants their resources just a block away. So there is a bigger wall that gets put up. Whereas in Newton,

they are a town over, so they have the suburban mentality. They drive into Boston but they really want to do the liberal thing. So they would maybe bus some folks into their schools or maybe some affordable housing or something and "Let's be nice to those people" or whatever but, don't have too many come through. But I think it's just a little bit different. In Brookline it really is quite a strong feeling: The classist feeling here. [Pauses] But I think other aspects of my background help in ways. I'm Jewish. I was raised in a Jewish community. I'm educated. So I can connect in other ways.

Unlike her first experience raising her daughter in Newton, Joy feels that she has developed strong friendships with other parents and a community in Brookline. Comparing the experiences she states,

I didn't want to be isolated in that way. This time around I have friends. I am totally honest with them. Friends here [in Brookline]. I have friends all around. But my daughter's friends' parents' I am honest with and have intimate relationships with. I express my real feelings about things. I draw them closer to me, into my inner circle. I can see that [my class status and angst] didn't get me anywhere in terms of my primary goal which is to have my daughter to be happy and not feel ostracized and for me to be happier too because I don't want that chip on my shoulder toward people that are my neighbors. It's not helpful for trying to belong here [Brookline].

In order to facilitate her daughter's access to social capital and upward mobility, Joy needed to integrate herself in the privileged community and social networks available to her. Although Joy did not fully conceal her welfare recipient or Section 8 housing status, she utilized the forms of capital available to her, her educational and ethnic capital to gain access to social capital for herself and her child. As a result, her daughter's peer network includes children of wealth who frequently offer to take her on paid trips and cultural excursions.

Conclusion

Historically access to welfare aid programs has been restricted and not democratically distributed to all social and racialized groups (Abramovitz 1988; Gordon 1998; Neubeck and Cazenave 2001; Ward 2005). The demographic statistics on Section 8 housing voucher recipients, in particular, reveal that those who qualify for whiteness are more likely to have access to these resources than those who do not. This may in part be due to one of the main eligibility requirements for the program: individuals who have a recent history of illegal drug use, alcohol abuse, or violent criminal behavior are deemed ineligible. Scholars have been quick to note that poor blacks and selected Latino groups (Mexican Americans, Puerto Ricans) are disproportionately incarcerated in the United States, especially for drug related offenses (Davis 2003; Pattillo et al. 2006 ; Alexander 2012). As such, in Massachusetts and in the city of Boston, whites are more likely to gain access to Section 8 housing vouchers than nonwhites. This key resource provides an opportunity for spatial and social mobility to predominantly poor whites, which already benefit from a racially segregated housing market by virtue of their racial privilege. Rather than residing in one of Boston's low-income, predominantly black or Latino neighborhoods, impoverished whites are given the opportunity to relocate to one of Greater Boston's many working-class or middle-class white communities, accessing all of the social, cultural, and material benefits of that particular community.

Impoverished whites are theoretically able via the Section 8 housing voucher program to gain access to subsidized housing in racially segregated and class exclusive communities, but the demographic composition of communities like Newton or Brookline, Massachusetts, reveal that very few do. Communities find formal and informal ways of maintaining racial and social class boundaries. To discourage low-income residents, local officials limit the development of low-income or affordable housing projects, landlords or realtors specifically price apartments out of the Section 8 housing voucher price range, and others may list their rentals with the following, albeit illegal, clause: "Section 8 need not apply." In response, welfare dependent white women who desire spatial and social mobility for themselves and their families devise strategies to gain access to housing in racially segregated and class privileged areas.

Welfare dependent white women, like Becca, Theresa, Leanne, and Joy, utilize their whiteness as a form of property and bodily capital to conceal and cover up welfare status, to manage stigma, and to facilitate spatial and social movement into racially segregated and class exclusive communities. These women employed a number of passing techniques: altering aspects of one's biography, withholding key information about one's current or previous welfare status, and modifying one's physical appearance, speech, and mannerisms to fit normative racial, gendered, and class expectations of a particular community. Passing did not only occur during their attempts to gain access to housing but also throughout their time in residence in these communities. Although the labor required to pass was physically, mentally, and emotionally taxing for the women involved, welfare dependent white women endured the process to gain important social, cultural, and material resources for their families unavailable in low-income communities and to the majority of welfare dependent women, white and nonwhite.

In this chapter, we identified six potential benefits white welfare dependent women gain from concealing their welfare status in a racially segregated housing market. First, it enabled them to secure access to Section 8 housing located in middle- and upper middle-class suburban communities that are often hostile to low-income residents. Second, it provided access to material resources due to reduced competition for donated food, clothing, gifts, and in-kind services provided by local charities and nonprofit organizations. Third, these neighborhoods provided access to physical safety, a key emotional resource, by reducing their exposure to physical violence and theft. Fourth, the children of welfare dependent women gained access to superior public education services, especially important for those children with special needs. Fifth, concealing one's welfare status provided access to privileged social networks and social capital. Finally, concealing one's welfare status mediated welfare stigma and provided welfare dependent white women with a form of respectability. The material, educational, cultural, social, and symbolic resources support the social mobility of the children of welfare dependent white women.

Our research findings contribute to the welfare, critical whiteness studies, social mobility, and impression management literatures by providing a more nuanced understanding of racial privilege in the housing market as it operates among impoverished women. The issue of how women who possess the bodily capital to represent themselves as "unhyphenated whites" utilized racial privilege to soften the blows of poverty and secure basic resources for their children has been relatively neglected in the literature on low-income women and welfare dependent families. For these impoverished women, their whiteness may still be a limited, but nonetheless a useful resource to ensure their survival. Whiteness can sometimes be converted into benefits not available to women perceived to be black, brown (Latina or Hispanic), or not qualified physically for whiteness.

Notes

1. Section 8 housing is subsidized by the federal government to support low-income and impoverished residents. They pay below-market rents for this housing which is in short supply.
2. To identify and recruit potential research participants one of the authors (MacDonald) sent letters to local social service organizations in the Greater Boston area including women's shelters, food banks, and welfare to work programs. MacDonald then posted weekly research advertisements under the volunteer section of the Boston Craigslist for a period of four months prior to field research in Boston. The requirements for inclusion in the study included the following: (a) participants self-identified as white, (b) participants were current or former ADFC or TAFDC recipients, and (c) participants resided within the Greater Boston area. Over thirty individuals responded to the research advertisement and of those, fourteen eventually participated in an in-person interview. Those who did not participate

in the study fell into one of the following categories: (a) they did not fit the criteria of the study, (b) they expressed initial interest but then, for an unknown reason, chose either not to schedule an interview or participate in a scheduled interview. Fourteen of the twenty respondents were gathered by this method. MacDonald then used a snow balling method to locate other participants.

The data presented in this chapter is based on in-depth, semistructured interviews with twenty white women living in the Greater Boston area in 2010 and 2011. All of the women were currently receiving or had previously received welfare (AFDC or TAFDC) benefits. None of the women were employed at the time of my interviews. Eight women were currently receiving TAFDC benefits, five women were receiving Social Security Disability Insurance (SSDI), four women were receiving Social Security Insurance (SSI), and three women were receiving Unemployment Insurance at the time of the research. Of the eight women currently receiving TAFDC benefits, three were also receiving SSI benefits (for themselves or their child or children). Five of the women had previously received welfare benefits prior to the 1996 Personal Responsibility and Work Opportunity Reconciliation Act (PRWORA). Twelve of the twenty women identified as welfare veterans (i.e. originating from multigenerational welfare recipient families). These women cited their mothers, aunts, sisters, and cousins as current or previous welfare recipients.

The women who agreed to participate ranged from twenty-two to sixty-nine years of age. Their marital status varied and included five divorced women, five married women, eight partnered women, and two single women. Nineteen women self-identified as heterosexual. One woman self-identified as lesbian. Ten of the twenty had current or previous relationships with men of color. And nine of the white mothers had children of multiracial heritage (including black, Native American, Puerto Rican, and Brazilian). The number of children per woman ranged from one to four. Ten of the twenty women reported a history of domestic violence and identified themselves as survivors.

Six women self-identified as Irish American, four self-identified as Italian American, three women as Irish and Italian, one woman self-identified as ethnically Portuguese American, one woman identified herself as culturally Jewish, and five identified as unhyphenated whites of no specific non-Anglo ancestry. Nine of the women also described their class background as poor and belonged to the impoverished rather than working classes. Four women identified their class background as working class. Seven women identified their class background as lower middle or middle class. Two women had earned master's degrees, three held bachelor's degrees, two held associate's degrees, three had some college education, four women held high school diplomas or G.E.D.'s, and six women had completed middle school.

3. Although each study explores the various stigma management strategies welfare dependent women employ, all focus on the need of welfare dependent women to manage stigma.

4. The 1896 U.S. Supreme Court decision that upheld the constitutionality of state laws requiring racial segregation in public facilities under the doctrine of "separate but equal."

5. The 1954 U.S. Supreme Court decision overturned the *Plessy v. Ferguson* decision and declared state laws establishing racially segregated public schools were unconstitutional.

6. Douglas, Craig M. "Greater Boston Gains Population, Remains 10th-largest Region in U.S." *Boston News | Boston Business Journal* March 24, 2010. http://boston.bizjournals.com/boston/stories/2010/03/22/daily22.html.

7. "Boston (city) QuickFacts from the US Census Bureau." State and County QuickFacts. August 16, 2010. http://quickfacts.census.gov/qfd/states/25/2507000.html

8. Gibson, Campbell. "Population of the 100 Largest Cities and Other Urban Places in the United States: 1790 to 1990." Census Bureau Home Page. June 1998. http://www.census.gov/population/www/documentation/twps0027/twps0027.html

9. "Boston (city) QuickFacts from the US Census Bureau." *State and County QuickFacts* August 16, 2010. http://quickfacts.census.gov/qfd/states/25/2507000.html

10. "Boston City, Massachusetts - DP-2. Profile of Selected Social Characteristics: 2000." *American FactFinder.* http://factfinder.census.gov/servlet/QTTable?_bm=y&-context=qt&-qr_name=DEC_2000_SF3_U_DP2&-ds_name=DEC_2000_SF3_U&-CONTEXT=qt&-tree_id=402&-redoLog=true&-all_geo_types=N&-geo_id=16000US2507000&-search_results=01000US&-_sse=on&-format=&-_lang=en

11. "Boston (city) QuickFacts from the US Census Bureau." State and County QuickFacts. August 16, 2010. http://quickfacts.census.gov/qfd/states/25/2507000.html

12. "Massachusetts QuickFacts from the US Census Bureau." State and County QuickFacts. August 16, 2010. http://quickfacts.census.gov/qfd/states/25000.html

13. Frank Hobbs and Nicole Stoops. *Demographic Trends in the 20th Century.* Washington, DC: U.S. Census Bureau, U.S. Census Special Reports. U.S. Government Printing Office. http://www.census.gov/prod/2002pubs/censr-4.pdf

14. "1.5.2 Degree of Residential Segregation, Boston and Metro Boston." *The Boston Indicators Project.* http://www.bostonindicators.org/Indicators2008/CivicVitality/Indicator.aspx?id=10722&sc=674&sct=Race/Ethnicity

15. "Boston (city) QuickFacts from the US Census Bureau." *State and County QuickFacts.* August 16, 2010. http://quickfacts.census.gov/qfd/states/25/2507000.html

16. "Dorchester Data Profile." City of Boston.gov. The Department of Neighborhood Development, May 1, 2006. http://www.cityofboston.gov/Images_Documents/Mattapan_PD_Profile_tcm3-12994.pdf

17. "Mattapan Data Profile." City of Boston.gov. The Department of Neighborhood Development, May 1 2006. http://www.cityofboston.gov/Images_Documents/Mattapan_PD_Profile_tcm3-12994.pdf

18. "Newton (city) QuickFacts from the US Census Bureau." *State and County QuickFacts.* http://quickfacts.census.gov/qfd/states/25/2545560.html

19. "Newton (city) QuickFacts from the US Census Bureau." State and County QuickFacts. Web. http://quickfacts.census.gov/qfd/states/25/2545560.html

20. "Brookline Massachusetts (MA) Census and Detailed Community Profile—AmericanTowns.com." AmericanTowns.com: Online Local Community Network—Connecting the Community Is What We Do Best. http://www.americantowns.com/ma/brookline-information#data

21. "Section 8 Housing for Residents of Massachusetts—An Overview." Massachusetts Section 8 Housing Programs. http://www.massresources.org/section_8_housing_massachusetts_d.html

22. Ibid.

23. See the October 2011 "Massachusetts Tenant Based Voucher." In *U.S. Department of Housing and Urban Development Resident Characteristics Report.* Washington, DC: U.S. Department of Housing and Urban Development.

References

Abramovitz, Mimi. 1988. *Regulating the Lives of Women: Social Policy from Colonial Times to the Present.* Boston: South End Press.

Alexander, Michelle. 2012. *The New Jim Crow.* New York: New Press.

Bourdieu, Pierre. 1984. *Distinction: A Social Critique of the Judgment of Taste.* Cambridge, MA: Harvard University Press.

Briar, Scott. 1966. "Welfare from Below: Recipients' Views of the Public Welfare System." *California Law Review* 54: 370–85.

Cleaveland, Carol. 2008. "'A Black Benefit': Racial Prejudice Among White Welfare Recipients in a Low-Income Neighborhood." *Journal of Progressive Human Services* 19 (2): 71–91.

Davis, Liane V., and Hagen, Jan L. 1996. "Stereotypes and Stigma: What's Changed for Welfare Mothers?" *Affilia* 11 (3): 319–37.

Du Bois, W. E. B. (1935) 1999. *Black Reconstruction in America, 1860–1880*. New York: Free Press.

Frank, Dana M. 1998. "White Working-Class Women and the Race Question." *International Labor and Working-Class History* 54: 80–102.

Goffman, Erving. 1963. *Stigma: Notes on the Management of Spoiled Identity*. Englewood Cliffs, NJ: Prentice-Hall.

Goodban, Nancy. 1985. "The Psychological Impact of Being on Welfare." *Social Service Review* 59: 403–22.

Gordon, Linda. 1998. *Pitied But Not Entitled: Single Mothers and the History of Welfare*. Cambridge, MA: Harvard University Press.

Hancock, Ange-Marie. 2004. *The Politics of Disgust: The Public Identity of the Welfare Queen*. New York: New York University Press.

Harris, Cheryl. 1993. "Whiteness as Property." *Harvard Law Review* 106 (8): 1707–95. doi: 10.2307/1341787

Hartigan, John. 1999. *Racial Situations: Class Predicaments of Whiteness in Detroit*. Princeton, NJ: Princeton University Press.

Jarrett, Robin L. 1996. "Welfare Stigma among Low-Income African American Single Mothers." *Family Relations* 45(4): 368–74.

Kaplan, Elaine Bell. 1997. *Not Our Kind of Girl: Unraveling the Myths of Black Teenage Motherhood*. Berkeley: University of California Press.

Latimer, Melissa. 2006. "'We Have Never Asked for Help That Was Not Desperately Needed': Patterns of Stigma Management among Former Welfare Recipients in West Virginia." *Journal of Appalachia Studies* 12 (2): 369–84.

Massey, Douglas, and Nancy Denton. 1993. *American Apartheid: Segregation and the Making of the Underclass*. Cambridge, MA: Harvard University Press.

McCormack, Karen. 2004. "Resisting the Welfare Mother: The Power of Welfare Discourse and Tactics of Resistance." *Critical Sociology* 30(2): 356–83.

———. 2005. "Stratified Reproduction and Poor Women's Resistance." *Gender and Society* 19 (5): 660–79.

McDermott, Monica. 2006. *Working-Class White: The Making and Unmaking of Race Relations*. Berkeley, CA: University of California Press.

Mink, Gwendolyn, and Rickie Solinger, eds. 2003. *Welfare: A Documentary History of U.S. Policy and Politics*. New York: New York University Press.

Neubeck, Kenneth J., and Noel A. Cazenave. 2001. *Welfare Racism: Playing the Race Card against America's Poor*. New York: Routledge.

Rank, Mark R. 1994. *Living on the Edge: The Realities of Welfare in America*. New York: Columbia University Press.

Reese, Ellen. 2005. *Backlash against Welfare Mothers: Past and Present*. Berkeley, CA: University of California Press.

Reutter, Linda I., Miriam J. Stewart, Gerry Veenstra, Rhonda Love Dennis Raphael, and Edward. Makwarimba. 2009. "Who Do They Think We Are, Anyway?": Perception of and Responses to Poverty Stigma." *Qualitative Health Research* 19 (3): 297–311.

Roediger, David. R. 1991. *The Wages of Whiteness: Race and the Making of the American Working-Class*. New York: Verso.

Roger-Dillons, Robin. 1995. "The Dynamics of Welfare Stigma." *Qualitative Sociology* 18(4): 439–56.

Seccombe, Karen. 1999. *So You Think I Drive a Cadillac? Welfare Recipients' Perspectives on the System and Its Reform*. Boston: Allyn & Bacon.

Twine, France Winddance. 2010. *A White Side of Black Britain: Racial Intimacy and Racial Literacy*. Durham, NC: Duke University Press.

Ward, Deborah. 2005. *The White Welfare State: The Racialization of U.S. Welfare Policy*. Ann Arbor: University of Michigan Press.

CHAPTER 10

From Racial Discrimination to Class Segregation in Postcolonial Urban Mozambique

DAVID MORTON

In 1968, Sebastião Chithombe left his family's farm in Mozambique's countryside and headed for the city of Lourenço Marques. Mozambique, stretching some 1,500 miles along the coast of southeast Africa, was at the time a colony of Portugal; Lourenço Marques, in the far south, was its capital. Chithombe was 14. He came to the city hoping to earn some cash, buy shoes and nice clothes, and then return to his parents' fields. But staying in the city soon became its own justification.

Chithombe's first home in Lourenço Marques was in the backyard of the Portuguese-owned cantina where he worked, at the edge of the city's shantytowns. Within a year he moved into the shantytowns, to a ramshackle compound built of zinc panels where he shared a small airless room with several other young men. There was no furniture. Between them they had a coal-burning stove, a cooking pot, dishes, a pail to fetch water with, and two reed mats for the five of them to sleep on. Chithombe opened a stall at a local market, made more money, and over the years moved into one larger room in the compound after another. By 1974, he was sharing a two-room unit with his brother. The roof did not leak as much as the other rooms he had lived in.

Mozambique became independent of Portugal in June 1975. In the months leading up to the scheduled handover, most of the Portuguese population left, many going to Portugal and many to neighboring South Africa. In Lourenço Marques, most whites lived in what was colloquially known as the City of Cement, the formalized part of the city, and as they departed, some left their homes in the care of African friends or employees. One of Chithombe's friends was gifted an apartment by a Portuguese friend. When Chithombe visited his friend at his new home, it was the first time Chithombe had ever been inside an apartment in the City of Cement as a welcome visitor, rather than as a laborer. The experience was bewildering. Entering through the apartment's front door, rather than the servants' entrance, Chithombe went to the bathroom and washed his hands. "It was the first time I'd ever been in a bathroom like that for a reason other than to wash the floors," he said in a recent interview. In the living room he turned the light switch on and off. He took pride in knowing the light was "ours," even though the apartment was not his.

Chithombe and thousands of other shantytown residents were soon offered an opportunity to acquire an apartment of their own in the City of Cement. On February 3, 1976, Chithombe was listening on the radio to Samora Machel, Mozambique's first president, as he spoke before thousands of supporters in a plaza at the edge of the city. Since independence from Portugal the year before, Frelimo, the armed independence movement Machel led, and which now governed the country, had nationalized all land, health clinics, schools, and even funeral parlors. Now the moment had come to nationalize rental housing. With most of the city's white population now gone, tens of thousands of homes and apartment units in the City of Cement were available for occupation. "The city must have a Mozambican face," declared the president. "The people will be able to live in their own city and not in the city's backyard!" (Machel 1976, 69). Lourenço Marques, Machel announced, would now be called Maputo.

If one were to write a global history of white flight, it might begin with a chapter on U.S. cities in the 1950s and 1960s, when court-mandated school integration and federal subsidies of suburbanization encouraged many white residents to leave urban centers and black neighbors behind. It would also have to include a chapter on South Africa in the 1980s and 1990s, as the fortified edifice of apartheid began to crumble and whites fled behind the walls of gated suburban communities. These are classic examples, and the similarities between them are clear: just as racial segregation was weakened, a new form of racial segregation took shape. The most dramatic episodes of white flight, however—dramatic because of how quickly and completely they took place—may have been those witnessed in the settler cities of colonial Africa during the era of decolonization. This chapter is about one of these cities. In Maputo in the mid-1970s tens of thousands of white residents didn't just pack up and move down the highway, but rather removed themselves from the country en masse and nearly overnight. Post independence Maputo raises an intriguing question about race and the urban landscape: What happens to racial privilege when there is no longer a privileged race?

There are only a handful of cities that share circumstances roughly comparable to Maputo's: cities such as Luanda, capital of Angola (which also became independent from Portugal in 1975), and the larger coastal cities of Algeria, from which the French withdrew in 1962 (Greger 1990; Lesbet 1990). Like Maputo, these were sizable African cities developed for the almost exclusive use of white settlers. Indigenous populations lived mostly in outlying shantytown slums (and in the case of Algiers, a centrally located ghetto as well). And these cities were all abandoned so rapidly that there was no significant period of transition from one situation to another; there was neither meaningful racial integration nor gradual racial turnover. In mid-1974, a year before Mozambique's independence from Portugal, a large majority of residents of the City of Cement—perhaps 70,000 people—were white (Rita-Ferreira 1988). By mid-1976, a year after independence, a large majority of residents of the City of Cement were black.

Rarely has a city found itself in a position to so utterly reorient itself. Nonetheless, the City of Cement remained a zone of privilege. It became the home to party elites, war veterans, military families, and those with better salaried work, generally as government functionaries—Mozambique's nascent African middle class. For most shantytown dwellers, the City of Cement remained out of reach. Many never even considered the possibility. Sebastião Chithombe, for instance, never did.

This chapter draws heavily from Lefebvre's (1991) and Foucault's (1980) insights regarding space: how the urban landscape, rather than simply reflecting existing social inequalities, at the same time, engenders them. This dynamic, furthermore, has as much to do with competing conceptions of the city as with the physical reality of the city itself—conceptions, for instance, of what constitutes modernity and civilization, and ideas about who is sufficiently "modern" or "civilized" to deserve the amenities of urban life. A central theme of this book is how such inequalities, once embedded in the urban environment, manage to persist, though perhaps in different forms. Maputo represents an extreme case in this regard.

It would be difficult to find circumstances that, at first glance, seemed more favorable to undoing a grossly unequal system of housing than the conditions that prevailed in Maputo in the years after independence. Following the Portuguese flight, Maputo was given what seemed to be a virtual blank slate, and it was governed by staunch Marxists often disposed to treating class privilege as a crime. Yet the new regime decided that for the tens of thousands of houses and apartment units of the City of Cement to be of any use at all they would need relatively privileged tenants capable of paying a rent sufficient to maintain them. And even when rents were lowered, most people still couldn't afford to live there. That Maputo remained during this revolutionary period a largely dual city, divided between the formal City of Cement and its shantytowns and, to a significant extent, between two different ways of life, lends further confirmation to just how rigid a social hierarchy can be once it has been reinforced in concrete.

Portuguese Colonialism, Whiteness, and Racial Segregation in Urban Spaces

Portugal is today, a small, economically marginal country on the western edge of Europe. It also had a marginal economy when it was one of the European powers claiming a controlling stake in Africa—the unlikeliest member of a select club. Portugal's African colonies in the twentieth century were a vestige of its dominance in the fifteenth and sixteenth centuries, when Portugal maintained a mercantilist empire with a truly global reach (Boxer 1973). Portuguese caravels were the first European vessels to explore the West African coast and, in 1497, to venture beyond the continent's southern tip, opening a seaborne trade with India and the Far East. Portugal initiated the trans-Atlantic slave trade as well, shipping Africans from present-day Angola and other parts of the west coast of Africa to Portugal's vast sugar plantations in Brazil. Dutch and English sea power eventually muscled Portugal out of most markets. The independence of Brazil in 1822 rendered Portugal's long and steep decline irreversible. Portugal nonetheless held on to a number of territories in various far-flung corners of Africa, India, and Southeast Asia.

For centuries, the Portuguese presence in these places was confined mostly to coastal towns and fortified trading posts. But in the late nineteenth century, during the Scramble for Africa, competition from Britain, France, and Germany threatened Portugal's tenuous positions on the continent. Only then was Portugal compelled to move beyond its coastal enclaves and exercise direct control over the interior of Mozambique, Angola, and Guinea, for fear that one of the other European powers would claim them instead. With most local populations in the various hinterlands violently "pacified" and the boundaries of European control settled, Mozambique and Angola became Portugal's most populous and important colonies. White settlement, however, proceeded slowly until the midtwentieth century, when Lisbon sponsored a series of ambitious efforts

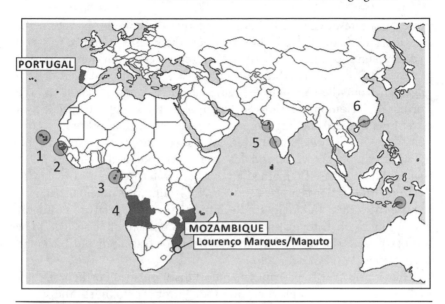

Figure 10.1 Portugal and its possessions in the twentieth century. Key: 1. Cape Verde, independent in 1975; 2. Portuguese Guinea (now Guinea-Bissau), independent in 1974; 3. São Tomé and Príncipe, independent in 1975; 4. Angola, independent in 1975; 5. Diu, Daman, and Goa, annexed by India in 1961; 6. Macau, transferred to China in 1999; 7. Portuguese Timor (now East Timor), independent in 1975. (Credit: Luciana Justiniani Hees and Wikimedia Commons)

to encourage immigration from the metropole to its territories overseas. By the eve of independence, the white population had reached 190,000 in Mozambique and 324,000 in Angola (Castelo 2007).

Portugal's long colonial career entered its terminal phase in 1961. That year, an armed revolt shook Angola and India annexed Portuguese possessions on the Indian coast. As in Angola, guerilla-based independence movements were soon launched in Guinea and then Mozambique, and Portugal waged three wars in Africa for more than a decade. In 1974, a coup in Lisbon led by left-wing army officers toppled Portugal's right-wing dictatorship, and the independence of Portugal's five African colonies—which also included two small island groups—followed in late 1974 and 1975. Mozambique, Angola, and Guinea-Bissau (as it was now called) entered the community of nations as some of the poorest, most underdeveloped countries in the world. (Perhaps the true end of empire, however, was in 1999, when Portugal's last colonial enclave, Macau, a city near Hong Kong, was ceded to China, 502 years after Vasco da Gama's first journey past the Cape of Good Hope.)

Portugal had been the first Europe-based power to colonize sub-Saharan Africa, and it was the last to leave. Portugal's tenacious staying power was a testament to the dominant role the colonies played in the imagination of successive Lisbon regimes; the country's future was said to depend on the preservation of an empire that echoed its heroic "Age of Discoveries" of centuries before (Duffy 1962). An oft-used item of propaganda, from the Colonial Exhibition held in Porto in 1934, showed Portugal's various possessions superimposed on a map of Europe and covering an area stretching from the Iberian Peninsula to Russia (Cairo 2006). The map's title: "Portugal is not a small country." Despite Portugal's past exploits, however, and despite the accumulated landmass flying its flag, Portugal itself remained a poor backwater, economically dependent on Britain. For centuries successive Lisbon governments struggled to raise the capital and maintain the administrative capacity to profitably exploit the colonies to Portugal's benefit. Colonialism often seemed to be an enterprise far beyond its means (Duffy 1962; Isaacman and Isaacman 1983; Newitt 1995; Castelo 2007).

After World War II, perhaps what most distinguished Portuguese colonialism in Africa from practices in other European colonies, and which for a time made Portugal something of a pariah nation, was the institution of forced labor. This was known in Mozambique as *chibalo*. According to laws in effect since the late nineteenth century, virtually all Mozambican men were subject to long spells as plantation workers or dockworkers or ditch diggers, and with men compelled to work away from home, or to flee Mozambique altogether, women were often left with the sole burden of compulsory cotton cultivation on their own small family fields (Penvenne 1995; Isaacman 1996; Sheldon 2002).

Chibalo differed from slavery; terms typically lasted six months (though sometimes years), and there was nominal compensation (which was often not paid). Like slavery under the Portuguese, the mortality rate on work gangs was high, and as one dissident Portuguese general put it in 1961, at least with slavery, masters valued their assets (Castelo 2007). Even after the official abolition of *chibalo* in 1961, long after the practice had been officially abolished in other European colonies in Africa, forms of coercive labor persisted in the countryside until independence (Vail and White 1980; Munslow 1983).

Other European colonial powers frequently portrayed Portugal as backward and inhumane and undeserving of its African possessions, and in the 1950s and 1960s, as the French, British, and Belgians departed Africa and their colonies became independent, Portugal faced mounting international pressure to do the same. The Portuguese regime stubbornly resisted. Lisbon argued that the Portuguese were exceptional, particularly suited for colonization in ways the other European powers had not been (Duffy 1962; Bender 1978).

Portugal's argument boiled down to a question of race. The Portuguese, asserted the regime's propagandists, had demonstrated over the course of centuries a genius for assimilating different cultures and peoples into Portuguese civilization. Large mixed-race populations in Brazil, Angola, and elsewhere were supposedly testament to Portugal's history of harmonious racial relations (Andrade 1961; Godinho 1962; Freyre 1961; Boxer 1963; Bender 1978; Castelo 2001). To advance this claim, a 1951 constitutional makeover changed the status of the African territories from "colonies" to "overseas provinces" of a single multicontinental, multiracial Portuguese nation. And following reforms in the 1960s, the laws of Portugal recognized as legal Portuguese citizens all those who lived within its many borders. The international community was generally cold to Portuguese claims. They saw African societies dominated and exploited by white minorities.

Declarations of racial harmony were in any case of little significance to the millions who lived in Mozambique's countryside, where in the 1960s perhaps one in three children died before the age of five and illiteracy neared 100 percent (Garenne, Coninx, and Dupuy 1996; Cross 1987). Only a small percentage of Mozambicans, fewer than 10 percent, lived in urban areas (Pinsky 1985). But the Portuguese presence was felt most directly in cities, where white populations were concentrated. Segregated Lourenço Marques cast in particularly sharp relief the contradictions of what Lisbon insisted was the colorblind character of its rule.[1] The population of Lourenço Marques, it must be said, could by no means be described in simple black and white. The 1960 census for both the city and shantytowns registered 41,165 whites, the vast majority of them Portuguese (Direcção Provincial dos Serviços de Estatística Geral 1960). Among recent arrivals to the city, some had been peasants in the Portuguese countryside who came and worked in cantinas or as day laborers, and some were young professionals or military men with their families, sent from Lisbon to work as government administrators (Castelo 2007). Others were second- and third-generation laurentinos who had never seen Portugal, and who worked in mid- and low-level jobs in the civil service or as shop-keepers or as railroad workers.

Since at least the early nineteenth century, cities all along Africa's Indian Ocean coast possessed significant Indian populations, and Lourenço Marques—with 6,565 Indians in 1960—was no exception. As elsewhere on the coast, many were involved in retail and other forms of trade, particularly in businesses with an African clientele, and occupied a kind of middle ground in colonial society: able to exercise great mobility in the economic sphere, though often marginalized as outsiders in civic and political affairs (Pereira Bastos 2005). The census also registered a small population of Chinese, like Indians largely involved in retail trade.

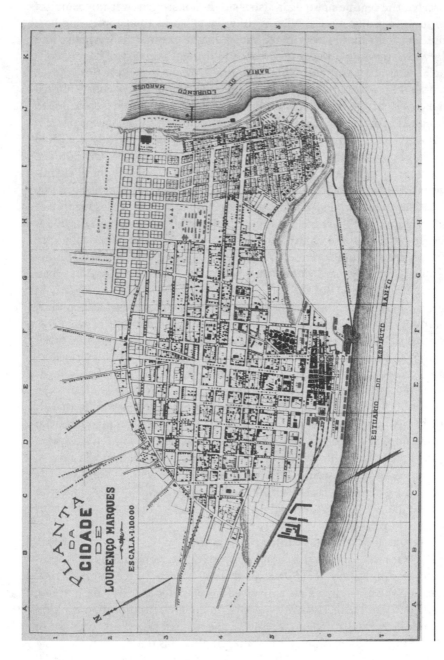

Figure 10.2 The city of Lourenço Marques in 1929, showing the curving street, later called Avenida Caldas Xavier, that divided the formalized city from its shantytowns. The shantytowns are represented in the map by blank spaces. (Credit: Morais 2001)

For a long time Portuguese immigrants to Mozambique were predominately men, and there were a number of people descended from the unions of these men and African women (Castelo 2007). In 1960, there were 7,440 residents of mixed race living in Lourenço Marques. Their level of schooling and employment, and thus their social standing, often depended on their relationship to white fathers (or kind-hearted godfathers), some of whom maintained multiple households—one with a white wife in the city, the other with an African companion in the slums (Honwana 1988; Penvenne 2005).[2] The rate of children born from interracial relationships in Lourenço Marques declined dramatically following World War II as more white women immigrated to the city, the white community grew, and with it the social stigma attached to unions that did not propagate whiteness (Castelo 2007).

The 1960 census counted 122,460 blacks living in Lourenço Marques. Most Africans in Lourenço Marques were from southern Mozambique, and as interviews with residents have borne out, many originating from the immediate vicinity of the city sometimes looked with condescension on "newcomers" from other districts, who were often in more desperate situations. African women were largely shut out of waged work, and single women lived in particularly precarious circumstances. Many brewed traditional beer illegally to get by, others resorted to prostitution (Sheldon 2002; Frates 2002). A number of Africans were from the distant

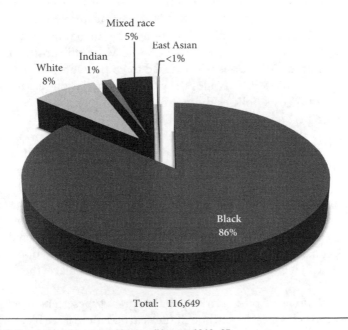

Figure 10.3 Population of Lourenço Marques/Maputo, 1940–97.

north of the colony and the nearby Comoros Islands and shared affinities with the Muslim Swahili culture of the East African coast, while those from the south tended to belong to the Catholic Church or Protestant denominations. Among the most important distinctions to be made, though, the one that for an African in Lourenço Marques was the ultimate determinant of one's place in the colonial-era hierarchy, was that between *indígena* and *assimilado*.

As with most European colonial regimes, the Portuguese had long cultivated a class of more privileged Africans (Honwana 1988; Penvenne 1989, 1991, 1995). Under the laws that prevailed until the early 1960s, blacks who officially "assimilated" were recognized as Portuguese citizens, with the limited rights that citizenship under a dictatorship conferred, including the right to live in the City of Cement. The path to assimilation was arduous, and few Mozambicans had either the resources or opportunity to attempt it. One had to achieve a certain level of formal education, formal employment, and literacy in Portuguese. After one achieved *assimilado* status, an official visited one's home to verify that only Portuguese was spoken, that meals were "Portuguese" and eaten with a knife and fork, and that husband and wife both dressed in appropriately Western clothing. The family also had to reside, at minimum, in a decently built wood-framed, zinc-paneled house, rather than a house built of reeds.

Assimilation was a degrading process, predicated on the complete disavowal of one's African traditions and values—at least outwardly. It was humiliating, too, that whites didn't also have to prove they were "civilized."[3] And so, though legal assimilation was a virtual requisite for better employment opportunities, there were some Mozambicans with many of the necessary qualifications who refused to go through with it (Penvenne 1995; Castelo 2007). For decades the path to assimilation served as Portuguese proof that its policies did not distinguish by race, since even Africans could become citizens.

In 1960 there were approximately 5,000 *assimilados* in a colony of about 6 million (Newitt 1995). All other blacks were identified as *indígenas* ("natives") and black men were subject to forced labor if not formally employed. The fact that fractionally few blacks met the Portuguese standard reinforced the notion that the essence of blackness was to be uncivilized. Whiteness, meanwhile, was linked to a bundle of practices and experiences—language, cuisine, dress, a specific educational curriculum, occupation—that defined what it meant to be civilized, or *evoluído*, evolved. And whiteness remained linked to a specific place: the formalized city.

Assimilados were office clerks, printing press typesetters, truck drivers, nurses, and schoolteachers. Though they earned more than black men who

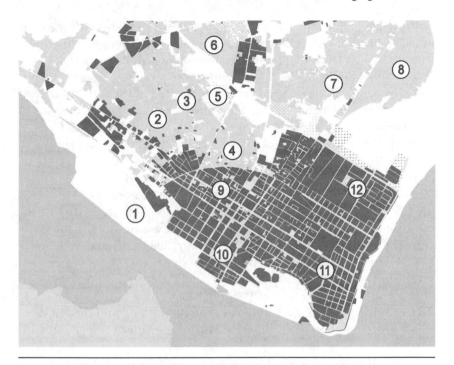

Figure 10.4 Lourenço Marques and its neighborhoods at independence, 1975. Key: 1. Port and rail facilities, *Subúrbios* (yellow); 2. Chamanculo; 3. Xipamanine; 4. Mafalala; 5. Munhuana; 6. Aeroporto; 7. Maxaquene; 8. Polana Caniço City of Cement (red); 9. Alto Maé; 10. Baixa (downtown); 11. Polana; 12. Sommershield. (Credit: Luciana Justiniani Hees, adapted from a map in Henriques 2008)

unloaded ships at the port, or black men who laundered the clothes for Portuguese families in town, or black women who worked on plantations at the city's edge, their incomes were still very modest by the standards of what most whites earned. In the 1960s, many better-off blacks stood with men of mixed race in the societal pecking order: working in jobs below whites in the civil service or as laborers, and often for a great deal less pay (Penvenne 1995; Castelo 2007). With few exceptions, white Portuguese received preference for job openings (Honwana 1988; Penvenne 1995).

The legal division of the black Mozambican population into *assimilado* and *indígena* was abolished along with the regime of forced labor in 1961. During the last decade or so of Portuguese rule, as the Lisbon regime battled Frelimo guerillas in northern Mozambique, Portuguese authorities attempted to win over Mozambican "hearts and minds" (Castelo 2007). Educational opportunities for Mozambicans in Lourenço Marques improved, and as wartime development boosted the city's economy, employment prospects improved as well. The numbers of relatively favored black Mozambicans, still commonly referred to as *assimilados*, grew. But, as Penvenne points out, a wage ceiling remained in place: with the continual swelling of the city's white population, the incomes of *assimilados* with the highest levels of formal education stagnated (Penvenne 2011).

The city, meanwhile, became perhaps more racially segregated than it had been before. The vast majority of whites lived in the City of Cement. Asians—those not living in the shantytown cantinas they owned—lived mostly in the two commercial neighborhoods within the City of Cement (Mendes 1985). Most people of mixed race as well as the great majority of Africans lived in the shantytowns. The lines were not definite: Hundreds of poor whites lived in the shantytowns and thousands of blacks lived as servants in the backyards of the City of Cement (Castelo 2007). But that the City of Cement was "the white city" was not a matter in dispute for those who actually lived in Lourenço Marques, black or white, in the 1960s and early 1970s (Rita-Ferreira 1967; Honwana 1988; Oliveira 1999; Frates 2002; Penvenne 2011). Antoinette Errante argues that racial segregation was part of the "artificial homogenization" of the diverse white population of Lourenço Marques (Errante 2003, 14). Establishing European superiority meant masking the class differences among whites, and this, in turn, meant rescuing poor, often illiterate Portuguese from comparison with Africans.

Segregation in Lourenço Marques was not achieved through overtly racial laws (Frates 2002). The city wasn't governed by anything similar to the ruthless legal apparatus of apartheid South Africa, which eliminated "black spots" in areas officially designated for white habitation. Rather, early dislocations of blacks from the city to the shantytowns were largely effected through the passage of new building codes, which outlawed the construction of lower-quality housing within city limits (Rita-Ferreira 1967; Frates 2002). Thereafter the racialized job market ensured that even better paid *assimilados* usually couldn't afford to build or rent a home in the city, and the reforms of the 1960s which opened up more opportunities for Africans did not at the same time open the doors to the City of Cement (Penvenne 2011). The few blacks with sufficient means were often blocked by the simple racism of landlords (or assumed they would be). Against such bigotry, ever more rigid with the continuing influx of white immigrants, there was no real recourse (Castelo 2007; Penvenne 2011).

In many respects, Portuguese colonial urbanism mirrored cities elsewhere on the continent. Whether ruled by France, Britain, Belgium, fascist Italy, or Portugal, cities in colonial Africa were usually organized on the basis of racial classification (Abu-Lughod 1980; Winters 1982; Prochaska 1990; Wright 1991; Çelik 1997; Myers 2003; Coquery-Vidrovitch 2005; Fuller 2007; Njoh 2008; Myers 2011). The logic of colonialism, like its apartheid variant, demanded separation of the races, at least where whites were present in any numbers. Without the notion of a hierarchy of peoples European control lacked a convincing self-justification. Cities maintained this social hierarchy through spatial hierarchy.

A typical settler-colonial city was consciously developed as the embodiment of what modernity and European civilization were said to represent and what African societies might eventually aspire to under European guidance: it was rationally planned, technologically superior, hygienic according to the latest principles of medical science. Until the 1930s, a "sanitation syndrome" guided urban development across the continent. Fear of Africans as vectors of malaria and other disease justified the demolition of African neighborhoods in city centers and the removal of their residents to undeveloped, unserviced, and usually low-lying land beyond the city's edge, often separated by a cordon sanitaire of open space. As if to enhance the contrast, some colonial cities were, architecturally, more deliberately "European" than European cities themselves.

Indigenous populations were to be kept close enough to be of use, while at the same time kept in their place—whether in backyards or the city's margins—and only for as long as their labor was needed. Movement was often strictly controlled. Until the 1960s, for instance, a person classified *indígena* was only permitted to live in the area of Lourenço Marques— including its shantytowns—if he or she carried an official pass granting that right, a pass predicated on formal employment. Getting caught without a pass could subject the offender to beatings, jail time, forced labor, or in extreme cases, deportation to the cocoa plantations of the island of São Tomé (Penvenne 1983, 1989, 1995; O'Laughlin 2000). The idea of an African city, a city populated mostly by Africans and shaped by the complexities of African life, was contrary to what a city was supposed to be.

The various European colonial powers did not share an identical vision. Some cities in Britain's African empire, notably Nairobi, opted for a standard apartheid-like arrangement (Myers 2003), and the British were in general less circumspect in using race as the criterion for spatial separation. The Portuguese (until the 1960s, at least) shared a great deal of affinity with the French. Like the French, the Portuguese provided some Africans with an avenue to citizenship and equal rights, including the right to live in European districts (Wright 1991; Çelik 1997; Morton 2000). But all these different legalisms were not nearly as significant as the ultimate de facto reality of racial residential segregation which so many white settler cities held in common until independence.

If Portuguese colonial urbanism set itself apart (i.e., apart from all but French Algeria) it was in the sheer size of white settler populations in its cities and the intensity of construction necessary to house them. By the 1960s the streetscape of Lourenço Marques was dominated by high-rise apartment buildings, a glaring contrast with the low-density neighbor-hoods of bungalows characteristic of white districts in many other African cities. One result was that the City of Cement—particularly images of its modernist architecture—played an unusually large role in giving mean-ing and content to being white and Portuguese in the Mozambican con-text (Frates 2002; Penvenne forthcoming). One might say that the City of Cement was built as it was for this very purpose. In any case, it gave the independent government of Mozambique an entrenched built legacy of considerable size to contend with.

The second significant difference pertained to shantytown growth. With greater industrialization and the greater need for African labor, nearly all urban areas in Africa experienced a dramatic increase in Afri-can population after World War II (Freund 2007). The growth was even more pronounced in the 1960s, in large part because newly independent governments abolished urban influx controls. In Portuguese cities in Africa, however, influx controls were eased years before independence. Shantytown populations exploded in size for a further generation while still under colonial rule, sharpening the distinction between the booming City of Cement and its booming shantytowns and between the daily lives of whites and the daily lives of blacks.

The Cement City and Its Shantytowns

> Lourenço Marques emerged in the late nineteenth century as the principal port city for the goldfields of neighboring South Africa. By World War II, it was one of the busiest ports in Africa, and it soon became one of southern Africa's most populous cities. With ever-increasing Portuguese immigration, it also possessed one of the largest white settler communities south of the Sahara (Duffy 1962; Castelo 2007; Penvenne 2005, 2011). During the last genera-tion or so of colonial rule, Lourenço Marques had the appearance of being two cities: one mostly white and the other mostly black—two distinct urban landscapes, divided for the most part by the curve of Avenida Caldas Xavier (Anon 1974).

The City of Cement was inside the curve, which for a number of years was also the official city limit. Nearly all buildings were built of concrete blocks or clay bricks, cars drove on a grid of paved roads, and homes were hooked up to electricity and running water. The neighborhood of Alto Maé, in the northwest part of the formalized city, was the one area with a notable degree of integration, a part of town where Indians, lower-income

Figure 10.5 Lourenço Marques's City of Cement, 1971. (Credit: F. Sousa/AHM)

whites, people of mixed race, and a small number of blacks lived side-by-side (Mendes 1985; Penvenne 1995; Frates 2002).

Outside the curve the shantytowns began. The *subúrbios*, as the shantytowns were often called, existed in the gray area of the law. Housing there was unauthorized, and therefore officially illegal, but it was tolerated (Morais 2001). Most houses were built of reed walls with zinc roofs, roads were mud tracks, homes were lit with paraffin lamps, and fetching water was a daily tribulation. In the absence of sewage and drainage systems, flooding and cholera outbreaks were common and malaria rampant. In the 1960s, the local press dubbed the shantytowns the *Cidade de Caniço*, the City of Reeds (Rangel 1996).

In the workplace and in bars after work, men from different backgrounds often mixed easily—particularly when the black men were *assimilados*. In private homes in the city it wasn't unusual for the children of black women to grow up with the children of the women's white employers. This kind of essentially human conviviality persists pretty much anywhere, but while people may have felt close to each other as individuals, they inevitably met on profoundly unequal terms (Errante 2003). In L. Lloys Frates's study (2002) of Mozambican women's memories of late colonial Lourenço Marques, the City of Cement was described as a place where one walked

Figure 10.6 The shantytowns of Lourenço Marques were built on poorly drained, flood-prone land that was deemed undesirable for European development. During the annual rainy season, African residents of many neighborhoods lived with standing water in their homes, and malaria and cholera took a heavy toll. This photo was taken in 1966, in the aftermath of the historically catastrophic Tropical Depression Claude. (Credit: AHM)

with caution if one went there at all. *Assimilados*, particularly men, could be seen at restaurants, the cinema, schools, and in shops.

The beach and government buildings, though, were strictly white places. Mozambican women without shoes or wearing traditional capulana wraps couldn't get on downtown buses or enter stores. "We were not relaxed in the city and we went to work and returned to the suburbs when the work was over," said Fernas Tembe. "When we walked in the street they did not pay any attention to us, but, for example, the children of Whites provoked us" (Frates 2002, 194–95). In more recent interviews, men described the tension of any encounter with authorities, when forgetting to remove one's cap in respect could result in physical punishment.

One former ranking official, João Pereira Neto, once the intelligence chief for Portugal's Overseas Ministry, recalled in a recent interview that he was shocked by the polarized racial climate that prevailed in Lourenço Marques, which seemed to have more in common with a city in South Africa than it did with its colonial sister city, Luanda. On a visit to Mozambique's capital in 1970 he was astonished by the sight of black workers rushing home to the *caniço* after work in the City of Cement, hoping to avoid being caught up by an informal nine p.m. curfew. "It wasn't an official curfew," said Neto, "but they knew that they ran the risk of running into a group of whites, those that the Mozambicans called a 'posse.'" Mozambique in the 1960s and 1970s functioned as a kind of renegade province, Neto said—a place where local officials and white civilians undermined Lisbon's attempts at reform.

The city's shantytowns were terra incognita for most Portuguese, less known and less well understood than many parts of the Mozambican countryside (Penvenne 2011). Maps of Lourenço Marques rarely showed anything beyond Avenida Caldas Xavier, as if the neighborhoods that sheltered the majority of the urban area's population were nameless, or did not exist (Morais 2001; Frates 2002). These neighborhoods were only a few miles from City Hall, but as one resident recalled, during the war for independence the Portuguese distributed propaganda in the shantytowns by dropping leaflets from helicopters.

The racial division of Lourenço Marques was visibly so stark in part because it was inscribed in the architecture. To build within city limits, one had to use permanent materials—hence the colloquial designation "City of Cement" (Rita-Ferreira 1967). In the shantytowns, however, construction in permanent materials required a builder to jump through so many costly regulatory hoops that it was effectively prohibited. The shantytowns were areas zoned for prospective expansion of the formal European city; concrete houses there would have made the work of bulldozers more difficult (Morais 2001).

But because the differentiation of African society was contained within the confines of the shantytowns, they were nonetheless places of great diversity in construction. Residents interviewed about the housing choices they made in the colonial era described what was essentially a three-tiered shantytown society.[4] The most destitute residents, often recent arrivals from the countryside, rented single-room units in cramped compounds. Many people shared the same room, and perhaps dozens of people would share the same latrine and, if one was available, a single water spigot. In the 1960s, rent for a single-room unit might run from 20 to 50 escudos a month.

Those with steadier employment and greater means generally lived in a one- or two-roomed reed shack built with their own hands. Many also rented such units, paying perhaps 150 escudos per month.

And in the older, more established neighborhoods, such as Chamanculo, Xipamanine, and Mafalala, half the homes or more were wood-framed, zinc-paneled houses. Some of these were featureless shacks, not much of a step up from the reed version. The grander examples, the homes of the shantytown elite, featured multiple-pitched roofs with high gables

Figure 10.7 Zinc-paneled houses in the Maputo Neighborhood of Minkadjuine, 1987. (Credit: CDFF)

and covered verandahs and wood floors and large pigeon coops, all of which spoke eloquently of the relative wealth and taste of its owner. Some people clandestinely built concrete walls behind the zinc panels. These finer houses, when rented out, might go for 500 escudos a month.

The disparities within the *caniço* were in some ways as striking as those that distinguished the *caniço* from the City of Cement. A kind of proto-middle class emerged: *assimilados* and *mestiços* who spoke fluent Portuguese, who in the workplace formed relationships with white Portuguese that exceeded the typically narrow dynamic of servant and *patrão*, and for whom the formalized city—predominately white though it might be—was, if not completely welcoming, at least not completely foreign. Stifled by the racial barriers of Lourenço Marques, this shantytown elite was, following independence, poised to enter Maputo with confidence.

The experience of personal racial humiliation in Lourenço Marques influenced many early policy decisions by Frelimo (Hall and Young 1997). Many leaders of the new government, including President Samora Machel, had themselves been *assimilados*, had been promised equality by the Portuguese in principle, and then denied it in practice. During Machel's 1976 speech announcing the nationalization of rental housing, he recalled for his audiences the apartheid structure of the colonial capital. Nationalization—which appropriated for the government not just abandoned properties around the country, but all rental housing in Mozambique's various Cities of Cement—would be an important victory over the legacy of colonialism, as it would end capitalist speculation and abolish racial and social

Figure 10.8 Mozambique's President Samora Machel addresses a Maputo crowd, 1980. (Credit: Martinho Fernando/CDFF)

discrimination in housing. The apartment buildings of the city were "built on top of our bones, and the cement, sand, and water in those buildings is none other than the blood of the workers, the sweat of the workers, the blood of the Mozambican people! Buildings are the highest forms of exploitation of our people" (Machel 1976, 60).

As Machel ended his speech, he issued a caveat. The president warned that not everyone who wanted an apartment or a house in the City of Cement would get one. Only those who made a reasonable income, he said, would be able to afford to live in a nationalized building. The buildings were state assets. The loans that had financed their construction somehow had to be paid off. Although rents were dramatically reduced from what they had been previously, the nationalization of rental buildings was still geared toward those who could recoup the government's investment and best maintain the physical condition of the colonial inheritance.

Much of the best vacant property was spoken for. Most of the posh districts, such as Polana and Sommerschield, were quickly occupied by Frelimo officials and various state institutions, or reserved for foreign diplomats and the many foreigners, Frelimo sympathizers, who arrived in Maputo to volunteer their skills to the socialist cause (Mendes 1989; Sidaway and Power 1995). Thousands of former Frelimo guerillas and their families were offered apartments in the rest of the city, as were the victims of flooding earlier in the year. Officials of APIE, the state agency created to manage the newly nationalized properties, became notorious for helping themselves, illegally, to many of the best units (Zunguza 1984).

The rental policy was soon made more equitable, with rent pegged to income. Families earning less were charged less than higher income families, no matter where in the City of Cement they were housed (Jenkins 1990). Yet, the formerly European core remained privileged territory (Mendes 1989). By 1980, only about 8 percent of the houses and apartments of the country's Cities of Cement were occupied by people who were officially categorized as "working class" (Carrilho 1987). The majority of units in formalized urban areas were occupied by people in the services sector (and the majority of these were government workers) the relatively few who earned a decent wage in the postcolonial order.[5]

As residents of the city recalled in interviews, rent wasn't the only cost to living in Maputo's City of Cement. One also had to factor in the costs of electricity and water. To cook the meals most people were accustomed to—and that they could afford—they would need their large mortars and pestles to make corn meal. But you were prohibited from bringing them into apartments because thousands of people pounding corn cobs on verandahs would compromise the structure of buildings. Nor could one use a coal-burning stove.

People like Sebastião Chithombe never even considered a move to the City of Cement. By 1976, he was living in the shabby backroom of a shantytown cantina he had purchased at a deep discount from a departing Portuguese the year before. His friends in the compounds were laborers, and not able to afford the rent in the city. There was some reluctance to make that move, even among those with greater means, people generally from *assimilado* backgrounds for whom such a move was potentially possible. Helena Macuacua, a young teacher living in the Aeroporto neighborhood, thought it was too risky. "I couldn't put the money together for it," she said in a recent interview. "I saw the rent was going to be very high, and also my husband wasn't someone I could trust. I preferred to plant myself here where things were accessible rather than go to the city and afterward suffer the consequences." Benjamim Benfica, another schoolteacher, lived in a zinc-paneled house in Chamanculo that his father, a truck driver, had built. He chose to honor his late father's wish that he never give up the house. "We didn't have electricity, we didn't have a sewage system, but it was my house. This is the fundamental part."

Benfica was young for a homeowner, only twenty-one at independence. Many of his friends, and many of Helena Macuacua's friends, jumped at the chance to live in the City of Cement—though many also returned to the *subúrbios* within a few years when costs proved too much to bear. (It was not unusual for people who had ventured a life in the City of Cement to return after a month or two.) Many others, like Benfica's father, had spent their adult lives saving up to build a house of their own in the shantytowns, and some families had lived on the same plot for decades. A house was the one solid investment that one could pass on to successive generations. For many people of this older generation, the City of Cement had been so distant and the lifestyle it required so unattainable that living there never took shape as an aspiration. A common anxiety that cropped up in interviews, far from unreasonable, was that the government would not survive and that the old order would return. Given that the new housing rules dictated that a family could only have one house,[6] the situation was too uncertain to exchange the home one had for a home one had not even hoped for.

For all the drama accompanying the nationalization of rental housing in the City of Cement, the real impact for most shantytown dwellers was the policy's consequences for shantytown housing. In some neighborhoods of the *caniço*, as much as 70 percent of the housing units were rentals (Rita-Ferreira 1967). According to a recent interview with former housing minister Júlio Carrilho, the nationalizations were never intended to apply to the shantytowns. But neighborhood-level activists, inspired by Machel's speech and Frelimo's characterization of rent as "exploitation of man by man," began "nationalizing" compounds and rental shacks in the *subúrbios* as well.

This spontaneous, grassroots phenomenon—rare under a government known for its heavy-handed, top-down approach (Hall and Young 1997)—spoke more to the nature of most people's expectations than the reoccupation of the City of Cement did. Shantytown nationalization, as Carrilho later reflected, addressed a long-held and heartfelt desire: it was a demand by shantytown dwellers for a meaningful form of citizenship, one in which the government acknowledged its responsibility for all parts of the city. Within a week of Machel's speech, the government became the reluctant landlord to a good share of the shantytown landscape.[7]

Frelimo in the first years of its rule regarded the seat of its power with suspicion (Hall and Young 1997; Sidaway and Power 1995). The capital city had been the colonial regime's beating heart—a place where the Portuguese influence had been most direct, and where, after independence, an African "petit bourgeoisie"—*assimilados*—with their supposedly colonized minds, lurked as a potential internal threat. Machel said he looked forward to the influence on the city of an influx of people from the countryside, who would bring with them their rural, communitarian values, and to putting city dwellers to work in the countryside, where they would learn what it meant to be authentically Mozambican (Machel 1976).

Yet it was this same petit bourgeoisie that was given the keys to the City of Cement. One of the contradictions of Portuguese propaganda had been that even those Africans considered "civilized" were effectively barred from living within the borders of the designated civilized enclave. That contradiction had now been resolved, so that the postindependence dispensation gave a measure of coherence to colonial-era attitudes linked to race—attitudes that distinguished between "civilized" and "uncivilized" ways of life, between the fixed city dweller and the rural sojourner who was best suited to the shantytowns.

Frelimo was itself marked by contradiction. For all its championing of traditional rural values, Frelimo also demonstrated a distaste—in word and in practice—for what it regarded as country backwardness,

Puxa o autoclismo
depois de utilizares a retrete

Figure 10.9 Following independence, apartment living was unfamiliar and uncomfortable for many of the new occupants of the City of Cement, where many accustomed practices were prohibited, such as cooking on open coals, pounding cornmeal, and keeping chickens and goats. Pictured is a detail from an undated poster demonstrating the proper use of flush toilets, distributed by Mozambique's Health Ministry. (Credit: Ministério de Saude/DNMP)

and Frelimo leaders considered themselves the clear-eyed agents of modernization (Hall and Young 1997; Pitcher 2002; Mahoney 2003; Sumich 2005). Perhaps populating central Maputo with civil servants was another example of how its ideas of what constituted modernity—and the modern city—echoed Portuguese notions (and not just Portuguese notions, of course). While listing the do's and don'ts of making a home in the City of Cement—such as not bringing livestock into buildings—the president instructed future tenants to not hang their colorful *capulanas* outside their apartments. "Otherwise the city will look as if it belongs to *monhés*," a common, though pejorative term for Indian and Arab Muslims (Machel 1976, 69).

But continuities with colonial-era mentalities can be overstated. The practical reasons to favor more privileged Mozambicans in the distribution of City of Cement housing were obvious: the City of Cement would likely fall apart otherwise. Given the limited number of apartments relative to the urban population, occupation of the City of Cement was never going to be more than a partial solution to Maputo's housing problems in any case (Jenkins 1990). And much was beyond Frelimo's ability to control. There was little the government could do, after lowering rents, to make apartment living affordable, or for that matter, livable.

It should be noted that the new tenants of the City of Cement were not all the so-called petit bourgeoisie. Many new residents (it is difficult to estimate how many) had come directly from the countryside, such as the many families of ex-guerillas. Or they were among the poorer households from the shantytowns, such as those evacuated from flooded neighborhoods. For them, the City of Cement was an uncomfortable fit. Despite prohibitions, many of these residents continued with their daily routines: cooking on open coals, raising goats and chickens in their apartments, and pounding grain on their verandahs. Common spaces of buildings became trash dumps (Anon. 1981). Journalists played up stories of simple Mozambicans baffled by the use of bathtubs and flushing toilets, and children who relieved themselves everywhere except where they were supposed to (Manuel 1985). Housing officials despaired of the threat to public health, and the damage to what they considered the nation's patrimony.

The building stock of the City of Cement was indeed deteriorating, and at a rapid pace (Jenkins 1990, 2011). It wasn't just the pounding of cornmeal contributing to the physical decline. The generalized collapse of the Mozambican economy following the Portuguese withdrawal resulted in dire shortages, including shortages of building materials. In Maputo, nails and cement mix and tools became scarce items (Tembe 1987). At the same time, when coal or cooking gas was short (which was often) cooking fires were often fueled by the wood of parquet floors (Ribas 1983).

And conditions continued to worsen. The decade of the 1980s was among the most trying in Mozambique's modern history. Apartheid South Africa bankrolled an anti-Frelimo insurgency, called Renamo, fueling a catastrophic war. Hundreds of thousands fled from the countryside to Maputo, seeking protection from the violence. The population of the city roughly doubled between 1980 and 1997 (Henriques 2008) and the capital and its shantytowns took on the character of a crowded refugee camp. Overwhelmed by the influx, Frelimo embarked in 1983 on a draconian program to purge Maputo of "unproductive elements"—people who could not prove they had formal employment. Tens of thousands of people lacking the proper documentation and who could not return to the rural homes from which many had fled were "evacuated" to remote provinces to work on state farms (Castanheira 1983a; 1983b; 1983c; Naroromele 1983).

By 1987, the Frelimo government, brought to its knees by war, drought, and economic hardship, gave up its socialist program, and adopted the market reforms imposed by the International Monetary Fund and the World Bank (Pitcher 2002). At the end of that year, the rent structure was adjusted to more closely reflect perceived market demand (Carrilho 1987). Rents, on average, more than doubled over the next five years (Sidaway and Power 1995). For many who had managed to endure in the City of Cement for a decade, the rent hike was the last straw, and it forced a move to the shantytowns (Mendes 1989).

Those who were able somehow to hang on during the brutal winnowing of Maputo were able to profit handsomely. In the 1990s, the government started selling rental properties to their occupants, and tenants, in turn, either sold or rented their apartments (Jenkins 2011). It was a seller's market, with home prices and rents boosted by the foreigners who came with the dizzying array of United Nations agencies and nongovernmental organizations that descended on Maputo, many after the end of the war with Renamo in 1992 (Hanlon 1997). Until then, living in the City of Cement had been a dubious luxury. Now, with an apartment an increasingly valuable asset to leverage, a relatively privileged group of city dwellers became even more privileged, and the social gap between themselves and those who lived in other parts of the city widened. For some an apartment became the primary source of income; some used the profits from selling an apartment, or the income from renting one out, to build a concrete-block house in the *subúrbios* or the city's distant and spacious exurbs (Jenkins 2011). The City of Cement didn't just house the African middle class. A generation after independence it also brought the middle class fully into being.

Theoretical Considerations: Transformations from a Racial System to a Class System

What can critical geographers and Marxist sociologists learn from the nationalization of housing in Maputo's City of Cement? The quick transformation after independence from a city divided principally by race to a city divided principally by class was not remarkable in itself: it was the common experience in cities throughout the decolonized world. African and Asian elites moved into neighborhoods built to house European elites (Coquery-Vidrovitch 2005). In most colonial cities, white districts were not particularly large, and their occupation by ruling parties amounted to little more than a changing of the guard. But in Maputo, after the new regime occupied the choicest real estate, much of the extensive City of Cement still remained to be parceled out. And as it distributed these properties, Frelimo favored an already favored class of people who in speeches it vilified as potential counterrevolutionaries.

Perhaps this decision reflected an inveterate modernizing impulse, one evident in so many state interventions after independence. Perhaps Frelimo envisioned a "modern" city as an essentially European one in its order, appearance, and stratification. If so, Frelimo's policy was an only slightly modified recapitulation of attitudes that shaped the city in the past, and those Mozambicans called *assimilados* were the natural inheritors of the "civilized" part of the city. Another, more important factor, however, was at work: Concrete. On the one hand, the buildings of the City of Cement weren't going anywhere. On the other hand, the buildings were subject to falling apart if not properly maintained, requiring an investment in the buildings themselves, in the almost 900 building superintendents to look after them, and in the bulky bureaucracy required to manage it all. To foot this bill, Frelimo was compelled to preserve the kind of economic and social segmentation that in other areas—such as public health and education—it refused to do. There is more to consider, furthermore, than Frelimo policy. Even for many people earning steady wages, life in a low-rent apartment, and even a rent-free apartment, proved considerably harder than life in the *subúrbios*. Inequality was seemingly hardwired into the city's structure.

One of the lessons to be learned from the case of Maputo (or rather, learned again) is the significance of the relative durability of urbanism itself: how a built legacy can convey the values of the past into the present, long after planners and builders are gone from the scene. Much of the work on colonial-era architecture and urbanism in Africa begins with Foucault as a starting point (whether he is acknowledged or not) with an emphasis on the intentions of colonial administrators and architects—the ideologies they brought to the drawing board, and that were embedded in the finished product (Wright 1991; Çelik 1997; Fuller 2007). As the work of Garth Myers (2003) suggests, one needs to examine, too, how people actually lived in colonial-era built environments over time, and reconfigured them to their own needs. His approach shares something of the spirit of Michel de Certeau (1984): ordinary people aren't the hapless victims of the spatial structures of control as Foucault makes them out to be.[8] The insight is an intuitively satisfying one, but in Maputo's City of Cement it finds an empirical test: there, even the new regime could not make the built landscape conform to new priorities; demolition, let alone construction, was a luxury. A converted movie theater served as the young nation's popular assembly.

Ultimately, though, the issue was not that most Mozambicans were ill-suited to the City of Cement, and the living arrangements it presupposed, but rather that the City of Cement was fundamentally unsuitable for Mozambique—a constant reminder of colonialism's colossally bad fit., The center of gravity of African life in Maputo has long been located on the city's margins, whether during the colonial era or afterward. Today, the "shantytown" designation is far less appropriate than it was before. Most houses are built of concrete block, and people from all walks of life live in them. Houses in the *subúrbios* are still unauthorized for the most part, still officially illegal, but the aspiration of the people who live in these neighborhoods is not to move to an apartment in what was once called the City of Cement. Rather, when most people in Maputo talk about their future, they imagine building a house on a larger plot of land in the peri-urban areas of Matola or Marracuene, even further from downtown, and that much closer to the countryside.

Acknowledgments

This chapter draws upon research that was generously supported by the Fundação Calouste Gulbenkian, the Fundação Luso-Americana, the University of Minnesota Office of International Programs, and a Fulbright Program grant sponsored by the Bureau of Educational and Cultural Affairs of the U.S. Department of State and administered by the Institute of International Education.

Glossary

APIE—Acronym for Administração do Parque Imobiliário do Estado, the Mozambican state agency that administered all state-owned real estate following the nationalization of rental buildings in 1976.

Assimilado—During most of the colonial era, one of several thousand black Mozambicans who were considered legal Portuguese citizens. To "assimilate," an African had to establish that he or she was sufficiently "civilized," a standard that included reading and writing Portuguese, eating and dressing as a European was said to eat and dress, and achieving a certain level of income and formal education.

Caniço—Portuguese for "reed," until recent decades the most common building material in Maputo's shantytowns. The band of shantytown settlements around the city was often called the caniço or the Cidade de Caniço ("City of Reeds").

Cidade de Cimento—"City of Cement." During the colonial era, the common term for the formalized, largely European part of the city where streets were paved and most buildings were built in concrete or brick.

Frelimo—The Frente da Libertação de Moçambique, or Mozambique Liberation Front, the one-time anticolonial guerilla force that, as a political party, has governed the country since independence.

Indígena—Portuguese for "native," the official classification of the vast majority of Mozambicans for most of the colonial era. Those with indígena status were denied the rights of Portuguese citizenship and subject to terms of forced labor, called *chibalo*.

Renamo—The Resistência Nacional Moçambicana, or Mozambican National Resistance, an armed insurgency assembled from Frelimo discontents by Rhodesia's white minority (the country became independent as Zimbabwe in 1980), and later backed by apartheid South Africa. From 1976 to 1992 the group sought to disable Frelimo's ability to govern, doing so mostly through attacks on civilian populations. The civil war that resulted—Frelimo calls it a "war of destabilization"—cost the lives of as many as one million Mozambicans and displaced millions more.

Subúrbios—Another, more official term for the Cidade de Caniço, still in common parlance. Unlike the English word *suburb*, which indicates a lack of urban density, *subúrbio* indicates a lack of urban infrastructure, such as paved roads, sewage systems, and water provision.

Notes

1. Historian Jeanne Penvenne is the widely recognized authority on colonial-era Maputo, particularly in matters of labor and class, and the rest of this section owes a particularly heavy debt to her work.

2. A number of people of mixed race were also of Indian or Chinese heritage.
3. Some 40 percent of the Portuguese who left Mozambique for Portugal in 1974–75 were illiterate (Errante 2003).
4. Frates (2002) describes a three-tiered society of the city as a whole: black, *assimilado*, and white.
5. By 1982, most of the country's economy was state-run (Pitcher 2002).
6. A second home was permitted if it was located in the countryside.
7. Nationalization of rental housing should not be confused with nationalization of land. In order to put a halt to speculation, the government has claimed since 1975 the sole right to buy and sell land.
8. See Martin Murray's observations regarding de Certeau and urban squatters in and around Johannesburg (Murray 2008, 106).

References

Abu-Lughod, Janet L. 1980. *Rabat: Urban Apartheid in Morocco*. Princeton, NJ: Princeton University Press.

Andrade, António Alberto Banha de. 1961. *Many Races–One Nation: Racial Non-Discrimination Always the Cornerstone of Portugal's Overseas Policy*. Lisbon: Tip. Silvas.

Anon. 1974. "'Apartheid' na habitação" [Apartheid in housing]. *Tempo*, October 27.

———. 1981. "Janela Aberta" [Open window]. *Notícias*, January 30.

Bender, Gerald J. 1978. *Angola under the Portuguese: The Myth and the Reality*. Berkeley: University of California Press.

Boxer, C. R. 1963. *Race Relations in the Portuguese Colonial Empire, 1415–1825*. Oxford, UK: Clarendon Press.

———. 1973. *The Portuguese Seaborne Empire, 1415–1825*. Harmondsworth, UK: Penguin.

Cairo, Heriberto. 2006. "'Portugal Is Not a Small Country': Maps and Propaganda in the Salazar Regime." *Geopolitics* 11 (3): 367–95.

Carrilho, Júlio. 1987. "Ajustar as rendas ao valor das casas" [Adjusting rents to the value of the houses]. *Tempo*, October 4.

Castanheira, Narciso. 1983a. "Operação Produção: punir os desvios" [Production Operation: punish deviations]. *Tempo*, July 24.

———. 1983b. "Operação Produção: de casa em casa" [Production operation: From house to house]. *Tempo*, August 14.

———. 1983c. "Operação Produção: até onde é que devemos intervir?" [Production operation: How far should we intervene?]. *Tempo*, August 28.

Castelo, Cláudia. 2001. *O modo português de estar no mundo: o luso-tropicalismo e a ideologia colonial portuguesa (1933–1961)* [The Portuguese way of being in the world: The Luso-tropical colonial ideology]. Porto: Afrontamento.

———. 2007. *Passagens para África: o povoamento de Angola e Moçambique com naturais da metrópole (1920–1974)* [Flights to Africa: the population of Angola and Mozambique with natural metropolis]. Porto: Edições Afrontamento.

Çelik, Zeynep. 1997. *Urban Forms and Colonial Confrontations: Algiers under French Rule*. Berkeley: University of California Press.

Certeau, Michel de. 1984. *The Practice of Everyday Life*, translated by Steven Rendall. Berkeley: University of California Press.

Coquery-Vidrovitch, Catherine. 2005. "Residential Segregation in African Cities." In *Urbanization and African Cultures*, edited by Steven J. Salm and Toyin Falola, 343–56. Durham, NC: Carolina Academic Press.

Cross, Michael. 1987. "The Political Economy of Colonial Education: Mozambique, 1930–1975." *Comparative Education Review*, 31 (4): 550–69.

Direcção Provincial dos Serviços de Estatística Geral. 1960. *III Recenseamento geral da população na Província de Lourenço Marques*. [III Population census in the province of Lourenço Marques]. Lourenço Marques: Author.

Duffy, James. 1962. *Portugal in Africa*. Baltimore: Penguin.

Errante, Antoinette. 2003. "White Skin, Many Masks: Colonial Schooling, Race, and National Consciousness among White Settler Children in Mozambique, 1934–1974." *The International Journal of African Historical Studies* 36 (1): 7–33.

Foucault, Michel. 1980. *Power/Knowledge*. Brighton, UK: Harvester Press.

Frates, L. Lloys. 2002. "Memory of Place, the Place of Memory: Women's Narrations of Late Colonial Lourenço Marques, Mozambique." PhD diss., University of California, Los Angeles.

Freund, Bill. 2007. *The African City: A History*. New York: Cambridge University Press.

Freyre, Gilberto. 1961. *Portuguese Integration in the Tropics*. Lisbon: Tip. Silvas.

Fuller, Mia. 2007. *Moderns Abroad: Architecture, Cities and Italian Imperialism*. London: Routledge.

Garenne, Michel, Rudi Coninx, and Chantal Dupuy. 1996. "Direct and Indirect Estimates of Mortality Changes: A Case Study in Mozambique." In *Demographic Evaluation of Health Programmes: Conference Proceedings*, edited by Myriam Khlat, 53–63. Paris: Committee for International Cooperation in National Research in Demography (CICRED).

Godinho, António Maria. 1962. *O ultramar português: uma comunidade multiracial* [The Portuguese overseas: A multiracial community]. Lisbon: Sociedade de Geografia de Lisboa, Semana do Ultramar.

Greger, Otto. 1990. "Angola." In *Housing Policies in the Socialist Third World*, edited by Kosta Mathéy, 129–45. Munich: Profil.

Hall, Margaret, and Tom Young. 1997. *Confronting Leviathan: Mozambique Since Independence*. Athens: Ohio University Press.

Hanlon, Joseph. 1997. "Mozambique: Under New Management." *Soundings* (7): 184–94.

Henriques, Cristina Delgado. 2008. *Maputo: cinco décadas de mudança territorial* [Maputo: Five decades of territorial change]. Lisbon: IPAD.

Honwana, Raúl Bernardo Manuel. 1988. *The Life History of Raúl Honwana: An Inside View of Mozambique from Colonialism to Independence, 1905–1975*, edited by Allen F. Isaacman, translated by Tamara L. Bender. Boulder, CO: Lynne Rienner.

Isaacman, Allen F. 1996. *Cotton Is the Mother of Poverty: Peasants, Work, and Rural Struggle in Colonial Mozambique, 1938–1961*. Portsmouth, NH: Heinemann.

———. Barbara Isaacman. 1983. *Mozambique: From Colonialism to Revolution, 1900–1982*. Boulder, CO: Westview Press.

Jenkins, Paul. 1990. "Mozambique." In *Housing Policies in the Socialist Third World*, edited by Kosta Mathéy, 147–79. Munich: Profil.

———. 2011. "Maputo and Luanda." In *Capital Cities in Africa: Power and Powerlessness*, edited by Simon Bekker and Göran Therborn, 141–66. Johannesburg, SA: HSRC Press.

Lefebvre, Henri. 1991. *The Production of Space*. Oxford, UK: Blackwell.

Lesbet, Djaffar. 1990. "Algeria." In *Housing Policies in the Socialist Third World*, edited by Kosta Mathéy, 249–73. Munich: Profil.

Machel, Samora. 1976. "Independência implica benefícios para as massas exploradas" [Independence implies benefits for the exploited masses]. Speech Given February 3, 1976. In *A nossa luta é uma revolução* [Our struggle is our revolution]. 33–70. Lisbon: CIDA-C.

Mahoney, Michael. 2003. "Estado Novo, Homem Novo [New State, New Man]: Colonial and Anti-Colonial Development Ideologies in Mozambique, 1930–1977." In *Staging Growth: Modernization, Development, and the Global Cold War*, edited by David C. Engerman, Nils Gilman, Mark H. Haefele, and Michael E. Latham, 142–175. Amherst, MA: University of Massachusetts Press.

Manuel, Fernando. 1985. "Habitação não é só a casa." [Housing is not only the house]. *Tempo*, April 7.

Medeiros, Eduardo. 1989. "L'évolution démographique de la ville de Lourenço-Marques (1894–1975). "[Demographic evolution in the city of Lourenço-Marques]. In *Bourgs et villes en afrique lusophone* [Market towns and cities of lusophone Africa], edited by Michel Cahen, 63–73. Paris: Editions L'Harmattan.

Mendes, Maria Clara. 1985. *Maputo antes da Independência: geografia de uma cidade* [Maputo before Independence: Geography of a colonial city], vol. 68. Memórias do Instituto de Investigação Científica Tropical 2) [Archives of the Institute of Tropical Research, 2]. Lisbon: IICT.

———. 1989. "Les répercussions de l'indépendance sur la ville de Maputo" [The repercussions of independence on the city of Maputo]. In *Bourgs et villes en afrique lusophone* [Market towns and cities in lusophone Africa], edited by Michel Cahen, 281–96. Paris: Editions L'Harmattan.

Morais, João Sousa. 2001. *Maputo: património da estrutura e forma urbana, topologia do lugar* [Maputo: Its heritage and the urban form of the structure, topology of the place]. Lisbon: Livros Horizonte.

Morton, Patricia A. 2000. *Hybrid Modernities: Architecture and Representation at the 1931 Colonial Exposition, Paris*. Cambridge, MA: MIT Press.

Munslow, Barry. 1983. *Mozambique: The Revolution and Its Origins*. London: Longman.

Murray, Martin J. 2008. *Taming the Disorderly City: The Spatial Landscape of Johannesburg after Apartheid*. Ithaca, NY: Cornell University Press.

Myers, Garth A. 2003. *Verandahs of Power: Colonialism and Space in Urban Africa*. Syracuse, NY: Syracuse University Press.

———. 2011. *African Cities: Alternate Visions of Urban Theory and Practice*. London: Zed Books.

Naroromele, Albano. 1983. "Operação Produção: uma missão histórica" [Operation Production: a historical mission]. *Tempo*, August 14.

Newitt, Malyn. 1995. *A History of Mozambique*. London: Hurst.

Njoh, A. J. 2008. "Colonial Philosophies, Urban Space, and Racial Segregation in British and French Colonial Africa." *Journal of Black Studies* 38 (4): 579–99.

O'Laughlin, Bridget. 2000. "Class and the Customary: The Ambiguous Legacy of the Indigenato in Mozambique." *African Affairs* 99 (394): 5–42.

Oliveira, Isabella. 1999. *M. & U., Companhia Ilimitada* [M & U, an unlimited company]. Porto: Edições Afrontamento.

Penvenne, Jeanne. 1983. "'Here We All Walked with Fear.' The Mozambican Labor System and the Workers of Lourenço Marques, 1945–1962." In *Struggle for the City: Migrant Labor, Capital, and the State in Urban Africa*, edited by Frederick Cooper, 131–66. Beverly Hills, CA: Sage.

———. 1989. "'We Are All Portuguese!' Challenging the Political Economy of Assimilation: Lourenço Marques, 1870–1933." In *The Creation of Tribalism in Southern Africa*, edited by Leroy Vail, 255–88. London: Currey.

———. 1991. *Principles and Passion: Capturing the Legacy of João dos Santos Albasini*. Boston: African Studies Center, Boston University.

———. 1995. *African Workers and Colonial Racism: Mozambican Strategies and Struggles in Lourenço Marques, 1877–1962*. Portsmouth, NH: Heinemann.

———. 2005. "Settling Against the Tide: The Layered Contradictions of Twentieth-Century Portuguese Settlement in Mozambique." In *Settler Colonialism in the Twentieth Century: Projects, Practices, Legacies*, edited by Caroline Elkins and Susan Pedersen, 79–94. New York: Taylor & Francis.

———. 2011. "Two Tales of a City: Lourenço Marques, 1945–1975." *Portuguese Studies Review* 19 (1–2): 249–69.

———. Forthcoming. "Fotografando Lourenço Marques: a cidade e os seus habitantes de 1960 a 1975" [Photographing Lourenço Marques: The city and its inhabitants from 1960 to 1975]. In *Os outros da colonização: ensaios sobre tardo-colonialismo em Moçambique* [The Others of colonization: Essays on late-colonialism in Mozambique], edited by Cláudia Castelo, Omar Ribeiro Tomaz, Sebastião Nascimento, and Teresa Cruz e Silva. Lisbon: Imprensa de Ciências Sociais.

Pereira Bastos, Susana. 2005. "Indian Transnationalisms in Colonial and Postcolonial Mozambique." *Stichproben: Wiener Zeitschrift für Kritische Afrikastudien* 8: 277–306.

Pinsky, Barry. 1985. "Territorial Dilemmas: Changing Urban Life." In *A Difficult Road: The Transition to Socialism in Mozambique*, edited by John S. Saul, 279–315. New York: Monthly Review Press.

Pitcher, M. Anne. 2002. *Transforming Mozambique: The Politics of Privatization, 1975–2000*. Cambridge, UK: Cambridge University Press.

Prochaska, David. 1990. *Making Algeria French: Colonialism in Bône, 1870–1920*. Cambridge, UK: Cambridge University Press.

Rangel, Ricardo. 1996. "Os primeiros passos de um fotojornalista famoso" [The first steps of a famous photojournalist]. In *140 anos de imprensa em Moçambique* [140 years of press in Mozambique], edited by Fátima Ribeiro and António Sopa, 121–123. Maputo: Associação Moçambicana da Língua Portuguesa.

Ribas, Filipe. 1983. "Não há gás, não há carvão, não há lenha" [No gas, no coal, no firewood]. *Tempo*, November 20.

Rita-Ferreira, António. 1967. "Os africanos de Lourenço Marques" [The Africans in Lourenço Marques]. *Memórias do Instituto Científica de Moçambique* [Archives of the Institute of Science of Mozambique] 9 (C): 95–491.

———. 1988. "Moçambique post-25 de Abril: causas do êxodo da população de origem europeia e asiática" [Mozambique following April 25: Reasons for the exodus of the European and Asiatic population]. In *Moçambique: cultura e história de um país* [Mozambique: Culture and history of a country], 119–169. (Publicações do Centro de Estudos Africanos No. 8. [Publication of the Center for African Studies]). Coimbra: Universidade de Coimbra.

Serviços de Centralização e Coordinação de Informações de Moçambique. 1973. *Moçambique na actualidade* [Mozambique today]. Lourenço Marques: Author.

Sheldon, Kathleen. 2002. *Pounders of Grain: A History of Women, Work, and Politics in Mozambique*. Portsmouth, NH: Heinemann.

Sidaway, J. D., and M. Power. 1995. "Socio-spatial Transformations in the 'Postsocialist' Periphery: The Case of Maputo, Mozambique." *Environment and Planning A* 27 (9): 1463–91.

Sumich, Jason Michael. "Elites and Modernity in Mozambique." PhD diss., London School of Economics, 2005.

Tembe, Alfredo. 1987. "Materiais de construção: quem não tem divisas fica 'a ver navios'" [Building materials: who has no foreign currency is "dust"]. *Tempo*, September 20.

Vail, Leroy, and Landeg White. 1980. *Capitalism and Colonialism in Mozambique: A Study of Quelimane District*. Minneapolis: University of Minnesota Press.

Winters, Christopher. 1982. "Urban Morphogenesis in Francophone Black Africa." *Geographical Review* 72 (2): 139–54.

Wright, Gwendolyn. 1991. *The Politics of Design in French Colonial Urbanism*. Chicago: University of Chicago Press.

Zunguza, Rui. 1984. "Doença da APIE: financeira não … de gestão talvez!" [Disease APIE: financial management maybe not …]. *Tempo*, August 19.

CHAPTER 11

Unsettling the Privilege of Self-Reflexivity

ANDREA SMITH

In my experience with a plethora of antiracist organizing projects over the years, I frequently found myself participating in various workshops in which participants were asked to reflect on their gender/race/sexuality/class/etc. privilege. These workshops had a bit of a self-help orientation to them: "I am so and so, and I have x privilege." It was never quite clear what the point of these confessions were. It was not as if other participants did not know the confessor in question had her or his proclaimed privilege. It did not appear that these individual confessions actually led to any political projects to dismantle the structures of domination that enabled their privilege. Rather, the confessions became the political project themselves. The benefits of these confessions seemed to be ephemeral. For the instant the confession took place, those who do not have that privilege in daily life would have a temporary position of power as the hearer of the confession who could grant absolution and forgiveness. The one who confessed could then be granted temporary forgiveness for her or his abuses of power and relief from white/male/heterosexual/etc. guilt. Because of the perceived benefits of this ritual, there was generally little critique of the fact that in the end, it primarily served to reinstantiate the structures of domination it was supposed to resist. One of the reasons there was little critique of this practice is that it bestowed cultural capital to those who seemed to be the "most oppressed." Those who had little privilege did not have to confess and were in the position to be the judge of those who did have privilege.

Consequently, people aspired to be oppressed. Inevitably, those with more privilege would develop new heretofore unknown forms of oppression from which they suffered. "I may be white, but my best friend was a person of color, which caused me to be oppressed when we played together." Consequently, the goal became not to actually end oppression but to be as oppressed as possible. These rituals often substituted confession for political movement-building. And despite the cultural capital that was, at least temporarily, bestowed to those who seemed to be the most oppressed, these rituals ultimately reinstantiated the white majority subject as the subject capable of self-reflexivity and the colonized/racialized subject as the occasion for self-reflexivity.

These rituals around self-reflexivity in the academy and in activist circles are not without merit. They are informed by key insights into how the logics of domination that structure the world also constitute who we are as subjects. Political projects of transformation necessarily involve a fundamental reconstitution of ourselves as well. However, for this process to work, individual transformation must occur concurrently with social and political transformation. That is, the undoing of privilege occurs not by individuals confessing their privileges or trying to think themselves into a new subject position, but through the creation of collective structures that dismantle the systems that enable these privileges. The activist genealogies that produced this response to racism and settler colonialism were not initially focused on racism as a problem of individual prejudice. Rather, the purpose was for individuals to recognize how they were shaped by structural forms of oppression. However, the response to structural racism became an individual one: individual confession at the expense of collective action. Thus the question becomes, how would one collectivize individual transformation? Many organizing projects attempt to do precisely this, such as Sisters in Action for Power, Sista II Sista, Incite! Women of Color Against Violence, and Communities Against Rape and Abuse, among many others. Rather than focus simply on one's individual privilege, they address privilege on an organizational level. For instance, they might assess whether everyone who is invited to speak is a college graduate. Are certain peoples always in the limelight? Based on this assessment, they develop structures to address how privilege is exercised collectively. For instance, anytime a person with a college degree is invited to speak, they bring with them a cospeaker who does not have that education level. They might develop mentoring and skills-sharing programs within the group. To quote one of my activist mentors, Judy Vaughn, "You don't think your way into a different way of acting; you act your way into a different way of thinking." Essentially, the current social structure conditions us to exercise what privileges we may have. If we want to undermine those privileges, we must change the structures within which we live so that we become different peoples in the process.

This essay will explore the structuring logics of the politics of privilege as they inform both activist and academic work. In particular, the logics of privilege rest on an individualized self that relies on the raw material of other beings to constitute itself. Although the confessing of privilege is understood to be an antiracist practice, it is ultimately a project premised on white supremacy. Thus, organizing and intellectual projects that are questioning these politics of privilege are shifting the question from what privileges does a particular subject have to what is the nature of the subject that claims to have privilege in the first place.

The Confessing Subject

As I have argued elsewhere, the academic industrial complex places the Native in the position of ethnographic entrapment (A. Smith 2009). Denise da Silva's *Toward a Global Idea of Race* (2007) informs my analysis of ethnographic entrapment, in which she holds that the Western subject is itself fundamentally constituted through race. She argues through her exhaustive account of enlightenment theory that the post-Enlightenment version of Subject as a sole self-determined actor exists by situating itself over and against "affectable" others who are subject to natural conditions as well as to the self-determined power of the Western subject. In essence, the Western subject knows itself because of (1) its apparent ability to exercise power over others; and (2) the inability of others to exercise power over it. The "others" meanwhile, are *affected* by the power of the Western subject (and hence are "affectable") but they cannot *effect* power themselves. The anxiety with which the Western subject struggles is that the Western subject is in fact not self-determining. After all, nobody is actually able to exercise power without being affected by others. Consequently, the manner in which the Western subject addresses this anxiety is to separate itself from conditions of "affectability" by separating from affectable others. This separation is fundamentally a racial one—both spatially and temporally. That is, the Western subject is spatially located in the West in relationship to the "affectable" Third World others. It is also temporally located in modernity in relationship to "primitive" others who are never able to enter modernity. The Western subject is a universal subject that determines itself without being determined by others; the racialized subject is particular, but aspires to be universal and self-determining (da Silva 2007).

Silva's analysis thus critiques the presumption that the problem facing Native peoples is that they have been "dehumanized." Antiracist intellectual and political projects are often premised on the notion that if people knew us better, we too would be granted humanity. But, according to Silva, the fundamental issue that does not get addressed is that "the human" is already a racial project. It is a project that aspires to universality, a project that can only exist over and against the particularity of "the other."

Consequently, two problems result. First, those who are put in the position of "affectable others," presume that liberation will ensue if they can become self-determining subjects; in other words, if they can become fully "human." However, the humanity to which we aspire still depends on the continued oppression of other affectable others. Thus, a liberation struggle that does not question the terms by which humanity is constituted becomes a liberation struggle that depends on the oppression of others.

Second, the assumption that "affectable others" have about liberation is that they will be granted humanity if they can prove their worthiness. If people understood us better, they would see we are "human" just like they are, and would grant us the status of humanity. As a result, antiracist activist and scholarly projects often become trapped in ethnographic multiculturalism, what Silva describes as a "neoliberal multicultural" representation that "includes never-before-heard languages that speak of never-before-heard things that actualize a never-before-known consciousness" (da Silva 2007, 169). This project rests on an inherent contradiction because this strategy, designed to demonstrate our worthiness of being universal subjects, actually rests on the logic that Native peoples are equivalent to nature itself, things to be discovered or to have an essential truth or essence. In other words, the very quest of full subjecthood that is implicit in the ethnographic project to tell our "truth" is already premised on a logic that requires us to be objects of discovery, unable to escape the status of affectable other. Consequently, as I will discuss later, Native Studies is in a position of ethnographic entrapment because Native peoples become almost unintelligible within the academy outside of this discursive regime.

Rey Chow (2002) notes that within this position of ethnographic entrapment, the only rhetorical position offered to the Native is that of the "protesting ethnic." The posture to be assumed under the politics of recognition is the posture of complaint. If we complain eloquently, the system will give us something. Building on Chow's work, this essay will explore how another posture that is created within this economy is the self-reflexive settler/white subject. This self-reflexive subject is frequently on display at various antiracist venues in which the privileged subject explains how much she or he learned about her complicity in settler colonialism or white supremacy because of her exposure to Native peoples. A typical instance of this will involve non-Native peoples who make presentations based on what they "learned" while doing solidarity work with Native peoples in their field research/solidarity work. Complete with videos and slide shows, the presenters will express the privilege with which they struggled. We will learn how they tried to address the power imbalances between them and the peoples with which they studied or worked. We will learn how they struggled to gain their trust. Invariably, the narrative begins with the presenters initially facing the distrust of the Natives because of their settler/white privilege. But through perseverance and good intentions, the researchers overcome this distrust and earn the friendship of their ethnographic objects. In these stories, of course, to evoke Gayatri Spivak, the subaltern does not speak (1994). We do not hear what their theoretical analysis of their relationship is. We do not hear about how they were organizing on their own before they were saved/studied by these presenters.

Native peoples are not positioned as those who can engage in self-reflection; they can only judge the worth of the confession. Consequently, the presenters of these narratives often present very nervously. Did they speak to all their privileges? Did they properly confess? Or will someone in the audience notice a mistake and question whether they have in fact become a fully developed antiracist subject? In that case, the subject would have to then engage in further acts of self-reflection that require new confessions in the future.

The Settler/White Subject and Self-Reflexivity

Thus borrowing from the work of Scott Morgensen (2011) and Hiram Perez (2005), the confession of privilege, while claiming to be antiracist and anticolonial, is actually a strategy that helps constitute the settler/white subject. In Morgensen's (2011) analysis, the settler subject constitutes itself through incorporation (or what Silva would term *engulfment*). Through this logic of settlement, settlers become the rightful inheritors of all that was indigenous: land, resources, indigenous spirituality, or culture. Thus, indigeneity is not necessarily framed as antagonistic to the settler subject; rather the Native is supposed to disappear into the project of settlement. The settler becomes the "new and improved" version of the Native, thus legitimizing and naturalizing the settler's claims to this land. Within the context of settler colonialism, Native peoples are the affectable others who become incorporated into settler subjectivity in order to establish settler claims to self-determination. Native peoples, by contrast, do not require self-determination because they are nothing more than the raw materials—the affectable others—of the settler project.

Hiram Perez similarly analyzes how the white subject positions itself intellectually as a cosmopolitan subject capable of abstract theorizing through the use of the "raw material" provided by fixed, brown bodies. The white subject is capable of being "ante-" or "postidentity," but understands their postidentity only in relationship to brown subjects that are hopelessly fixed within identity. Brown peoples provide the "raw material" that enables the intellectual production of the white subject (Perez 2005).

Thus, self-reflexivity enables the constitution of the white/settler subject. Antiracist/colonial struggles have created a colonial dis-ease that the settler/white subject may not in fact be self-determining. As a result, the white/settler subject reasserts her or his power through self-reflection. In doing so, his or her subjectivity is reaffirmed against the foil of the "oppressed" people who still remain the "affectable" others who provide the occasion for this self-reflection.

Oftentimes, the white/settler subject of self-reflexivity positions her- or himself in relationship to those settler subjects that appear to fail in their responsibilities toward self-reflection. For instance, a plethora of work has been published that critiques "New Age" appropriation of Native spirituality. These critiques have addressed the manner in which aspects of Native "culture" are severed from their context and commodified as objects that can assist in the healing or personal development of non-Natives. While these analyses are very valuable, it can also be easy for those in the academy to ridicule "New Agers" while not considering the way in which academic engagement with Native peoples often replicates these same New Age logics.

Micaela Di Leonardo (1998) makes the connections between these operations by exploring how the treatment of Native peoples within the academy does not sharply differ in its logics from the New Age movement. She critiques the tendency for social scientists to study "exotics" as a means for those in the dominant culture to learn more about themselves. Either Native communities have "ancient wisdom" to bestow upon others or they represent the "savage" which proves the superiority of the dominant society. "Primitives are ourselves, or our worse or best selves, or our former selves, undressed: human nature in the buff" (Di Leonardo 1998, 147). She critiques many feminist ethnographies for portraying cultures disconnected from the global political economy. She notes, for instance, that Ruth Behar's *Translated Woman* (1993) tells the story of an indigenous woman in Mexico with almost no reference to Mexican history or political economy (310). Instead, the ethnography becomes the occasion for Behar to authorize her own identity as an "oppressed" woman of color. Esperanza's story becomes the occasion to tell Behar's story. "Esperanza challenged me continually to articulate the connections between who she is as a visibly invisible Indian street peddler and who I am as an academic woman with a certain measure of power and privilege ... Esperanza and I were in many ways exaggerated, distorted mirrors of each other" (Behar 1993, 302).

Ironically, however, even Di Leonardo's critique replicates some of these same logics in that her analysis appears to dismiss the possibility that indigenous peoples' may have any intellectual contributions to make. It is noteworthy that in her critique of the exoticizing practices of anthropologists in their relations with Native peoples, she fails to intellectually engage Native academics (with the lone exception of Vine Deloria, Jr.), who have been making similar critiques about anthropology for years. For example, in her discussion of Frank Boaz and his students, she does not mention Dakota anthropologist Ella Deloria. The one Native scholar she does cite, Vine Deloria, she dismisses completely because he does not cite specific anthropologists in his analysis, even though such a task was completely beyond the scope of his project. She dismisses the efforts of any scholars to uncover contributions Native peoples might make to discussions of political economy as simply arguing that Native peoples "are better off" (Di Leonardo 1998, 243). From her perspective, the only thing of importance to say about Native peoples is that "They simply have less power and fewer resources than their interlocutors ... [they] are engaged on the losing ends of the varying institutions of international political economy" (35). Hence, in the end, while critiquing the primitivist stereotypes that undergird even many feminist anthropological works, she essentially holds on to the same stereotypes, implicitly claiming that Native peoples are somehow outside of history and are therefore incapable of contributing to understandings of global historical processes. Audra Simpson's germinal essay "On Ethnographic Refusal" (2007) thus questions whether or not to call for greater "accuracy" in anthropology's depiction of Native peoples. Instead, she suggests the project may be to refuse anthropological intelligibility in the first place.

Of course, this essay itself does not escape the logics of self-reflexivity either. Rhetorically, it simply sets me up as yet another judge of the inadequacies of the academic/activist confessions of others. Thus, what is important in this discussion is not so much how particular individual scholars engage Native Studies. If Native peoples are represented problematically even by peoples who espouse antiracist or antisettler politics, it is not an indication that the work of those peoples is particularly flawed or that their scholarship has less value. Similarly, those privileged "confessing" subjects in antiracism workshops do so with a commitment to fighting settler colonialism or white supremacy and their solidarity work is critically needed. Furthermore, as women of color scholars and activists have noted, there is no sharp divide between those who are "oppressed" and those who are "oppressors." Individuals may find themselves variously in the position of being the confessor or the judge of the confession depending on the context since these positions are not ontologically fixed to particular bodies but are contingent, discursive positions. Rather, the point of this analysis is to illustrate the larger dynamics by which Native Studies is even intelligible in the academy in particular and in society at large in the first place. As mentioned previously, Native Studies is in a position of ethnographic entrapment because Native peoples become almost unintelligible within the academy outside of this discursive regime. In our desire to prove our worthiness to be deemed human, we constantly put ourselves in the position of ethnographic objects who have no value other than to enable self-determining settler subjects to constitute themselves. In addition, because we do not more fundamentally question the colonialist and white supremacist constructions of humanity to which we aspire, we find that our engagements in antisettler/racist struggle ultimately reinstantiate the logics we seek to deconstruct. In other words, we fail to imagine a liberatory politic that does not ultimately rest on the oppression of others.

From "Self"-Determination to Radical Relationality

Denise Da Silva's work suggests that the settler/white supremacist logics of confession and self-reflexivity rest on an epistemological understanding of the self as being constituted over and against other selves. Furthermore, the trap facing racial/colonial "affectable" others is that they also seek liberation by positioning themselves against others that they perceive to be affectable. For example, many racial justice groups have either supported or been complicit with sexism or homophobia within their communities. The project of self-reflexivity is another instantiation of the self-determining subject seeking to transcend the affectability created by conditions of white supremacy and colonialism. Affectable others aspire for self-determination by becoming the judges of those deemed capable of self-reflexivity. While this position can be attractive, ultimately, as Antonio Viego (1998) notes, "it helps render the ethnic-racialized subject as a thoroughly calculable and exhaustible—that is, dead-subject"(Kindle locations 1424–25). In other words, this mode sets up the racial subject as one that is to be fully known and understood by the self-reflexive subject, who remains indeterminate and hence self-determining. Essentially, the presupposition is that, "If only others knew us better, we [whoever we is] would be free."

In fact, however, the quest for the knowable racialized subject is part of racial discourse itself. As Viego argues, our goal may not be to "understand" the Native but to challenge the grid of intelligibility under which the Native is known. "Given what I have been arguing thus far regarding how racism depends on a certain representational capture of the ethnic-racialized subject—rendered as transparent to the signifier, potentially whole and unified—in order to manage this subject more masterfully in discourse, then this insistence on the incalculable and indeterminate should be very welcome in our antiracist analyses" (Viego 1998, Kindle locations 698–700). Similarly, as Alexander Weheliye notes, the goal is not to secure the well-being of the oppressed class to which we belong, but to create new forms of humanity by practicing "a politics of being that ... introduces invention into existence.... This is a battle to supplant the current instantiation of the human as synonymous with the objective existence of white, western Man and his various damned counterparts ... offering in its stead new styles of human subjectivity and community" (Weheliye 2009, 174).

Thus, da Silva's analysis implies that "liberation" would require different selves that understand themselves in radical relationality with all other peoples and things. The goal then becomes not the mastery of antiracist/anticolonialist lingo but a different self-understanding that sees one's being as fundamentally constituted through other beings. An example of the political enactment of this critique of the Western subject could be glimpsed at the 2008 World Social Forum that I attended. The indigenous peoples made a collective statement calling into question the issue of the nation-state. In addition to challenging capitalism, they called on participants to imagine new forms of governance not based on a nation-state model. They contended that the nation-state has not worked in the last 500 years, so they suspected that it was not going to start working now. Instead, they called for new forms of collectivities that were based on principles of interrelatedness, mutuality, and global responsibility. These new collectivities (nations, if you will, for lack of a better world) would not be based on insular or exclusivist claims to a land base; indeed they would reject the contention that land is a commodity that any one group of people should be able to buy, control, or own. Rather, these collectivities would be based on responsibility for and relationship with land. The indigenous people's statement echoed that of Patricia Monture-Angus (1999) who argued:

> Although Aboriginal Peoples maintain a close relationship with the land ... it is not about control of the land.... Earth is mother and she nurtures us all ... it is the human race that is dependent on the earth and not vice versa.
>
> Sovereignty, when defined as my right to be responsible ... requires a relationship with territory (and not a relationship based on control of that territory).... What must be understood then is that the Aboriginal request to have our sovereignty respected is really a request to be responsible. I do not know of anywhere else in history where a group of people have had to fight so hard just to be responsible. (36)

But they suggested that these collectivities could not be formed without a radical change in what we perceived ourselves to be. That is, if we understand ourselves to be transparent, self-determining subjects, defining ourselves in opposition to who we are not, then the nations that will emerge from this sense of self will be exclusivist and insular. However, if we understand ourselves as being fundamentally constituted through our relations with other beings and the land, then the nations that emerge will also be inclusive and interconnected with each other. Interestingly, the spokespeople at the WSF specifically stated that their goal was not to tell nonindigenous peoples to "go home." They articulated an expansive notion of indigeneity by stating that all are welcome to their lands if they live in good ways with the land. Of course, these kinds of statements can be troubling in the New Age context in North America where they might be heard as "everyone can be indigenous by doing a pipe ceremony, sweat lodge, etc." Essentially, this expansive understanding of indigeneity could be understood to erase the specificity of indigenous peoples and their struggles today.

But in this context, I would argue that while this call might be more open and affirming than the typical calls to confess settler privilege, it is also a more difficult demand. This demand is something more akin to Weheliye's call: a complete transformation of subjectivity and humanity. Indigenity then in this call does not become an easily calculable category that the privileged subject can become through a simple process of appropriation and commodification. Rather, to borrow from the work of Justine Smith (2005), indigenity becomes the performance of transformation itself. Their call then was less about critiquing settler privilege and more about gesturing toward a political project that requires global and collective participation to move beyond the conditions of settler colonialism.

Beyond Recognition

If we question the self as a self-determining subject that uses others as the occasion to constitute itself through self-reflection, then we might develop alternatives to confession and self-reflexivity as a means to dismantle white supremacy and settler colonialism. Queer and indigenous futurities provide some possible directions because they question the assumption that the goal of oppressed groups is to become recognized or to be bestowed humanity within the current social order. Rather, this work suggests that our project may be to disrupt the order itself. For instance, queer theorist Lee Edelman (2004) contends futurity acts as a guarantor of the current oppressive social order that articulates the Child as the anchor for reproductive futurity.

For politics, however radical the means by which specific constituencies attempt to produce a more desirable social order, remains, at its core, conservative insofar is it works to affirm a structure, to *authenticate* social order, which intends to transmit to the future in the form of its inner Child. That Child remains the perpetual horizon of every acknowledged politics, the fantasmic beneficiary of every political intervention. (2–3)

He contends that "queerness takes the side of those *not* fighting for the children ... the side outside the consensus by which all politics confirms the absolute value of reproductive futurism" (3). Of course there has been much critique, particularly queer of color critique of Edelman's call for "no future" as vacating any possibilities for social or political transformation as well as being premised on a disavowed whiteness whose futurity is not under threat (Munoz 2007). However, it may be possible to view his call as being less about a call against futurity and more about a call to end the social order. That is, the problem we face in struggling for social transformation is that we do so within the terms set by the current system. Consequently, our calls for a better future are necessarily limited to the terms predetermined by the present. Hence a call for "no future" may be described more accurately as a call to the end of our very grid of intelligibility that does not allow us to conceptualize "another world" because to do so would simply be another rearticulation of the current world. Thus it follows that under this analysis, one would regard all political programs with suspicion: "Political programs are programmed to reify difference and thus to secure in the form of the future, the order of the same "(Edelman 2004, 151).

Kara Keeling's (2009) work, while sharing much of this analysis, provides another approach toward the symbolic order. A call for a "no future" or a complete end to political programs tends to situate the "outside" of the social order as its opposite. That is, when we try to imagine ourselves outside the current system, we often imagine it to be the complete opposite of the current system. For instance, many Native activist and intellectual projects often call for "decolonization." While decolonization is an important project for denaturalizing and thus dismantling the structures and logics of settler colonialism, it is sometimes interpreted to mean that Native peoples must reject everything that is not "indigenous" in order to be properly authentic.

As Kiri Sailiata (2010) notes, this understanding of decolonization imagines itself as an extractive process whereby we must remove anything from lives that is tainted by colonialism. Similarly, Scott Lyons's *X-Marks* (2010) contends that a politics of decolonization has the danger of lapsing into a politics of purity in which any engagement with the current legal and economic system is dismissed as co-opted. "If you happen to live away from your homeland, speak English, practice Christianity, or know more songs by the Dave Matthews Band than by the ancestors, you effectively 'cease to exist' as one of the People" (139). While Lyons does not dismiss the importance of decolonization, he argues that such politics do not begin from an imagined precolonial past but under the conditions in which we currently live. Rather than articulate contemporary Native identity as an "impure" version of traditional identity, Lyons argues that such a framework locks Native identity in the past and cedes the "modern" to whiteness. Decolonization entails not a going backward to a precolonial past, but a commitment to building a future for indigenous peoples based on principles of justice and liberation.

Keeling (2009) suggests that the "outside" should not be seen as the opposite of the current system, but instead imagined as being in noncorrespondence to the current order. Thus, since it is not the opposite of our current grid of intelligibility, we may be able to see glimpses of the outside—ghosts that gesture toward a beyond—within the current systems. And, as a result, we do not have to reject everything within the current system in our quest for liberation. Some theoretical concepts within Native Studies can help elucidate her arguments.

The work of Vine Deloria Jr. has provided much of the theoretical grounding for Native Studies. He argued that decolonization required a fundamental epistemological shift that questioned the very logic systems of Western thought itself (1977, 17). In *God is Red*, he articulated what he viewed as some of the distinctions between Western and indigenous thought systems such as the distinction between spatial versus temporal orientations, circular versus linear time, and practice versus belief centered traditions (Deloria 1992).However, as Scott Lyons (2010) notes, these concepts started to become taken very literally such that Native scholars started insisting that Native people "think in circles." However, I think Deloria's analysis could be better understood not as a literal reading of indigenous epistemologies but as a gesture toward a beyond the colonial order. Because of colonization, one must articulate these frameworks within colonial terms. Yet, colonialism cannot contain them either. What Keeling (2009) suggests then is that these gestures toward the beyond are critically important, but we should not mistake the gestures for the "beyond" itself.

Based on this analysis then, our project becomes less of one based on self-improvement or even collective self-improvement, and more about the creation of new worlds and futurities for which we currently have no language. In addition, the "new" worlds may exist within this world. For instance, at the 2005 World Liberation Theology Forum held in Porto Alegre, Brazil, indigenous peoples from Bolivia stated that they know another world is possible because they see that world whenever they do their ceremonies. Native ceremonies can be a place where the present, past, and future become copresent, thereby allowing us to engage in what Native Hawaiian scholar Manu Meyer calls a radical remembering of the future, a beyond that where we currently live. Thus, as Alexander Weheliye (2009) notes, global oppression is not complete. In fact, perhaps one way global oppression perpetuates itself is through its appearance of universality, which can cloud us from seeing those spaces in which liberatory praxis does exist.

Alternatives to Confession for Dismantling Settler Colonialism/White Supremacy

There is no simple antioppression formula that we can follow; we are in a constant state of trial and error and radical experimentation. In that spirit then, I offer some possibilities that might speak to new ways of undoing privilege, not in the sense of offering the "correct" process for moving forward, but in the spirit of adding to our collective imagining of a "beyond." These projects of decolonization can be contrasted with that of the projects of antiracist or anticolonialist self-reflexivity in that they are not based on the goal of "knowing" more about our privilege, but on creating that which we cannot now know.

As I have discussed elsewhere, many of these models are based on "taking power by making power" models particularly prevalent in Latin America (A. Smith 2005). These models, which are deeply informed by indigenous peoples' movements, have informed the landless movement, the factory movements, and other peoples' struggles. Many of these models are also being used by a variety of social justice organizations throughout the United States and elsewhere. The principle undergirding these models is to challenge capital and state power by actually creating the world we want to live in now. These groups develop alternative governance systems based on principles of horizontality, mutuality, and interrelatedness rather than hierarchy, domination, and control. In beginning to create this new world, subjects are transformed. These "autonomous zones" can be differentiated from the projects of many groups in the United States that create separatist communities based on egalitarian ideals in that people in these "making power" movements do not just create autonomous zones, but they *proliferate* them.

These movements developed in reaction to the revolutionary vanguard model of organizing in Latin America that became criticized as "machismo-leninismo" models. These models were so hierarchical that in the effort to combat systems of oppression, they inadvertently re-created the same systems they were trying to replace. In addition, this model of organizing was inherently exclusivist because not everyone can take up guns and go the mountains to become revolutionaries. Women, who have to care for families, could particularly be excluded from such revolutionary movements. So, movements began to develop organizing models that are based on integrating the organizing into one's everyday life so that all people can participate. For instance, a group might organize through communal cooking, but during the cooking process, which everyone needs to do anyway in order to eat, they might educate themselves on the nature of agribusiness.

At the 2005 World Social Forum in Brazil, activists from Chiapas reported that this movement began to realize that one cannot combat militarism with more militarism because the state always has more guns. However, if movements began to build their own autonomous zones and proliferated them until they reached a mass scale, eventually there would be nothing the state's military could do. If mass-based peoples' movements begin to live life using alternative governance structures and stop relying on the state, then what can the state do? Of course, during the process, there may be skirmishes with the state, but conflict is not the primary work of these movements. And as we see these movements literally take over entire countries in Latin America, it is clear that it is possible to do revolutionary work on a mass scale in a manner based on radical participatory rather than representational democracy or through a revolutionary vanguard model.

Many leftists will argue that nation-states are necessary to check the power of multinational corporations or will argue that nation-states are no longer important units of analysis. These groups, by contrast, recognize the importance of creating alternative forms of governance outside of a nation-state model based on principles of horizontalism. In addition, these groups are taking on multinational corporations directly. An example would be the factory movement in Argentina where workers have appropriated factories and seized the means of production themselves. They have also developed cooperative relationships with other appropriated factories. In addition, in many factories all of the work is collectivized. For instance, a participant from a group I work with who recently had a child and was breastfeeding went to visit a factory. She tried to sign up for one of the collectively organized tasks of the factory, and was told that breastfeeding was her task. The factory recognized breastfeeding as work on par with all the other work going on in the factory.

This kind of politics then challenges the notions of "safe space" often prevalent in many activist circles in the United States. The concept of safe space flows naturally from the logics of privilege. That is, once we have confessed our gender/race/settler/class privileges, we can then create a safe space where others will not be negatively impacted by these privileges. Of course because we have not dismantled heteropatriarchy, white supremacy, settler colonialism or capitalism, these confessed privileges never actually disappear in "safe spaces." Consequently, when a person is found guilty of his and her privilege in these spaces, the person is accused of making the space "unsafe." This rhetorical strategy presumes that only certain privileged subjects can make the space "unsafe" as if everyone isn't implicated in heteropatriarchy, white supremacy, settler colonialism, and capitalism. Our focus is shifted from the larger systems that make the entire world unsafe, to interpersonal conduct. In addition, the accusation of "unsafe" is also levied against people of color who express anger about racism, only to find themselves accused of making the space "unsafe" because of their raised voices. The problem with safe space is the presumption that a safe space is even possible.

By contrast, instead of thinking of safe spaces as a refuge from colonialism, patriarchy, and white supremacy, Ruthie Gilmore suggests that safe space is not an escape from the real, but a place to practice the real we want to bring into being. "Making power" models follow this suggestion in that they do not purport to be free of oppression, only that they are trying to create the world they would like to live in now. To give one smaller example, when Incite! Women of Color Against Violence, organized, we questioned the assumption that "women of color" space is a safe space. In fact, participants began to articulate that women of color space may in fact be a very dangerous space. We realized that we could not assume alliances with each other, but we would actually have to create these alliances.

One strategy that was helpful was rather than presume that we were acting "nonoppressively," we built a structure that would presume that we were complicit in the structures of white supremacy/settler colonialism/heteropatriarchy etc. We then structured this presumption into our organizing by creating spaces where we would educate ourselves on issues in which our politics and praxis were particularly problematic. The issues we have covered include: disability, anti-Black racism, settler colonialism, Zionism, and anti-Arab racism, transphobia, and many others. However, in this space, while we did not ignore our individual complicity in oppression, we developed action plans for how we would *collectively* try to transform our politics and praxis.

Thus, this space did not create the dynamic of the confessor and the hearer of the confession. Instead, we presumed we are all implicated in these structures of oppression and that we would need to work together to undo them. Consequently, in my experience, this kind of space facilitated our ability to integrate personal and social transformation because no one had to anxiously worry about whether they were going to be targeted as a bad person with undue privilege who would need to publicly confess. The space became one that was based on principles of loving rather than punitive accountability.

Conclusion

The politics of privilege have made the important contribution of signaling how the structures of oppression constitute who we are as persons. However, as the rituals of confessing privilege have evolved in academic and activist circles, they have shifted our focus from building social movements for global transformation to individual self-improvement. Furthermore, they rest on a white supremacist/colonialist notion of a subject that can constitute itself over and against others through self-reflexivity. While trying to keep the key insight made in activist/academic circles that personal and social transformation are interconnected, alternative projects have developed that focus less on privilege and more the structures that create privilege. These new models do not hold the "answer," because the genealogy of the politics of privilege also demonstrates that our activist/ intellectual projects of liberation must be constantly changing. Our imaginations are limited by white supremacy and settler colonialism, so all ideas we have will not be "perfect." The ideas we develop today also do not have to be based on the complete disavowal of what we did yesterday because what we did yesterday teaches what we might do tomorrow. Thus, as we think not only beyond privilege, but beyond the sense of self that claims privilege, we open ourselves to new possibilities that we cannot imagine now for the future.

References

Behar, Ruth. 1993. *Translated Woman*. Boston: Beacon Press.

Chow, Rey. 2002. *The Protestant Ethnic and the Spirit of Capitalism*. New York: Columbia University Press.

da Silva, Denise Ferreira. 2007. *Toward a Global Idea of Race*. Minneapolis: University of Minnesota Press.

Deloria, Vine Jr. 1977. "A Native American Perspective on Liberation." *Occasional Bulletin of Missionary Research* 1: 15–17.

———. 1992. *God is Red*. Golden: North American Press.

———. (1973) 2003. *God Is Red: A Native View of Religion*. Golden, CO: Fulcrum.

Di Leonardo, Micaela. 1998. *Exotics at Home: Anthropologies, Others, and American Modernity*. Chicago: University of Chicago Press.

Edelman, Lee. 2004. *No Future: Queer Theory and the Death Drive*. Durham, NC: Duke University Press.

Keeling, Kara. 2009. "Looking for M--: Queer Temporality, Black Political Possibility, and Poetry from the Future." *GLQ* 15 (4): 565–582.

Lyons, Scott. 2010. *X-Marks*. Minneapolis: University of Minnesota Press.

Mohanty, Chandra. 2003. *Feminism without Borders*. Durham, NC: Duke University Press.

Monture-Angus, Patricia. 1999. *Journeying Forward*. Halifax, Nova Scotia: Fernwood.

Morgensen, Scott. 2011. *Spaces between Us*. Minneapolis: University of Minnesota Press.

Munoz, Jose Esteban. 2007. "Cruising the Toilet: Leroi Jones/Amiri Baraka, Radical Black Traditions, and Queer Futurity." *GLQ* 13 (2–3): 353–68.

Perez, Hiram. 2005. "You Can Have My Brown Body and Eat It, Too." *Social Text* 23 (Fall–Winter): 171–91.

Sailiata. Kiri. 2010. Conference Paper: *Pacific Destiny: A Strategic Sea of Islands, NAISA Conference, Sacramento, CA.*

Simpson, Audra. 2007. "On Ethnographic Refusal: Indigeneity, 'Voice' and Colonial Citizenship." *Junctures* 9 (December): 67–80.

Smith, Andrea. 2005. *Conquest: Sexual Violence and American Indian Genocide.* Cambridge, MA: South End Press.

———. 2009. "Queer Theory and Native Studies: The Heteronormativity of Settler Colonialism." *GLQ* 61 (1–2): 41–68.

Smith, Justine. 2005. "Indigenous Performance and Aporetic Texts." *Union Seminary Quarterly Review* 59 (1–2): 114–24.

Spivak, Gayatri. 1994."Can the Subaltern Speak?" In *Colonial Discourse and Post-Colonial Theory*, edited by Patrick Williams and Laura Chrisman, 66–111. New York: Columbia University Press.

Viego, Antonio. 2007. *Dead Subjects: Toward a Politics of Loss in Latino Studies*. Durham, NC: Duke University Press.

Weheliye, Alexander G. 2009. "My Volk to Come: Peoplehood in Recent Diaspora Discourse and Afro-German Popular Music." In *Black Europe and the African Disapora*, edited by Darlene Clark Hine, Tricia Danielle Keaton, and Stephen Small, 169–79. Champaign: University of Illinois Press.

PART IV

Gendered Privileges and Gendered Vulnerabilities

Public and Private Spaces

CHAPTER 12

Gendered Vulnerabilities and Muslim American Civil Rights Advocacy

ERIK LOVE

In the autumn of 1996, two women strolled down the street in Portsmouth, Virginia. They walked from their mosque toward a nearby convenience store to buy some candy for their children. Just before they reached the store's entrance, some police officers stopped them. One of the officers told the women that the veils covering most of their faces were illegal masks that could not be worn in public (American-Arab Anti-Discrimination Committee [ADC] 1996, 17). The women tried to explain that they always wear niqab veils, in keeping with their Muslim faith. The officer replied, "I don't care what you say. It's a mask and you can't wear it in the Commonwealth of Virginia" (Ferris 1996, D.02). The women refused to remove their niqabs, and the police officers promptly placed them under arrest, handcuffed them, and took the women to the police station. The police eventually released the women without filing any criminal charges. Later, the women complained that when an officer frisked them to check for weapons, he also fondled their breasts and buttocks (ADC 1996, 17).

Shortly after this incident, two advocacy organizations, one an Arab American organization and the other a Muslim American organization, sent a joint letter to the chief of police in Portsmouth, Virginia. "This incident is outrageous and demonstrates a complete lack of sensitivity to Islam," the letter said (ADC 1996, 17). An assistant to the police chief responded by insisting that the arrests were "not based on religious or ethnic hostility but rather a single officer's interpretation of a State Code forbidding the concealment of one's face in public" (17). This officer's interpretation of the law apparently was in error, because the letter also admitted that there is an exemption in the antimask law for religious observance. (The law was originally intended to prevent Ku Klux Klan members from wearing their hoods.) The department had already begun to instruct its officers about the religious exemption. The allegations of sexual harassment were investigated by the police as well, and a spokesperson disputed those claims (Ferris 1996). American Arab Anti-Discrimination Committee (ADC) sent educational materials to the Portsmouth police department to help them in teaching their officers about Arab and Muslim culture (ADC 1996).

Versions of this story, where gendered performances cause Muslim women and men to become vulnerable to discrimination and unjustified harassment, have taken place again and again in the United States. These stories show, in sometimes horrifying detail, how so-called Islamophobia closely connects with gender and space.[1] While *Islamophobia* is generally defined as xenophobic fear, bigotry, hatred, and discrimination directed toward Islam and Muslims, Islamophobia as it occurs in the United States, directly affects a wide range of groups because of race. Moreover, the term *Islamophobia* centers the religion of Islam as the site of discrimination, while race is often the primary reason that Arab, Muslim, Sikh, and South Asian Americans are affected by discrimination.[2]

Islamophobia, like other forms of political and social power, interacts with different types of space in complex ways. For these Virginia women, gendered discrimination impacted them in typical, everyday space—on the sidewalk near a convenience store. Public spaces often become contested sites where gender and Islamophobia interact. Places such as streets and sidewalks, places of worship, shops, restaurants, and the like. However, Islamophobic discourses also invade private and semiprivate spaces including offices and private workplaces, the home, classrooms, and so on. Advocacy work that attempts to confront Islamophobia, then, must also take account of differing gendered vulnerabilities these spaces. The question that animates this research centers on the ways in which political and social advocacy around Islamophobia is shaped by space.

Why is it that the advocacy organizations took up the case of the two women in Virginia? The interpretation of the public arrest as an affront to civil rights required a sense that public spaces should remain open to individuals and communities who express a gendered Islam. The particular actions taken by the advocacy organizations—sending educational materials for police training sessions and issuing an open letter to the police—fit into established patterns for civil rights advocacy for gendered discrimination cases in public spaces. The privilege to confront Islamophobia in this way is also shaped by gendered processes of privilege. How (and whether) gendered issues become an active area of engagement for advocacy organizations is a central question for this research. What about advocacy centered on other gendered issues that impact private spaces, such as domestic violence, sexual harassment, and workplace discrimination?

The conceptualization of physical space by civil rights advocates can play an important role in deciding what types of issues to confront, and which issues remain unchallenged. Indeed, the political, social, and legal application of civil rights is highly dependent upon the organization and articulation of physical space (Delaney 1998). The general focus of mainstream civil rights advocacy is on rights that are most visible in public, such as equal protection, religious expression, and freedom from unreasonable searches. This for us reflects in many ways a masculine understanding of the social world and civil rights, where the private sphere of the home is seen as a refuge where the individual and the family should exist without intervention from institutions such as civil rights advocacy organizations and government agencies. A masculine interpretation can exclude gendered inequalities that are practiced in private spaces (Goldsack 1999). Gendered inequality and Islamophobia exist in spaces considered both public and private. This means that conceptualizing the work of civil rights advocacy as engaged only with public spaces draws from and contributes to the masculine interpretation of social space as divided between "work" and "home," or public and private (Massey 1994). In this way, the issue of religious expression (as in the case in Virginia) is seen as an appropriate site for civil rights advocacy work, but issues like domestic violence and sexual harassment are not. When civil rights advocacy fails to include advocacy around gendered issues, gendered vulnerabilities remain in place.

This chapter discusses the work of two Muslim American advocacy organizations and how they organize their work around gendered issues including domestic violence, gender discrimination, and sexual harassment among other issues. I find that the largest Muslim American advocacy organization, the Council on American Islamic Relations (CAIR), engaged in only superficial advocacy work on these issues. In the process, CAIR centers nearly all of its advocacy work in public space—its (limited) work on gendered issues is almost exclusively seen in the arena of the workplace, law enforcement, and in public policy. It is therefore a rather unsurprising to find that smaller Muslim American advocacy organizations like Karamah: Muslim Women Lawyers for Human Rights, emerged to "fill the gap" on gendered issues not addressed by CAIR. Karamah's advocacy work centers on gendered issues in private spaces, particularly the home, especially. This difference in spatial orientation is a reflection of the main finding in this research: a de facto division of labor between CAIR and Karamah on advocacy that attempts to address gendered vulnerabilities. In addition, this research has larger implications for the study of privilege. Privilege also plays an important role in how organizations deal with gendered issues. Perhaps, CAIR advocates believe they lack the privilege to address gendered issues such as domestic violence because of the stereotype that Muslims are uniquely oppressive towards women. If CAIR engages such issues in a sustained way, the organization's actions might unintentionally work to affirm that stereotype. If this is the case, then Karamah advocates might perceive that they have sufficient privilege to take on these sorts of issues. In this way, gender privilege might create a deprioritizing of advocacy centered on private spaces in favor of public spaces, in ways that help to reproduce gender inequality where masculine issues are assigned more weight. The chapter considers these explanations while describing empirical research derived from qualitative interviews with advocates working at these two organization's along with a content analysis of documents produced by each organization.

The chapter begins with a discussion of gender, privilege, and Islamophobia, and then moves into the details of the organizations' anti-Islamophobia advocacy work and their relationship with specific gendered issues including domestic violence and sexual harassment. The concluding section considers how this research fosters a better understanding of the relationship between gendered inequality and advocacy work.

Gender, Privilege, and Islamophobia

Feminist scholarship has repeatedly shown that in nearly all aspects of life, the social construction of gender causes women's experiences to differ systematically from those of men (Smith 1977; Davis 1981; hooks 1981; Stacey and Thorne 1985), and the experiences of women of color are affected by multiple systems of oppression including race as well as gender (Flax 1990; Jayawardena 1986; Minh-ha 1989; Mohanty, Russo, and Torres 1991; Collins 2000). It follows that Islamophobia is inextricably linked with sexism and patriarchy, and that it signals a unique set of challenges for Arab, Muslim, Sikh, and South Asian Americans of all genders. For example, because Muslim women are often visibly marked—especially if they wear hijab or other traditional forms of clothing—ethnographic and survey work has shown that they are more likely than men to experience hate crimes (Naber 2008). Similarly, gender makes Muslim men more likely to face racial profiling and discrimination, especially if they have the masculine features associated with the stereotypical "Islamic terrorist" image, including a beard, dark hair and skin, or a turban (Abu-Lughod 2002).

This gendered racialization process begins to explain why there have been so many attacks against Sikhs motivated by desires to harm someone "from the Middle East." Similarly Chaldeans, Druze, Kurds, Pakistanis, Turks, Zoroastrians, and people representing dozens of national, ethnic, and religious identities have to a large extent found themselves "lumped in" to a common category in the American context—largely due to the familiar patterns of racial formation (Omi and Winant [1986] 1994; Love 2009; Rana 2011).

At the center of this racialized Islamophobia is the pervasive, highly gendered stereotype that women from a racially collectivized "Middle Eastern" world live in a (singular) culture from which they need special salvation (Shakir 1997; Suleiman 1999; Abu-Loughod 2002; Read 2002). Mahmood (2005) describes how women's agency is a central issue in some recent feminist literature, which carries the implication that some women (Muslims) contend with cultures that deny them agency more thoroughly than would another culture (Western). Mahmood shows how Muslim women are too often seen as the unwitting objects of a patriarchal culture, a perspective which often uses Muslim women who participate in Islamist movements as an exemplar for women who should be properly educated with (Western) feminist ideals to disabuse them of their commitment to Islam. Similarly, Razack (2008) illustrates how "Muslim women have been singled out as needing protection from their violent and hyper patriarchal men" (4). Effectively, gender and Islamophobia combine in such a way that men in these groups are considered extra dangerous, and women are considered extra oppressed.

Privilege takes on multiple meanings in the case of gendered Islamophobia. Patricia Hill Collins observed that privilege is constantly bound up in various oppressive systems: "Each individual derives varying amounts of penalty and privilege from the multiple systems of oppression which frame everyone's lives" (2000, 287). First, there is the contextualized articulation of restriction and permission in everyday life. For Muslim American communities, that often comes into play with the pervasive stereotype of a supposedly singular "Islamic culture" that is somehow uniquely patriarchal and extremely oppressive of women. The power of this stereotype to impact the lives of individuals should not be underestimated, implicating all aspects of gender performance, from attire to public displays of affection. This study, which focuses on the efforts of advocacy work to confront these sorts of harmful discourses, is concerned with a second kind of privilege that can influence the development of gender and Islamophobia—the privilege to advocate for change.

Very often, the privilege to engage in advocacy is perceived as male-dominated. However, in other civil rights struggles, for example, during the 1950s and 1960s women played significant roles in the African American Civil Rights Movement. Their efforts have largely gone unnoticed until recent scholarship on the subject (Irons 1998; Payne 1995; McAdam 1992; Barnett 1993; Robnett 1996). However, male privilege contributed to a "glass ceiling" that was observed in many civil rights organizations that prevented women from attaining senior leadership positions in advocacy organizations. Robnett found that although women frequently presented new ideas and initiated activism, they then would often "recede into the background" (1996, 1677). Whether a similar "glass ceiling" is in place at Muslim American organizations working today is an empirical question addressed later in this chapter. Even if the metaphorical glass ceiling is not in place, however, the perception that men have greater ability to participate in advocacy work. The perception that Muslim men are uniquely oppressive toward women might also affect the advocacy strategies taken by male-dominated advocacy organizations. This could manifest in an attempt to recruit women into leadership positions; for example, the attempt to showcase women as community leaders. It might also lead organizations to take up (or avoid) advocacy around certain gendered issues in an attempt to highlight (or downplay) their significance.

In this chapter, I follow in the footsteps of Jenny Irons (1998), who engages with issues of gender roles and privilege in her groundbreaking work on gender in the African American civil rights movement in Mississippi. Irons concludes her study by suggesting that in-depth interviews and other qualitative measures will provide additional "explanatory power" (708). "[P]rivileging the voices of movement actors themselves," she writes, "develop[s] a more complete picture of the ways social matrices of domination are infused into social movements" (708). Indeed, only recently has gender been given significant attention in scholarly literature around advocacy organizations. Gender issues were neglected by social scientists for decades (Taylor and Whittier 1998). In part, the neglect of gender stemmed from what McAdam says was a general failure to consider differences between activists working in the same organized protest groups (McAdam 1992; Wiltfang and McAdam 1991). Verta Taylor (1999) was among the first to note that "even in movements that purport to be gender-inclusive, the mobilization, leadership patterns, strategies, ideologies, and even the outcomes of social movements are gendered" (9). My research also addresses the under representation of Muslim Americans in the civil rights advocacy literature.

These theoretical questions lend themselves to empirical investigations of how gender and privilege actually impact advocacy work at Muslim American advocacy organizations. Recent empirical research suggests that

Muslim American women are not uniquely excluded from the privilege to participate in advocacy work.

Several recent studies have shown that images of the subjugation of women in these communities are little more than overblown stereotypes (Read 2002; Kurien 2003; Jamal 2005; Wadud 2006). While patriarchy affects women of all backgrounds, Jen'nan Ghazal Read's extensive study of Arab American communities shows that the idea that women from these communities are especially oppressed is "severely overstated" and such images of Muslim Arab women in particular are "flawed" (Read 2002, 34). The stereotypical presumption is that women in these communities are less likely to work outside the home, less likely to be politically active, and more likely to suffer from domestic violence. Read illustrates this by saying, "Too many, the veil symbolizes a patriarchal religious culture that universally oppresses Arab women" (2002, 19). Read's survey finds that Arab American women in fact have a wide range of beliefs about gender roles, and "progressive" gender ideologies are quite common (2002, 34). She also finds that "differences in religiosity and ethnicity are more significant" in predicting gender role beliefs than whether one identifies as Muslim or not (2003, 218). More deeply religious Arab American women, whether Muslim or Christian, were more likely to have traditionalist beliefs around gender, Read concludes.

Similarly, Amaney Jamal's study (2005) of Arab Muslim women living near Detroit found that gender attitudes as related to religion did not necessarily lead to a lack of political activism. In fact, she found that involvement in mosques can increase political participation for Arab Muslim American women. Through interviews with dozens of women, Jamal found that Arab Muslim American women were more likely than men to be involved in community organizations. Those women more involved in mosques and community centers, or "ethnic institutions," were more likely to become involved in advocacy work. Jamal explains that, "ethnic institutions serve as vehicles of cultural and identity preservation while simultaneously increasing levels of female political capital in ways that bode well for mainstream political participation" (2005, 74). The details of these gendered Islamophobic stereotypes, and how widespread and persistent they are, remain important open questions requiring more study. The role that gender plays in the reproduction of Islamophobia urgently needs to be further unpacked.

Confronting Islamophobia

In this section, I focus my analysis on the Muslim American advocacy organizations, the Council on American Islamic Relations (CAIR). As it works to confront Islamophobia. What can we learn about certain forms of privilege and advocacy by studying the dynamics of work at this advocacy organizations that deal with Islamophobia?

The Council on American Islamic Relations (CAIR) is an organization that considers itself within the legacy of civil rights movement organizations. Founded in Washington, DC in 1994, CAIR has grown to become one of the leading Muslim American advocacy organizations, with thirty-two chapters across twenty states (CAIR 2011). CAIR's website describes its mission simply: "to enhance understanding of Islam, encourage dialogue, protect civil liberties, empower American Muslims, and build coalitions that promote justice and mutual understanding" (2011). CAIR credibly claims to be the Muslim American advocacy organization with the largest grassroots following, processing more than 9,500 civil rights discrimination cases and working with more than 300 active volunteers and sixty paid staff across the country (2011). The analysis of CAIR featured in this chapter is grounded in a multimethod, qualitative study carried out between 2007 and 2009. This research includes interviews, a content analysis of CAIR's website and other documents, and ethnographic observations from time I spent with executive CAIR staff in the national office.[3] It is important to note that even though CAIR represents a wide spectrum of demographic groups that exist under the racialized Islamophobia umbrella, it is by no means representative of the entire field of Muslim American advocacy.[4] The study discussed here refers specifically to the national headquarters of CAIR, and each individual chapter might have a very different relationship with gender, advocacy, and privilege. Furthermore, it is important to caution that the findings here are preliminary, and additional research will refine the conclusions presented below.

Confronting or Ignoring Gendered Vulnerabilities?

Like any advocacy organization, CAIR must carefully balance its desire for creating social and political change with the need to retain legitimacy in the eyes of its constituents. It is possible to conceive of this advocacy work as trading privilege for change. Privilege, in this view, takes on some aspects of cultural currency, where more privilege is gained by successfully bringing about social change, but unsuccessfully moving to make change can result in "wasting" privilege. Taking a chance, spending privilege, and ending up with nothing might end an advocacy organization's legitimacy. Riskier actions can cause a large loss of prestige that can reduce the privilege available for future actions. In keeping with this interpretation, most actions that CAIR takes, in general terms, always have the dual goals of creating change and improving legitimacy as part of the motivation.

CAIR's civil rights work involves using the justice system to advocate for individuals and groups disparately impacted by policy and practice (CAIR 2006). This kind of legal advocacy is an efficient use of CAIR's resources (including privilege), because legal cases can result in tangible benefits, and use of the courts to resolve disputes is considered legitimate by nearly everyone involved. Most of CAIR's paid staff are lawyers by profession, and they work with or refer discrimination cases brought to their attention by the Muslim American communities they serve. Legal advocacy is not the only avenue CAIR takes, however. CAIR has also engaged in legislative lobbying, direct consultations with executive branch agencies tasked with enforcing civil rights laws, and it has worked with public and private service providers to advocate for social change through educational and cultural programs. CAIR also publishes research and opinion statements. CAIR's advocacy work, in short, is extensive and represents a large amount of privilege that the organization has gained on the basis of building legitimacy among its constituents. CAIR's large grassroots footprint gives it a large base of support from which to work. Despite all of its available privilege and other resources it could bring to bear, according to the analysis of CAIR documents, very little advocacy work is carried out on gendered issues by CAIR's national office.

Searching through the sample of CAIR documents produced between 1996 and 2008 by keyword, very few instances were found that describe specific CAIR advocacy actions on gendered issues. Many of the documents described the actions of CAIR standing in support of work done by other organizations and institutions. There were some instances when CAIR took direct action on gendered issues uncovered by my study. For example, CAIR took action to stop the continued publication of a college textbook, that falsely (and offensively) claimed that "In Islam, the most male-oriented of the modern religions, a woman is nothing but a vehicle for producing sons" (CAIR n.d.). Another example came in 2007 when CAIR issued a statement from its Executive Director supporting a bill in the House of Representatives that would call "for an end to female genital mutilation, domestic violence, so-called 'honor killings,' and other gender-based human rights violations against women" (CAIR 2007). Other CAIR press releases describe panels attended by CAIR representatives where gender and Islam are discussed, and a few CAIR publications meant to provide cultural competency training providing some introductory cultural information on gender in Islam.

Most mentions of advocacy on issues relating to gender seen in newsletters, pamphlets, conference programs, and other publications produced by CAIR since 2001 have an ad hoc quality to them, with gender mostly dealt with either in larger projects dealing with public spaces, or in one-off incidents that had no campaign built around them. These projects did not have a sustained focus on gender specifically. For example, the story from Portsmouth, Virginia described at the beginning of this chapter shows ADC and CAIR taking action on that single case, but there is no dedicated coalition between these two organizations to create a sustained campaign against gender discrimination and sexual harassment by law enforcement. The activism around the Portsmouth incident and others like happen sporadically and reactively rather than proactively. CAIR's activism in this area is thus ad hoc, not part of a larger campaign around gendered issues.

Interview data gathered in this study show that one of CAIR's most active projects is cultural awareness training. For this sustained campaign, educators, employers, public servants, and people involved in discrimination cases learn about Islamic culture at a seminar (or series of seminars) moderated by CAIR advocates. As part of that effort, CAIR published *An Employer's Guide to Islamic Religious Practices*, which was distributed at cultural awareness trainings (CAIR [1997] 2005a). This guide includes information on gender and Islam, stating that "Islam prescribes that both men and women behave and dress modestly. Muslims believe men and women should be valued and judged by their intelligence, skills and contributions to the community, not by their physical attributes" (13). The guide suggests amending company policies against hats to allow Muslims to wear kufis and hijabs. Once again, the focus on public spaces is apparent here, with the *Employer's Guide* avoiding mention of gendered issues that get articulated in private spaces.

Another area of concerted advocacy around gender at CAIR is the issue of gender roles within Islamic worship. A series of documents describe CAIR's commissioned studies on American Islamic culture. For example, in 2001 CAIR published *The Mosque in America: A National Portrait*, with extensive survey data on the ways women engaged in worship, and women's roles on mosque governing boards was given specific attention (Bagby, Perl, and Froehle 2001). Later, in 2005, CAIR distributed a pamphlet, *Women Friendly Mosques and Community Centers* (CAIR 2005b), aimed at religious leaders to help them provide a more welcoming atmosphere for women in places of worship. This provides an example of the documents describing CAIR's work to promote and highlight gender diversity within the public space of American Islamic institutions, actively countering the idea that women are singularly oppressed within Islam.

Not all of CAIR's work has exclusively centered on public spaces. CAIR has occasionally conducted advocacy work to reject Islamophobic discourses that claim Islam and Muslims are by nature sexist and violent toward women. In one example of many CAIR documents produced to oppose these frequent claims, CAIR published a response to an article produced by a right-wing fringe group that claimed rape is condoned under Islamic law (CAIR 2005c). The twenty-page CAIR publication is a thorough debunking of the right-wing report, with a point-by-point discussion of inaccuracies, much of which centered on the treatment of women in mosques and within Islamic tradition. This report clearly focuses on the gendered issue of rape and does so in a way that impacts private space. Additionally, CAIR does some work on gender discrimination, especially when specific incidents are brought to its attention. Usually, CAIR's advocacy work on gendered issues takes place within the overall framework of countering discrimination. Most of this advocacy work centers around the interaction between Islamic theology, practice, and gender. There is no record, however, showing that CAIR has frequently engaged in a direct, proactive way with gendered issues articulated in private space: domestic violence, sexual harassment, and rape.

The examples mentioned here represent nearly all of the substantive mentions of advocacy work on gendered issues in the sample of documents covering a decade of CAIR's public-facing activities. There are simply very few substantive mentions of CAIR doing advocacy work around gendered issues, and no evidence of any sustained advocacy campaign centered on domestic violence, sexual harassment, gendered discrimination, or a similar issue.

This result is surprising CAIR's reputation as an advocacy organization with a great deal of grassroots support means that it would be expected to have programs and campaigns dedicated to gendered issues that impact people of all religious backgrounds; for example, domestic violence, sexual harassment, and so on. In interviews, I asked CAIR staff about the role of gender in CAIR itself as well as within Muslim American communities.

I aksed CAIR staff about the impact of gender in American Islamic institutions (including CAIR) generally was described to me as a "controversial" issue that was "in flux." Everything from wearing hijab, to praying in separate sections often at the rear of mosques, to appropriate contact with men, to the role of women outside the home were seen as a matters up for debate among CAIR advocates. At the national headquarters of CAIR, it seems that some had conservative views on the appropriate role for women that may have resulted in some difficulty for women working in the organization.

I noted some discomfort in interviews with CAIR staff, which suggested some ongoing tensions within CAIR on gender issues that staff did not want to discuss with me. One CAIR staff member told me that she felt proud to be a "strong woman" working at CAIR, but she remarked that it was "also sometimes difficult to be a woman" in a leadership role in CAIR. Another woman revealed that she had dealt with "serious gender stuff" while working at CAIR's national office. I asked for clarification, as to whether she meant "usual gender issues about women in leadership, or something more serious?" She replied, "More serious gender stuff," and I took her to mean that she had experienced sexual harassment (she was uncomfortable discussing this, so I did not press for extensive details). One man told me that he personally did not know of "gender issues" at CAIR, but he did acknowledge that the role of women for many Muslims was a "touchy issue for some in the community." In short, there is some compelling evidence that there is a rather strong "glass ceiling" at CAIR, with very few women in the top leadership positions. Women who have been in executive positions have experienced discomfort, and at least one resigned after only one year at the national office. The difficulty for women at CAIR might help to explain why several other nationally prominent Muslim American advocacy organizations have been founded by women, and why staff at those organizations seem to include women almost exclusively. One such organization is Karamah: Muslim Women Lawyers for Human Rights.

The Division of Labor between Organizations Confronting Gendered Vulnerabilities

The contrasts between Karamah and CAIR are extensive. Karamah is a relatively small organization, with a smaller grassroots presence. Karamah's mission statement (and indeed its name) both mention Muslim women specifically, while CAIR's list of Core Principles mentions only support for "equal and complementary rights and responsibilities for men and women" (CAIR 2011; Karamah 2012). While CAIR was founded by a group of men, Karamah grew out of the Feminist Arab American Network, an activist group founded in the 1980s (the same founder started each group). Technically, Karamah's founding predates CAIR with an official start date of 1993, but Karamah did not undertake much U.S.-based advocacy work until 2001. The organization was born during the UN's "Decade for Women," at a time when many secular NGOs were pushing a focus on the "oppression of Muslim women," and Karamah's founders saw a need to provide a vehicle for Muslim women to speak for themselves. Whether the executive staff has intentionally been limited to mostly women is unclear, and although three men served on the organization's board of directors in 2008, most of the executive staff have been women throughout the organization's history (Karamah 2008).

In a 2008 interview, a founding member of the organization told me that "not much happened with Karamah until 9/11," and it remained very small with "only two or three people" in its early years. But after 2001 the organization became more formally structured, and for the first time it began doing advocacy work around civil rights issues in the United States. While the organization remains "nonpolitical," meaning that it does no legislative lobbying or electoral activism, Karamah has presented several consciousness-raising and educational activities around women's rights in the United States. This kind of activism focused around gender stands in stark contrast to the work carried out by CAIR, much of which has not centered on gender.

Based on the vastly different women's participation between them, there appears to be a de facto gendered division of labor between CAIR and Karamah. By this, I mean that people working at Karamah believe that CAIR (and similar, large Muslim American advocacy organizations) do not meet the needs of women in the community. Therefore, organizations focused on gender must help fill that need with a staff that is almost exclusively women. I learned in my interview with a founding member of the organization that the Board of Directors decided in late 2002 or early 2003 to narrow the organization's focus from civil rights generally to women's rights in particular. At that time, the board felt that "no one is really watching the store about women's rights." She went on:

> [S]o we wanted to go back to that [working exclusively on women's rights]. Especially since Muslim women were having issues with marriage and divorce, immigration, abuse, et cetera, and no one was really caring about those issues. So we decided that we are a women's organization that for now will focus on that, since others are doing the heavy lifting in the other field.

This respondent told me that while the organization doesn't coordinate its activities directly with CAIR or any other advocacy organization, she and the board "receive their emails" and the organizations are in contact with one another occasionally. So while there is not a formal division of labor along gendered lines and no specific coordination between CAIR and Karamah on gender issues, clearly the lack of attention to women's issues from CAIR informed Karamah's decision to work in that niche. Based on the data on women's participation at CAIR and at Karamah, there are quite sharp differences in the involvement of women between these two organizations.

Perhaps not surprisingly, documents from Karamah indicate that domestic violence is a primary issue for the organization, and they engage in sustained campaigns designed to impact private as well as public spaces to confront this issue. Karamah maintained a webpage specific to the resources it provides on domestic violence (Karamah 2004a). Together with the Asian and Pacific Islander Institute on Domestic Violence, in

2004 Karamah held a "National Summit of American Muslim Women Leaders" (Karamah 2005). The resulting Final Report from that summit was a document describing top advocacy priorities, including "Family: Marriage and Divorce," "Violence Against Women (National and International)," "Empowerment of Women through Education," "Domestic Violence," and other issues (Karamah 2004b). Nearly all of these Karamah priorities require a focus on private space, an area that CAIR has allowed to remain largely invisible in its advocacy work.

These documents, among others published by Karamah, support an image of the organization as focused specifically on gendered issues, particularly violence against and oppression of women. Karamah, like CAIR, has produced a great number of reports debunking the myth that Muslim women are always and everywhere uniquely oppressed by Islamic culture, but Karamah goes further to advocate on issues that CAIR only infrequently addresses. In this way, the gendered division in the staff of these two organizations can be seen to follow in some of the advocacy work done by these two Muslim American organizations.

Conclusion

Overall, the preliminary data presented in the limited space available above provides a general picture of the ways gender operates in Muslim American advocacy organizations fighting against racialized Islamophobia in the United States. This chapter has offered an initial effort to bring together data on gender dynamics within a wide range of groups seeking to confront Islamophobia in the United States. I find that advocacy work that privileges public over private places is inadequate to the task of changing the ways that Islamophobia and gender privilege operate. At the outset of this chapter, I argued that privilege significantly affects how organizations like CAIR and Karamah advocate around gendered Islamophobic stereotypes. The contribution of Patricia Hill Collins (2000) and others toward understanding privilege as a multifaceted and contextual process allows for a conception of privilege that incorporates issues of gender.

While I must emphasize that my empirical data cannot directly speak to this, there remains the possibility that the stereotype of a uniquely oppressive singular "Islamic culture" might have led CAIR to avoid sustained advocacy campaigns speaking to gendered issues like domestic violence. CAIR's leadership might see a sustained campaign on this issue as feeding the stereotype that Muslim Americans have a unique problem with these issues. If this is indeed the case, then CAIR effectively would not have the privilege to take exception to these gendered issues. Karamah, on this view, would have the privilege to build sustained campaigns around domestic violence, sexual harassment, and other gendered issues. The nuanced approach taken by Karamah, which defines itself as a women's organization, allows it to make private space a site of advocacy, thereby sidestepping concerns of reifying stereotypes about Islam. The privilege to take exception would then be rearticulated by gender in surprising ways, with a smaller women's organization effectively finding more privilege than the larger mainstream Muslim American civil rights advocacy organization.

The work presented here provides a preliminary look at these issues, which require far more research. I have argued elsewhere (Love 2009) that in order to understand work that confronts Islamophobia it is necessary to understand the connections, fractures, similarities, and differences between and within the communities impacted under the racialized Islamophobia umbrella. More research that includes additional communities and organizations is clearly needed.

Additional research in this area will contribute further to not only an understanding of gender dynamics within these communities, but also toward a greater general understanding of gender and civil rights advocacy organizations working in the twenty-first century (a supposedly "post-civil rights" and even "post-feminist" era). Research on confronting Islamophobia also contributes to unpacking the intersectionality of race and gender in the contemporary United States. When racialized dynamics cause Arab American men and South Asian women to face similar discriminatory actions in the workplace, at airports, and at schools and universities, then political advocacy that attempts to change social conditions such that discrimination and hate crimes cannot thrive is a crucial nexus in which race, gender, and many other axes of social difference are important. Researching how this advocacy work happens requires a great deal of qualitative work that "privilege[es] the voices of movement actors themselves" (Irons 1998, 708). This chapter represents an important step in this direction.

Notes

1. Sexuality, which is coconstituted with gender, is also an important factor to consider when analyzing Islamophobia. Some excellent scholarship examining these issues has been produced in recent years (Husain 2006; Jadallah 2000; Naber 2006). Unfortunately, my empirical data are far too insufficient to make a meaningful contribution to this literature, other than to say that sexuality (especially sexuality as a civil rights issue) remains largely neglected among the advocacy organizations that I have studied.
2. I use the term *Islamophobia* in this article despite its problems because it has attained currency in much of the contemporary scholarship on this issue, and in part to emphasize the racialized nature of Islamophobia without attempting to introduce a new term to replace Islamophobia.
3. I interviewed seven staff members at CAIR. The interviews were conducted between 2007

and 2008. Most interviews were voice recorded and transcribed, and all respondents were assured that their names would not be included in any published material resulting from this study. In addition to the interview data, this article references the results of a content analysis of a large sample of documents. Types of documents in the analysis include newsletters, press releases, conference programs, and research impressions. I made copies of dozens of documents at CAIR's headquarters in Washington, DC. In addition, CAIR's website was downloaded in 2008 and added to the sample of documents. Content analysis was conducted using a computer-aided design. Optical character recognition was performed to create machine-readable versions of paper documents. These machine-readable archives were searched by keyword, and the results were coded to create descriptions in several categories. Legal advocacy, legislative advocacy, research reports, opinion pieces, and "action alerts" were the categories in which most advocacy on gender issues was observed. The results of the keyword searches were carefully reviewed to find substantive occurrences indicating action on the part of the organization. The archival record which forms the basis of the content analysis is, of course, not a perfect representation of the advocacy work performed by these organizations. The records are by nature very incomplete. For example, legal advocacy on gender discrimination would likely remain confidential: no organization would publish specific details for most of their casework. However, published information can provide some valuable insights into the decisions made by the organizations.

4. Muslim advocacy organizations with primarily African American constituencies, in particular, are absent in this analysis (although many local chapters of CAIR have an African American constituency). In addition, many nationally prominent organizations are not included here. Some of the organizations not included in this analysis were active in 2009 and some were no longer active, but all have a role in confronting Islamophobia. To name a few of these organizations: Islamic Society of North America (ISNA), Muslim Public Affairs Council (MPAC), Muslim American Society (MAS), National Arab American Association (NAAA), National Association of Muslim Lawyers/Muslim Advocates (NAML/MA), and many others. Future research will incorporate additional organizations into the analysis.

References

Abu-Lughod, Lila. 2002. "Do Muslim Women Really Need Saving?" *American Anthropologist* 104 (3): 783–90.

American-Arab Anti-Discrimination Committee (ADC). 1996. "ADC, CAIR Protest Arrest of Two Veiled Muslim Women." *ADC Times* 17: 7. Washington, DC: Author.

Bagby, Ihsan, Paul M. Perl, and Bryan T. Froehle. 2001. *The Mosque in America: A National Portrait*. Washington, DC: Council on American Islamic Relations.

Barnett, Bernice McNair. 1993. "Invisible Southern Black Women Leaders in the Civil Rights Movement: The Triple Constraints of Gender, Race, and Class." *Signs* 7 (2): 162–82.

Collins, Patricia Hill. 2000. *Black Feminist Thought: Knowledge, Consciousness, and the Politics of Empowerment*. 2nd ed. New York: Routledge.

Council on American Islamic Relations (CAIR). (1997) 2005a. *An Employer's Guide to Islamic Religious Practices*. Washington, DC: Author. www.cair.com/Portals/0/pdf/employment_guide.pdf

———. 2005b. *Women Friendly Mosques and Community Centers: Working Together to Reclaim Our Heritage*. Washington, DC: Author.

———. 2005c. *American Mosque Response to Freedom House Report: "Saudi Publications on Hate Ideology Fill American Mosques."* Washington, DC: Author.

———. 2006. *Results that Speak for Themselves: 2006 Annual Report*. Washington, DC: Author.

———. 2007. "Statement of CAIR Executive Director Supporting H. Res. 32." http://www.cair.com/ArticleDetails.aspx?mid1=777&&ArticleID=23361

———. 2011. "Our Vision, Mission, and Core Principles." Washington, DC: Author. www.cair.com/AboutUs/VisionMissionCorePrinciples.aspx

———. n.d. "Publisher Stops Distribution of Textbook that Defames Muslim Women." http://www.cair.com/DesktopModules/Articles/Print.aspx?ArticleID=8637

Davis, Angela. 1981. *Women, Race, and Class.* New York: Vintage.

Delaney, David. 1998. *Race, Place, and the Law, 1836–1948.* Houston: University of Texas Press.

Ferris, Gerrie. 1996. "Region in Brief: Veiled Muslim Women Arrested." *Atlanta Journal-Constitution* September 19: D.02.

Flax, Jane. 1990. *Thinking Fragments: Psychoanalysis, Feminism, and Postmodernism in the Contemporary West.* Berkeley: University of California Press.

hooks, bell. 1981. *Ain't I a Woman: Black Women and Feminism.* Boston: South End Press.

Husain, Sarah, ed. 2006. *Voices of Resistance: Muslim Women on War, Faith and Sexuality.* Emeryville, CA: Seal.

Goldsack, Laura. 1999. "A Haven in a Heartless World? Women and Domestic Violence." In *Ideal Homes? Social Change and the Experience of the Home,* edited by Tony Chapman and Jenny Hockey, 121-32. New York: Routledge.

Irons, Jenny. 1998. "The Shaping of Activist Recruitment and Participation: A Study of Women in the Mississippi Civil Rights Movement." *Gender and Society* 12 (6): 692–709.

Jadallah, Huda. 2000. "Queer Arab Women in the US: Struggles With Honor and Shame." PhD Diss., University of California, Santa Barbara.

Jamal, Amaney. 2005. "Mosques, Collective Identity, and Gender Differences among Arab American Muslims." *Journal of Middle East Women's Studies* 1 (1): 53–78.

Jayawardena, Kumari. 1986. *Feminism and Nationalism in the Third World.* London: Zed Books.

Karamah: Muslim Lawyers for Human Rights. 2004a. "Domestic Violence within the Muslim American Community." Washington, DC: Author. www.karamah.org/newsletter_may2005.pdf

———. 2004b. *Final Report of the First American Muslim Women Leadership Summit.* Washington, DC: Author. www.karamah.org/docs/Final_Report_of_Summit.pdf

———. 2005. "Muslim Women at Home and Abroad: National Summit of American Muslim Leaders." *Karamah: The Circle* 1 (1): 2–3. Washington, DC: Author. www.karamah.org/docs/newsletter_may2005.pdf

———. 2008. "Karamah Directors and Officers." Washington, DC: Author. www.karamah.org/directors.htm

———. 2012. *Vision and Mission.* Washington, DC: Author. www.karamah.org/about/vision-and-mission

Love, Erik. 2009. "Confronting Islamophobia in the United States: Framing Civil Rights Activism among Middle Eastern Americans." *Patterns of Prejudice* 43 (3&4): 401–25.

Kurien, Prema. 2003. "To Be or Not to Be South Asian: Contemporary Indian American Politics." *Journal of Asian American Studies* 6 (3): 261–88.

Mahmood, Saba. 2005. *Politics of Piety: The Islamic revival and the Feminist Subject.* Princeton, NJ: Princeton University Press.

Massey, Doreen B. 1994. *Space, Place, and Gender.* Minneapolis: University of Minnesota Press.

McAdam, Doug. 1992. "Gender as Mediator of Activist Experience: The Case of Freedom Summer." *American Journal of Sociology* 95: 1211–30.

Minh-ha, Trinh. 1989. *Woman, Native, Other.* Bloomington: Indiana University Press.

Mohanty, Chandra Talpade, Ann Russo, and Lourdes Torres, eds. 1991. *Third World Women and the Politics of Feminism.* Bloomington: Indiana University Press.

Naber, Nadine. 2008. "'Look, Mohammed the Terrorist is Coming!': Cultural Racism, Nation-Based Racism, and the Intersectionality of Oppressions after 9/11." In *Race and Arab Amer-*

icans before and after 9/11, edited by Amaney Jamal and Nadine Naber, 276–317. Syracuse, NY: Syracuse University Press.

———. 2006. "Arab American Femininities: Beyond Arab Virgin/American(ized) Whore." *Feminist Studies* 32 (1): 87–112.

Omi, Michael, and Howard Winant. (1986) 1994. *Racial Formation in the United States*. New York: Routledge.

Payne, Charles. 1995. *I've got the Light of Freedom: The Organizing Tradition and the Mississippi Struggle*. Los Angeles: University of California Press.

Rana, Junaid. 2011. *Terrifying Muslims: Race and Labor in the South Asian Diaspora*. Durham, NC: Duke University Press.

Razack, Sherene H. 2008. *Casting Out: The Eviction of Muslims from Western Law and Politics*. Toronto, Canada: University of Toronto Press.

Read, Jen'nan Ghazal. 2002. "Challenging Myths of Muslim Women: The Influence of Islam on Arab American Women's Labor Force Activity." *The Muslim World* 92: 19–37.

———. 2003. "The Sources of Gender Role Attitudes among Christian and Muslim Arab-American Women." *Sociology of Religion* 64 (2): 207–22.

Robnett, Belinda. 1996. "African-American Women in the Civil Rights Movement, 1954–1965: Gender, Leadership, and Micromobilization." *American Journal of Sociology* 101 (6): 1661–93.

Shakir, Evelyn. 1997. *Bint Arab: Arab and Arab American Women in the United States*. Westport, CT: Praeger.

Smith, Dorothy. 1977. *Feminism and Marxism: A Place to Begin, a Way to Go*. Vancouver, Canada: New Star Books.

Stacey, Judith, and Barrie Thorne. 1985. "The Missing Feminist Revolution in Sociology." *Social Problems*, 32: 301–16.

Suleiman, Michael. 1999. "Introduction: The Arab Immigrant Experience." In *Arabs in America: Building a New Future*, edited by Michael Suleiman, 1–21. Philadelphia: Temple University Press.

Taylor, Verta. 1999. "Gender and Social Movements: Gender Processes in Women's Self-Help Movements." *Gender and Society* 13 (1): 8–33.

———. Nancy Whittier. 1998. "Guest Editors' Introduction." *Gender and Society* 12(6): 622–25.

Wadud, Amina. 2006. *Inside the Gender Jihad: Women's Reform in Islam*. Oxford, UK: Oneworld.

Wiltfang, Gregory L., and Doug McAdam. 1991. "The Costs and Risks of Activism: A Study of Social Movement Activism." *Social Forces* 69 (4): 987–1010.

CHAPTER 13

Masculine Privilege

The Culture of Bullying at an Elite Private School

BRETT G. STOUDT

A broadly defined study of privilege—not only class, but the intersection of race, gender, sexual orientation, religion, nationality (to name a few)—represents an important pursuit of social justice scholarship. In 1946, Kurt Lewin (founder of modern social psychology) recognized this: "In recent years we have started to realize that so-called minority problems are in fact majority problems, that the Negro problem is the problem of the white, that the Jewish problem is the problem of the non-Jew, and so on" (Lewin 1946, 44). Despite his early claims, privilege has long remained an underscrutinized topic in the social sciences. However, an increasing body of critical research has emerged in areas like hegemonic masculinity (Connell and Messerschmidt 2005), whiteness (Fine et al. 2004), the ruling class (Domhoff 2002), private schools (Howard and Gaztambide-Fernandez 2010), and hetero-normativity (Kimmel 2001). New to this encouraging wave of scholarship has been the use of participatory action research (PAR)[1] to directly study privilege *with* those individuals and *inside* those institutions that are most structurally advantaged (see Kuriloff et al. 2009; Stoudt et al. 2010).

The Rockport Bullying Study is one illustration of the critical study of privilege bridged with PAR. This project involved a faculty research team and a student research team from Rockport, an elite private school educating mostly white, economically advantaged boys.[2] Together, the student and faculty researchers set out to examine how students experienced bullying and how it was connected to masculine performances at Rockport (see Stoudt 2006, 2007, 2009; Stoudt et al. 2010).

The student researchers and I identified four types of verbal and physical bullying, which we defined broadly as ridiculing/teasing, bullying/intimidation, hazing/initiations, and fighting/physical violence (Stoudt 2007, 2009). We created an instrument based on our understanding of bullying at Rockport[3] and then used it informally throughout the day (e.g., halls, cafeteria, classrooms, locker-rooms) to interview a sample of ninety-six classmates in ninth through twelfth grade. Faculty researchers and I developed a set of interview questions inspired by the student researchers' broad conceptualization of bullying. The faculty research team[4] conducted semistructured interviews with ten faculty colleagues (7 males and 3 females; 8 teachers and 2 administrators).

Student and faculty researchers then collaborated with me to systematically analyze the collected data together; taking turns to read aloud and review quotes, stopping to discuss surprising or interesting results, reflecting upon personal experiences, and summarizing the general themes that emerged. This chapter will illustrate the conversations student and faculty researchers had as they engaged with their data and their own experiences as well as direct quotes from one of the administrators interviewed in the study. Labels in parentheses are included throughout the text to help readers identify who made the quotes: SR=student researcher; FR=faculty researchers; AD=administrator. The quotes offered in the following sections exemplify the type of research spaces that can evolve when community data mediate and anchor a critical discussion about one's local environment.

In the follow sections we examine the intersection between masculinity, privilege, and space as it is learned and reproduced through the enactment of masculine-oriented bullying and within a school culture of hegemonic masculinity and bullying. By focusing on such institutional spaces as sports locker-rooms, classrooms, and student clubs, I will contextualize the reproduction of privilege within the geography of the school. By focusing on bullying not as an outlying activity by some individual students, but as a common masculine expression of a hegemonic culture among boys within this elite space, I will reveal the production of privilege as a social interaction, co-constructed between students, faculty, and the administration.

Rockport as a Privilege (Re)Producing Space

People in the American upper class have a disproportionate amount of power, privilege, and influence (Domhoff, 2002). Those most advantaged are increasingly concentrated and the gap between the wealthy and poor continues to widen (Rose 2007). Domhoff (2002) argued that "families can rise and fall in the class structure, but the institutions of the upper class persist" (67–68). Elite private schooling represents one of the persistent "institutions of the upper class." While not all of the students in private schools become members of the power elite (e.g., politicians, CEOs, corporate leaders), these *were* the spaces where many of those individuals traditionally emerged from (Cookson and Persell 1985). These remain important spaces for the (re)production of upper class privilege (Kuriloff and Reichert 2003).

The Privileged Curriculum

Mills (1956) wrote that the private school "is the most important agency for transmitting the traditions of the upper social classes and regulating the admissions of the new wealth and talent" (64–65). Similarly, Baltzell (1958) suggested, "These private educational institutions serve the latent function of acculturating the members of the younger generation, especially those not quite to the manor born, into an upper-class style of life" (293). Elite private schools serve as gatekeepers to the upper class as well as a type of inheritance transferred to children by their wealthy families; what Shapiro (2004) called "head-start assets" because they give individuals a nonmeritorious lead in the race to get ahead. McNamee and Miller (2004) explained that families from the upper class, "Convert economic advantages into social and cultural advantages that help their children go further in school than others usually do, and then reconvert school credentials into economic (occupational, income, and wealth) advantages" (110). Sending children to private schools is an act of class consciousness by upper class parents. It is an expensive investment and there is a lot at stake.

The evidence collected by students and faculty indicated that the traditional purposes for private schooling persist at Rockport. All of the faculty researchers agreed with Jill (FR) when she said that the "socioeconomic piece is huge, HUGE." Sara (FR) added, "Yes, social-economic is much bigger here." The importance of socioeconomic status emerged as a dominant theme in our research data. As an administrator, Mike (AD) perceived Rockport's mission, at least in part, as preparing students for privilege, "I think there is an implicit message.... I mean it is like, you are training these people socially in a way that they don't even realize they are getting trained. But they are developing outlooks on life." He continued, "The implicit curriculum here is an elite." And at least some of the students we spoke to, such as this white senior, indicated they were absorbing these messages: "I think, not to use like, a stereotype of a blue-collar job, but I would say that most of the kids here are not going to graduate Rockport, go to an Ivy League school, and then work at McDonalds."

This "implicit curriculum" that Mike (AD) referenced is Rockport's "hidden curriculum." Giroux (Giroux and Pena 1979) described a school's hidden curriculum as "the unstated norms, values and beliefs that are transmitted to students through the underlying structure of meaning in both the formal content as well as the social relations of school and classroom life" (Giroux and Penna 1979, 22). As Mike (AD) indicated, the norms, values and beliefs conveyed through the hidden curriculum at Rockport are not neutral but designed to prepare students for their role in the reproduction of class structure (Anyon 1980) where they are being educated to sit atop of a system with vast amounts of social and material inequality (Bowles and Gintis 1976). Mike (AD) continued with an example of how the school helps to teach privilege: "We don't drag kids onto the carpet for not absolutely following the rules all the time. I mean it is not because we are lax, it's because I think it's almost an expectation." He explains, "You are just kind of implying, 'Hey, you are going to be in this station in life—well sure you are supposed to show up on time; but, if you don't people are going to wait for you or people are going to make exceptions for you.'"

Education and the uneven distribution of economic and sociocultural resources are strongly connected. Bowles and Gintis (1977) believed that schools reproduced privilege through what they called a "façade of meritocracy." "The educational system legitimates economic inequality by providing open, objective, and ostensibly meritocratic mechanisms for assigning individuals to unequal economic positions" (103). Cookson and Persell (1985) argued that the hidden curriculum for elite schools like Rockport is largely designed to justify and legitimate the students' disproportionate amount of advantages: "Privilege must appear to be earned, because the only real justification for inequality is that it is deserved— payment for sacrifices" (125). Zweigenhaft and Domhoff (1991) got the sense that prep school students understood themselves as having "rights and privileges which other people can't trample over...a feeling of specialness that is best characterized as a sense of superiority" (159). Cookson and Persell (1985) similarly found that, "For those who survive the prep ordeal, there is a sense that they are entitled to the privileges and position that they attain. Their 'specialness' has been confirmed by their experience" (206).

We heard comparable narratives from students at Rockport. Students often spoke of strong expectations for both personal success as well as the success of their peers. We heard narratives of elevated moral standards and superior academic achievement as compared to, for example, public school students. Many of the students expressed an overall sense of confidence in personal merit. Mike (AD) described what the performance of such values can look like in the workplace, "One of the things I once heard an employer say, he said he could always tell independent schools—not college—but independent school kids from public school kids because at twenty-four years old they are hired and they are participating in meetings." Mike attributed this to a sense of confidence gotten in their private school training, "Not because they're arrogant but because—it's like it's not arrogance its confidence. There is an expectation that you want to hear my voice, you want to hear my opinions, you want to hear what I have to say. You want my analysis of the situation."

It is not to say that private school students do not "earn" their diploma, many if not most certainly work hard for their success, but so do most working- and middle-class public school students. However, values such as entitlement, individualism, and meritocracy that are taught in many elite private schools are troubling, particularly given the disproportionate amount of affluence and influence many will have not only nationally but also internationally. The research we conducted at Rockport helped us to scratch beneath the formal curriculum to closely observe the culture that was developed, the values that were reinforced, and the ways through which these were embodied, performed, and resisted by its community members as "normal."

Masculinity, Privilege, and Space

Elite schools have long held traditions of defining particular types of "ruling" masculinities for the preparation of power and privilege (Gathorne-Hardy 1978). Thus, becoming "an elite member of society" for students at Rockport rests not only on class but also on many types of systemic privileges, most especially on gendered privileges. And the privileges given to men are inseparably linked to another type of privilege, heterosexuality. Hegemonic representations of manhood are rooted in heterosexual versions of love, romance, sexual prowess, marriage, and family, and therefore to be gay is to be "insufficiently" male (Kimmel 2001).

Bullying among boys represents one important and prevalent enactment of hegemonic masculinity within schools (Garbarino and deLara 2003; Phoenix, Frosh, and Pattman 2003). Particularly revealing is the meaning of bullying within privileged educational environments. Enduring the aggressive masculine environment noted at private schools contributes to the feeling of "making it" or "earning it" and a sense of meritocracy. Cookson and Persell (1985) observed bullying among boys at the multiple private schools they studied. They concluded that "students learn the real lessons of power and privilege from their fellow [classmates] … students socialize each other for power in the total institution, and as long as the competition does not become too intense, the school gives their tacit approval by allowing them to continue" (130). They explained:

> There are few tender mercies among boys, who establish finely graded pecking orders. Big, strong, and aggressive boys often demand deference from smaller boys and, as a group, seniors tend to band together and lord it over the rest. Violations of the pecking order may be punished physically and verbally…. The threat of this kind of humiliation has a sobering effect on potential mavericks or troublemakers. (154)

Cookson and Persell (1985) argued that masculine performances expressed through bullying in prep schools was an important part of the upper class training since it helped to develop a strong sense of "collective identity" while minimizing "divergent thinkers" (106). Ultimately, it helped to prepare for future enactments of privilege:

> What one boy described as the "dog-eat-dog" elements in the boy culture provide ample opportunities to learn that survival and success do not go to the weak but to the strong, a philosophy of life well suited to managing power relations in the financial and business world. (154)

New (2001) similarly linked traditional representations of masculinity with the reproduction of privilege, "The social construction of such constricted [masculine] selves does indeed produce subjects who can function well in capitalistic, patriarchal organizations" (740).

We found in our data that hegemonic values were entrenched within the institution and reinforced systemically by the entire Rockport community, often through broadly defined version of bullying. Mike (AD) *also* implied a relationship between elite schooling and aggression at Rockport: "We are setting you up to be an elite member of society, which means recognizing this competition, which means recognizing that you've got to try and get advantages." He explained further, "You are taking kids from incredibly competitive, high driven families and you are putting them together." It is an environment, he argued, that makes eliminating bullying very difficult, "To say that you are going to get those kids to stop snapping at, competing with, and bullying or teasing and ridiculing each other is never going to happen." Mike (AD) connected this with the parents' belief system, "I mean a lot of these families are firm believers in capitalism, it's sinking or swimming. It's about competition; it's about crushing the other guy." Indeed, as part of Rockport's power elite education, teaching hegemonic masculinity that includes giving and enduring aggression may serve students well within our violent and hierarchical neoliberal economy. If so, it reveals bullying at Rockport not as an unwanted and deviant break from the norm by some rogue students but instead as an expression of the "normal" masculine culture as part of privileged training.

How boys' masculinities are performed, directed, and limited in schools like Rockport is an important research question to ask because it is fundamental to the establishment and maintenance of hegemony. Mills (1956), as one of the first scholars to study the power elite, noted that most vital aspects of prep school are not located in the formal curriculum but "in a dozen other places, some of them queer places indeed: in the relations between boys and faculty; in who the boys are and where they come from; in a Gothic chapel or a shiny new gymnasium" (65). His latter reference to a chapel or gymnasium—in other words, what meanings are taken from and conveyed in the experience of space—deserves deeper consideration as it pertains to privilege. Space can produce and communicate power and help define the meaning of social relationships (Creswell 2004). Rockport's beautifully manicured and tree-lined campus, with well-funded athletic facilities, old architecture, and a central location in a prestigious zip code projects to the students, parents, and passersby a sign of wealth, power, and importance.

Examples of spatial meaning emerged from our data. Students made the receptionist's office at the entrance of Richmond Hall (Rockport's primary academic building) an informal communal space. This area tended to become rowdy, "basically out of control" as suggested by Paul (SR). In response, Mary (FR) reacted to the message it presented about the school, "I think places matter, so that when it happens in the reception area of the school I think there is some specific understanding, 'This is who we are. This is my best foot forward.'" She linked the receptionist's office with the image the school is selling, "Its function in the institution is to be a welcoming spot for visitors and many of these visitors are prospective customers since we have a product that we sell at a very expensive cost."

The symbolic significance of how physical space is used can contribute to indoctrinating students into a privileged lifestyle and can provide important clues about the institution's values. Mary (FR) and other faculty researchers recognized this in Rockport's use of the nearby country club for official venues. Mary (FR) described the country club's relationship to exclusionary attitudes, "I've always boycotted [the country club], I just hate it.... I think they probably have one Jewish family, one Korean family, one Black family." Jill (FR) argued, "It's those kinds of things in our system,

I think, that if we continue to allow to go on, what message are we sending?" Mike (AD) illustrated a similar point, again reflecting on Richmond Hall, "Straight in front of you are two huge rooms dedicated to the college office. Hello, I mean, what is important to Rockport? Getting your kid into college, ... but service learning is buried in the basement." He admitted that these "are strong implicit messages which I think oftentimes get overlooked or just taken for granted." In the next section, bullying within institutional spaces will be explored in order to discuss the transference of hegemonic masculinity and privilege and its relationships to bullying.

Bullying and Aggression in Sports Related Spaces

As part of our research, student researchers asked their peers how often and in what contexts they experienced the broadly defined versions of bullying. From this data, they used the campus map to graph the "hot zones" of bullying.[5] Through this mapping process we found that the far majority of physical violence, fighting, hazing, and initiations occurred in sports related spaces like the locker-rooms, athletic fields, or buses. The student researchers described how these athletic spaces helped to facilitate bullying.

The crew locker-room was geographically located on the river far from the school. The room, as described by Steve (SR), was "big and it's dark, and kids are getting changed, so you can do so much stuff, like you are so exposed." He explained, "There are always people pushing each other and it's such a competitive sport anyway so I mean ... it's like a breeding ground." John (SR) depicted the space as unsupervised, "There is absolutely nobody around.... This is sort of an accepted thing that like this is a place that is outside of school, so the rules of school don't really apply as much there." And the behavior within the space, by students and the coaches, seemed to draw from stereotypical masculine values where, as Steve (SR) explained, "If you are soft, you just won't—yea, you'll just get eaten alive."

Within a sports context, the boys at Rockport taught each other how to be masculine, how to be "real" men, through more physical and aggressive forms of bullying. Steve (SR) described the expectations placed on freshmen by seniors to embody toughness, emotional stoicism, aggression, and respect for hierarchy. John (SR) explained:

> When I was a freshman what they did was they took us all into this room with the lights out, the TV was on static, the alarm clock was beeping and we had to sit in the room and do nothing and wait our turn and go to another room. They took freshmen one by one and

shaved their heads and told them to come back and tell the rest how like, "oh my god it is so terrible." I remember there was a senior who came into the room and like we were getting out of hand because we were talking and it was just like we had to sit still and so he made us sit on the bed and hold hands. And when he got really pissed off he took the alarm clock, ripped it out of the wall, and threw it into the wall and left a dent.

We heard stories of hazing and other forms of bullying conducted throughout Rockport's sports program including crew, wrestling, soccer, and lacrosse. However, the athletes were not the only group at Rockport endorsing these traditions. For example, one of the faculty members and also the wrestling coach explained that in male-oriented spaces like Rockport, "there is a certain pecking order, there is a dominance that needs to be established. It's a pack mentality and everybody has to seek their own level.... I don't think I would really construe [it] as bullying as much as trying to establish a normal order of things."

Steve (SR) told us a story of his coach (also an administrator) who, along with the older students, helped to uphold and reaffirm the socially constructed, hierarchical power that older students yielded over the younger students, despite complaints by parents and resistance by freshmen. His story took place during one of the athletic bus trips:

> Whenever the bus stops the seniors race to get out first. So the seniors try to get off first and the freshmen always have to wait to get off last, and the sophomores get off second last. So the seniors, as they are walking down [the isle] hit the freshmen and like it's bad, it's really bad.

On one occasion, Steve (SR) explained, when the bus driver opened the door, "the freshman kids see that their parents' cars are right there so a couple of kids thought it would be funny to jump off the bus and run into the car and get away." The break in the seniors' perceived entitlement to their privileged status caused a strong reaction:

> Some of the seniors thought this was ridiculous. So they [seniors] were like taunting them [freshmen] in school and then the bus rides were hell for these kids. They made them do so many things. They took one kid and pulled him out of his seat and put him in the aisle and put book bags on him and sat on him and stuff.

It got so bad that the freshmen's parents got involved and called the coach, "Mr. Smith [administrator] and the school got involved somewhat."

Steve (SR) thought the seniors would be reprimanded for their behavior, "I seriously thought that the next day all the seniors, whether you were involved in it or not, were going to be like this is wrong and [the seniors] would be made to run [during practice as punishment]." However instead, Steve (SR) found Rockport's hegemonic masculine culture—in this case represented by the seniors' privileged and violent status amongst lower-classmen—upheld by faculty and the institution:

> When I got [to practice the next day] the coach (who had gone to Rockport) took me inside and he said, "What happened yesterday?" and I told him the truth about what happened and he said, "That's ridiculous." I was like "I know" and I meant that the seniors were abusing the freshmen. And he's like, "That's ridiculous that they [the freshmen] disrespected you guys and it shouldn't be like that." He made the freshmen run [extra] for the next week. [Those] freshmen ran like a total of 40 miles in a week because they rebelled against the seniors.

Steve's (SR) description of how forcefully the resistance to the norms were disciplined between peers was striking. John (SR) commented on the bus incident, "Yeah and those kids [freshmen] have never adjusted—ever since those incidents—haven't adjusted." Steve (SR) added, "And the kids who keep their mouth shut and just let people hit them are the ones who get respect." Our data suggested silence and conformity gain greater respect than resistance to and departure from the traditional boundaries. What is most striking about Steve's (SR) story is that it exemplifies how the students at Rockport are expected to handle a certain amount of physical or verbal bullying not only from their peers *but also* from the adults at Rockport. In this case, it *was also* the adults that assisted in legitimating violent bullying between boys along with the messages about masculinity it conveyed.

Civilized Oppression from the Cafeteria to the Classroom

The student researchers' "hot zone" maps also revealed that verbal bullying such as hurtful ridiculing, teasing, and joking was pervasive, and was found nearly everywhere throughout the campus but especially in hallways, by the lockers, in the cafeteria, even in the classroom. The student and faculty researchers eventually came to understand this pervasiveness as "the white noise of bullying" because of how widespread and taken-for-granted it was at Rockport. However, much of what the student researchers described as verbal bullying also seemed intertwined with friendship and fun; making these forms of bullying particularly pervasive and invisible. Our analysis of the verbal content of this bullying revealed it to be what Harvey (1999) called *civilized oppression*. Neither explicitly violent nor illegal, civilized oppression thrives in the unexamined habits of conversation, the subtlety of many power relationships, nonverbal behavior, and the tacit assumptions often found in such "neutral" places as humor and ridicule. Through small, normalized, hidden, and cumulative acts, its victims are systemically harmed while boosting the systemic privileges of others.

The student researchers acknowledged that competitive verbal bullying often existed in the classroom; however, like Steve (SR), they believed witty comments made in class were often so malicious (and funny) because the students were "all really close to each other, and know so much about each other, and like their everyday lives, and they take out those funny things." John (SR) spoke of the person taking the brunt of ridicule as the sacrificial cost for the larger advantage of classroom bonding, "But what happens is you bond.... The witty comments benefit the whole entire class except for one person, and then that sort of—the bonding thing—you are adding something else to the class." And Steve (SR) agreed suggesting that traditional classes without ridiculing would not be as conducive to building relationships, "Everyone is comfortable with each other and the environment is different and I just feel like a really structured class wouldn't be the same." The students made meaning from bullying; they built friendships even in the midst of aggression.

The student researchers also recognized the way faculty contributed to both a culture of competition and a culture of bullying. The student researchers used one of their classes to exemplify how ridiculing could be closely linked to a competitive classroom culture that the teacher helped to facilitate. They described a game played by a teacher and her students, as Paul (SR) explained, to "chalk up on the board for rude comments ... to keep a running tally, like, anytime someone does a witty thing." John (SR) added, "It's like, malicious too." Steve (SR) elaborated on this competitive classroom game of put-downs, "We'll be in class, so like, the teacher will be teaching, and ... if you say something really funny, everyone is like, 'Oh put it up, put it up' and then some kid will stand up.... Totally accepted." Steve (SR) recalled one recent incident with a student who "tries ten times harder than anyone else. He just doesn't get it all the time." He explained, "When he gets picked on it's just like, ohhh, like you can tell it just nails him. They say, 'Thanks for like, helping our curve, I'm so glad you're in our class.'" Dave (SR) reported that the teacher is not passive in this competition, "The teacher's on the board too. She's on the board a lot." Steve (SR) added, "But hers' aren't hurtful, they are just funny. But ours are, the kids are hurtful like, they are specific to a certain person, stuff like that.

And she's just like ohhhhh." Mary (FR) interviewed their teacher, "She said there is a lot of vicious teasing that boys recognize and she used the term the *soft underbellies of the boys* and they go for them." The student researchers did not believe their description of this classroom experience was uncommon. John (SR) said he could "name six or seven teachers [whose classes are similar to this]."

Faculty researchers reflected on their classroom experiences and in-class banter. They described it as "quick" or "sarcastic" responses toward the students as a way to discipline the class and earn respect. Greg (FR) suggested that, "When we say 'quick' we are not just saying in terms of time but it has to be a comment that stops the kid. Stops the kid dead. It puts him in his place; it shows your authority over that situation." Mary (FR) explained this kind of "verbal sparring is currency around here." She believed that "one of the ways you are well regarded by students [is] if they see you are able to be verbally really quick and verbally not necessary mean but clever." Sara (FR) agreed and suggested, "When I first came here that was something I felt like I had to learn how to do. To literally get control of my classroom I had to be quick because the people who aren't are the ones who get run over by the kids." Jill (FR) added, "Sometimes I have to turn that off on a weekend with my husband. Like this morning I said something quick back to him and he said you're not in school. I'm like oh my god why did I [do that]? Sarcasm is actually currency around here."

The student researchers suggested that these types of bullying were so prevalent that they always needed to be on guard. Steve (SR) felt like, "It could be anything … no matter who you are, you are always vulnerable because it could be anyone who takes a shot at you … from any side pretty much." Although at first glance it seemed to student researchers that boys could be picked on indiscriminately for any way they differed from the norm. However, these actions were often not arbitrary. When we looked at the verbal content of the bullying closer, we found it also served to discipline masculine boundaries (as well as other hegemonic boundaries such as race/ethnicity, socioeconomic status, religion, and sexual orientation (see Stoudt et al. 2010).

The Rockport community often held unspoken and spoken expectations about gender and what it means to be a male. It became clear throughout my discussion with the student researchers that masculine expectations were present in their lives. For example, and as might be predicted, they explained that emotionally expressive signs of weakness such as crying among the boys was strongly ridiculed. John (SR) described, "Yeah, then the story goes around that this person cried. Everybody hears that this person cried. I hear stories about people crying over everything." Dave (SR) suggested that, "Rockport has so many added pressures besides making sure that all of your homework is done. On top of the demands that the teachers put on you, the students subconsciously put pressures on other students." He described pressures that "include making sure your tie is not considered a 'gay' tie because of its coloring, or that the car you are getting out of is up to the standards of a [local wealthy] community." He explained that on days when they don't have to wear their uniform "there is the added pressure of wearing a certain pair of jeans that won't be considered tough enough, or [worrying] the saying on your sweatshirt is as 'gay' as the pink tie you wore two days ago."

Student researchers suggested that their peers frequently held sexist and also heterosexist attitudes. Paul (SR) explained, "I think people definitely talk about women a lot differently when they are not around. Yeah [sort of degrading]. Just like it is almost normal. Yeah like 'she was being such a bitch yesterday.' You hear that all the time." Dave (FR) connected it to masculine performance by commenting that "It is the manly thing to do." A common putdown among the students as explained both by the student researchers and the faculty researchers was to call someone "gay" or "a girl." Steve (SR) said, "It's a word you use so much." The faculty researchers were very aware of how often the students used it in their discourse. Greg (FR) explained, "'You're gay, that's gay'—that's something I hear all the time." Sara (FR) agreed, "I hear that all the time, you're gay, you're a girl.... So many teachers that we interviewed said they commonly hear that one of the biggest put downs is 'that's gay.'"

The female faculty researchers suggested that their experiences with sexist jokes and other inappropriate verbal comments about women—not only by students but also male faculty—reinforced the male-oriented culture. Jill (FR) explained, "Yeah, the women here, give me a break. There is just stuff that we put up with, you know comments all the time, jokes it's like.... It's always underlying. Some days it's worse than others. We've all been around on a couple of those days." Sara (FR) reported that one of her male interviewees admitted, "We are totally insensitive to what we say about females in the presence of female teachers." For example, all of the faculty researchers told of gender insensitive e-mails forwarded by male faculty and administration that were intended to be "humorous." Sara (FR) suggested some prominent adult males in the community such as administrators have given what Jill (FR) called "tacit approval" around sexist attitudes, "Oh things that are said in assemblies that kids are allowed to say, remarks that the kids, that literally male faculty and administrators will laugh at instead of stopping it or saying that's inappropriate to say."

Mike (AD) often noticed that "kids who come new in ninth grade or seventh grade from middle class environments can't believe some of the things that are said, which kids who have been here for a while are like,

'He's just joking.'" The students at Rockport often disciplined institutional and cultural values through the way they joked and insulted each other. The student researchers defined casual teasing about race, ethnicity, class, gender, religion, and sexual identity as forms of verbal bullying. Deconstructing the tacit assumptions often found in such "neutral" places as humor, ridiculing or playful insults such as calling someone "a fag" or "gay" or "a girl" forced us to ask what lies beneath such a statement, who is disadvantaged by it, who is empowered by it?

Rockport students' (and some faculty's) use of homophobic, antifeminine, or misogynistic insults (among others like race and class) helped to impose the boundaries of who's in and who's out, what is acceptable and what is unacceptable, who is "normal" and who is marginalized. These insults contributed in subtle and not so subtle ways to marginalizing women and people who identify as gay by defining them as something undesirable, negative, or less than whole. These insults and jokes were forms of "civilized oppression" (Harvey, 1999) and helped to directly (re) produce a local culture embedded in hegemonic stereotypical values.

Controlling School Space

At Rockport, not all masculine performances are equally valued. Boys gain or lose social standing depending on how they are positioned with gendered norms. It does not come as a surprise, given the vast amount of "men and masculinities" literature, that some of the most valued qualities of manhood at Rockport are those embodying strength, individuality, skill, aggression, and emotional reserve as well as standing in distinction to things feminine. Drawing lines between what is masculine and feminine includes, obviously women *but also* homosexuality and other subordinated versions of masculinity. Hegemonic masculinity is not only about masculine qualities, it is also about power and privilege; the systemic advantages and opportunities given to men (particularly wealthy, white, American, straight men) at the expense of women and marginalized men (Connell and Messerschmidt 2005). In this final section we explore one of the most dominant themes in our work: the enactment of elite masculinity training at Rockport as drawn in contrast to homosexuality.

As described in the previous section, a common putdown among the students as described both by the student researchers and the faculty researchers was to call someone a "girl" or "gay." Mary (FR) explained, "Everybody's, 'you're a girl' or 'you're gay.' 'You're a girl' or 'you're gay' that is the worst possible put down." I asked one of the only openly gay students (Jason) at Rockport during an interview why homophobic insults were so common among his peers. Jason told me:

I just think because it's like against the norm, and I think it's kind of looked down upon if you are gay, so if you want to get a point across you're not going to be like "stop being straight," because it really wouldn't do any good—what does that mean? But everyone knows that if you call someone "gay," what you're implying and what the actions are.

The students (including the student researchers) often expressed difficulty understanding why using homophobic insults was inappropriate even in the absence of someone who is gay or even if using the word was not a punishable offense. For example one of Jason's classmates explained:

Yea, you got to be careful, there's like a gay kid in our school— there's actually a couple— but there's one who is pretty outwardly gay and like—he like bothered someone and someone called him a faggot and there was like this huge deal—like the kid got suspended and all that. So when you know you're in the vicinity of those people you've got to watch your words.

For many of the students, they draw clear distinctions between calling someone gay as in homosexual and gay as in doing something negative. Another of Jason's peers explained, "Gay in our school doesn't mean homosexual, it means stupid."

The student researchers also had a difficult time seeing this distinction. John (SR) argued, "Yeah 'gay' is something like an anecdote or takes on connotations.... Like you can tell by context where 'gay' is meant to be negative or 'gay' is meant to homosexual." Paul (SR) agreed, "You are not actually saying someone is actually gay you are just saying what you are doing is gay. It's just like if they are annoying you." The use of the word *gay* was so pervasive that it erased for the students how their definition of "gay" was connected to and because of the marginalization of homosexuality. These invisible homophobic insults helped control the representational spaces for how gender was interpreted and performed by defining the boundaries of "normal" masculinity at Rockport as heterosexual masculinity.

Students who directly and maliciously insulted gay students at Rockport were punished. However, the faculty often contributed to or accepted the homophobic environment. Mike (AD) illustrated this:

[Rockport is] a conservative institution, it's always going to be a conservative institution. Like I said, don't fight the market. If you don't want that go to [a less conservative school]. You know, it is what it is and I accept that ... I don't think you'll ever have lots of kids coming out and saying they are gay here, not because it is not safe or they are worried about being beat up, just because it's not Rockport, it's a conservative place.

Our evidence did not support Mike's (AD) belief that Rockport is a safe place for young people who identify as gay.

Mary (FR) described a student of color who came out as gay to which not all of the faculty were responsive. Mary (FR) explained:

> We have an African American kid who's come out as gay and he wrote this little thing up about "I'm queer and I'm here" and nobody reacted.... Kids have been mean to him.... He put this thing in every faculty member's mailbox... I mean, everyone knew he was gay, nobody could care less.... But [one of the older male faculty members] loudly and publicly—of course he is deaf so he's speaks really loudly—he got this thing in his mailbox and he's the only person on campus that didn't know he's gay—he said, "He's black and queer?" He was saying, "Oh it must be really hard for him around here to be black *and* queer."

Jill (FR) added, "[He gave us] a packet of reading material for faculty to read through, for awareness.... [Faculty] never discussed it. We never brought it up at our faculty [meeting]. You know, good for him but whatever." Though the student tried to build awareness among the faculty with a packet of reading material, the faculty researchers explained that his effort was met with little reaction. While on the one hand it was positive that many of the teachers were neither surprised nor cared about the student's sexual identity, by not properly acknowledging the presence of homosexuality in the institution—in faculty meetings or in the classroom—they were helping to silence (make invisible) his and others' unique, often difficult experiences within the Rockport community.

Sara (FR) told us a story about the resistance of some faculty to discussing homosexuality as part of the science curriculum:

> We meet once a month with the lower school science and the middle school science teachers and the upper school science and [one of the faculty members] brought [the student's letter about being gay up] and said, "I think really as science teachers it is our duty to [address this]. [If] we are going to get asked these questions it's our duty to [answer them]. So we need to be empathic to this and we need to teach kids the correct things."

Sara (FR) explained that other faculty members in the meeting were adamantly opposed to this proposal based on their personal values that homosexuality should not be legitimized, "Afterwards [other faculty] came up to him and were flabbergasted. They said to him, 'I'm sorry but this is absolutely unacceptable and it will never be brought up in my class.' I mean totally would not even hear of the fact that [homosexuality] should ever be something that is condoned." Sara (FR) was shocked that some faculty, "would come out and say 'I will not support this kid.'" Actions such as these minimize sexual identity as a single student's deviance rather than an issue that has important relevance for the entire institution. Sara's (FR) story revealed how important it is for gay-friendly faculty to encourage rather than silence discussion about homosexuality since silence favors, in this case, intolerant attitudes and ignorance. Jason's story at Rockport (introduced earlier in this section) further helps to illustrate this point.

Jason reflected upon coming out in such a conservative place as Rockport, "It was tricky. I had some scuffles in past years with kids and like, there were some suspensions and stuff.... I'm pretty sure that people do talk about me behind my back and say things." But he explained, "It doesn't really matter because they know that I will fight back, and I have gotten kids suspended and I've gotten them in trouble, and maybe that's a lesson that gay people are not powerless." When Jason first realized what his sexual orientation was he sought the safe space of a Gay Student Alliance that met in a nearby city:

> It was just like something that struck me one day—like all the pieces of the puzzle fit together, like "that's why—O.K." So then there is, "where do I go from here?" Yea, it was like a relief. And, I mean, there was no-one here [Rockport] I could really talk to, so there is a Gay Student Alliance in [a nearby town] that meets on Friday nights.

Jason explained that at Rockport and the larger community, there is a need for a "total overhaul of the value system," "There is homophobia and there is sexism and there is racism but there's not a whole lot you can do without the whole area changing.... I mean, granted I'm in school more than I'm at home, so school could have a very big effect." So he attempted to claim physical institutional space that would also represent a symbolically safe space to discuss sexual orientation at Rockport. He initiated a Gay Students Alliance on campus.

However, Jason's initiative was ultimately denied by the school from becoming an extracurricular club. Mike (AD) explained how faculty contributed to an environment not fully supportive of homosexuality by controlling the use of school space:

That one still really bothers me because he came out as a junior, was very well liked, very popular.... Essentially this young man wanted to start a club. He was the perfect kid to do it...[So he gets up in front of the student body] and says, "Gay Students Alliance if anyone is interested it starts next Tuesday." It became this enormous thing. The headmaster basically said, "Well I'll do it if the board says it's okay." So the kid and I met with a board member with my personal understanding ... [that] Rockport supports him as long as he made a reasonable case. So he explained the rationale for it, why it's healthy, and why it's not going to ruin the school.

This meeting did not go as planned. The outward presence of homosexuality at Rockport sent aftershocks that even reached beyond the immediate community, as one alumnus of ten years told me, "Rockport is getting soft." Mike (AD) continued:

It became a political issue. The headmaster was saying, "Well I support it but I need board approval" and the board would say, "We'd support it but this is really an institutional issue we need the headmaster to say it is okay." And in the end no one was willing to step up and say, "Yeah sure go ahead and do it."

In this case, not taking a stand had severe consequences. Mike (AD) recalled that that he felt this incident contributed to Jason's attempted suicide:

In retrospect if I had to do it over again, I would have taken the heat personally after the fact.... But instead it became an issue and I think the kid tried taking his life because he felt betrayed by [Rockport]. I mean there were many other issues in his life, but I think had that club been accepted, ... I think he would have still felt supported and secure here.... You know I don't think it would ruin the school. I don't think it would have any impact on the school. I think everyone is more afraid of what it will do than it really will do.

The boundaries of hetero-normative masculinity at Rockport were controlled in both symbolic and physical spaces: symbolic—by devaluing homosexuality through the values conveyed in homophobic insults, physical—by disallowing the use of institutional property or classroom time for the purposes of opening up conversation about male sexualities. In terms of the reproduction of privileged space, these acts of control are most telling for what is absent; what goes left unsaid, what is made invisible, what is left without interpretation. Homophobic slurs such as "that's gay" are so normalized by students that the connection of "something bad" to "homosexual" is explicitly lost. Yet, rendering homosexuality invisible in this equation still implicitly reproduces heterosexual privilege by serving as a general warning about breaking "acceptable" masculine boundaries while remaining explicitly hurtful and subordinating to those who identify as gay or questioning. Failing to actively create spaces inside the school to have critical discussions about sexuality, to gain knowledge about sexual identities, and to celebrate multiple human expressions of sexuality—through student clubs or teacher validation or through the academic curriculum—is not a passive vote of acceptance or indifference. Institutionally, it is a clear endorsement and reproduction of dominant values. This was made evident, for example, when neither the board nor the headmaster would approve the Gay Students Alliance without the other's consent. Neither acted; in their inaction not only was heterosexual privilege maintained but homosexuality was overtly marginalized and even denigrated within the institution.

During the time of this study, hetero-normative values had a strong presence at Rockport and topics like homosexuality were rarely discussed, either as a lack of awareness or as described by some faculty members, out of resistance because of personal belief. Our data suggested that safe spaces for gay students were not widely available at Rockport. Most concerning, developing initiatives to address issues around homosexuality and homophobia continued to be, as one faculty researcher recently told me, "off limits."

Conclusion

This chapter revealed, through intensive discussion with student and faculty researchers and mediated by collected data from at least three levels of the institutional hierarchy (students, faculty, and administration), that verbal and physical bullying was widespread at Rockport and related to the reproduction of hegemonic masculinity and privilege. Our data suggested that masculine oriented bullying and Rockport's hidden curriculum designed to teach privilege were connected to space: the of use space, the messages space conveyed and the types of social interactions space facilitated. Our data also revealed the ways in which not only students *but also* faculty and administrators helped to co-construct, communicate, and discipline the institution's hegemonic values. What emerged clearly in our work was that school bullying was not only a student problem; it was also a faculty problem and an institutional problem. As Jill (FR) and the other faculty researchers conclude, "From the headmaster on down … it is systemic."

The reproduction of cultural privilege is likely to occur in subtle spaces at schools like Rockport through institutionalized discourse around meritocracy or hetero-normative violence. These processes may be embedded in the hidden curriculum and embodied in students', teachers' and administrators' performances of masculinity, whiteness, heterosexuality, and wealth. Research within elite schools can help expose the hidden curriculum and bring to the school community's awareness the ways in which it may have damaging social, cultural, and political implications. The participatory work described in this chapter helped to carve open spaces for a school-wide conversation not only about bullying, but also about the ways that restrictive versions of masculinities were encouraged as part of the institutional culture and relationships.

Notes

1. PAR is a form of collaborative research that has a long history in social psychology. PAR researchers use critical research with community members to better understand and improve their own communities. It pursues democratic participation at each phase of the research from the framing of research questions to the analyses of the data (Cammarota and Fine 2008; Reason and Bradbury 2006).
2. This research was conducted in close partnership with the Center for the Study of Boys' and Girls' Lives (CSBGL). CSBGL supports an ongoing consortium of independent schools throughout the country to conduct research and facilitate critical discussion on behalf of boys and girls.
3. The survey used a range of closed and open-ended questions designed to address the frequency of bullying, the contextual prevalence of bullying throughout the school, emotional experiences with bullying, experiences with bullying from the standpoint of victim, observer, and perpetrator as well as other social, cultural, or institutional factors that may have contributed to bullying.
4. Faculty interviewees were asked about their experiences with bullying personally, their observations of bullying at Rockport, their interpretations of bullying, and what, if anything, should the school do about bullying. In addition, faculty interviewees were asked to react to some of the data collected by student researchers.
5. The student researchers' "hot zone" maps, as we referred to them, were maps of the school that were color coded for the frequency of bullying. The students created four maps, one for each of the four types of bullying we identified. The survey asked respondents to indicate where at Rockport the four types of bullying were most likely to happen. Given that data, six colors were used to represent varying degrees of frequency across different buildings and open spaces throughout the campus.

References

Anyon, Jean. 1980. "Social Class and the Hidden Curriculum of Work." *Journal of Education* 162 (1): 67–92.

Baltzell, Edward D. 2002. *Philadelphia Gentlemen: The Making of a New Upper Class.* New Brunswick, NJ: Transaction.

Bowles, Samuel and Herbert Gintis. 1977. *Schooling in capitalist America: Educational reform and the contradictions of economic life.* New York: Basic Books.

Cammarota, Julio and Michelle Fine. 2008. *Revolutionizing Education: Youth Participatory Action Research in Motion.* Routledge: New York.

Connell, Raewyn W., and James W. Messerschmidt. 2005. "Hegemonic Masculinity: Rethinking the Concept." *Gender and Society* 19 (6): 829–59.

Cookson, Peter W., and Caroline H. Persell. 1985. *Preparing for Power: America's Elite Boarding Schools.* New York: Basic Books.

Creswell, Tim. 2004. *Place: A Short Introduction.* Oxford, UK: Blackwell.

Domhoff, G. William. 2002. *Who Rules America?* New York: McGraw Hill.

Fine, Michelle, Lois Weis, Linda. P. Pruitt, and M. Wong. 2004. *Off-White: Readings on Power, Privilege, and Resistance.* New York: Routledge.

Garbarino, James, and Ellen deLara. 2003. *And Words Can Hurt Forever: How to Protect Adolescents from Bullying, Harassment, and Emotional Violence.* New York: Free Press.

Gathorne-Hardy, Jonathan. 1978. *The Old School Tie: The Phenomenon of the English Public School.* New York: Viking Press.

Giroux, Henry, and Anthony Penna. 1979. "Social Education in the Classroom: The Dynamics of the Hidden Curriculum." *Theory and Research in Social Education* 7 (1): 21–42.

Harvey, Jean. 1999. *Civilized Oppression.* New York: Rowman and Littlefield.

Howard, Adam, and Reuben Gaztambide-Fernandez. 2010. *Class Privilege and Education Advantage.* New York: Rowman and Littlefield.

Kimmel, Michael. S. 2001. "Masculinity as Homophobia: Fear, Shame, and Silence in Theodore F. Cohen, 29–41. Stamford, CT: Wadsworth.

Kuriloff, Peter, and Michael Reichert. 2003. "Boys of Class, Boys of Color: Negotiating the Academic and Social Geography of an Elite Independent School." *Journal of Social Issues* 59 (4): 1–11.

———, ———, Brett G. Stoudt, and Sharon Ravitch. 2009. "Building Research Collaboratives Among Schools and Universities: Lessons from the Field." *Mind, Brain and Education* 3 (1): 33–43.

Lewin, K. 1946. Action research and minority problems. *The Journal of Social Issues* 2 (4): 34–46.

McNamee, Stephen. J. and Robert. K. Miller. 2004. *The Meritocracy Myth.* New York: Rowman and Littlefield.

Mills, C. Wright. 1956. *The Power Elite.* New York: Oxford University Press.

New, C. 2001. Oppressed and oppressors? The systematic mistreatment of men. *Sociology* 35 (3): 729–48.

Phoenix, Ann, Stephen Frosh, and Rob Pattman. 2003. "Producing Contradictory Masculine Subject Positions: Narratives of Threat, Homophobia and Bullying in 11–14 Year Old Boys." *Journal of Social Issues* 59 (1): 179–96.

Reason, Peter, and Hilary Bradbury. 2006. *Handbook of Action Research.* New York: Sage.

Rose, Stephen. J. 2007. *Social Stratification in the United States.* New York: New Press.

Shapiro, Thomas. M. 2004. *The Hidden Cost of Being African American: How Wealth Perpetuates Inequality.* New York: Oxford University Press.

Stoudt, Brett. G. 2006. "'You're Either In or You're Out': School Violence, Peer Discipline, and the (Re)Production of Hegemonic Masculinity." *Men and Masculinities* 8 (3): 273–87.

———. 2007. "The Co-Construction of Knowledge In 'Safe Spaces': Reflecting On Politics and Power in Participatory Action Research." *Children, Youth and Environments* 17 (2), 280–97.

———. 2009. "The Role of Language in the Investigation of Privilege: Using Participatory Action Research to Discuss Theory, Develop Methodology, and Interrupt Power." *The Urban Review* 41: 7–28.

———, Peter Kuriloff, Michael Reichert, and Sharon Ravitch. 2010. "Educating For Hegemony,

Researching For Change: Collaborating With Teachers and Students to Examine Bullying at an Elite Private School." In *Class Privilege and Education Advantage,* edited by Adam Howard and Rubin Gaztambide-Fernandez, 31–53. New York: Rowman and Littlefield.

Zweigenhaft, Richard, and G. William Domhoff. 1991. *Blacks in the White Establishment: A Case Study of Race and Class in America.* New Haven, CT: Yale University Press.

CHAPTER 14

Zones of Exclusion[1]

The Experiences of Scottish Girls

HAZEL McFARLANE AND NANCY HANSEN

Geography and Disability in Context

Whether or not group membership is valued can have profound social and personal consequences. Throughout history various racial, social, and religious groups have been singled out as unacceptable (Young 1997). The disabled body, and within that context the disabled female body, are often not seen as a "natural" part of the community (Asch and Fine 1997). Indeed space has evolved largely in the absence of disabled people. Examining and reframing perceptions of women with disabilities blends well with the social citizenship understanding of Disability Studies. The reality of disability and impairment in daily life is acknowledged and discussed without becoming fixated on medical conditions. Community, education, and domestic spaces cannot be explored in isolation. Moving beyond the arbitrary borders of public community spaces and private domestic spaces, we are able to recognize linkages and elements that simultaneously impact all of these spaces (Hansen 2002).

Geographical studies of everyday life are changing the field of disability studies. Geographers are escaping the rigid isolated disciplinary boxes of medical geography in favor of a multidimensional approach that incorporates social and cultural aspects of human geography. Scholars are examining embodied geographies of disability and impairment moving well beyond individual incapacity and looking at wider social perceptions and attitudes (Hansen 2002).

This chapter is part of a qualitative study exploring how disabled women's bodies are understood, "normalized," controlled, and excluded in terms of gender, sexuality, and space from the perspectives of disabled women.

Normalizing "Different" Bodies: The Power of the Privileged Body

> Averted and silenced, the disabled body presents a threat to the very idea of the body. (Porter 1997, xiii)

The nondisabled or "able" body is rarely characterized as privileged. However, open public spaces with little or no seating, many stairs, and poor signage mark social expectations of physicality (Chouinard and Grant 1997). Systems of segregated housing, education, transportation, and employment keep those who do not fit the mold in their place (Baird 1992). This process effectively privileges able bodyness.

The medical model frames disability as something wrong with the body and thus constructs disability as a medical problem that must be addressed to minimize the noticeable difference, such as physical appearance or body function (Barnes and Mercer 2003; Swain, French, and Cameron 2003). This "normalization" process may be regarded as a form of governance and control; indeed, disabled people may be subjected to medical intervention without being consulted or involved in the decision-making process (Basnett 2001). Normalization of the body has become naturalized as a logical and advantageous measure as unnoticeable difference equates with ordinary bodies, meaning that ordinariness is inextricably linked with social acceptability and humanness (Michalko and Titchkosky 2001), whereas physical difference signifies the extraordinary and social unacceptability (Hansen 2002; Bruegemann 2001).

Normalization of the body's physical appearance or function may be prioritized over all other aspects of an individual's life. For example, Ellen was selected for surgery by an orthopedic surgeon on a regular visit to her special school. As a result Ellen spent two and a half years in hospital, and during this time her education and relationship with her parents were adversely affected. Societal pressure to minimize physical difference also led to Elizabeth's parents undertaking an extreme treatment widely believed in the late 1950s to improve circulation. Elizabeth had clear memories of the painful and somewhat barbaric practice of applying rags soaked in boiling water to her leg:

I remember lying on the kitchen table, I'd be about four or five at the time, and this went on for years … really boiling hot, he had to use the washing tongs to get it out. He'd throw this rag on the top of my leg and I would be lying there screaming, covered in blisters, but they thought that they were doing good. (Elizabeth 51–56 years)

In an attempt to normalize Hannah's appearance she was advised to hang from the wall bars in her school gym each break-time, and she was also instructed to swim the backstroke. Her PE teacher's words convey a social misconception that disabled people themselves, if they try hard enough in pursuit of normality, can attain acceptance through alteration of their physical form (Philips 1999). Hannah recalled that: "I can remember her [PE teacher] shouting at me "you know you are just not trying hard enough, how do you ever expect to get better if you just don't try hard?" (Hannah 41–46 years). Normalization would appear to be the overarching imperative promoting and naturalizing the absence of disability.

Gender and Sexuality Enforcing the Normative

As children we learn of our expected (hetero)sexuality and gendered roles; girls are often encouraged to play house and play with dolls in a caring mothering way. Nondisabled girls are subtly encouraged to aspire to marriage through stories such as Cinderella and her marriage to the handsome prince. For disabled women, some of this early socialization is present, but, crucially, not all of it. Indeed, although almost every woman mentioned playing with dolls, none remembered being encouraged to aspire to marriage or indeed to think of themselves as potential partners. These women also recalled that as children there were very few, if any, positive images of disabled children or adults in story books. Hence, the "natural" absence of disability is again equated with normalcy.

Rather, they grew up with stories that portrayed physical difference as negative and a reason for social ostracism or segregation, such as "The Hunchback of Notre Dame" and "Snow White and the Seven Dwarfs" (SPOD 1990a). Therefore as children they had few points of reference in terms of a positive body image or meaningful disabled adult role models. Disability is usually linked with something not right or unnatural.

The unnaturalness carries through disability and sexuality, therefore, and disabled girls learn and are reminded of their asexual status in various contexts and social interactions of everyday life from professionals, families, relatives, friends, and strangers. A number of women hence had strong memories of others' responses to their physicality, particularly when approaching adolescence and becoming self-aware of their physical difference.

The body acts as a site of capture between others' responses to our bodies and internalized interpretations of these responses (Hall 1999, 143). These accumulated experiences may influence an individual's present or future self-image and sexual identity, an aspect of how personal pasts weigh upon individual futures.

Normalizing Absences

Many of the women interviewed recalled that sex or any topics related to sex were never discussed within their family. This led them to understand that sex was not for them; although this was not directly communicated to them, the nonmention of sex evidently conveyed family expectations of them as asexual (Gillespie-Sells, Hill, and Robbins 1998).

Parents convey their expectations to children through direct communication, but often it is what remains unspoken that most strongly conveys parental expectations. The nonmention of sex, sex education, or the possibility of their daughter having children passes on a clear message that disabled girls are not expected to participate in sexually active relationships. In general parental expectations may subtly pressure nondisabled girls to incorporate marriage and children into their future, while the converse seems to be the case for disabled girls.

As Micheline, a participant in Campling's (1981) study, recalled from her childhood at the age of 12 years old: "Sex was distinctly not talked about nor was the issue of my having children, which I had started to worry about from that day onwards" (quoted in Campling 1981, 24). Teachers may also prove significant influences in conveying societal expectations of disabled girls' asexual status. Beth's future expectations were significantly influenced by the comments of a special school teacher:

> [M]y best friend happened to say one day, "Well when I have children," and she was basically shot down in flames for it by the teacher … who said, "Well you know girls you won't, you can't have children, so you will have to think of other things in life because you can't have children." (Beth 36–41 years)

Such comments by an authoritative and influential figure impressed upon the girls that they were not expected to participate in intimate relationships, effectively fortifying the myth that participating in sex is something that disabled people do not do (Cooper and Guillebaud 1999). Thus, the girls were not given permission or approval to aspire to an active, enjoyable sex life. The teacher by implication communicated another social misunderstanding by insinuating that disabled female bodies are incapable of reproduction, and are therefore unsuited to pursuing feminized social roles of wife, mother, or homemaker (Lonsdale 1990).

Disabled young people may also learn of their asexual status from their peer group. Sara was educated in a mainstream school where she was the only disabled pupil. She recalled a fellow pupil making an inadvertent comment to her, verbalizing her presumed asexuality and implying her unsuitability as a prospective sexual partner:

> [O]ne of the boys that I was dancing with said, "You know you'll never be able to have babies" ... he wasn't being mean or anything... that just stuck with me.... I thought it was just hurtful. He didn't say it to be hurtful, but it was. (Sara 41–46 years)

Boadicea, a teenager in the late-1960s, remarked that, although the '60s heralded the beginnings of a sexual revolution for women, societal attitudes toward disabled girls and young women remained unaffected. Societal responses to her impairment, and the asexual identity imposed upon her as a result, made it difficult for Boadicea to develop a positive sexual identity:

> Disabled young women ... were generally and continue to be perceived as asexual beings ... seen as vulnerable, needing to be protected, asexual. Disabled young people don't indulge in sex, they don't need to and, also, it would be totally wrong if they did, it would be immoral if they did. (Boadicea, 46–51 years, her emphasis)

A number of the older women in the study clearly remembered being totally unprepared for the bodily changes that puberty would bring. Some women reported receiving absolutely no sex education from their parents or preparation for the onset of menstruation, indicating a lack of expectation that disabled girls would experience the physical consequences of being female (Morris 1994).

Hurried, necessary explanations may also simply be indicative of a social reluctance to discuss bodily functions that are culturally taboo rather than a deliberate denial of sexuality or sexual potential; but the impression is nonetheless of a particular intensity or awkwardness bound up in the nontransmission of relevant information on such matters to disabled girls, as revealed by the interviewees.

While at school very few nondisabled or disabled people receive good sex education (SPOD 1990b). Most of the women aged over fifty years old reported that they received no sex education at all, and that it was common for young people to be uninformed and totally ignorant about sexual intimacy. Younger women recalled receiving limited sex education in the guise of biology or personal hygiene classes. Many women referred to gaining information about the facts of life or mechanics of sex, but not in a form that was necessarily relevant or useful to them. These are given, taken for granted bodily functions for nondisabled girls and women but not for disabled girls or women. These were usually just one or two classes and tended to be sex segregated. Only one woman who attended special school recalled sex education being part of the educational curriculum, included in a biology course. It is perhaps significant that for subjects such as science and biology, pupils walked the short distance from the segregated special unit to join mainstream classes in the neighboring school. Therefore, the special school had no involvement in the delivery of sex education.

Disabled people in general and disabled women in particular are often perceived as childlike or asexual. Hence, systems of social regulation evolve that exercise normative control over individuals (Turner 2001), and in the case of disabled women normative controls involve conformity with expected social rolelessness (Fine and Asch 1988). Disabled women are rarely seen as appropriate for traditional female roles of motherhood or reproduction (Hansen 2002). Consequently, girls feel like they had to normalize their bodies. Family members, or those in a position of influence, may assume the role of societal supervisors who explicitly or more subtly convey their lack of expectation with respect to future adult lives. These beliefs, based upon the presumption of disabled women's deficiency in intimate relationships, childbearing, or mothering, may involve attempts to influence women's decisions and self-expectations through supervisory approval or disapproval. Parents may protect their daughters from potential male attention by dressing them in a dowdy or old-fashioned manner, but in the case of young disabled women, the same may be the case for other reasons. Where girls or young women require personal assistance to dress, due to a disability, it appears that clothes are often chosen on the basis of ease of dressing rather than style or fashion (Campling 1979, 1981). Boadicea, for example, identified her mother as the main person who chose and purchased her clothes, tending to buy items that reflected her own views on practicability rather than Boadicea's own taste or age.

As a young teenager in the early 1960s Elizabeth recalled being conscious that the prospect of her becoming a nun was far more palatable to her parents, as the subject was constantly discussed, than were the possibilities of her marrying and having children—possibilities that were never mentioned.

> [H]e [a priest] always thought I would make a good nun, because I was disabled, that was the reason ... she will never get married, she'll never have a family of her own, she might as well come into

the convent and he was always on at my parents'.... I think my parents did believe that I would go into the convent. (Elizabeth 51–56 years)

Similarly, in the mid-1960s, Boadicea became acutely aware of her family's lack of expectations for her adult life when she overheard a group of her female relatives discussing her future prospects: "[they were] saying that of course she will never get a husband, nobody is going to want to marry a blind girl" (Boadicea 46–51 years). These remarks were evidently made on the assumption that Boadicea's visual impairment rendered her undesirable to potential partners and unsuitable as a sexual partner or wife.

Beth also mentioned subtle expectations for her adult life as conveyed by her parents and teachers. Beth's interpretation of these messages was that her adult life would not include relationships or social roles of wife or mother: "I wouldn't get married, I wouldn't have relationships, and I certainly would never be a mother, that's the sort of message that you got—and sex, but disabled people don't have sex [laughs]" (Beth 36–41 years).

Beth noted that teachers in her special school subtly and more often explicitly conveyed their expectations of her adult life. Angie, a participant in Campling's (1981) study, recalled that when she was fourteen a teacher had intimated the social expectation of her nonparticipation in any feminized roles. At the end of a cooking lesson in which Angie had prepared a salad, the teacher remarked: "What a good job you've made of that, you would have made someone a good wife" (Campling 1981, 9).

The teacher's turn of phrase that Angie would have made a good wife conveys to the young teenager that the teacher's expectation is that she will not aspire to or indeed attain the role of a wife, an assumption made upon the basis of Angie's impairment and consequent supposed inappropriate role.

Normalizing Lack of Space and Place

A number of women made reference to the fact that their parents and close relatives had never mentioned or discussed the possibility of them marrying or having children. Kent has suggested that it is the subjects that are not spoken about which shape disabled women's self-expectations and voice others' expectations of disabled women. Kent has written of her own experience of the way in which unspoken expectations conveyed a clear message to her as a young blind woman:

I was seldom encouraged to say: "When I grow up I'll get married and have babies." Instead, my intellectual growth was nurtured. I

very definitely received the unspoken message that I would need
the independence of a profession, as I could not count on having the
support of a husband. (Kent 1987, 82)

It is noteworthy that in Kent's case there was an expectation that she
could be academically "bright" and could have a career whereas, for many
of the women who participated in this study neither was considered an
option by their families. The "natural" or "traditional" adult female wife
and motherhood roles were perceived as privileged spaces for disabled
women.

Disabled women's active participation as partners, wives, or mothers
at the center of the domestic sphere continues to be regarded as an exception to the rule. Their presence in the capacity of wife or mother is often
regarded as extraordinary (Michalko 2002): and, put bluntly and using a
construction that should now be familiar, they are matter "out of place"
(Creswell 1996; Sibley 1995) in the context of the domestic environment
with an active woman supposedly at its heart.

Limiting Domestic Space

Despite young disabled women's exclusion from family assumptions of
marriage and childbearing, some are nonetheless taught the basics of
housekeeping (Rae 1993). Yet, even here it has been found that low parental
expectations of an individual's ability to contribute to the domestic routine adversely impacts opportunities to do so (Hirst and Baldwin 1994).
Individuals who require personal assistance or adaptation to the physical
environment are likely to have very limited or no experience of managing
domestic affairs.

Susan was clear that her mother did not expect her to be able to "cope"
living out of the parental home. Boadicea had a similar experience following the breakdown of her marriage: when she was offered a local authority house, her mother voiced her expectation that Boadicea "would never
be able to manage by herself," and as a result she agreed to remain in the
parental home. Susan noted that the inaccessibility of the kitchen in her
parents' home also presented a barrier to her participation in this space.
More telling from her narrative is the construction of the kitchen as a dangerous place, full of potential hazards. Perhaps prompted by her mother's
desire to protect Susan from harm, this approach is arguably more fitting
toward the education of a small child rather than that of a young woman.
Exclusion from the kitchen created a barrier to Susan's opportunities to
learn to cook, a basic skill required for independent living:

"When I lived with my mother, it was a big 'no no' for me to go into the kitchen because there was so many things that could happen, I could spill pots over me" (Susan 41–46 years). Boadicea recounted something similar: "She [mother] would do the cooking, I would ask her if it was okay for me to do the cooking but she said no" (Boadicea 46–51 years).

The exclusion of these women from the domestic space may well have been intended to protect them, but would inevitably lead to their dependence upon others to prepare and cook meals for them, with all manner of consequences later on. "Normal" in public space is the art of "passing": "Even though we are all different, not all differences are noticed" (Michalko and Titchkosky 2001, 202). The normalization process inherently magnifies physical difference because it focuses primarily on alteration of the body's physical appearance (Tremain 2002).

Asexual stereotypes of disabled women are sustained by contemporary media images where they are often portrayed as being in need of care and assistance, being unable to undertake feminized roles. For example, a Royal National Institute of Blind People (RNIB) 2002 poster campaign to "raise awareness of sight loss" implied blind women could not fulfill the roles of wife or mother because amongst other things, they could not host a dinner party, undertake housework, care for children, read their children stories, or make their child smile (Jennings 2002). The very nature of charity advertising tends to fortify negative attitudes toward disabled women's sexual eligibility and capabilities as lovers, wives, and mothers.

Positive images of disabled women and men rarely appear in mainstream media such as magazines, newspapers, films, or television (Butler 1999). On the rare occasions when they do appear, they are asexually objectified, whereas nondisabled women's bodies are sexually objectified. Women are bombarded with physical images of "beauty" and "femininity" through media representations. While these images represent an ideal unobtainable to the majority of the female population, disabled women are often physically displaced from what constitutes a "normal" body, let alone from those highly valued as beautiful, desirable, and sexually eligible (Lonsdale 1990; Shakespeare, Gillespie-Sells, & Davies 1996; Wendell 1996; Gillespie-Sells et al. 1998). The body beautiful fixation in heterosexual, gay, and lesbian sexualized environments effectively displaces disabled women as potential sexual partners (Finger 1992; Watson 2000), in a similar manner to how pregnant women are placed off limits as suitable sexual partners, being equally regarded as sexually unavailable (Longhurst 2001).

Although attitudes toward sex are more liberal in contemporary society, attitudes toward disabled people having sex have changed at a much slower pace. As a result disabled people are often spatially and socially excluded from sexual expression. Drawing further upon in-depth interviews, we will explore in detail the spatial and social processes that influence disabled women's sexual expression and participation in intimate relationships.

> Disabled people are not often welcome in contexts where sex is on the agenda. For example, nightclub and social venues may aim to cater for young people, fashionable people and beautiful people. Steps, narrow entrances, flashing lights, smoke and loud noise may all prove barriers to disabled people's participation. (Shakespeare et al. 1996, 88)

The inaccessible nature of the built environment has a significant influence on disabled individuals' presence and participation in social spaces. Factors such as inaccessible social venues and a lack of accessible public transport exacerbate social exclusion. Even today, when affordable accessible transport is available, for example Handicabs (based in Edinburgh), the service does not facilitate social inclusion or spontaneity; it can only be used for two journeys per week, and must be booked forty-eight hours in advance. Taxis, as an alternative mode of transport to social venues or events, may be prohibitively expensive for disabled people, especially for those with low incomes or those who are reliant upon benefits as their main source of income. Therefore, for some women, their opportunities to meet others, form relationships, and participate in sexually intimate relationships will be strongly dependent upon the nature of the physical environment to be negotiated in the process.

The advent of the Disability Discrimination Act (DDA 1995) has positively influenced new building and adaptations to existing venues, and this has resulted in an increase in accessible social venues. Although social spaces are becoming increasingly accessible, disabled people's participation in such spaces nonetheless often requires planning. Jenny talked about some of the environmental and practical considerations that had to be made when socializing with visually impaired friends:

> [Y]ou end up going to the same places because you know it's easy to get to the loo, it's easy to get to the bar, the staff will read you the menu…. You want to sit where there's room for the guide dogs, those of us that are long cane users getting to the loo, getting somewhere near a taxi rank or near transport and that is a major consideration…. You have got to be psyched up to try somewhere new because you are never really sure of the reaction of the staff. (Jenny 41–46 years)

Some adaptations to the built environment may be compliant with legislation, but their design or installation undertaken without consideration for, or consultation with, disabled people may render the facilities unusable. Taken-for-granted facilities available to nondisabled patrons are often not available to disabled customers, a prime example being the provision of accessible toilet facilities, the lack of which restricts disabled peoples' participation in social spaces. As Sara commented:

> [M]ost pubs and clubs I can't get into or I can't go to the toilet in, and it's fine to get into some place but you have to be able to go to the toilet in order to be socially free: to go out you have to be able to pee. (Sara 41–46 years)

Furthermore, these facilities are often kept locked, reducing disabled adults to a childlike status where they have to seek permission to use the toilet, which may be regarded as a subtle form of abuse toward disabled people (MacFarlane 1994). The wider social environment has very much evolved in the absence of disabled people, and as a consequence the presence of diverse physicalities disrupts mainstream social spaces (Chouinard 1999) because nondisabled people are often unsure of how to respond to disabled people's presence. Therefore, while changing the physical environment is essential to facilitate the access of disabled people in social settings, attitudes and behavior toward disabled people also need to change (Butler and Bowlby 1997). As Sara again commented: "but as far as going out and stuff, it's always a novelty to see a disabled person out.... They are amazed that we're out mixing among the other humans you know" (Sara 45 years).

For some disabled women, the very nature of their impairment, for example, a visual impairment, can create difficulties in responding to or even noticing initial contact from others such as eye contact, facial expressions, or some other engaging flirtatious communication. Due to a general lack of social disability awareness, a visually impaired woman's lack of response may be misinterpreted by nondisabled men as disinterest, aloofness, or unfriendliness (Butler 1999).

Negative ascriptions are compounded by social understandings of pieces of equipment that enable women to retain their independence. Long canes, crutches, and wheelchairs, for instance, are socially ascribed symbols of dependence, confinement, and limitation rather than associated with independence, liberation, and ability (Thomas 2002). These cold metallic pieces of equipment are not socially regarded as an integral part of a sexually attractive body. Sara declared that, as a disabled woman, she was conscious that men did not always regard her as a sexual being or as a prospective sexual partner:

With so much emphasis and value placed upon physical appearance, the women interviewees noted that it was during their teenage years that they became aware of "feeling different" from their nondisabled peers. Sara spoke of the moment that she realized her physicality was noticeably different from those around her in the mainstream secondary school that she attended:

> I was 11 or 12 … I walked into the school gym for a dance and I thought, "I'm not like these people," and believe it or not it's the first time I remember and, it's just weird, before that I was totally oblivious to the fact that I didn't move around the way everybody else did. (Sara 41–46 years)

Hannah also spoke of first noticing her physical difference as a teenager when she started to dress in a sexualized way, wearing tight fitting clothes: "It was at that point that I realized my body was a different shape on either side, because I've got a wee short side and I've got a long side so for the first time I really noticed" (Hannah 41–46 years). Hannah also felt "different" because of her feelings around her sexuality and her dawning sense of sexual attraction toward other women. She felt she had "buried" this unnoticeable difference, and "latched onto" her physical difference as an explanation of her feelings of being set apart from her nondisabled peers. A number of the women referred to their teenage years as a particularly painful and upsetting time in their lives, much of which may be attributed to society's response to their impairment. Claire, who also attended mainstream school, talked similarly of experiencing disablist attitudes. She had clear memories of regular humiliation, verbal abuse, and ridicule by nondisabled contemporaries, and this treatment had adversely affected her self-esteem and confidence during her teenage years.

The manner in which we communicate may be considered a noticeable difference: for instance, where an individual's speech is impaired or he or she uses symbol boards or books of pictures, sign language, or other human aids to communication, such as lip speakers or sign language interpreters. There is an assumption that speech impairment equates with lower intellectual capacity, and this results in social interactions where people adopt a patronizing tone similar to one used by adults when they are engaging with children (Knight and Brent 1998). Annie spoke of being conscious about the links that society makes between physical appearance, mode of communication, and intellectual capacity:

> I think people see my impairment and they make assumptions about what I can and cannot do, and I think that, with a speech impairment, quite a lot of them probably see me as being stupid or mentally retarded [sic] in some way. (Annie 26–31 years)

Annie noted that people often spoke to her in a patronizing or condescending manner, negating her status as an adult, and at the same time potentially negating her possibilities for developing relationships and sexual partnerships. Sara also spoke of societal assumptions that erroneously equate physical appearance with intellectual capacity: "people assuming that, [because] I walk differently than they do, that I also think differently than they do" (Sara 41–46 years).

Laura spoke of concealing her visual impairment as a means of protecting herself from societal responses to impairment, especially disablist attitudes. "Passing" as nondisabled facilitates social acceptance and inclusion in everyday life (Bruegemann 2001). The energy, time, and effort involved in passing is immense, however, and is usually expended at great personal cost to the individual (Hansen 2002). Passing may be regarded as "an act of repression" (Michalko 2002, 10) where individuals deliberately conceal part of their identity. To return to Laura, she revealed that: "from that day on for several, well for the next fifteen years, I kind of denied that I had a visual impairment and actually put myself under a tremendous amount of strain to do it" (Laura 46–51 years).

French wrote of her childhood denial of her visual impairment as a means of self-protection from negative responses to her impairment, and as a means of gaining societal acceptance and approval primarily from her family: "By denying the reality of my disability I protected myself from the anxiety, disapproval, frustration and disappointment of the adults in my life" (French 1993, 70). Thomas also spoke of concealing her impairment in response to social messages regarding "noticeable difference":

> I was born without a left hand, an impairment which I began to conceal at some point in my childhood (probably around 9 or 10 years of age). This childhood concealment strategy has left a long legacy. I still struggle with the "reveal or not to reveal" dilemma, and more often than not will hide my "hand" and "pass" as normal. (Thomas 1999, 54)

Many people act as conduits of social messages, primarily parents, doctors, teachers, and friends, but even complete strangers may display a resistance to embracing diversity and in effect tell the disabled person that, in order to gain social acceptance, noticeable difference should be minimized (Thomas 1999). Claire spoke of differential treatment depending on whether she was using her long cane or not. If she walked into someone when not using it, this would usually be met with a hostile or abusive response, whereas when using her long cane, identifying herself as a blind person, other people tended to move out of her way or treated her in a patronizing manner. Thus, there was further demonstration of how disabled women can be in effect set aside or ignored. It would seem that disability is often treated as disruptive, out of place, or unnatural in public space.

Resistance Contesting Space Breach Body Privilege

Many of the women interviewed talked of developing positive self-identities primarily through involvement in the disabled people's movement and disability arts. It became apparent, that as the women had grown older, they had begun to work more constructively with the difference caused by their disability, relating to it in a more self-conscious manner perhaps. The conscious creation of positive self-identities was often borne out of a negative normalizing past where as girls, women were subjected to normalizing assumptions and techniques, persuading them that their bodily difference was bad, inappropriate, in need of correction, rendering it invisible if at all possible so that they might be socially accepted.

Some women spoke of consciously making space for themselves on their own terms, so that they no longer feel obliged to conceal their impairments but, rather, feel able to assert their positive self-identities as disabled women. Adele spoke of using callipers [braces] and crutches to coerce her body into the normative standing position, something drilled into her as the right thing to do when younger. Now, she talked positively of her decision to discard these mobility aids in favor of using a wheelchair: "So they [the crutches and callipers (braces)] got put in the bin and I just used my wheelchair and that was like a liberation" (Adele 51–56 years).

Although Adele's decision was liberating for her, she made reference to her immediate family's disapproval and disappointment at her decision, which was perceived by them to indicate that she had "given up on trying to be like one of them." She remade and reclaimed space on her own terms

Laura spoke positively of her decision to stop hiding her impairment, but instead to be proud of her identity as a disabled woman: "I thought, Sod it, this not being able to see is part of me and I'm not denying it anymore and I'm not going to be embarrassed about it, so I sort of came out the closet and started doing Disability Equality Training" (Laura 46–51 years).

Laura had discussed the tremendous strain that hiding her impairment had caused her, emphasizing her sense of relief at making a decision to come out as a visually impaired woman. Veronica put much time and energy into concealing her sexuality. As a wheelchair user concealing her impairment was not an option. It would seem that any act of repression may be detrimental to an individual's well-being, although in psychoanalytic theory there may be good reasons why an individual may repress things; for example, as part of a self-survival mechanism regardless of whether it be denial of an impairment or sexuality.

Veronica spoke positively of coming out of the closet. Brown suggests that the closet describes the denial, concealment, erasure, or ignorance of lesbians and gay men (Brown 2000, 1). Likewise, the need to pass as non-disabled reflects the socially valued visible attributes of "normalcy."

The notion of hiding or concealment of those who do not have a place in the world unless they pass as something they are not, can also be translated to disability. By coming out Laura self-identified as a disabled person. Choosing to come out of the closet represents a powerful act of positive self-identification (Linton 1998), and also serves to turn socially valued physicality on its head. In addition, for Veronica, her self-identification as a lesbian freed her from heteronormative sexual oppression and enabled her to explore and express her lesbian sexuality.

> I used to be anorexic ... when I came out all the kind of things like that disappeared ... I feel like I've come alive within the past four years ... because I feel I can finally be me, I can finally be the person I want to be. (Veronica 21–26 years)

Boadicea spoke of resisting societal expectations that were impressed upon her by close family members to glamorize her body. She considered it ironic that as a blind woman she was nonetheless expected to present a sighted image of femininity. She talked of her decision to stop wearing makeup:

> What made it really ridiculous is that I had to present a sighted image, what they thought as beauty, what they thought as feminine.... [The decision not to wear makeup] was a conscious effort on my part to reject all of that sighted stuff. (Boadicea 46–51 years)

Although Sara spoke positively of her self-identity, she was conscious that contemporary society remains transfixed by physical appearance. Gill (2001, 353) refers to the insider experience of disability as "a persistent and disquieting sense of mistaken identity," where disabled people find the identities they have forged and present to society are dismissed by others in favor of stereotypical identity ascriptions:

"I love living my life, they [nondisabled society] see my crutches, they see that I walk differently, and my friends that are really my friends are the ones that are really clued up: they see the other person that I am.... I don't mind that I walk differently, I just wish they could see who I am, I'm proud of me, every inch of me, I just wish they could get away from the superficial stuff" (Sara 41–46 years). Laura echoed such claims: "They say your impairment shapes you, and I don't think I would want to be a different person, you know I'm happy in my skin now, I'm happy with who I am" (Laura 46–51 years).

It would appear that the adoption of positive self-identities enable disabled women to challenge and to counteract the negative identities and stereotypes imposed on them by others (Swain, French, and Cameron 2003). A positive self-concept is often in conflict with wider social understandings of disability: "[G]uys … they think of disabled women as being nice people or whatever, or courageous people, but I don't think that at first glance would think of them as being dating material" (Sara 41–46 years).

A participant in Gow's (2000) study was acutely aware that in sexualized social environments, where sex is on the agenda (Shakespeare et al. 1996), her presence was peripheral. Although she shared the space, she was not regarded as sexually equitable: "I wear lipstick, I wear everything. And they still think you're a wee girl. Because you're in a wheelchair, I'm a young child. Because I'm in a wheelchair" (Gow 2000, 164).

Socially relegated to childlike status, sexuality is considered to be inappropriate or absent. Despite her best efforts to counteract the asexual identity imposed upon her, this young woman was acutely aware of her asexual status through a complex mix of social responses to both her body and her wheelchair.

Leslie, a participant in Watson's (2000) study, noted a change in her sexual status when she acquired an impairment: "meeting up with guys and things like that—that virtually has not happened since I've become disabled" (Watson 2000, 147).

In the highly sexualized social scene of Western culture, perfect, glamorous, and beautiful bodies are welcomed, celebrated, and sought after as sexual partners (Limaye 2003; Gillespie-Sells et al. 1998). Disabled women's bodies are not regarded in these terms; rather they are not considered to be sexually available, akin to the manner in which pregnant women's bodies are regarded as sexually unavailable (Longhurst 2001; Watson 2000). Disabled women are similarly placed off limits in terms of sexual availability and are therefore not considered to be part of the game in terms of flirtation, sexual initiation, or courtship rules (Longhurst 2001). Disabled women are effectively sexually set aside (Michalko 2002): "In a sense, to be treated as a sexual object is a 'privilege' that non-disabled women have, and disabled women do not" (Tremain 1992, 26).

The notion of disabled women being off limits in terms of sexual availability, or their assumed unsuitability as appropriate sexual partners, seems to have changed little over time; as Elizabeth experienced in the nineteen sixties and as Theresa currently experiences: "I was standing at a bus stop this night going out to the dancing at the time, and I heard this guy at the back saying, 'Oh! She's all right, but oh! Oh! Look, look she's got a calliper (brace) on her leg'" (Elizabeth 51–56 years).

Theresa talked of numerous occasions in her local pub where men had approached her, chatted her up, and were interested in her. However, when Theresa harnessed up her guide dog making herself identifiable as a blind woman, men usually responded by sexually setting her aside:

> [He said] "oh I'm so sorry, I'm so sorry," and I'm like, "Why are you sorry?" I get that a lot, people apologizing for having spoken to me.... Or they've been chatting me up and they're like, "Oh I shouldn't have been chatting you up, you're blind," and I'm like "Why?" I find that one a weird one. (Theresa 36–41 years)

The notion of disabled women as substandard or unsuitable sexual partners is also illustrated in Goffman (1968), where a young woman recalls her realization of being sexually set aside:

> I think the first realization of my situation, and the first intense grief resulting from this realization, came one day, very casually, when a group of us in our early teens had gone to the beach for the day. I was lying on the sand, and I guess the fellows and girls thought I was asleep. One of the fellows said, "I like Domenica very much, but I would never go out with a blind girl." I cannot think of any prejudice which so completely rejects you. (quoted in Goffman 1968, 47)

Similar experiences were recalled by many of the women, revealing a theme to do with the intertwining of social space and the complexities of sexual citizenship. In some instances, nondisabled men who find disabled women attractive may possibly be considered to have deviant sexual tendencies, as Theresa's experience illustrates:

> One of the guys in the pub had been chatting me up he was really interested in me.... Another guy had told me that someone was slagging him and calling him a pervert because he was wanting to go out with a blind girl, and I was like "so how does that make him a pervert?" (Theresa 36-41 years)

This being said, a high proportion of blind women who participated in this study also reported experience of domestic abuse. It seems that men with controlling tendencies or abusive behaviors may pursue a blind woman as they consider her to be easily controlled (Claire Jennings,

Personal communication with Hazel McFarlane, January 2002). Although Jenny did not explicitly discuss domestic abuse, she was conscious of this element in social space:

> I'm always suspicious of people who pester us. You do get folk who will come and chat you up ... chatting up the wee blind bird.... Sometimes you tend to attract folk that think "Oh! Well this is one, I can do her a favor and ask her out and manipulate her." (Jenny 36–41 years)

In social space, disabled women, perhaps more so than nondisabled women, have to be able to decipher the difference between genuine individuals and those with ulterior motives, something that may be particularly problematic for some women who may have experienced sexual rejection in the past and may be flattered by sexual attention and the prospect of a relationship. The very presence of disabled women on the social scene is slowly shifting the social terrain. No longer as tightly constrained by social regulation and domestic dictate, disabled women are making and shaping public and private space on their own terms (Creswell 1997; Hansen 2009).

Conclusion

Social and cultural attitudes toward disabled people and disabled women in particular, remain largely unchanged. The able body is a privileged body and disability is perceived as naturally absent. Many women are dealing with entrenched social attitudes and perceptions of normality, traditional gender roles, sexuality (or the lack thereof), on a daily basis. Indeed, the very presence of disabled women is often framed as unnatural or disruptive. These spaces have evolved with little or any consideration of disability except as an add-on or afterthought. Caught up in a legacy of limitation, abnormality, and lack of expectation many disabled women have had few if any opportunities to be in social spaces or public spaces to claim even the most traditional female roles of partner, wife, or mother. However, even in the face of strong negative social pressures, disabled women are reclaiming, rebuilding, and reshaping these spaces to fit their needs in positive ways that suit them.

Note

1. Utilizing a participatory action research approach through the lens of disability geography and with twenty women, aged twenty-one to sixty-six living in central Scotland. Nine women had vision impairments, and eleven had physical impairments. All the women chose their own pseudonyms (McFarlane, 2004).

References

Asch, Adrienne, and Michelle Fine. 1997. "Nurturance, Sexuality and Women with Disabilities." In *The Disability Studies Reader*, edited by Lennard Davis, 241–55. New York: Routledge.

Baird, V. 1992. "Difference and Defiance." *The New Internationalist* 233 (July): 4–7.

Barnes, Colin, and Geof Mercer. 2003. *Disability*. Cambridge, UK: Polity Press.

Basnett, Ian. 2001. "Health Care Professionals and Their Attitudes toward Decisions Affecting Disabled People." In *Handbook of Disability Studies*, edited by Gary L. Albrecht, Katherine D. Seelman, and Michael Bury, 450–67. London: Sage.

Brown, Michael P. 2000. *Closet Space: Geographies of Metaphor from the Body to the Globe*. London: Routledge.

Brueggemann, Brenda J. 2001. "Deafness, Literacy, Rhetoric: Legacies of Language and Communication." In *Embodied Rhetorics: Disability in Language and Culture*, edited by James C. Wilson and Cynthia Lewiecki-Wilson, 115–34. Carbondale: Southern Illinois University Press.

Butler, Ruth. 1999. "Double the Trouble or Twice the Fun? Disabled Bodies in the Gay Community." In *Mind and Body Spaces: Geographies of Illness, Impairment and Disability*, edited by Ruth Butler and Hester Parr, 203–20. London: Routledge,

———, and Sophie Bowlby. 1997. "Bodies and Spaces: An Exploration of Disabled People's Experience of Public Space." *Environment and Planning D: Society and Space* 15: 411–33.

Campling, Jo. 1979. *Better Lives for Disabled Women*. London: Virago.

———, ed. 1981. *Images of Ourselves: Women with Disabilities Talking*. London: Routledge and Keegan Paul.

Chouinard, Vera. 1999. "Life at the Margins: Disabled Women's Explorations of Ableist Spaces." In *Embodied Geographies: Spaces, Bodies and Rites of Passage*, edited by Elizabeth Kenworthy Teather, 142–57. London: Routledge.

Chouinard, V. and A. Grant. 1997. "On Not Being Anywhere Near the Project: Revolutionary Ways of Putting Ourselves in the Picture." In *Space, Gender and Knowledge: Feminist Readings*, edited by L. McDowell and J. Sharp, 147–70. London: Arnold.

Cooper, Elaine, and John Guillebaud. 1999. *Sexuality and Disability: A Guide for Everyday Practice*. Abingdon, UK: Radcliffe Medical Press.

Creswell, Tim. 1996. *In Place/Out of Place: Geography, Ideology and Transgression*. Minneapolis: University of Minnesota Press.

Fine, Michelle, and Adrienne Asch, eds. 1988. *Women with Disabilities: Essays in Psychology, Culture and Politics*. Philadelphia: Temple University Press.

Finger, Anne. 1992. "Forbidden Fruit." *The New Internationalist* 233 (July): 8–10.

French, Sally. 1993. "Can You See the Rainbow: The Roots of Denial." In *Disabling Barriers, Enabling Environments*, edited by John Swain, Vic Finkelstein, Sally French, and Mike Oliver, 69–77. London: Sage.

Gill, C. J. 2001. "Divided Understandings: Social Understandings of Disability." In *Handbook of Disability Studies*, edited by Gary L. Albrecht, Katherine D. Seelman, and Michael Bury, 351–72. London: Sage.

Gillespie-Sells, Kath, Mildrette Hill, and Bree Robbins. 1998. *She Dances to Different Drums: Research into Disabled Women's Sexuality*. London: Kings Fund.

Goffman, Erving. 1968. *Stigma: Notes on the Management of Spoiled Identity*. Harmondsworth, UK: Penguin Books.

Gow, J. 2000. "A Study Examining the Views about Reproductive Screening Programmes of Young Women Affected with Congenital Conditions for which a Screening Programme is Currently Offered, Compared with Those of Professionals in the Related Fields of Medicine and Disability, and Those of Young Women in the General Public." PhD diss., University of Glasgow, Scotland.

Hall, Edward. 1999. "Workspaces: Refiguring the Disability-Employment Debate." In *Mind and Body Spaces: Geographies of Illness, Impairment and Disability*, edited by Ruth Butler and Hester Parr, 138–54. London: Routledge.

Hansen, Nancy. 2002. "Passing Through Other Peoples' Spaces: Disabled Women Geography and Work." PhD diss., Department of Geography and Geomatics, University of Glasgow, Scotland.

———. 2009. "Remapping the Medical Terrain on Our Terms." *Aporia* 3: 28–34.

Hirst, Michael, and Sally Baldwin, 1994. *Unequal Opportunities: Growing Up Disabled*. Social Policy Research Unit. London: Her Majesty's Stationery Office.

Jennings, Claire. 2002. "Do They Mean Us?" *New Beacon* 86 (1014): 22–23.

Kent, Debra. 1987. "In Search of Liberation." In *With Wings: An Anthology of Literature by and about Women with Disabilities*, edited by Marsha Saxton and Florence Howe, 82–83. New York: The Feminist Press at the City University of New York.

Knight, John, and Martine Brent. 1998. *Access Denied: Disabled Peoples' Experience of Social Exclusion*. London: Leonard Cheshire.

Limaye, Sandhya. 2003. "Sexuality and Women with Sensory Disabilities." In *Women, Disability and Identity*, edited by Asha Hans and A. Patri, 89–102., New Delhi, India: Sage.

Linton, Simi. 1998. *Claiming Disability Knowledge and Identity*. New York: New York University Press.

Longhurst, Robyn. 2001. *Bodies: Exploring Fluid Boundaries*. London: Routledge.

Lonsdale, Susan. 1990. *Women and Disability: The Experience of Physical Disability among Women*. London: Macmillan Education.

MacFarlane, Ann. 1994. "Subtle Forms of Abuse and Their Long Term Effects." *Disability and Society* 9: 85–88.

McFarlane, Hazel. 2004. "Disabled Women and Socio-Spatial 'Barriers' to Motherhood." PhD diss., University of Glasgow, Scotland.

Michalko, Rod. 2002. *The Difference that Disability Makes*. Philadelphia: Temple University Press.

———, and Tayna Titchkosky. 2001. "Putting Disability in Its Place; It's Not a Joking Matter." In *Embodied Rhetorics: Disability in Language and Culture*, edited by James C Wilson and Cynthia Lewiecki-Wilson, 200–29. Carbondale: Southern Illinois University Press.

Morris, Jenny. 1994. "Gender and Disability." In *On Equal Terms: Working with Disabled People*, edited by Sally French, 207–20. London: Butterworth Heinemann

Philips, Marilynn J. 1992. "Try Harder: The Experience of Disability and the Dilemma of Normalization." In *Interpreting Disability: A Qualitative Reader*, edited by Philip M. Ferguson, Dianne L. Ferguson, and Steven J. Taylor, 213–32. New York: Teachers College Press.

Porter, James. 1997. Foreword. In *The Body and Physical Difference: Discourses of Disability*, edited by David Mitchell and Sharon Snyder, ix–xiv. Ann Arbor: University of Michigan Press.

Rae, Anne. 1993. "Independent Living, Personal Assistance and Disabled Women: The Double Bind?" *Disability, Handicap and Society* 8: 431–34.

Shakespeare, Tom, Kath Gillespie-Sells, and Dominic Davies, eds. 1996. *The Sexual Politics of Disability: Untold Desires*. London: Cassell.

Sibley, David. 1995. *Geographies of Exclusion: Society and Difference in the West*. London: Routledge.

SPOD. 1990a. *Disability and Body Image* (Resource and Information Leaflet No.1). The Association to Aid The Sexual and Personal Relationships of People with a Disability.

———. 1990b. *Physical Handicap and Sexual Intercourse: Methods and Techniques*. (Resource and Information Leaflet No.3). The Association to Aid the Sexual and Personal relationships of People with a Disability.

Swain, John, Sally French, and Colin Cameron. 2003. *Controversial Issues in a Disabling Society*. London: Open University Press.

Thomas, Calvin. 1998. "Disabled Women's Stories about Their Childhood Experiences." In *Growing Up with Disability*, edited by Carol Robinson and Kirsten Stalker, 85–96. London: Jessica Kingsley.

———. 1999. "Narrative Identity and the Disabled Self." In *Disability Discourse*, edited by Mairian Corker and Sally French, 47–56. Buckingham, UK: Open University Press.

———. 2002. "The 'Disabled' Body." In *Real Bodies: A Sociological Introduction*, edited by Mary Evans and Ellie Lee, 64–78. Basingstoke, UK: Palgrave.

Tremain, Shelley. 1992. "Creating Our Own Images." In *Women Sexuality and Disability: Peeling off the Labels—Summary of a Two Day Symposium*, Disabled Women's Network Toronto (DAWN), 23–28.

Turner, Bryan S. 2001. "Disability and the Sociology of the Body." In *Handbook of Disability Studies*, edited by Gary L Albrecht, Katherine D. Seelman, and Michael Bury, 252–66. London: Sage.

Watson, Nick. 2000. "Impairment, Disablement and Identity," PhD diss., University of Edinburgh, Scotland.

Wendell, Susan. 1996. *The Rejected Body: Feminist Philosophical Reflections on Disability* London: Routledge.

Young, Iris. 1997. "The Scaling of Bodies and the Politics of Identity." In *Space, Gender and Knowledge: Feminist Readings*, edited by L. McDowell and J. Sharp, 218–31. London: Arnold.

The Contributors

Max Andrucki earned his PhD in the School of Geography at the University of Leeds, UK, in 2011, where his research focused on the transnational practices of white, English-speaking South Africans in the postapartheid period. He has an MA in geography from the University of Vermont and a BA in East Asian Languages and Cultures from Columbia University. He has taught at the University of Leeds, Leeds Metropolitan University, Temple University, and Rutgers University and has published on sexuality and space, citizenship, and geographies of whiteness. An Irish citizen born in Maine, he has lived in Japan, South Africa, and the UK and is currently based in New York City.

Donald Martin Carter is a Professor of Anthropology and Africana Studies, and is currently serving as Chief Diversity Officer at Hamilton College in New York. He is the author of *States of Grace: Senegalese in Italy* and the *New European Immigration* (1997), and *Navigating the African Diaspora: The Anthropology of Invisibility* (2010). His recent work explores an emergent Black Europe and the cultural, social, and human contours of a global African Diaspora.

John Dixon is a Professor of Social Psychology at the Open University, UK, and Coeditor (with Professor Jolanda Jetten) of the *British Journal of Social Psychology*. His research has focused on the social psychology of contact and desegregation in historically divided societies and, relatedly, on the relationship between places, identities, and resistance to social change.

Kevin Durrheim is Professor of Psychology at the University of KwaZulu-Natal, where he teaches social psychology and research methods. He writes on topics related to racism, segregation, and social change. He has coauthored *Race Trouble* (Durrheim, Mtose, and Brown 2011, Lexington Press) and *Racial Encounter* (Durrheim and Dixon 2005, Routledge).

Bradley Gardener earned his PhD in the Earth and Environmental Sciences Program at the CUNY Graduate Center. He has taught at several CUNY schools and has been employed as writing fellow at Medgar Evers College in Brooklyn, New York. His research focuses on the intersections between race, migration, place, and identity.

Nancy Hansen is an Associate Professor and Director of the Interdisciplinary Master's Program in Disability Studies at the University of Manitoba. Nancy obtained a PhD (Human Geography) from the University of Glasgow. Her thesis examined the impact of education and social policy on the employment experiences of disabled women through CIHR. Nancy's postdoctoral research examined disabled women's access to primary health care. Nancy received an Einstein research fellowship examining Disability Studies and the Legacy of Nazi Eugenics. Nancy received the ICUF Sprott Asset Management Scholarship examining disability history. She has worked on defining disability ethics and literacy research projects related to quality of life and disability. She is now researching disabled persons' access to primary care in Manitoba.

Pauline Leonard is Reader in Sociology in the School of Social Sciences and Director of the Work Futures Research Centre at the University of Southampton, UK. She is also a member of the ESRC Third Sector Research Centre, University of Southampton. She has longstanding research interests in diversity, identity, and space across a broad range of international contexts. A particular area of interest is in how these play out in work and organizations, and she has written widely in this area, including *Gender. Power and Organizations* (Palgrave 2001 with Susan Halford), and *Negotiating Gendered Identities at Work: Place, Space and Time* (Palgrave 2006, with Susan Halford), and *Expatriate Identities in Postcolonial Organizations* (Ashgate 2010). She is currently working on a research project funded by the British Academy (with Daniel Conway) exploring British migrants in South Africa, and a book *The British in South Africa: Continuity or Change?* is forthcoming from Palgrave in 2013. Pauline is also a steering group member of the WUN "White Spaces" network (http://www.wun.ac.uk/research/white-spaces-network) which explores the role of careers and diversity in international work contexts.

Erik Love is an Assistant Professor of Sociology at Dickinson College in Pennsylvania. He earned his PhD in Sociology from the University of California at Santa Barbara. His research focuses on civil rights advocacy in the United States. He has presented his research at academic conferences, in peer reviewed journals, and has contributed to a wide range of media including Jadilliyya and Al Jazeera. He is currently completing a book on this topic.

Catrin Lundström is an Associate Professor in Sociology and a researcher at the Department for Studies of Social Change and Culture at Linköping University, Sweden. She is working with a comparative ethnographic research project on first-generation Swedish migrant women in the Western part of the United States, Singapore, and Costa del Sol, Spain (Palgrave). During the 2007–08 academic year she was a visiting scholar in the Sociology Department at the University of California at Santa Barbara. Her research interests include cultural studies, postcolonial studies, migration studies, critical race and whiteness studies, urban ethnography, Latina/o studies, and feminist sociology. Within these theoretical fields, she has published articles in *Social Identities, Gender, Place and Culture, Journal of Intercultural Studies,* and *European Journal of Women's Studies.*

Melissa MacDonald is a doctoral candidate in the Department of Sociology at the University of California, Santa Barbara. She earned her BA in Women and Gender Studies from Smith College. Her research interests include critical race and whiteness studies, sociology of the body, and the intersection of race, gender, and class. She is currently conducting field research on how welfare dependent white women construct, perform, and reproduce white racialized identities in the Greater Boston area.

Pardis Mahdavi is Associate Professor of Anthropology at Pomona College. Her research interests include gendered labor, migration, sexuality, human rights, youth culture, transnational feminism, and public health in the context of changing global and political structures. Mahdavi has published two books, *Passionate Uprisings: Iran's Sexual Revolution* (Stanford University Press 2008) and *Gridlock: Labor, Migration and 'Human Trafficking' in Dubai* (2011). Mahdavi teaches courses on Medical Anthropology, Sociocultural Anthropology, and Ethnographic Methods, and has designed new courses titled "Sexual Politics of the Middle East" and "Love, Labor and the Law." She has published in the *Journal of Middle East Women's Studies, Encyclopedia of Women in Islamic Cultures, Culture, Health and Sexuality, Social Identities, Comparative Studies of South Asia Africa and the Middle East, Anthropology News,* and the *Institute for the Study* *of Islam in the Modern World Review.* She has received fellowships and awards from institutions such as the American Council of Learned Societies, the Woodrow Wilson International Center for Scholars, the National Drug Research Institute, the American Public Health Association, and the Society for Applied Anthropology.

Hazel McFarlane earned her PhD in 2005. Her research examined disabled women's experiences of social and spatial barriers to motherhood. Employed in the Centre for Disability Research, University of Glasgow until 2010, Hazel undertook diverse disability related research projects on behalf of the Scottish Government and National Health Service. Hazel retains honorary research status at the Centre. Hazel is currently Coordinator of the Centre for Sensory Impaired People, where she is engaged in the management, development, and delivery of person-centered, responsive services to sensorily impaired people across Glasgow.

Heather Merrill is an Associate Professor of Africana Studies at Hamilton College, trained as a Cultural Anthropologist and Human Geographer at the University of Chicago and the University of California at Berkeley. Dr. Merrill's book, *An Alliance of Women: Immigration and the Politics of Race* (2006, University of Minnesota) examines the spatial politics of identity and the challenges of collective struggle among an interethnic group of women in Turin. She has published numerous articles in journals of geography. Her research centers on struggles and negotiations over place, identity, and belonging in the African Diaspora in Italy. Her current research in Italy is focused on African diasporic politics and the plight of refugees from the Horn of Africa. She is also working on an edited volume on Power, Culture, and Practice in Critical Geography. From 2006 to 2008 she was Executive Director of the Clarke Forum for Contemporary Studies at Dickinson College, and from 2009 to 2011 Irwin Chair in Women's Studies at Hamilton College. She teaches courses on race, gender, identity, space, place, and globalization in relation to the African Diaspora.

David Morton is a PhD candidate in African history at the University of Minnesota. In his career as a journalist, his work appeared in media such as *The New Republic, Foreign Policy,* Slate.com, and *Architectural Record.* He writes about his current research in the *subúrbios* of Maputo, Mozambique, on his website: hoteluniverso.wordpress.com.

Tamaryn Nicholson is currently completing her MA degree in social sciences at the University of Kwazulu-Natal. Her fields of interest include feminism, gender, and popular culture.

Clinton Rautenbach is an English teacher and school guidance counselor, and is currently completing his postgraduate studies in Critical Social Psychology under the supervision of Professor Kevin Durrheim at the University of KwaZulu-Natal, where he also teaches part of a Psychology Service Learning course. His primary research interests are in race, gender, and social change. This is his debut as a published author.

Brett G. Stoudt is an Associate Professor in the Psychology Department with a joint appointment in the Gender Studies Program at John Jay College of Criminal Justice as well as the Environmental Psychology Doctoral Program at the CUNY Graduate Center. He has worked on numerous participatory action research projects with community groups, lawyers, and policy-makers nationally and internationally. His interests include the social psychology of privilege and oppression as well as aggressive and discriminatory policing practices. He is also interested in critical methodologies, particularly critical approaches to quantitative research. His work has been published in volumes such as *Class Privilege and Education Advantage* and *Conflict, Interdependence and Justice* as well as journals such as *The Journal of Social Issues*, *The Urban Review*, and *Men and Masculinities*.

France Winddance Twine is Professor of Sociology at the University of California at Santa Barbara and a documentary filmmaker. Twine, a theorist and an ethnographer is the author of five books and an editor of eight volumes. Her recent books include: *A White Side of Black Britain: Interracial Intimacy and Racial Literacy* (2010), *Outsourcing the Womb: Race, Class and Gestational Surrogacy in a Global Market* (2011), and *Girls with Guns: Feminism and Militarism* (2012). She is an editor of *Retheorizing Race and Whiteness in the 21st Century* (with Charles Gallagher, 2011), *Feminism and Anti-Racism International Struggles for Justice* (2000), *Ideologies and Technologies of Motherhood* (1999), and *Racing Research, Researching Race: Methodological Dilemmas in Critical Race Studies* (1999a). Her articles have appeared in *The Dubois Review: Social Science Research On Race, Ethnic and Racial Studies*, *Estudos Afro-Asiaticos*, *European Journal of Women Studies*, *Ethnicities*, *Feminist Studies*, *Gender, Place and Culture: Journal of Feminist Geography*, *Gender and Society*, *Meridians*, *Social Identities*, *Race and Class*, *Journal of Black Studies*, and *Signs*. She currently serves on the editorial boards of *American Sociological Review*, *Ethnic and Racial Studies*, *Identities: Global Studies in Culture and Power* and *Sociology: The Official Journal of the British Sociological Association*.

Henk van Houtum is Research Professor Geopolitics of Borders, University of Bergamo and Associate Professor Geopolitics and Political Geography, and Head of the Nijmegen Centre for Border Research, Radboud University, Nijmegen. In addition, he is editor of the *Journal of Borderlands Studies* (JBS). He has published extensively on the ontology and (in) justice of borders, on migration and cross-border mobility, national identity, (divided) cities, and the geopolitics of cartography. He is a columnist and commentator for various media. For more information, see www. henkvanhoutum.nl

David Wilson is Professor of Geography, Urban Planning, African American Studies, and the Unit for Criticism and Interpretive Theory at the University of Illinois at Urbana-Champaign. His current research focuses on contemporary urban politics in the neoliberal era, the politics of competing discursive formations that generate gentrified neighborhoods and poverty communities, and the racializing of the contemporary urban issues of crime and city growth. At the moment, he serves on the editorial boards of *Urban Geography, Professional Geographer, Social and Cultural Geography,* Syracuse University Press (Society, Space, and Place Book Series), *Inter-Cultural Studies,* the *International Encyclopedia of Human Geography* project, and *Acme: International Journal for Critical Geography.*

Index